SEX IN GLOBAL HISTORY

Modern Sources and Perspectives

Bassim Hamadeh, CEO and Publisher
David Miano, Senior Field Acquisitions Editor
Michelle Piehl, Project Editor
Alia Bales, Production Editor
Miguel Macias, Senior Graphic Designer
Stephanie Kohl, Licensing Coordinator
Gustavo Youngberg, Interior Designer
Natalie Piccotti, Senior Marketing Manager
Kassie Graves, Vice President of Editorial
Jamie Giganti, Director of Academic Publishing

Cover image copyright © 2016 iStockphoto LP/f9photos.

Printed in the United States of America.

ISBN: 978-1-5165-2010-7 (pbk) / 978-1-5165-2011-4 (br)

cognella® | ACADEMIC PUBLISHING

SEX IN GLOBAL HISTORY

Modern Sources and Perspectives

FIRST EDITION

Laura L. Lovett

University of Massachusetts—Amherst

TABLE OF CONTENTS

PART V: "NEW WOMEN" 142

PART VI: INVENTING SEXOLOGY 204

INTRODUCTION

Laura L. Lovett

We are at a moment when scholars, students, and activists are challenging us think "beyond the binary" when it comes to biological sexes, gender identities, and sexual orientations. Juxtapositions of male and female do not easily incorporate the complexities of intersexuality, just as the binary categories of masculine and feminine fail to adequately represent all transgender identities. Sexuality has also failed to conform to any simple juxtaposition of hetero- and homosexuality, and may in fact be more fluid than even Alfred Kinsey realized. Informed by social activism, on campus and off, these challenges are not purely academic; they make the history of sex, gender, and sexuality particularly important and relevant.

As fascinating as it might be to guide a class through the contemporary culture wars on sex, gender, and sexuality, as historians, our task is to historically contextualize the very categories themselves, their shifting interrelations, and their use and abuse in the name of empire, modernity, and science. Although courses on the history of sexuality are a staple in many history departments, and global history of sexuality courses are becoming more common, these courses tend to focus on sexuality instead of the combination of sexuality, sex, and gender, and they tend to be aimed at students with some history training and an appreciation of some of the major trends in world history. This collection is designed to be used in an *introductory* history course that uses sex, gender, and sexuality as an interpretive framework for global history over the past four centuries. As such, this collection addresses the challenge of gathering accessible sources that speak to a range of themes and regions.

This book is a collection of primary and secondary sources intended for courses that approach the history of the world since the seventeenth century in terms of sex, gender, and sexuality. I have used it in conjunction with Robert M. Buffington, Eithne Luibheid, and Donna J. Guy's *A Global History of Sexuality: The Modern Era* (Wiley Blackwell, 2014), which offers an excellent set of essays framing key issues in the history of sexuality within a world history framework.

Rather than aim for a comprehensive survey of sex in global history, this collection concentrates on selected historical episodes where sex, gender, and sexuality illuminate major features of global history. Themes of colonialism, representation, scientific inquiry and authority, and rights and regulations bind together material from the Spanish Conquest of North America to contemporary transgender history.

Consider, for instance, the history of conquest and slavery in North America. Whereas a typical treatment of this topic might rightly center on issues of race and economic history, here we integrate issues of gender representation and reproductive order using Jennifer Morgan's richly illustrated and insightful essay, "'Some Could Suckle over Their Shoulder': Male Travelers, Female Bodies, and the Gendering of Racial Ideology, 1500–1770." Morgan explains how European colonizers represented black women's bodies, held them up against an ideal of European womanhood, and then used the perceived differences as means to legitimate conquest- and race-based chattel slavery. Variations on this theme easily extend to other colonial contexts, such as Africa in the eighteenth century and India in the nineteenth and twentieth centuries.

The theme of representation cuts across a number of sources in this collection, including Hiratsuka Raicho's "Restoring Women's Talents," Huda Shaarawi's *Harem Years*, and Vicki Ruiz's "The Flapper and the Chaperone." In these sources, women's appearance acts as a source of social and political resistance. Raicho's embrace of the "modern girl," for instance, places her in a global dialogue concerning women's sexuality and its representations. These "new women" of the early twentieth century challenged prevailing ideas of women's roles and sexual expression that were at once locally specific and yet globally recognized.

Appreciating the range of sexual expression in different societies goes hand in hand with understanding the condition under which states and societies sought to categorize, name, and regulate what became alternative expressions of gender, sex, and sexuality. The practice of "norming" was especially important in colonial contexts where norms of femininity, masculinity, and heterosexuality were imposed on colonial subjects. State-dictated reproductive norms also played a central role in the regulation of birth control, abortion, and population in eugenic efforts developed in the United States, Europe, India, and China. These eugenic and population control efforts enforced often-racialized procreative norms with important implications for ideas of heterosexuality and women's and men's broader social and political roles.

The scientific construction of sex, sexuality, and gender played a crucial role in the legitimation of certain social norms as well as the legitimation of resistance to those norms. From Aristotle and Barclay to Krafft-Ebbing, through Hirschfeld and Freud to Kinsey, the sources in this collection highlight major developments in scientific understanding of sex and sexuality and their social implications. These primary sources are placed in wider historical context by secondary essays by Vernon Rosario and Veronika Fuechtner. These essays demonstrate that the science of sex and sexuality was steadily changing and always deeply immersed in its social and political context. These sources and Genny Beemyn's "Transgender History in the United States" allow us to appreciate how the very categories of sex, gender, and sexuality have changed over the course of the past four centuries, how they have been deployed by states as tools of empire and social control, and how they have been incorporated into or resisted by countless lives in a wide range of times and places.

The preparation of this collection has been aided by the generous assistance of colleagues and students. I am grateful for thoughtful suggestions from Julio Capo Jr. and Priyanka Srivastava, as well as my students in my initial offerings of Sex in Global History who helped fine-tune this course. A Mellon Mutual Mentoring grant awarded to myself, Julio Capo Jr., Priyanka Srivastava, and Tanisha Ford offered the initial impetus to think broadly about the history of sex, gender, and sexuality. The editorial staff at Cognella has been invaluable in the process of seeing this collection into print.

PART I

COLONIAL ENCOUNTERS AND "NEW WORLDS"

The sources in this section include descriptions of the Americas and Africa from the diaries of a colonizer, Christopher Columbus, and an enslaved subject, Olaudah Equiano, respectively. Jennifer Morgan's essay analyzes how these and other representations use gender and race to justify processes of colonization.

READING 1

Diary of Christopher Columbus, Entries for
August 3rd and October 11th and 13th.

Recorded in 1493, Columbus's journal describes his travel to the "New
World." Excerpts include descriptions of the Native American people
that Columbus and his crew met when they landed on October 11th
and 13th, 1492.

Diary of Christopher Columbus

Christopher Columbus

FRIDAY 3 AUGUST

We left the bar of Saltés at eight o'clock on Friday 3 August 1492. We sailed with a strong sea breeze until sunset, S for 60 miles, which is 15 leagues, then SW and S by W, which was the route to the Canaries.

THURSDAY 11 OCTOBER

He sailed WSW. They had a rough sea, rougher than any they had had throughout the voyage. They spotted some petrels and a green reed near the flagship. The crew of the caravel Pinta spotted a cane and a twig and they fished out another piece of stick, carved with iron by the looks of it, and a piece of cane and other vegetation that grows on land, and a small plank. The crew of the caravel Niña also saw signs of land and a branch covered in barnacles. At these signs they breathed again and all took heart. They sailed 27 leagues today, until sunset. After sunset he set his former course due W. They were making about twelve miles an hour and until two in the morning they made about 90 miles, that is 22 leagues and a half. And because the caravel Pinta was faster and sailed ahead of the Admiral, she sighted land and gave the signals that the Admiral had commanded. The first man to see this land was a sailor by the name of Rodrigo de Triana,[1] although the Admiral had seen a light at ten in the evening on the poop deck, but

---

1   The name Rodrigo de Triana does not appear in the crew lists and the evidence of the pleitos suggests that the correct name was Juan Rodriguez Bermejo, a native of the town of Molinos. 'Rodrigo de Triana' may have been a nickname. In the event, Columbus claimed the reward on the grounds that he had seen a light the previous evening.

Christopher Columbus, *from the Diary of Christopher Columbus*, ed. Barry Ife.

it was so indistinct that he would not swear that it was land.[2] But he called Pero Gutiérrez, His Majesty's chamberlain, told him that it seemed to be a light and asked him to look, which he did, and he did see it. He also called Rodrigo Sánchez de Segovia, whom the King and Queen had sent as comptroller, and he saw nothing as he was not in a position from which he could see it. After the Admiral had spoken, the light was spotted a couple of times, and it was like a small wax candle being raised and lowered, which struck very few people as being a sign of land, but the Admiral was certain that he was near land. So when they had said the Salve, which all sailors are accustomed to say or chant in their own way, and they were all gathered together, the Admiral urged them to keep a good lookout from the forecastle and watch for land, saying that he would give the first man to tell him that he could see land a silk doublet, quite apart from the other rewards which the King and Queen had promised, such as the annual payment of ten thousand maravedís to the first man to see land. Two hours after midnight land appeared at a distance of about two leagues. They shortened all sail, kept the mainsail without the bonnets and lay to, waiting for Friday to dawn, the day on which they finally reached a small island of the Lucayos which was called in the language of the Indians Guanahaní.[3] Then they saw some naked people and the Admiral went ashore in the armed boat with Martín Alonso Pinzón and Vicente Yáñez, his brother, who was the captain of the Niña. The Admiral brought out the royal standard, and the captains unfurled two banners of the green cross, which the Admiral flew as his standard on all the ships, with an F and a Y, and a crown over each letter, one on one side of the + and one on the other. When they landed they saw trees, very green, many streams and a large variety of fruits. The Admiral called the two captains and the others who landed, and Rodrigo de Escobedo, secretary of the expedition, and Rodrigo Sánchez de Segovia, and made them bear witness and

---

2   This light has variously been attributed to Columbus's imagination, wishful thinking, or refusal to accept that someone else had spotted land first. If the light did exist, it may have been caused by a fire lit by native fishermen to attract fish to the vicinity at night. It would have to be a large fire, since the ships were over 50 miles from landfall at 10 pm the previous evening.

3   The exact location of this island remains uncertain, and no contemporary source identifies Guanahani, presumably because its identity was common knowledge; there is no hint of doubt in Las Casas's mind about which island is being referred to. Many islands in the Bahamas and the Turks and Caicos group fit the description given by Columbus - low, green and surrounded by a reef, and connected to another island by a narrow isthmus. In all, nine islands have been suggested as the site of the first landfall, but only two, Watlings and Samana Cay, have attracted convincing arguments from respected scholars. The arguments have been summarised by John Parker in De Vorsey and Parker, *In the Wake of Columbus*, pp. 1–34, and by Robert Fuson in *The Log of Christopher Columbus*, Southampton: Ashford Press Publishing, 1987, pp. 199–221. Columbus visited four main islands before reaching Cuba on 28 October. He called these islands San Salvador, Santa María de la Concepción, Fernandina, and Isabela. If the first island is assumed to be Watlings, the others are Rum Cay, Long Island and Crooked Island; if the first island is Samana Cay, the others are Crooked Island, Long Island and Fortune Island. The Watlings theory is supported by S.E. Morison, *Admiral of the Ocean Sea*, Boston: Little, Brown and Co., 1942. The Samana Cay theory was first proposed by Gustavus V. Fox in 1882 and was endorsed by Joseph Judge in the November 1986 issue of the *National Geographic*. All landfall theories involve stretching the evidence of the text to some degree.

testimony that he, in their presence, took possession, as in fact he did take possession, of the said island in the names of the King and Queen, His Sovereigns, making the requisite declarations, as is more fully recorded in the statutory instruments which were set down in writing. Then, many islanders gathered round. What follows are the Admiral's own words from the journal of his first voyage and discovery of these Indies. In order to win their good will, he says, because I could see that they were a people who could more easily be won over and converted to our holy faith by kindness than by force, I gave some of them red hats and glass beads that they put round their necks, and many other things of little value, with which they were very pleased and became so friendly that it was a wonder to see. Afterwards they swam out to the ships' boats where we were and brought parrots and balls of cotton thread and spears and many other things, and they bartered with us for other things which we gave them, like glass beads and hawks' bells. In fact they took and gave everything they had with good will, but it seemed to me that they were a people who were very poor in everything.[4] They go as naked as their mothers bore them, even the women, though I only saw one girl, and she was very young. All those I did see were young men, none of them more than thirty years old. They were well built, with handsome bodies and fine features. Their hair is thick, almost like a horse's tail, but short; they wear it down over their eyebrows except for a few strands behind which they wear long and never cut. Some of them paint themselves black, though they are naturally the colour of Canary Islanders,[5] neither black nor white; and some paint themselves white, some red and some whatever colour they can find; some paint their faces, some their whole bodies, some only the eyes and some only the nose. They do not carry arms and do not know of them because I showed them some swords and they grasped them by the blade and cut themselves out of ignorance. They have no iron: their spears are just shafts without a metal tip, and some have a fish tooth at the end, and some have other things. They are all fairly tall, good looking and well proportioned. I saw some who had signs of wounds on their bodies and in sign language I asked them what they were, and they indicated that other people came from other islands nearby and tried to capture them, and they defended themselves.[6] I believed then and still believe that they come here from the mainland to take them as slaves. They ought to make good slaves for they are of quick intelligence since I notice that they are quick to repeat what is said to them, and I believe that they could very easily become Christians, for it seemed to me that they had no religion of their own. God willing, when I come

4   The original inhabitants of the Bahamas were Tainos, members of the Arawak cultural and linguistic group.

5   Columbus assumed, along with his contemporaries, a correlation between skin colour and latitude. The idea derived from Aristotle via Pierre D'Ailly's Imago Mundi.

6   Columbus is quick to form the notion that these people are preyed upon by another, superior, culture in the vicinity (identified as cannibals on 23 November) and the theory governs much of his decision-making for the rest of the first voyage (see Peter Hulme, 'Columbus and the Cannibals' in Colonial Encounters, London and New York: Methuen, 1986, pp. 13–43).

to leave I will bring six of them to Your Highnesses so that they may learn to speak. I have seen no animals of any kind on this island, except parrots. These are all the Admiral's own words.

SATURDAY 13 OCTOBER

At sunrise many of these men, all youths, as I have said, came to the shore. They were all of good stature, very handsome people, with hair which is not curly but thick and flowing like a horse's mane. They all have very wide foreheads and heads, wider than those of any race I have seen before; their eyes are very beautiful and not small. None of them is black, rather the colour of the Canary islanders, which is to be expected since this island lies E-W with the island of Ferro in the Canaries on the same latitude.[7] They all have very straight legs; they are not pot-bellied, but very well formed. They came to the ship in dugouts[8] which are made out of a tree-trunk, like a long boat, and all in one piece and wonderfully well carved in the local manner. Some are large, to the extent that 40 or 45 men came in some of them, and others are smaller, so small that there were some with only one man in them. They paddle with a kind of baker's peel and it goes along wonderfully, and if one overturns they all swim around and right it and bale it out with gourds which they carry. They brought balls of cotton thread and parrots and spears and other things which it would be tedious to list and they gave anything in exchange for whatever was given to them. I watched intently and tried to find out if there was any gold and I saw that some of them wore a small piece hanging from a hole in the nose. By sign language I gathered that to the south, or rounding the southern end of the island, there was a king who had great quantities of it in large pots. I tried to get them to go there but I subsequently saw that they were not interested in going.[9] I decided to wait until tomorrow afternoon and then leave for the SW, where from what many of them pointed out to me, they said there was land to the S and SW and NW, and that from these islands to the NW they very often came to attack them; and so to the SW, to look for the gold and precious stones. This island is very large and very flat, the trees are very green, and there is much water; there is a very large lake[10] in the centre. There are no mountains and it is all so green that it is a pleasure to see. And these people are so gentle, and out of a desire to have some of our things and fear that they will not be given anything without their giving something in exchange, and they have nothing to give, they grab whatever they can

---

7 Both Watlings and Samana Cay are 3–40 south of the latitude of Ferro, but Columbus is speaking in general terms.

8 The native word 'canoa' is not used in the text at this point, but appears only in Las Casas's marginal note. The word used by Columbus to describe the Indian dugout, 'almadia', is of Arabic origin and was normally used to refer to a raft rather than a boat made from a single piece of wood.

9 Or possibly: 'that they did not know the way'.

10 Some authorities prefer to translate 'laguna' as 'lagoon'; the Samana Cay theory requires this interpretation.

and set off swimming. They give everything they have for whatever we give them, even pieces of broken bowls and glass cups they will barter for. I even saw 16 balls of cotton given for three Portuguese coins worth a few farthings in Castile, but there must have been more than 25 pounds of cotton thread there. I would forbid this and not allow anyone to take any of it, but order it all to be kept for Your Highnesses, if there were plenty of it. It grows here on this island but for lack of time I could not make a full investigation; the gold which they wear hanging from their noses is also found here, but, in order not to waste time I want to go and see if I can find the island of Cipangu. Now since it is night they have all gone ashore in their canoes.

READING 2

Olaudah Equiano, *The Interesting Narrative of the
Life of Olaudah Equiano, or Gustavus Vassa,
the African* (1789), Ch. 1, Excerpts.

Olaudah Equiano's (1745–1797) autobiography is one of the best-known
narratives of slavery. Published in 1789, this excerpt describes the
"manners and customs" of his people in Guinea before he was forced
into slavery.

The Interesting Narrative of the Life of Olaudah Equiano, or Gustavus Vassa, the African

Olaudah Equiano

That part of Africa, known by the name of Guinea, to which the trade for slaves is carried on, extends along the coast above 3400 miles, from the Senegal to Angola, and includes a variety of kingdoms. Of these the most considerable is the kingdom of Benen, both as to extent and wealth, the richness and cultivation of the soil, the power of its king, and the number and warlike disposition of the inhabitants. It is situated nearly under the line, and extends along the coast about 170 miles, but runs back into the interior part of Africa to a distance hitherto I believe unexplored by any traveller; and seems only terminated at length by the empire of Abyssinia, near 1500 miles from its beginning. This kingdom is divided into many provinces or districts: in one of the most remote and fertile of which, called Eboe, I was born, in the year 1745, in a charming fruitful vale, named Essaka. The distance of this province from the capital of Benin and the sea coast must be very considerable; for I had never heard of white men or Europeans, nor of the sea: and our subjection to the king of Benin was little more than nominal; for every transaction of the government, as far as my slender observation extended, was conducted by the chiefs or elders of the place. The manners and government of a people who have little commerce with other countries are generally very simple; and the history of what passes in one family or village may serve as a specimen of a nation. My father was one of those elders or chiefs I have spoken of, and was styled Embrenche; a term, as I remember, importing the highest distinction, and signifying in our language a mark of grandeur. This mark is conferred on the person entitled to it, by cutting the skin across at the top of the forehead, and drawing it down to the eye-brows; and while it is in this situation applying a warm hand, and rubbing it until it shrinks up into a thick weal across the lower part of the forehead. Most of the judges and senators were thus marked;

Olaudah Equiano, *The Interesting Narrative of the Life of Olaudah Equiano*, or *Gustavus Vassa*, the African (1789), pp. 4-22, 30-32, 37-44, 1789.

my father had long born it: I had seen it conferred on one of my brothers, and I was also destined to receive it by my parents. Those Embrence, or chief men, decided disputes and punished crimes; for which purpose they always assembled together. The proceedings were generally short; and in most cases the law of retaliation prevailed. I remember a man was brought before my father, and the other judges, for kidnapping a boy; he was the son of a chief or senator, he was condemned to make recompense by a man or woman slave. Adultery, however, was sometimes punished with slavery or death; a punishment which I believe is inflicted on it throughout most of the nations of Africa:[1] so sacred among them is the honour of the marriage bed, and so jealous are they of the fidelity of their wives. Of this I recollect an instance:—a woman was convicted before the judges of adultery, and delivered over, as the custom was, to her husband to be punished. Accordingly he determined to put her to death: but it being found, just before her execution, that she had an infant at her breast; and no woman being prevailed on to perform the part of a nurse, she was spared on account of the child. The men, however, do not preserve the same constancy to their wives, which they expect from them; for they indulge in a plurality, though seldom in more than two. Their mode of marriage is thus:—both parties are usually betrothed when young by their parents, (though I have known the males to betroth themselves). On this occasion a feast is prepared, and the bride and bridegroom stand up in the midst of all their friends, who are assembled for the purpose, while he declares she is thenceforth to be looked upon as his wife, and that no other person is to pay any addresses to her. This is also immediately proclaimed in the vicinity, on which the bride retires from the assembly. Some time after she is brought home to her husband, and then another feast is made, to which the relations of both parties are invited: her parents then deliver her to the bridegroom, accompanied with a number of blessings, and at the same time they tie round her waist a cotton string of the thickness of a goose-quill, which none but married women are permitted to wear: she is now considered as completely his wife; and at this time the dowry is given to the new married pair, which generally consists of portions of land, slaves, and cattle, household goods, and implements of husbandry. These are offered by the friends of both parties; besides which the parents of the bride-groom present gifts to those of the bride, whose property she is looked upon before marriage; but after it she is esteemed the sole property of her husband. The ceremony being now ended the festival begins, which is celebrated with bonefires, and loud acclamations of joy, accompanied with music and dancing.

We are almost a nation of dancers, musicians, and poets. Thus every great event, such as a triumphant return from battle, or other cause of public rejoicing is celebrated in public dances, which are accompanied with songs and music suited to the occasion. The assembly is separated into four divisions, which dance either apart or in succession, and each with a character peculiar to itself. The first division contains the married men, who in their dances frequently exhibit seats of arms, and the

---

1   *See Benezet's "Account of Guinea" throughout.*

representation of a battle. To these succeed the married women, who dance in the second division. The young men occupy the third; and the maidens the fourth. Each represents some interesting scene of real life, such as a great achievement, domestic employment, a pathetic story, or some rural sport; and as the subject is generally founded on some recent event, it is therefore ever new. This gives our dances a spirit and variety which I have scarcely seen elsewhere.[2] We have many musical instruments, particularly drums of different kinds, a piece of music which resembles a guitar, and another much like a stickado. These last are chiefly used by betrothed virgins, who play on them on all grand festivals.

As our manners are simple, our luxuries are few. The dress of both sexes is nearly the same. It generally consists of a long piece of callico, or muslin, wrapped loosely round the body, somewhat in the form of a highland plaid. This is usually dyed blue, which is our favourite colour. It is extracted from a berry, and is brighter and richer than any I have seen in Europe. Besides this, our women of distinction wear golden ornaments; which they dispose with some profusion on their arms and legs. When our women are not employed with the men in tillage, their usual occupation is spinning and weaving cotton, which they afterwards dye, and make it into garments. They also manufacture earthen vessels, of which we have many kinds. Among the rest tobacco pipes, made after the same fashion, and used in the same manner, as those in Turkey.[3]

Our manner of living is entirely plain; for as yet the natives are unacquainted with those refinements in cookery which debauch the taste: bullocks, goats, and poultry, supply the greatest part of their food. These constitute likewise the principal wealth of the country, and the chief articles of its commerce. The flesh is usually stewed in a pan; to make it savoury we sometimes use also pepper, and other spices, and we have salt made of wood ashes. Our vegetables are mostly plantains, eadas, yams, beans, and Indian corn. The head of the family usually eats alone; his wives and slaves have also their separate tables. Before we taste food we always wash our hands: indeed our cleanliness on all occasions is extreme; but on this it is an indispensable ceremony. After washing, libation is made, by pouring out a small portion of the food, in a certain place, for the spirits of departed relations, which the natives suppose to preside over their conduct, and guard them from evil. They are totally unacquainted with strong or spirituous liquours; and their principal beverage is palm wine. This is gotten from a tree of that name by tapping it at the top, and fastening a large gourd to it; and sometimes one tree will yield three or four gallons in a night. When just drawn it is of a most delicious sweetness; but in a few days it acquires a tartish and more spirituous flavour; though I never saw any one intoxicated by it. The same tree also produces nuts and oil. Our principal luxury is in perfumes; one sort of these is an odoriferous wood of delicious fragrance: the other a kind of earth; a small portion of which thrown into

---

2   When I was in Smyrna I have frequently seen the Greeks dance after this manner.

3   The bowl is earthen, curiously figured, to which a long reed is fixed as a tube. This tube is sometimes so long as to be born by one, and frequently out of grandeur by two boys.

the fire diffuses a most powerful odour.[4] We beat this wood into powder, and mix it with palm oil; with which both men and women perfume themselves.

In our buildings we study convenience rather than ornament. Each master of a family has a large square piece of ground, surrounded with a moat or fence, or enclosed with a wall made of red earth tempered; which, when dry, is as hard as brick. Within this are his houses to accommodate his family and slaves; which, if numerous, frequently present the appearance of a village. In the middle stands the principal building, appropriated to the sole use of the master, and consisting of two apartments; in one of which he sits in the day with his family, the other is left apart for the reception of his friends. He has besides these a distinct apartment in which he sleeps, together with his male children. On each side are the apartments of his wives, who have also their separate day and night houses. The habitations of the slaves and their families are distributed throughout the rest of the enclosure. These houses never exceed one story in height: they are always built of wood, or stakes driven into the ground, crossed with wattles, and neatly plastered within, and without. The roof is thatched with reeds. Our day-houses are left open at the sides; but those in which we sleep are always covered, and plastered in the inside, with a composition mixed with cowdung, to keep off the different insects, which annoy us during the night. The walls and floors also of these are generally covered with mats. Our beds consist of a platform, raised three or four feet from the ground, on which are laid skins, and different parts of a spungy tree called plaintain. Our covering is calico or muslin, the same as our dress. The usual seats are a few logs of wood; but we have benches, which are generally perfumed, to accommodate strangers: these compose the greater part of our household furniture. Houses so constructed and furnished require but little skill to erect them. Every man is a sufficient architect for the purpose. The whole neighbourhood afford their unanimous assistance in building them and in return receive, and expect no other recompense than a feast.

As we live in a country where nature is prodigal of her favours, our wants are few and easily supplied; of course we have few manufactures. They consist for the most part of calicoes, earthern ware, ornaments, and instruments of war and husbandry. But these make no part of our commerce, the principal articles of which, as I have observed, are provisions. In such a state money is of little use; however we have some small pieces of coin, if I may call them such. They are made something like an anchor; but I do not remember either their value or denomination. We have also markets, at which I have been frequently with my mother. These are sometimes visited by stout mahogany-coloured men from the south west of us: we call them Oye-Eboe, which term signifies red men living at a distance. They generally bring us fire-arms, gunpowder, hats, beads, and dried fish. The last we esteemed a great rarity, as our waters were only brooks and springs. These articles they barter with us for odoriferous

---

4 *When I was in Smyrna I saw the same kind of earth; and brought some of it with me to England; it resembles musk in strength, but is more delicious in scent, and is not unlike the smell of a rose.*

woods and earth, and our salt of wood ashes. They always carry slaves through our land; but the strictest account is exacted of their manner of procuring them before they are suffered to pass. Sometimes indeed we sold slaves to them, but they were only prisoners of war, or such among us as had been convicted of kidnapping, or adultery, and some other crimes, which we esteemed heinous. This practice of kidnapping induces me to think, that, notwithstanding all our strictness, their principal business among us was to trepan our people. I remember too they carried great sacks along with them, which not long after I had an opportunity of fatally seeing applied to that infamous purpose.

Our land is uncommonly rich and fruitful, and produces all kinds of vegetables in great abundance. We have plenty of Indian corn, and vast quantities of cotton and tobacco. Our pine apples grow without culture; they are about the size of the largest sugar-loaf, and finely flavoured. We have also spices of different kinds, particularly pepper; and a variety of delicious fruits which I have never seen in Europe; together with gums of various kinds, and honey in abundance. All our industry is exerted to improve those blessings of nature. Agriculture is our chief employment; and every one, even the children and women, are engaged in it. Thus we are all habituated to labour from our earliest years. Every one contributes something to the common stock; and as we are unacquainted with idleness, we have no beggars. The benefits of such a mode of living are obvious. The West India planters prefer the slaves of Benin or Eboe to those of any other part of Guinea, for their hardiness, intelligence, integrity, and zeal. Those benefits are felt by us in the general healthiness of the people, and in their vigour and activity; I might have added too in their comeliness. Deformity is indeed unknown amongst us, I mean that of shape. Numbers of the natives of Eboe now in London might be brought in support of this assertion: for, in regard to complexion, ideas of beauty are wholly relative. I remember while in Africa to have seen three negro children, who were tawny, and another quite white, who were universally regarded by myself, and the natives in general, as far as related to their complexions, deformed. Our women too were in my eyes at least uncommonly graceful, alert, and modest to a degree of bashfulness; nor do I remember to have ever heard of an instance of incontinence amongst them before marriage. They are also remarkably cheerful. Indeed cheerfulness and affability are two of the leading characteristics of our nation.

. . .

We practised circumcision like the Jews, and made offerings and feasts on that occasion in the same manner as they did. Like them also, our children were named from some event, some circumstance, or fancied foreboding at the time of their birth. I was named Olaudah, which, in our language, signifies vicissitude or fortune also, one favoured, and having a loud voice and well spoken. I remember we never polluted the name of the object of our adoration; on the contrary, it was always mentioned with the greatest reverence; and we were totally unacquainted with swearing, and all those terms of abuse and reproach which find their way so readily and copiously into the languages of more civilized people. The only expressions of that kind I remember were 'May you rot, or may you swell, or may a beast take you.'

I have before remarked that the natives of this part of Africa are extremely cleanly. This necessary habit of decency was with us a part of religion, and therefore we had many purifications and washings; indeed almost as many, and used on the same occasions, if my recollection does not fail me, as the Jews. Those that touched the dead at any time were obliged to wash and purify themselves before they could enter a dwelling-house. Every woman too, at certain times, was forbidden to come into a dwelling-house, or touch any person, or any thing we ate. I was so fond of my mother I could not keep from her, or avoid touching her at some of those periods, in consequence of which I was obliged to be kept out with her, in a little house made for that purpose, till offering was made, and then we were purified.

. . .

Such is the imperfect sketch my memory has furnished me with of the manners and customs of a people among whom I first drew my breath. And here I cannot forbear suggesting what has long struck me very forcibly, namely, the strong analogy which even by this sketch, imperfect as it is, appears to prevail in the manners and customs of my countrymen and those of the Jews, before they reached the Land of Promise, and particularly the patriarchs while they were yet in that pastoral state which is described in Genesis—an analogy, which alone would induce me to think that the one people had sprung from the other. Indeed this is the opinion of Dr. Gill, who, in his commentary on Genesis, very ably deduces the pedigree of the Africans from Afer and Afra, the descendants of Abraham by Keturah his wife and concubine (for both these titles are applied to her). It is also conformable to the sentiments of Dr. John Clarke, formerly Dean of Sarum, in his Truth of the Christian Religion: both these authors concur in ascribing to us this original. The reasonings of these gentlemen are still further confirmed by the scripture chronology; and if any further corroboration were required, this resemblance in so many respects is a strong evidence in support of the opinion. Like the Israelites in their primitive state, our government was conducted by our chiefs or judges, our wise men and elders; and the head of a family with us enjoyed a similar authority over his household with that which is ascribed to Abraham and the other patriarchs. The law of retaliation obtained almost universally with us as with them: and even their religion appeared to have shed upon us a ray of its glory, though broken and spent in its passage, or eclipsed by the cloud with which time, tradition, and ignorance might have enveloped it; for we had our circumcision (a rule I believe peculiar to that people:) we had also our sacrifices and burnt-offerings, our washings and purifications, on the same occasions as they had.

As to the difference of colour between the Eboan Africans and the modern Jews,

I shall not presume to account for it. It is a subject which has engaged the pens of men of both genius and learning, and is far above my strength. The most able and Reverend Mr. T. Clarkson, however, in his much admired Essay on the Slavery and Commerce of the Human Species, has ascertained the cause, in a manner that at once solves every objection on that account, and, on my mind at least, has produced the fullest conviction. I shall therefore refer to that performance for the theory,[5] contenting myself with extracting a fact as related by Dr. Mitchel.[6] "The Spaniards, who have inhabited America, under the torrid zone, for any time, are become as dark coloured as our native Indians of Virginia; of which I myself have been a witness." There is also another instance[7] of a Portuguese settlement at Mitomba, a river in Sierra Leona; where the inhabitants are bred from a mixture of the first Portuguese discoverers with the natives, and are now become in their complexion, and in the woolly quality of their hair, perfect negroes, retaining however a smattering of the Portuguese language.

These instances, and a great many more which might be adduced, while they shew how the complexions of the same persons vary in different climates, it is hoped may tend also to remove the prejudice that some conceive against the natives of Africa on account of their colour. Surely the minds of the Spaniards did not change with their complexions! Are there not causes enough to which the apparent inferiority of an African may be ascribed, without limiting the goodness of God, and supposing he forbore to stamp understanding on certainly his own image, because "carved in ebony." Might it not naturally be ascribed to their situation? When they come among Europeans, they are ignorant of their language, religion, manners, and customs. Are any pains taken to teach them these? Are they treated as men? Does not slavery itself depress the mind, and extinguish all its fire and every noble sentiment? But, above all, what advantages do not a refined people possess over those who are rude and unculti- vated. Let the polished and haughty European recollect that his ancestors were once, like the Africans, uncivilized, and even barbarous. Did Nature make them inferior to their sons? and should they too have been made slaves? Every rational mind answers, No. Let such reflections as these melt the pride of their superiority into sympathy for the wants and miseries of their sable brethren, and compel them to acknowledge, that understanding is not confined to feature or colour. If, when they look round the world, they feel exultation, let it be tempered with benevolence to others, and gratitude to God, "who hath made of one blood all nations of men for to dwell on all the face of the earth;[8] and whose wisdom is not our wisdom, neither are our ways his ways."

----

5   *Page 178 to 216.*

6   *Philos. Trans. No. 476, Sect. 4, cited by Mr. Clarkson, p. 205.*

7   *Same page.*

8   *Acts, c. xvii, v. 26.*

READING 3

Jennifer Morgan, "'Some Could Suckle over Their Shoulder': Male Travelers, Female Bodies, and the Gendering of Racial Ideology, 1500–1770," *The William and Mary Quarterly* 54 (1997): 167–192.

Reprinted in its entirety, this essay by historian Jennifer Morgan considers how colonial representations of bodily difference, especially among women, were used to justify racial superiority and European colonization.

"Some Could Suckle over Their Shoulder"

Male Travelers, Female Bodies, and the Gendering
of Racial Ideology, 1500–1770

Jennifer L. Morgan

I n June 1647, the Englishman Richard Ligon left London on the
ship *Achilles* to establish himself as a planter in the newly settled
colony of Barbados. En route, Ligon's ship stopped in the Cape Verde
Islands for provisions and trade. There Ligon saw a black woman
for the first time; as he recorded the encounter in his *True and Exact
History of ... Barbadoes,* she was a "Negro of the greatest beauty and
majesty together: that ever I saw in one woman. Her stature large, and
excellently shap'd, well favour'd, full eye'd, and admirably grac'd....
[I] awaited her comming out, which was with far greater Majesty and
gracefulness, than I have seen Queen Anne, descend from the Chaire
of State."[1] Ligon's rhetoric may have surprised his English readers, for
seventeenth-century images of black women did not usually evoke the
ultimate marker of civility—the monarchy—as the referent.

Early modern English writers conventionally set the black female
figure against one that was white—and thus beautiful. In *Pseudodoxia
Epidemica* (1646), Sir Thomas Browne argued that blackness and beauty
were mutually dependent, each relying on the other as antithetical

---

1 Ligon, *A True and Exact History of the Island of Barbadoes* (London, 1657), 12–13.

Jennifer L. Morgan is a postdoctoral fellow in the Department of History at the Uni-
versity of Maryland, College Park. Versions of this article were presented at the
1994 Caribbean Studies Association meeting; at Interrogating the Nation—Feminist
Perspectives, a symposium sponsored by the Program in Women's Studies at The
Johns Hopkins University; and at the Tenth Berkshire Conference on the History of
Women, Chapel Hill, North Carolina. She thanks participants in the Institute of Early
American History and Culture's Constructing Race seminar, the anonymous *William
and Mary Quarterly* referees, and Herman Bennett, Antoinette Burton, Shelly Evers-
ley, Kirsten Fischer, and Robert Reid-Pharr for being both friends and critics.

Jennifer L. Morgan, "'Some Could Suckle over Their Shoulder': Male Travelers,

Female Bodies, and the Gendering of Racial Ideology, 1500-1770," *The William and*

Mary Quarterly, vol. 54, no. 1, pp. 167-192. Copyright © 1997 by Omohundro Institute

of Early American History and Culture. Reprinted with permission.

proof of each one's existence.[2] Recently, depictions of black women in early modern England have attracted scholarly attention. Peter Erickson calls the image of the black woman a trope for disrupted harmony. Lynda Boose sees black women in early modern English writing as symbolically "unrepresentable," embodying a deep threat to patriarchy. Kim Hall finds early modern English literature and material culture fully involved with a gendered racial discourse committed to constructing stable categories of whiteness and blackness.[3] As these and other scholars have shown, male travelers to Africa and the Americas contributed to a European discourse on black womanhood. Femaleness evoked a certain element of desire, but travelers depicted black women as simultaneously un-womanly and marked by a reproductive value dependent on their sex. Writers' recognition of black femaleness and their inability to allow black women to embody "proper" female space composed a focus for representations of racial difference. During the course of his journey, Ligon came to another view of black women. As he saw it, their breasts "hang down below their Navels, so that when they stoop at their common work of weeding, they hang almost to the ground, that at a distance you would think they had six legs." For Ligon, their monstrous bodies symbolized their sole utility—their ability to produce both crops and other laborers.[4]

Ligon's narrative is a microcosm of a much larger ideological maneuver that juxtaposed the familiar with the unfamiliar—the beautiful woman who is also the monstrous laboring beast. As the tenacious and historically deep roots of racialist ideology become more evident, it becomes clear also that, through the rubric of monstrously "raced" Amerindian and African women, Europeans found a means to articulate shifting perceptions of themselves as religiously, culturally, and phenotypically superior to those black or brown persons they sought to define. In the discourse used to justify the slave trade, Ligon's beautiful Negro woman was as important as her six-legged counterpart. Both imaginary women marked a gendered whiteness that accompanied European expansionism.[5] Well before the publication of Ligon's work, New World and African narratives that relied on gender to convey an emergent notion of racialized difference had been published in England and Europe.

---

2 Browne, *Pseudodoxia Epidemica: or Enquiries into very many received tenents and commonly presumed truths* (1646), cited in Kim F. Hall, *Things of Darkness: Economies of Race and Gender in Early Modern England* (Ithaca, 1995), 12.

3 Erickson, "Representations of Blacks and Blackness in the Renaissance," *Criticism*, 35 (1993), 514–15; Boose, "'The Getting of a Lawful Race': Racial Discourse in Early Modern England and the Unrepresentable Black Woman," in Margo Hendricks and Patricia Parker, eds., *Women, "Race," and Writing in the Early Modern Period* (London, 1994), 49; Hall, *Things of Darkness*, 4, 6–7.

4 Ligon, *True and Exact History ... of Barbadoes*, 51.

5 In regard to "whiteness" as defined by "blackness," Toni Morrison asserts that "the fabrication of an Africanist persona is reflexive; an extraordinary meditation on the [white] self; a powerful exploration of the fears and desires that reside in the writerly conscious. It is an astonishing revelation of longing, of terror, of perplexity, of shame, of magnanimity. It requires hard work not to see this," in *Playing in the Dark: Whiteness and the Literary Imagination* (Cambridge, Mass., 1992), 17.

Although this article is primarily concerned with England and its imperial expansion, by the time English colonists arrived in the Americas they already possessed the trans-European ethnohistoriographical tradition of depicting the imagined native in which Ligon's account is firmly situated.[6]

Ligon's attitude toward the enslaved has been characterized by modern historians as "more liberal and humane than [that] of the generality of planters."[7] Nevertheless, his text indicates the kind of negative symbolic work required of black women in early modern English discourse. As Ligon penned his manuscript while in debtors' prison in 1653, he constructed a layered narrative in which the discovery of African women's monstrosity helped to assure the work's success. Taking the female body as a symbol of the deceptive beauty and ultimate savagery of blackness, Ligon allowed his readers to dally with him among beautiful black women, only seductively to disclose their monstrosity over the course of the narrative. Travel accounts, which had proved their popularity by the time Ligon's *History ... of Barbadoes* appeared, relied on gendered notions of European social order to project African cultural disorder. I do not argue here that gender operated as a more profound category of difference than race. Rather, this article focuses on the way in which racialist discourse was deeply imbued with ideas about gender and sexual difference that, indeed, became manifest only in contact with each other. White men who laid the discursive groundwork on which the "theft of bodies" could be justified relied on mutually constitutive ideologies of race and gender to affirm Europe's legitimate access to African labor.[8]

Travel accounts produced in Europe and available in England provided a corpus from which subsequent writers borrowed freely, reproducing images of Native American and African women that resonated with readers. These travelers learned to dismiss the idea that women in the Americas and Africa might be innocuous, unremarkable,

---

6   Peter Hulme, *Colonial Encounters: Europe and the Native Caribbean, 1492–1797* (London,(1986), 11, 18.

7   P. F. Campbell, "Richard Ligon," *Journal of the Barbados Museum and Historical Society, 37* (1985), 259. For more on Ligon see Campbell, "Two Generations of Walronds," ibid., 38 (1989), 253–85.

8   Arguments about the primacy of race or gender regarding the original construction of difference comprise an enormous theoretical literature. See, for example, Henry Louis Gates, Jr., "Writing, 'Race,' and the Difference It Makes," in Gates, ed., *"Race," Writing and Difference* (Chicago, 1985), 5, who asserts that "race has become a trope of ultimate, irreducible difference." Hortense J. Spillers similarly argues that slavery—the theft of the body—severed the captive from all that had been "gender-related [or] gender-specific" and thus was an "ungendering" process, in "Mama's Baby, Papa's Maybe: An American Grammar Book," *Diacritics*, 17 (Summer 1987), 65–81. I would posit that, rather than creating a hierarchy of difference, simultaneous categories of analysis illuminate the complexity of racialist discourse in the early modern period. See, for example, Anne McClintock, *Imperial Leather: Race, Gender and Sexuality in the Colonial Conquest* (New York, 1995), 61, on the connections between categories of difference; Elsa Barkley Brown, "Polyrhythms and Improvisation: Lessons for Women's History," *History Workshop Journal*, 31 (Spring 1991), 85–90, on simultaneous categories of analysis; and Ania Loomba, "The Color of Patriarchy: Critical Difference, Cultural Difference, and Renaissance Drama," in Hendricks and Parker, eds., *Women, "Race," and Writing*, 17–34, for cautions on the dangers of erecting hierarchies of difference.

or even beautiful. Rather, indigenous women bore an enormous symbolic burden as writers from Walter Ralegh to Edward Long employed them to mark metaphorically the symbiotic boundaries of European national identities and white supremacy. The struggle with perceptions of beauty and assertions of monstrosity such as Ligon's exemplified a much larger process through which the familiar became unfamiliar as beauty became beastliness and mothers became monstrous, all ultimately in the service of racial distinctions. Writers who articulated religious and moral justifications for the slave trade simultaneously grappled with the character of the female African body—a body both desirable and repulsive, available and untouchable, productive and reproductive, beautiful and black. This article argues that these meanings were inscribed well before the establishment of England's colonial American plantations and that the intellectual work necessary to naturalize African enslavement—that is, the development of racialist discourse—was deeply implicated by gendered notions of difference and human hierarchy.

Europe had a long tradition of identifying Others through the monstrous physiognomy or sexual behavior of women. Pliny the Elder's ancient collection of monstrous races, *Historia Naturalis,* catalogued the longbreasted wild woman alongside the oddity of Indian and Ethiopian tribal women who bore only one child in their lifetime.[9] Medieval images of female devils included sagging breasts as part of the iconography of danger and monstrosity. The medieval wild woman, whose breasts dragged on the ground when she walked and could be thrown over her shoulder, was believed to disguise herself with youth and beauty in order to enact seductions that would satisfy her "obsessed ... craving for the love of mortal men."[10] The shape of her body marked her deviant sexuality; both shape and sexuality evidenced her savagery.

Thus, writers commonly looked to sociosexual deviance to indicate savagery in Africa and the Americas and to mark difference from Europe. According to *The Travels of Sir John Mandeville,* "in Ethiopia and in many other countries [in Africa] the folk lie all naked ... and the women have no shame of the men." Further, "they wed there no wives, for all the women there be common ... and when [women] have children they may give them to what man they will that hath companied with them."[11] Deviant sexual behavior reflected the breakdown of natural laws—the absence of shame, the inability to identify lines of heredity and descent. This concern with deviant sexuality, articulated almost always through descriptions of women, is a constant theme in the travel writings of early modern Europe. Explorers and travelers to the New World

9   Pliny, *Natural History in Ten Volumes,* vol. 2, trans. H. Rockham (Cambridge, Mass., 1969), 509–27; Herodotus, *The History,* trans. David Grene (Chicago, 1987) 4, 180, 191.

10   Richard Bernheimer, *Wild Men in the Middle Ages: A Study in Art, Sentiment, and Demonology* (Cambridge, Mass., 1952), 33–41, quotation on 34. See also Peter Mason, *Deconstructing America: Representations of the Other* (New York, 1990), 47–56.

11   *The Travels of Sir John Mandeville: The Version of the Cotton Manuscript in Modern Spelling,* ed. A. W. Pollard (London, 1915), 109, 119.

and Africa brought expectations of distended breasts and dangerous sexuality with them. Indeed, Columbus exemplified his reliance on the female body to articulate the colonial venture at the very outset of his voyage when he wrote that the earth was shaped like a breast with the Indies composing the nipple.[12]

Richard Eden's 1553 English translation of Sebastian Münster's *A Treatyse of the Newe India* presented Amerigo Vespucci's voyage to English readers for the first time. Vespucci did not mobilize color to mark the difference of the people he encountered; rather, he described them in terms of their lack of social institutions ("they fight not for the enlargeing of theyr dominion for asmuch as they have no Magistrates") and social niceties ("at theyr meate they use rude and barberous fashions, lying on the ground without any table clothe or coverlet"). Nonetheless, his descriptions are not without positive attributes, and when he turned his attention to women, his language bristles with illuminating contradiction:

> Theyr bodies are verye smothe and clene by reason of theyr often washinge. They are in other thinges fylthy and withoute shame. Thei use no lawful coniunccion of mariage, and but every one hath as many women as him liketh, and leaveth them agayn at his pleasure. The women are very fruiteful, and refuse no laboure al the whyle they are with childe. They travayle in maner withoute payne, so that the nexte day they are cherefull and able to walke. Neyther have they theyr bellies wimpeled or loose, and hanginge pappes, by reason of bearinge manye chyldren.[13]

The passage conveys admiration for indigenous women's strength in pregnancy and their ability to maintain aesthetically pleasing bodies, and it also represents the conflict at the heart of European discourse on gender and difference. Vespucci's familiarity with icons of difference led him to expect American women with hanging breasts; thus he registers surprise that women's breasts and bodies were neither "wimpeled" nor "hanginge." That surprise is inextricable from his description of childbearing. His admiration hinges on both a veiled critique of European female weakness and a dismissal of Amerindian women's pain. The question of pain in childbirth became a central component of descriptions of Africa and Africans. Vespucci presented a preliminary, still ambiguously laudatory account of Amerindian

---

12   See McClintock, *Imperial Leather*, 22–23, for more on what she labels the "pornotropic" tradition of European eroticized writing on Africa and the Americas.

13   *A Treatyse of the Newe India by Sebastian Münster* (1553), trans. Richard Eden (microprint), (Ann Arbor, Mich., 1966), [57]. See also Mason, *Deconstructing America*, 55, who links Vespucci's surprise at Indian women's firm breasts with expectations grounded in medieval imagery of wild women with sagging breasts. The language of "fylth" and shame also evoked sodomy and treachery for English readers. See Alan Bray, "Homosexuality and the Signs of Male Friendship in Elizabethan England," in Jonathan Goldberg, ed., *Queering the Renaissance* (Durham, N. C., 1994), 48. The wording of Münster's passage materializes many axes of difference.

women. Nonetheless, he mobilized the place of women in society as a cultural referent that evoked the "fylth" and shamelessness of all indigenous people. Thus the passage exposes early modern English readers' sometimes ambivalent encounters with narratives that utilized women's behavior and physiognomy to mark European national identities and inscribe racial hierarchy.[14]

In the narration of Columbus's voyage that appears in A Treatyse, Münster situated women both as intermediaries between the intrusive and indigenous peoples and as animal-like reproductive units.[15] On arriving at Hispaniola, Columbus's men "pursewinge [the women and men who had come down to the shore] toke a womanne whom they brought to theyr shyppe ... fyllinge her with delicate meates and wyne, and clothing her in fayre apparel, & so let her depart ... to her companie."[16] As Stephen Greenblatt has illustrated, the female "go-between" was crucial in encounter narratives. This woman figured as a pliable emissary who could be returned to her people as a sign of Spanish generosity (in the form of food and wine) and civility (in the form of clothes). She could be improved by the experience. Indeed, her ability to receive European goods—to be made familiar through European intervention—served as evidence of her own people's savagery, disorder, and distance from civility.[17]

In a passage that closely follows, Münster considered another role for indigenous women and children, a role whose proximate contradiction evokes the complicated nature of European assessment of women and their bodies. Describing the behavior of so-called cannibals, Münster avowed that "such children as they take, they geld to make them fat as we doo cocke chikyns and younge hogges.... Such younge women as they take, they keepe for increase, as we doo hennes to laye egges."[18] The

---

14   It is significant that this association with sagging breasts, unusual childbearing, and monstrosity emerged so early. Not until the 16th century, for example, did elite European women begin to use corsets to impose an elevated shape to their bodies, and only then did the elevated breasts of corseted women became a marker of refinement, courtliness, and status; Georges Vigarello, "The Upwards Training of the Body from the Age of Chivalry to Courtly Civility," in Michel Feher, Ramona Naddaff, and Nadia Tazi, eds., Fragments for a History of the Human Body, Part Two (Cambridge, Mass., 1989), 154–55. Very soon thereafter, the "unused" breast, preserved among the elite by employing wet-nurses for their children, embodied the "classic aesthetic ideal," according to Londa Schiebinger, "Why Mammals Are Called Mammals: Gender Politics in Eighteenth-Century Natural History," American Historical Review, 98 (1993), 401.

15   Two years after the publication of Münster's Treatyse, Eden translated and published Peter Martyr, The Decades of the New Worlde of West India (1533), (London, 1555), another description of the Columbus encounters.

16   Münster, Treatyse, trans. Eden, [4]; Martyr, Decades of the New Worlde, trans. Eden, 2.

17   Greenblatt discusses the role of the "go-between" through his analysis of Bernal Díaz's conquest narrative. He argues that Doña Marina, a native woman who becomes connected to the Spaniards, is the "object of exchange, agent of communication, model of conversion, the only figure who appears to understand the two cultures, the only person in whom they meet.... the site of the strategic symbolic oscillation between self and Other is the body of this woman," in Marvelous Possessions: The Wonder of the New World (Chicago, 1991), 143.

18   Münster, Treatyse, trans. Eden, [5]; Martyr, Decades of the New Worlde, trans. Eden, 3.

metaphor of domesticated livestock introduced a notion that became an *ideé fixe* concerning indigenous and enslaved women's twofold value to the European project of expansion and extraction.[19] This metaphor, however, did not fully encompass the complexity of dangers indigenous women presented for Europe. Despite his respect for female reproductive hardiness, at the end of the volume Vespucci fixed the indigenous woman as a dangerous cannibal:

> there came sodeynly a woman downe from a mountayne, bringing with her secretly a great stake with which she [killed a Spaniard.] The other wommene foorthwith toke him by the legges, and drewe him to the mountayne…. The women also which had slayne the yong man, cut him in pieces even in the sight of the Spaniardes, shewinge them the pieces, and rosting them at a greate fyre.[20]

Vespucci made manifest the latent sexualized danger embedded by the man-slaying woman in a letter in which he wrote of women biting off the penises of their sexual partners, thus linking cannibalism—an absolute indicator of savagery and distance from European norms—to female sexual insatiability.[21]

The label savage was not uniformly applied to Amerindian people. Indeed, in the context of European national rivalries, the indigenous woman became somewhat less savage. In the mid-to late sixteenth century, the bodies of women figured at the borders of national identities more often than at the edges of a larger European identity. The Italian traveler Girolamo Benzoni, in his *History of the New World* (a 1572 narrative that appeared in multiple translations), utilized sexualized indigenous women both as markers of difference and indicators of Spanish immorality. His first description of a person in the Americas (in Venezuela in 1541) occurs at the very beginning of his story:

> Then came an Indian woman … such a woman as I have never before nor since seen the like of; so that my eyes could not be satisfied with looking at her for wonder…. She was quite naked, except where modisty forbids, such being the custom throughout all this country; she was old, and painted black, with long hair down to her waist, and her ear-rings had so weighed her ears down, as to make them reach her shoulders, a thing

---

19   Indeed, the language of "increase" permeated 17th- and 18th-century slaveowners' probate records as planters in the West Indies and the southern colonies laid claim to enslaved women's productive and reproductive value; Jennifer Lyle Morgan, "Laboring Women: Enslaved Women, Reproduction, and Slavery in Barbados and South Carolina, 1650–1750" (Ph.D. diss., Duke University, 1995.)

20   Münster, *Treatyse*, trans. Eden, quoted in Louis Montrose, "The Work of Gender in the Discourse of Discovery," *Representations*, No. 33 (1991), 4.

21   Montrose, "Work of Gender," 5. For more on gender and cannibalism see Carla Freccero, "Cannibalism, Homophobia, Women: Montaigne's *'Des cannibales'* and *'De l'amitié*," in Hendricks and Parker, eds., *Women, "Race, " and Writing*, 73–83; for the etymological relationship between Caribs and cannibalism see Hulme, *Colonial Encounters*, 13–42.

> wonderful to see.... her teeth were black, her mouth large, and she had a ring in her nostrils ... so that she appeared like a monster to us, rather than a human being.[22]

Benzoni's description invokes a sizable catalogue of cultural distance packed with meaning made visible by early modern conventions of gendered difference. His inability to satisfy his gaze speaks to an obfuscation Ligon enacted one hundred years later and Greenblatt argues is the defining metaphor of the colonial encounter. His "wonder" situated her distance.[23] In the context of a society concerned with the dissemblance of cosmetics, as Hall argues, her black-faced body was both cause for alarm and evidence of a dangerous inversion of norms. Her nakedness, her ears, and her nose—all oddities accentuated by willful adornment—irrevocably placed her outside the realm of the familiar. Her blackened teeth and large mouth evoked a sexualized danger that, as Benzoni himself explicitly states, linked her and, by implication, her people to an inhuman monstrosity.[24]

In evoking this singular woman—the like of whom he had never seen—Benzoni departed from his contemporaries. He used his description of her to open his narrative and, through her, placed his reader in the realm of the exotic. This "wonderful" woman alerted readers to the distance Benzoni traveled, but he deployed another, more familiar set of female images to level a sustained critique of Spanish colonial expansion and thereby to insist on the indigenous woman's connection, or nearness, to a familiar European femininity.

> Capt. Pedro de Calize arrived with upwards of 4000 slaves.... It was really a most distressing thing to see the way in which these wretched creatures naked, tired, and lame were treated [by the Spaniards]; exhausted with hunger, sick, and despairing. The *unfortunate mothers*, with two or three children on their shoulders or clinging round their necks, overwhelmed with tears and grief, all tied with cords or with iron chains.... Nor was there a girl but had been violated by the depredators; wherefore, from too much indulgence, many Spaniards entirely lost their health.[25]

---

22 Benzoni, *History of the New World* (1572), trans. W. H. Smyth (London, 1857), 3–4.

23 Greenblatt argues that "wonder is ... the central figure in the initial European response to the New World, the decisive emotional and intellectual experience in the presence of radical difference," in *Marvelous Possessions,* 14.

24 Hall argues that "the painted woman often represents concerns over female unruliness, [and] the power of whiteness.... Male writers continually accuse women of hiding their 'blackness' under the fair disguise of cosmetics," in *Things of Darkness,* 89–90. See also PaulGabriel Bouce for an early 18th-century reference to popular English beliefs correlating the size of a woman's mouth to that of her vagina, in "Some Sexual Beliefs and Myths in Eighteenth-Century Britain," in Bouce, ed., *Sexuality in Eighteenth-Century Britain* (Manchester, Eng., 1982), 29–46, esp. 31–32.

25 Benzoni, *History of the New World,* trans. Smyth, 8. For an example of the consequences of the Black Legend for English settlers in the Americas see Karen Ordahl Kupperman, *Providence Island, 1630–1641: The Other Puritan Colony* (Cambridge, 1993), 92–96.

Benzoni utilized the pathetic figure of the fecund mother and the sexually violated young girl against the Spaniards. Such a move was common in the aftermath of Las Casas's *In Defense of the Indians* (circa 1550) and amid the intensified resentment over access to the Americas directed toward Spain by other European nations. In "Discoverie of the ... Empire of Guiana" (1598), Ralegh stated that he "suffered not any man to ... touch any of [the natives'] wives or daughters: which course so contrary to the Spaniards (who tyrannize over them in all things) drewe them to admire her [English] majestie."[26] While permitting himself and his men to gaze upon naked Indian women, Ralegh accentuated their restraint. In doing so, he used the untouched bodies of Native American women to mark national boundaries and signal the civility and superiority of English colonizers—in contrast to the sexually violent Spaniards. Moreover, in linking the eroticism of indigenous women to the sexual attention of Spanish men, Ralegh signaled the Spaniards' "lapse into savagery."[27] Benzoni, too, inscribed the negative consequences of too-close associations with indigenous women. For him, sexual proximity to local women depleted Spanish strength. As he prepared to abandon the topic of Indian slavery for a lengthy discussion of Columbus's travels, he again invoked motherhood to prove Spanish depravity: "All the slaves that the Spaniards catch in these provinces are sent [to the Caribbean] ... and even when *some of the Indian women are pregnant by these same Spaniards*, they sell them without any consciences."[28]

This rhetorical flourish, through female bodies, highlighted the contradictions of the familiar and unfamiliar in the Americas. The woman who opened Benzoni's narrative, in her nakedness and her monstrous adornments, could not be familiar to conquistadors and colonizers, yet in her role as mother, sexual victim, or even sexually arousing female, she evoked the familiar. Benzoni sidestepped the tension inherent in the savage-violated-mother by mobilizing her in the service of publicizing Spanish atrocity. In effect, the Black Legend created (among other things) this confusing figure of pathos—the savage mother whose nurturing quality is both recorded and praised. In order to facilitate the ultimate roles of extractors and extracted, the indigenous woman's familiarity had to be neutralized. Thus the pathos of raped mothers ultimately reverberated back onto Europe, signifying disdain for the Spanish and disregard for monstrous women.[29]

---

26   Ralegh, "The discoverie of the large, rich, and beautifull Empire of Guiana," in Richard Hakluyt, *The Principal Navigations Voyages Traffiques & Discoveries of the English Nation* (1598–1600), 12 vols. (Glasgow, 1903–1905), 10:391, cited in Montrose, "Work of Gender," 20.

27   Karen Robertson, "Pocahontas at the Masque," *Signs,* 21 (1996), 561, argues that "representation of an Indian woman does involve a dilemma for a male colonist, as expression of the erotic may signal his own lapse into savagery." See also Montrose, "Work of Gender," 21.

28   Benzoni, *History of the New World,* trans. Smyth, 11 (emphasis added).

29   In 18th-century England, writers intent on displaying the *natural* role of motherhood for English women idealized the "savage mother" and in doing so created tension as the dichotomy of civilized-English and savage-Other slipped; Felicity A. Nussbaum, *Torrid Zones: Maternity, Sexuality, and Empire in Eighteenth-Century English Narratives* (Baltimore, 1995), 48–53.

The monstrosity of the native mother had an important visual corollary. A mid-sixteenth-century Portuguese artist, for example, depicted the Devil wearing a Brazilian headdress and rendered his demonic female companions with long, sagging breasts.[30] Toward the end of the century, a multivolume collection of travel accounts, published in Latin and German, augmented the evolving discourse of European civility with visual images of overseas encounters.[31] As Bernadette Bucher has shown, the early volumes of Theodor de Bry's *Grand Voyages* (1590) depicted the Algonkians of Virginia and the Timucuas of Florida as classical Europeans: Amerindian bodies mirrored ancient Greek and Roman statuary, modest virgins covered their breasts, and infants suckled at the high, small breasts of young attractive women (see Figures 3.1, 3.2). These images were always in flux. In the third de Bry volume, *Voyages to Brazil,* published in 1592, the Indian was portrayed as aggressive and savage, and the representation of women's bodies changed. The new woman was a cannibal with breasts that fell below her waist. She licks the juices of grilled human flesh from her fingers and adorns the frontispiece of the map of Tierra del Fuego (see Figures 3.3, 3.4). Bucher argues that the absence of a suckling child in these depictions is essential to the image's symbolic weight.[32] Their childlessness signified their cannibalism—consumption rather than production. Although cannibalism was not exemplified by women only, women with long breasts marked such savagery among Native Americans for English readers. Other images of monstrous races, such as the headless Euaipanonoma, the one-footed Sciopods, and the Astomi who lived on the aroma of apples, slowly vanished from Europe's imagined America and Africa. Once in Africa, however, the place of motherhood in the complex of savagery and race became central to the figure of the black woman. Unlike other monstrosities, the long-breasted woman—who, when depicted with her child, carried the full weight of productive savagery—maintained her place in the lexicon of conquest and exploration.

---

30 Hugh Honour, *The New Golden Land: European Images of America from the Discoveries to the Present Time* (New York, 1975), 54–55.

31 Theodor de Bry, ed., *Grand Voyages,* 13 vols. (Frankfurt am Main, 1590–1627). De Bry also published the series *Small Voyages,* 12 vols. (Frankfurt am Main, 1598–1628), chronicling voyages to Africa and the East Indies. Language training among the elite, particularly in Latin, meant that those with access to de Bry's volumes would possess the capacity to understand them. See Lawrence Stone, *The Crisis of the Aristocracy 1558–1641* (Oxford, 1965), 672–702. For a discussion of the availability of books on reproduction and physiognomy see Patricia Crawford, "Sexual Knowledge in England, 1500–1750," in Roy Porter and Mikulas Teich, eds., *Sexual Knowledge, Sexual Science: The History of Attitudes to Sexuality* (Cambridge, 1994), 86.

32 Bucher, *Icon and Conquest: A Structural Analysis of the Illustrations of de Bry's Great Voyages,* trans. Basia Miller Gulati (Chicago, 1981), 135, 145. Bucher's analysis includes a complex discussion of the morphology of consumption and an explanation that locates the reversal at the heart of anthropophagy in the icon of the sagging breast. See Bucher, "Savage Women with Sagging Breasts," ibid., 73–120. For the formulation of the long-breasted woman in the Americas see also Mason, *Deconstructing America,* 47–60.

FIGURE 3.1 Young virgin covering her breast, from Thomas Hariot, *A brief and True Report of the New Found Land of Virginia,* in Theodor de Bry, *Grand Voyages,* vol. 1 (Frankfurt am Main, 1590), plate 6. Courtesy of The John Work Garrett Library of The Johns Hopkins University.

American narratives contributed to a discursive triangulation among Europe, America, and Africa. English travelers to West Africa drew on American narrative traditions. Richard Hakluyt's collection of travel narratives, *Principall Navigations* (1589), brought Africa into the purview of English readers. *Principall Navigations* portrayed Africa and Africans in positive and negative terms. The authors' shifting assessments of Africa and Africans "produc[ed] an Africa which is familiar and unfamiliar, civil and savage, full of promise and full of threat." Sixteenth-century ambivalence concerning England's role in overseas expansion required a forceful antidote. In response, Hakluyt presented texts that, through an often conflicted depiction of African peoples, ultimately differentiated Africa and England and erected a boundary that made English expansion in the face of confused and uncivilized peoples reasonable, profitable, and moral.[33]

---

33 Emily C. Bartels, "Imperialist Beginnings: Richard Hakluyt and the Construction of Africa," *Criticism,* 34 (1992), 519. See Winthrop D. Jordan, *White over Black: American Attitudes toward the Negro, 1550–1812* (Chapel Hill, 1968), 3–43, for further discussion of the fluidity of images of Africa in the early modern European imaginary. See also David Armitage, "The New World and British Historical Thought: From Richard Hakluyt to William Robertson," in *America in European Consciousness, 1493–1750,* ed. Karen Ordahl Kupperman (Chapel Hill, 1995), 52–75. The Hakluyt collection served

FIGURE 3.2   Woman suckling child, from *Eorum Quae in Florida* ..., in Theodor de Bry, *Grand Voyages*, vol. 2 (Frankfurt am Main, 1591), plate 20. Courtesy of The John Work Garrett Library of The Johns Hopkins University.

On the West African coast, women's bodies, like those of their New World counter-parts, symbolized the shifting parameters of the colonizing venture. English writers regularly directed readers' attention to the sexually titillating topic of African wom-en's physiognomy and reproductive experience. In doing so, they drew attention to the complex interstices of desire and repulsion that marked European men's gaze on Amerindian and African women. Sixteenth- and seventeenth-century writers con-veyed a sexual grotesquerie that ultimately made African women indispensable, in that it showed the gendered ways of putting African savagery to productive use. Although titillation was certainly a component of these accounts, to write of sex was also to define and expand the boundaries of profit through productive and reproductive labor.

The symbolic weight of indigenous women's sexual, childbearing, and child-rear-ing practices continued to be brought to bear on England's literary imagination.

as "a mythico-historical amalgam intended to introduce ... conquest and colonization to Europeans"; Bucher, *Icon and Conquest*, 22.

FIGURE 3.3   Woman (at left) holding leg, from *Memorabile Proviniciae Brasilae ...* , in Theodor de Bry, *Grand Voyages*, vol. 3 (Frankfurt am Main, 1592), 179. Courtesy of The John Work Garrett Library of The Johns Hopkins University.

John Lok, in his account of his 1554 voyage to Guinea, published forty years later in Hakluyt's collection, re-inscribed Africans' place in the human hierarchy. Borrowing verbatim from Richard Eden's 1555 translation of Peter Martyr, Lok described all Africans as "people of beastly living." He located the proof of this in *women's* behavior: among the Garamantes, women "are common: for they contract no matrimonie, neither have respect to chastitie."[34] Eden's Martyr has a long descriptive passage on African oddities; in it the reference to Garamante women is followed by one to a tribe who "have no speeche, but rather a grynnynge and chatterynge. There are also people without heades cauled Blemines, havyinge their eyes and mouth in theyr breast."[35] By not reproducing the entire paragraph, Lok's abbreviation suggests that, by the end of the sixteenth century, the oddities of Africa could be consolidated into the particular symbol of women's sexual availability.

---

34   "The second voyage [of Master John Lok] to Guinea 1554," in Hakluyt, *Principal Navigations* (1598–1600), 6:167, 168; see also Martyr, *Decades of the New Worlde*, trans. Eden, 356. "Garamantes" originally occur in Pliny, who describes them as an Ethiopian race that did not practice marriage. See John Block Friedman, *The Monstrous Races in Medieval Art and Thought* (Cambridge, Mass., 1981), 15.

35   *Decades of the New Worlde*, trans. Eden, 356. In this paragraph, Martyr clearly borrows from Herodotus and Pliny.

Women on the map of Tierra del Fuego, from *Vera et Accurate Descriptio e orum omnius Quae Acciderunt Quinque navibus, Anno 1598,* in Theodor de Bry, *Grand Voyages*, vol. 9 (Frankfurt am Main, 1602), 56. Courtesy of The John Work Garrett Library of The Johns Hopkins University.

William Towrson's narrative of his 1555 voyage to Guinea, also published by Hakluyt, further exhibits this kind of distillation. Towrson depicted women and men as largely indistinguishable. They "goe so alike, that one cannot know a man from a woman but by their breastes, which in the most part be very foule and long, hanging downe low like the udder of a goate."[36] This was, perhaps, the first time an Englishman

36 "The first voyage made by Master William Towrson Marchant of London, to the coast of Guinea … in the yeere 1555," in Hakluyt, *Principal Navigations* (1598–1600), 6:184. Jordan notes that "many chroniclers [of Africa] made a point of discussing the Negro women's long breasts and ease of child-bearing," in *White over Black*, 39–40. Schiebinger places the equation of African women's breasts with the udders of goats in a continuum of European imagery of, and relationship to, the breast. She notes that 19th-century ethnologists compared and classified breast size and shape much as they did skulls. Not surprisingly, they used African breasts, like African heads, to prove the linkage between Africans and animals. See Schiebinger, "Why Mammals Are Called Mammals," 402–03, 394. Philip D. Morgan asserts that "[Beginning with Richard Ligon,] Barbadians were the first coherent group within

in Africa explicitly used breasts as an identifying trait of beastliness and difference. He goes on to maintain that "diverse of the women have such exceeding long breasts, that some of them wil lay the same upon the ground and lie downe by them."[37] Lok and Towrson represented African women's bodies and sexual behavior so as to distinguish Africa from Europe. Towrson in particular gave readers only two analogies through which to view and understand African women—beasts and monsters.

Some thirty years after the original Hakluyt collections were published, other writers continued to mobilize African women to do complex symbolic work. In 1622, Richard Jobson's *The Golden Trade* appeared in London, chronicling his 1620–1621 trading ventures up the Gambia River.[38] Jobson described strong and noble people on the one hand and barbarous and bestial people on the other, and African women personified his nation's struggle with the familiar and unfamiliar African—a struggle that can also be located along the axis of desire and repulsion. Jobson's association with the "Fulbie" and "Maudingo" people furnishes evidence of this struggle. He described Fulbie men as beastlike, "seemingly more senselesse, then our Country beasts," a state he attributed to their close association with the livestock they raised.[39] Unlike many of his contemporaries, Jobson regarded African women with admiration. In contrast to Fulbie men, the women were "excellently well bodied, having very good features, with a long blacke haire."[40] He maintained that the discovery of a "mote or haire" in milk would cause these dairywomen to "blush, in defence of her cleanely meaning."[41] This experience of shame encapsulated a morality and civility to which only women had access. Among the Maudingos of Cassan, newly married women "observ[e] herein a shamefast modestie, not to be looked for, *among such a kinde of blacke or barbarous people*."[42] Despite his well-meaning description of African women, Jobson recorded their behaviors associated with English civility only inasmuch as they deviated from that which he, and his readers, expected. His appreciation of Fulbie women and Maudingo people was predicated on their ability to exceed his expectations. To Jobson, African women proved the precarious nature of African civility. His narrative, even at its most laudatory, always returned to inferiority. While describing the history of kingship and the great importance of ancestral

---

the Anglo-American world to portray blacks as beasts or as beastlike," in "British Encounters with Africans and African-Americans, circa 1600–1780," in Bernard Bailyn and Morgan, eds., *Strangers within the Realm: Cultural Margins of the First British Empire* (Chapel Hill, 1991), 174.

37   Towrson, "The first voyage made by Master William Towrson," 187. Once he categorized them, Towrson relegated women to a passive role in the background of his interactions with Africans, despite the fact that they "worke as well as the men"; ibid., 185.

38   Jobson, *The Golden Trade or a Discovery of the River Gambra ... by Richard Jobson* (1628), (Amsterdam, 1968).

39   Ibid., 35.

40   Ibid., 33.

41   Ibid., 36.

42   Ibid., 56 (emphasis added).

honor among the Maudingos, Jobson still contended that "from the King to the slave, they are all perpetuall beggers from us." His "wonder" at women's modesty alerted his readers to the culture's abnormality and, implicitly, to its larger absence of civility. Even as he depicted them positively, women became part of the demonstration that, despite kings and history, these Africans were barbarous and ripe for exploitation.[43]

Other English publications continued to locate evidence of savagery and legitimated exploitation in women. After Hakluyt died, Samuel Purchas took up the mantle of editor and published an additional twenty volumes in Hakluyt's series in 1624.[44] In his translation of a fourteenth-century narrative by Leo Africanus, Purchas presented a West Africa sharply delineated from the civilized. Discussion of "the Land of Negros," for example, is preceded by, and thus set apart from, a long section on North Africa. "Negros," unlike their northern neighbors, lived "a brutish and savage life, without any King, Governour, Common-wealth, or knowledge of Husbandry." To confirm this savagery, Leo Africanus asserted that they were "clad ... in skinnes of beasts, neither had they any peculiar wives ... and when night came they resorted ... both men and women into one Cottage together ... and each man choosing his [woman] which hee had most fanciee unto."[45] This indictment opened the descriptive passages on "Ghinea," thereby making women's sexual availability the defining metaphor of colonial accessibility and black African savagery.

In the following volume, Purchas published Andrew Battell's "Strange Adventures."[46] Battell spent seventeen years in Angola, from 1590 to 1607, some as captive, some as escapee, and some in service to King James. For sixteen months, Battell stayed near "Dongo" with the "Gaga" people, "the greatest Canibals and man-eaters that bee in the World."[47] Like sixteenth-century observers in Brazil, he highlighted women's unnatural reproductive behavior. This "tribe" of fighters and cannibals rejected motherhood. According to Battell, "the women are very fruitfull, but they enjoy none of their children: for as soon as the woman is delivered of her Childe, it is

---

43 Unlike many of his contemporaries, Jobson leveled his open-eyed gaze primarily at male African sexuality. In a unique twist on the consequences of the Curse of Ham, Jobson maintained that African men carried the mark of the curse in the size of their sexual organs: "[They] are furnisht with such members as are after a sort burthensome unto them, whereby their women being once conceived with child … accompanies the man no longer, because he shall not destroy what is conceived." Jobson's interpretation of the penis corresponded to others' ideas about women's breasts. Both sexual organs are seen as pendulous and distended, somehow disembodied from their owner, and physically burdensome. Subsequently he returned to the subject of women only in terms of their subjugation to men, certain that "there is no other woman [that] can be under more servitude"; ibid., 58, 52, 54, and Greenblatt, *Marvelous Possessions*, 14.

44 Samuel Purchas, *Hakluytus Posthumus, or Purchas His Pilgrimes* (1624), 20 vols. (Glasgow, 1905).

45 "Observations of Africa, taken out of John Leo his nine Bookes, translated by Master Pory … ," ibid., 5:517.

46 "The Strange Adventures of Andrew Battell …" (1625), ed. E. G. Ravenstein, in *Hakluytus Posthumus*, 6:367–517.

47 Ibid., 377–78.

presently buried quicke [alive]; So that there is not one Childe brought up."[48] Battell positioned his discussion of this unnatural behavior in such a way as to close the debate on African savagery. Gaga savagery began, in his account, with cannibalism and ended with mothers who consented to the killing of the children they bore.

Purchas also provided a translation of Pieter de Marees's "A description and historicall declaration of the golden Kingedome of Guinea." This narrative was first published in Dutch in 1602, was translated into German and Latin for the de Bry volumes (1603–1634), and appeared in French in 1605. Plagiarism by seventeenth- and eighteenth-century writers gave it still wider circulation.[49] Here, too, black women embody African savagery. De Marees began by describing the people at Sierra Leone as "very greedie eaters, and no lesse drinkers, and very lecherous, and theevish, and much addicted to uncleanenesse; one man hath as many wives as hee is able to keepe and maintaine. The women also are much addicted to leacherie, specially, with strange Countrey people.... [and] are also great Lyers, and not to be credited."[50] As did most of his contemporaries, de Marees invoked women's sexuality to castigate the incivility of both men and women: all Africans were savage. The passage displays African males' savagery alongside their multiple access to women. Similarly, De Marees located evidence of African women's savagery in their unrestricted sexual desire. Given the association of unrestricted sexuality with native savagery, black female sexuality alone might have been enough to implicate the entire continent. But de Marees further castigated West African women: they delivered children surrounded by men, women, and youngsters "in [a] most shamelesse manner ... before them all."[51] This absence of shame (evoked explicitly, as here, or implicitly in the constant references to nakedness in other narratives) worked to establish distance. Readers, titillated by the topics discussed and thus tacitly shamed, found themselves further distanced from the shameless subject of the narrative. De Marees dwelt on the brute nature of shameless African women. He marveled that "when the child is borne [the mother] goes to the water to wash & make cleane her selfe, not once dreaming of a moneths lying in ... as women here with us use to doe; they use no Nurses to helpe them when they lie in child-bed, neither seeke to lie dainty and soft.... The next day after, they goe abroad in the streets, to doe their businesse."[52] This testimony to African women's physical strength and emotional indifference is even more emphatic in the original Dutch. In the most recent translation from the Dutch, the passage continues: "This

---

48   Ibid., 32.

49   Pieter de Marees, *Description and Historical Account of the Gold Kingdom of Guinea* (1602), trans. and ed. Albert van Dantzig and Adam Jones (Oxford, 1987), xvii.

50   De Marees, "Description and historicall declaration of the golden Kingedome of Guinea," in Purchas, ed., *Hakluytus Posthumus*, 6:251. I cite the Purchas edition rather than the modern edition so as to draw on the narrative that early modern English readers encountered.

51   Ibid., 258–59.

52   Ibid., 259.

shows that the women here are of a cruder nature and stronger posture than the Females in our Lands in Europe."[53]

De Marees inscribed an image of women's reproductive identity whose influence persisted long after his original publication. "When [the child] is two or three moneths old, the mother ties the childe with a peece of cloth at her backe…. When the child crieth to sucke, the mother casteth one of her dugs backeward over her shoulder, and so the child suckes it as it hangs."[54] Frontispieces for the de Marees narrative and the African narratives in de Bry approximate the over-the-shoulder breastfeeding de Marees described, thereby creating an image that could symbolize the continent (see Figures 3.5, 3.6, 3.7). The image was a compelling one, offering in a single narrative-visual moment evidence that black women's difference was both cultural (in this strange *habit*) and physical (in this strange *ability*). The word "dug" (which by the early 1660s was used, according to the *Oxford English Dictionary* to mean both a woman's breasts and an animal's teats) connoted a brute animality that de Marees reinforced through his description of small children "lying downe in their house, like Dogges, [and] rooting in the ground like Hogges" and of "boyes and girles [that] goe starke naked as they were borne, with their privie members all open, without any shame or civilitie."[55]

African women's African-ness seemed contingent on the linkages between sexuality and a savagery that fitted them for both productive and reproductive labor. Women enslaved in the seventeenth and early eighteenth centuries did not give birth to many children, but descriptions of African women in the Americas almost always highlighted their fecundity along with their capacity for manual labor.[56] Seventeenth-century English medical writers, both men and women, equated breastfeeding and tending to children with work.[57] Erroneous observations about African women's propensity for easy birth and breastfeeding reassured colonizers that these women could easily perform hard labor in the Americas while simultaneously erecting a barrier of difference between Africa and England. Sixteenth- and seventeenth-century English women and men anticipated pregnancy and child-birth with extreme uneasiness and fear of death, but at least they knew that the experience of pain in childbirth marked women as members of a Christian community.[58] African women entered the developing discourse of national resources via an emphasis on their mechanical and

53 De Marees, *Description and Historical Account of the Gold Kingdom of Guinea,* ed. Dantzig and Jones, 23.

54 De Marees, "Description and historicall declaration of the golden Kingdome of Guinea," 259.

55 Ibid., 261.

56 Jordan, *White over Black,* 39.

57 Marylynn Salmon, "The Cultural Significance of Breastfeeding and Infant Care in Early Modern England and America "*Journal of Social History,* 28 (1994), 247–70.

58 Linda Pollock, "Embarking on a Rough Passage: The Experience of Pregnancy in Early Modern Society," in Valerie Fildes, ed., *Women as Mothers in Pre-Industrial England* (New York, 1990), 45.

FIGURE 3.5 Woman breastfeeding over her shoulder, title page from *Verum et Historicam Descriptionem Avriferi Regni Guineaa*, in Theodor de Bry, *Small Voyages*, vol. 6 (Frankfurt am Main, 1604). Note the contrast between this later depiction and the early representation of a Native American woman in Figure 3.7. Courtesy of The John Work Garrett Library of The Johns Hopkins University.

meaningless childbearing. Early on, metaphors of domestic livestock and sexually located cannibalism relied on notions of reproduction for consumption. By about the turn of the seventeenth century, as England joined in the transatlantic slave trade, assertions of African savagery began to be predicated less on consumption via cannibalism and more on production via reproduction. African women were materialized in the context of England's need for productivity. The image of utilitarian feeding implied a mechanistic approach to both childbirth and reproduction that ultimately became located within the national economy. Whereas English women's reproductive work took place solely in the domestic economy, African women's reproductive work could, indeed, embody the developing discourses of extraction and forced labor at the heart of England's national design for the colonies.[59]

59 Ruth Perry argues that the valuation of "Motherhood" developed in England alongside empire so that not until the 19th-century did "the production of children for the nation and for the empire constitute childbearing women as a national resource," in "Colonizing the Breast: Sexuality and Maternity in Eighteenth-Century England," *Journal of the History of Sexuality,* 2 (1991), 204, 205; see also Greenblatt, *Marvelous Possessions,* 7. Miranda Chaytor maintains that in 17th-century England only poor women had "laboring bodies," for as elite women withdrew from household production, their "entire mental and physical lives" became sexualized and thus defined as nonproductive, in "Husband(ry): Narratives of Rape in the Seventeenth-Century," *Gender and History,* 7 (1995), 378–407, esp. 396–98.

FIGURE 3.6 Women in Africa, from *Verum et Historicam Descriptionem Avriferi Regni Guineaa*, in Theodor de Bry, *Small Voyages*, vol. 6 (Frankfurt am Main, 1604), plate 3. Courtesy of The John Work Garrett Library of The Johns Hopkins University.

By the eighteenth century, English writers rarely employed black women's breasts or behavior for anything but concrete evidence of barbarism in Africa. In *A Description of the Coasts of North and South-Guinea* ..., begun in the 1680s and completed and published almost forty years later, John Barbot "admired the quietness of the poor babes, so carr'd about at their mothers' backs ... and how freely they suck the breasts, which are always full of milk, over their mothers' shoulders, and sleep soundly in that odd posture."[60] William Snelgrave introduced his *New Account of Some Parts of Guinea and the Slave-trade* with an anecdote designed to illustrate the benevolence of the trade. He described himself rescuing an infant from human sacrifice and reuniting the child with its mother, who "had much Milk in her Breasts." He accented the

---

60 Barbot, *A Description of the Coasts of North and South-Guinea* ... , in A. Churchill, ed., *A Collection of Voyages* (London, 1732), 36. See also J. D. Fage, "'Good Red Herring': The Definitive Barbot," *Journal of African History*, 34 (1993), 315–20.

FIGURE 3.7   Native American woman with her child, two views, from Thomas Hariot, *A brief and True Report of the New Found Land of Virginia,* in Theodor de Bry, *Grand Voyages,* vol. i (Frankfurt am Main, 1590), plate 10. Courtesy of The John Work Garrett Library of The Johns Hopkins University.

barbarism of those who attempted to sacrifice the child and claimed that the reunion cemented his goodwill in the eyes of the enslaved, who, convinced of the "good notion of White Men," caused no problems during the voyage to Antigua.[61] Having utilized the figure of the breastfeeding woman to legitimize his slaving endeavor, Snelgrave went on to describe the roots of Whydah involvement in the slave trade and its defeat in war at the hands of the Kingdom of Dahomey (both coastal cities in present-day Ghana). "Custom of the Country allows Polygamy to an excessive degree … whereby the land was become so stocked with people" that the slave trade flourished. More-over, the wealth generated by the trade made the beneficiaries so "proud, effeminate and luxurious" that they were easily conquered by the more disciplined (read masculine) nation of Dahomey.[62] Thus women's fecundity undermined African society from without and within as they provided a constant stream of potential slaves.

---

61   Snelgrave, introduction, *A New Account of Some Parts of Guinea and the Slave-trade* (1734), (London, 1971).

62   Ibid., 3–4.

Abolitionist John Atkins similarly adopted the icon of black female bodies in his writings on Guinea. "Childing, and their Breasts always pendulous, stretches them to so unseemly a length and Bigness that some … could suckle over their shoulder."[63] Atkins then considered the idea of African women copulating with apes. He noted that "at some places the Negroes have been suspected of Bestiality" and, while maintaining the ruse of scholarly distance, suggested that evidence "would tempt one to suspect the Fact." The evidence lay mostly in apes' resemblance to humans but was bolstered by "the Ignorance and Stupidity [of black women unable] to guide or controll lust."[64] Abolitionists and antiabolitionists alike accepted the connections between race, animality, the legitimacy of slavery, and black women's monstrous and fecund bodies. By the 1770s, Edward Long's *History of Jamaica* presented readers with African women whose savagery was total, for whom enslavement was the only means of civility. Long maintained that "an oran-outang husband would [not] be any dishonour to an Hottentot female; for what are these Hottentots?"[65] He asserted as fact that sexual liaisons occurred between African women and apes. Nowhere did he make reference to any sort of African female shame or beauty. Rather, Long used women's bodies and behavior to justify and promote the mass enslavement of Africans. By the time he wrote, the association of black people with beasts—via African women—had been cemented: "Their women are delivered with little or no labour; they have therefore no more occasion for midwifes than the female oran-outang, or any other wild animall…. Thus they seem exempted from the course inflicted upon Eve and *her daughters*."[66]

If African women gave birth without pain, they somehow sidestepped God's curse upon Eve. If they were not her descendants, they were not related to Europeans and could therefore be forced to labor on England's overseas plantations with impunity. Elaine Scarry has persuasively argued that the experience of pain—and thus the materiality of the body—lends a sense of reality and certainty to a society at times of crisis.[67] Early modern European women were so defined by their experience of pain in childbirth that an inability to feel pain was evidence of witchcraft.[68] In the case

---

63   Atkins, *A Voyage to Guinea, Brazil, and the West-Indies* (1735), (London, 1970), 50.

64   Ibid., 108.

65   Edward Long, "History of Jamaica, 2, with notes and corrections by the Author" (1774), Add. Ms. 12405, p364/f295, British Library, London. Long was not alone in his delight at suggesting interspecies copulation. Schiebinger details 17th- and 18th-century naturalists' investigations of apes. She notes that naturalists "ascribed to [simian] females the modesty they were hoping to find in their own wives and daughters, and to males the wildest fantasies of violent interspecies rape," in her *Nature's Body: Gender in the Making of Modern Science* (Boston, 1993), 75–114, quotation on 78.

66   Long, "History of Jamaica," p380/f304 (emphasis added).

67   Scarry, *The Body in Pain: The Making and Unmaking of the World* (New York, 1985), 15, 185–91; see also Spillers, "Mama's Baby, Papa's Maybe," 67–68, on the role of inflicted pain as a process of ungendering "female flesh" in slavery.

68   Lyndal Roper, *Oedipus and the Devil: Witchcraft, Sexuality and Religion in Early Modern Europe*

of England's contact with Africa and the Americas, the crisis in European identity was mediated by constructing an image of pain-free reproduction that diminished Africa's access to certainty and civilization, thus allowing for the mass appropriation that was the transatlantic slave trade.

After Richard Ligon saw the black woman at Cape Verde, he pursued her around a dance hall, anxious to hear her voice, though she ultimately put him off with only "the loveliest smile that I have ever seen." The following morning he came upon two "prettie young Negro Virgins." Their clothing was arranged such that Ligon viewed "their breasts round, firm, and beautifully shaped." He demurred that he was unable "to expresse all the perfections of Nature, and Parts, these Virgins were owners of." Aware of the image of African womanhood already circulating in England, he assured his readers that these women should not be confused with the women of "high Africa ... that dwell nere the River of Gambia, who are thick lipt, short nos'd, and commonly [have] low foreheads."[69] As though their breasts did not adequately set these women apart, Ligon used these qualifiers to highlight the exception of their beauty. As were many of his contemporaries, Ligon was quite willing to find beauty and allure in women who were exceptional—not "of high Africa," but whose physiognomy and "education" marked them as improved by contact with Europe.[70]

In the face of Ligon's pursuit, these women, like the beautiful woman he met the evening before, remained silent. Ligon tried, unsuccessfully, to test the truth of their beauty through the sound of their speech. Language had been a mark of monstrosity for centuries; Pliny identified five of his monstrous races as such simply because they lacked human speech.[71] It appears that decent language, like shame, denoted civility

---

(London and New York, 1994), 203–04. See also Mary Poovey, *Uneven Developments: The Ideological Work of Gender in Mid-Victorian England* (Chicago, 1988), 24–50, who shows that, during mid-19th-century debates over anesthesia for women in childbirth, members of the medical and religious professions argued that to relieve women of pain would interfere with God and deprive women of the pain that ultimately civilized them. See also Diane Purkiss, "Women's Stories of Witchcraft in Early Modern England: The House, the Body, the Child," *Gender and History*, 7 (1995), 408–32, for the connection between pain-free childbirth and accusations of witchcraft. On the connection between midwifery and accusations of witchcraft, Carol F. Karlsen notes that "the procreative nurturing and nursing roles of women were *perverted* by witches," in *The Devil in the Shape of a Woman: Witchcraft in Colonial New England* (New York, 1989), 144.

69   Ligon, *True and Exact History ... ofBarbadoes*, 13, 15–16.

70   Another example can be found in John Gabriel Stedman's relationship to the mulatto woman Johanna in his *Narrative of a Five Years Expedition Against the Revolted Negroes of Surinam: Transcribed ... from the Original 1790 Manuscript,* ed. Richard Price and Sally Price (Baltimore, 1988). His attempts to persuade this almost-English woman to return to Britain with him failed in part because she understood what he did not—that her status as "exceptional" was contingent on her location in Surinam. Had she gone to England, she would have become, in effect, a "high African" woman. See Homi Bhabha, "Of Mimicry and Man: The Ambivalence of Colonial Discourse," *October*, 28 (Spring 1984), 108, for a discussion of the symbolic importance of those who occupy the borders of colonial spaces.

71   Friedman, *Monstrous Races in Medieval Art and Thought,* 29.

for Ligon in the face of this inexplicable specter of female African beauty. Finally, Ligon begged pardon for his dalliances and remarked that he "had little else to say" about the otherwise desolate island.[72] To speak of African beauty in this context, then, was justified.

When Ligon arrived in Barbados and settled on a 500-acre sugar plantation with one hundred slaves, African beauty—if it ever really existed—dissolved in the face of racial slavery. He saw African men and women carrying bunches of plantains: "'Tis a lovely sight to see a hundred handsom Negroes, men and women, with every one a grasse-green bunch of these fruits on their heads ... the black and green so well becoming one another." African people became comparable to vegetation and only passively and abstractly beautiful as blocks of color. Ligon attested to their passivity with their servitude: they made "very good servants, if they be not spoyled by the English."[73] But if Ligon found interest in beauty, as Jobson did in shame, he ultimately equated black people with animals. He declared that planters bought slaves so that the "sexes may be equall ... [because] they cannot live without Wives," although the enslaved choose their partners much "as Cows do ... for, the most of them are as near beasts as may be."[74] When Ligon reinforced African women's animality with descriptions of breasts "hang[ing] down below their Navels," he tethered his narrative to familiar images of black women that—for readers nourished on Hakluyt and de Bry—effectively naturalized the enslavement of Africans. Like his predecessors, Ligon offered further proof of Africans' capacity for physical labor—their aptitude for slavery—through ease of childbearing. "In a fortnight [after giving birth] this woman is at worke with her Pickaninny at her back, as merry a soule as any is there."[75] In the Americas, African women's pain-free childbearing thus continued to be central in the gendering of racism.

By the time the English made their way to the West Indies, decades of ideas and information about brown and black women predated the actual encounter. In many ways, the encounter had already taken place in parlors and reading rooms on English soil, assuring that colonists would arrive with a battery of assumptions and

---

72 Ligon, *True and Exact History ... of Barbadoes*, 17. Henry Louis Gates, Jr., argues that the primary theme in Afro-American literature is the quest for literacy, a response to white assertions that blacks lacked "reason." Just as Phillis Wheatley's literacy had to be authenticated by thirteen white male signatories, so all Afro-American writing was an oppositional demonstration of authentic intellect that "was a political act." Ligon's need to hear the voices of the black women who excited his lust and curiosity suggests a precursor to the black literary link between reading and reason. "The *spoken* language of black people had become an object of parody at least since 1769," says Gates, in *Figures in Black: Words, Signs, and the "Racial" Self* (New York and Oxford, 1987), 5–6 (emphasis added). Ligon wrote out of a period that predated that tradition of parody and instead located reason and civility in spoken language.

73 Ligon, *True and Exact History ... of Barbadoes*, 44.

74 Ibid., 47.

75 Ibid., 51

predispositions about race, femininity, sexuality, and civilization.[76] Confronted with an Africa they needed to exploit, European writers turned to black women as evidence of a cultural inferiority that ultimately became encoded as racial difference. Monstrous bodies became enmeshed with savage behavior as the icon of women's breasts became evidence of tangible barbarism. African women's "unwomanly" behavior evoked an immutable distance between Europe and Africa on which the development of racial slavery depended. By the mid-seventeenth century, that which had initially marked African women as unfamiliar—their sexually and reproductively bound savagery—had become familiar. To invoke it was to conjure up a gendered and racialized figure who marked the boundaries of English civility even as she naturalized the subjugation of Africans and their descendants in the Americas.

---

76 Greenblatt, *Marvelous Possessions*, 55.

PART II

CHANGING ROLES IN CHINA

The sources in this section describe the imposition of gender norms in China during the nineteenth and twentieth centuries. Two of the sources are written from a Western colonial perspective, whereas the third takes aim at Chinese norms of the family in the name of social revolution. Susan Mann's essay places these and similar efforts in the context of movements to "civilize" Chinese society.

READING 4

"The Natural History of the Chinese Girl," *North China Herald and Supreme Court and Consular Gazette*, July 4, 1890.

Written by an unknown author in Shanghai for the foreign community, this excerpt from a newspaper article from 1890 criticizes the position of women under Confucian social norms in China as "Seven Deadly Sins."

The Natural History of a Chinese Girl

North China Herald and Supreme Court and Consular Gazette

W̲e must regard the position of women, and especially of wives, in China as the ultimate outcome and most characteristic fruitage of the Confucian system. In our view it has been a bitter fruit; and in recapitulating we wish to lay especial emphasis upon the Seven Deadly Sins of Confucianism in its relation to women.

I. It provides them with no education. Their minds are left in a state of nature, until millions of them are led to suppose that they have no minds at all, an opinion which their husbands often do much to confirm, and upon which they habitually act.

II. The sale of wives and daughters. This comes about so naturally, and it might almost be said so inevitably, when certain conditions prevail, that it is taken by the Chinese as a matter of course. Except in years of famine it appears in some parts of the empire to be rare, but in other parts it is the constant and the normal state of things for daughters to be as really sold as are horses and cattle.

III. Too early and too universal marriages. A considerable part of the unhappiness caused by Chinese marriages may fairly be charged to the immaturity of the victims. To treat children as if they were adults, while at the same time treating them as children who require the same watch and ward as other children, does not appear to be a rational procedure, nor can it be claimed that it is justified by its results. That a new pair constitute a distinct entity, to be dealt with independently, is a proposition which Confucianism treats with scorn, if indeed it ever entertains such a conception at all. The compulsory marriage of all girls forces all Chinese society into cast-iron grooves, and leaves no room for exceptional individual development.

"The Natural History of the Chinese Girl," *North China Herald and Supreme Court and Consular Gazette*, 1890.

It throws suspicion around every isolated struggle against this galling bondage, and makes the unmarried woman seem a personified violation of the decrees of Heaven and of the laws of man.

IV. Infanticide of female infants. This is a direct, if not a legitimate result of the tenet that male children are absolutely indispensable, applied in a social system where dire poverty is the rule, and where an additional mouth frequently means impending starvation. In a chapter in her "Pagoda Shadows" on "The extent of a Great Crime" Miss Fielde combines a great variety of testimony taken from several different provinces, in the following paragraph. "I find that a hundred and sixty Chinese women, all over fifty years of age, had borne six hundred and thirty-one sons, and five hundred and thirty-eight daughters. Of the sons, three hundred and sixty-six, or nearly sixty per cent, had lived more than ten years; while of the daughters only two hundred and five, or thirty-eight per cent, had lived ten years. The hundred and sixty women, according to their own statements, had destroyed a hundred and fifty eight of their daughters; but none had ever destroyed a boy. As only four women had reared more than three girls, the probability is that the number of infanticides confessed to is considerably below the truth. I have occasionally been told by a woman that she had forgotten just how many girls she had had, more than she wanted. The greatest number of infanticides owned to by any one woman is eleven."

Infanticide will never cease in China, until the notion that the dead are dependent for their happiness upon sacrifices offered to them by the living shall have been totally overthrown.

V. Secondary wives. Concubinage is the natural result of the Confucian theory of ancestral worship. The misery which it has caused and still causes in China is beyond comprehension. Nothing can uproot it but a decay of faith in the assumption underlying all forms of worship of the dead.

VI. Suicides of wives and daughters. The preceding causes, operating singly and in combination, are wholly sufficient to account for the number of suicides among Chinese women. The wonder rather is that there are not more. But whoever undertakes to collect facts on this subject for any given district will not improbably be greatly surprised a the extraordinary prevalence of this practice. It is even adopted by children, and for causes relatively trifling. At times it appears to spread, like the small pox, and the thirst for suicide becomes virtually an epidemic. According to the native newspapers, there are parts of China in which young girls band themselves into a secret league to commit suicide within a certain time after they have been betrothed or married. The wretchedness of the lives to which they are condemned is thoroughly appreciated in advance, and fate is thus effectually checkmated. It would be wrong to overstate the evils suffered by women in China, evils which have indeed many alleviations, and which are not to be compared to those of her sisters in India or in Turkey. But after all abatements have been made it remains true that the death-roll of suicides is the most convincing proof of the woes endured by Chinese women.

VII. Overpopulation. The whole Chinese race is and always has been given up with a single devotion to the task of raising up a posterity, to do for the fathers what the fathers have done for the grandfathers. In this particular line, they have realised Wesley's conception of the ideal church in its line, where as he remarked the members are 'All at it, and always at it.' War, famine, pestilence sweep off scores of millions of the population, but a few decades of peace seem to repair the ravages of the past, which are lost to sight like battle-fields covered with wide areas of waving grain. However much we may admire the recuperative power of the Chinese people as a whole, and individually, it is impossible not to feel righteous indignation toward a system which violates those beneficent laws of nature, which would mercifully put an end to many branches of families when such branches are unfitted to survive. It is impossible to contemplate with equanimity the deliberate, persistent, and uniform propagation of poverty, vice, disease and crime, which ought rather to be surrounded with every restriction to prevent its multiplication, and to see this propagation of evil and misery done, too, with an air of virtue, as if this were of itself a kind of religion, often indeed the only form of religion on which the Chinese take any vital interest.

It is this system which loads down the rising generation with the responsibility for feeding and clothing tens of thousands of human beings who ought never to have been born, and whose existence can never be other than a burden to themselves, a period of incessant struggle without respite and without hope.

To the intelligent foreigner, the most prominent fact in China is the poverty of its people. There are too many villages to the square mile, too many families to the village, too many 'mouths' to the family. Wherever one goes, it is the same weary tale with interminable reiteration. Poverty, poverty, poverty, always and evermore poverty. The empire is broad, its unoccupied regions are extensive, and its undeveloped resources undoubtedly vast. But in what way can these resources be so developed as to benefit the great mass of the Chinese people? By none, with which we are acquainted, or of which we can conceive, without a radical disturbance of the existing conditions. The seething mass of overpopulation must be drawn off to the regions where it is needed, and then only will there be room for the relief of those who remain. It is impossible to do anything for people who are wedged together after the manner of matches in a box. Imagine a surgeon making the attempt to set the broken leg of a man in an omnibus in motion, which at the time contained twenty other people, most of whom also had broken legs which likewise require setting! The first thing to do would be to get them all unloaded, and to put them where they could be properly treated, with room for the treatment, and space for breathing. It is, we repeat, not easy to perceive how even the most advanced political economy can do anything of permanent benefit for the great mass of the Chinese without a redistribution of the surplus population. But at this point practical Confucianism intervenes, and having indeed the begetting of this swarm of human beings, it declares that they must not abandon the graves of their ancestors, who require their sacrifices, but must in the same spot continue to propagate a number their posterity to continue the interminable process.

The world is still large, and it has, and for ages will doubtless continue to have, ample room for all the additional millions which its existing millions can produce. The world was never so much in need of the Chinese as to day, and never, on the other hand, were the Chinese more in need of the world. But if China is to hold its own, much more if it is to advance as other nations have advanced, and do advance, it must be done under the head of new forces. Confucianism has been a might power to build up, and to conserve. But Confucianism with its great merits has committed many 'Deadly Sins,' and of those sins it must ultimately suffer the penalty. Confucianism as a developing force is a force which is spent. Sooner or later it must give way to something stronger, wiser, and better.

READING 5

"Small Feet of the Chinese Females: Remarks on the Origin of the Custom of Compressing the Feet; the Extent and Effects of the Practice; with an Anatomical Description of a Small Foot." *Chinese Repository* 3 (1835): 537–539.

Published in a missionary journal in Canton for foreigners in China and religious groups in the United States and China, the unknown author of this article criticizes foot-binding among Chinese women as physical and moral perversion of divine law.

Small Feet of the Chinese Females

Remarks on the Origin of the Custom of Compressing the Feet; the Extent and Effects of the Practice; with an Anatomical Description of a Small Foot.

Chinese Repository 3

rt. I. Small feet of the Chinese females: remarks on the origin of the custom of compressing the feet; the extent and effects of the practice; with an anatomical description of a small foot.

Ample evidence of the inefficiency of the ethical systems of the Chinese is found in their national and domestic customs. Not only the minds of the people, but their bodies also, are distorted and deformed by unnatural usages; and those laws, physical as well as moral, which the Creator designed for the good of his creatures, are perverted, and, if possible, would be annihilated. The truth of these remarks is presented to our view in a clear light by the anatomical description, which forms a part of this article. Historians are not agreed as to the time or place in which the practice of compressing the feet originated. Du Halde states, but on what authority he does not inform us, that the practice originated with the infamous Take, the last empress of the Shang dynasty, who perished in its overthrow, B.C. 1123. "Her own feet being very small, she bound them tight with fillets, affecting to make that pass for a beauty which was really a deformity. However, the women all followed her example; and this ridiculous custom is so thoroughly established, that to have feet of the natural size is enough to render them contemptible." Again, the same author remarks, "The Chinese themselves are not certain what gave rise to this odd custom. The story current among us, which attributes the invention to the ancient Chinese, who, to oblige their wives to keep at home, are said to have brought little feet into fashion, is by some looked upon as fabulous. The far greater number think it to be a political design, to keep women in continual subjection. It is certain that they are extremely confined, and seldom stir out of their apartments, which are in the most retired place in the house; having no

"Small Feet of the Chinese Females: Remarks on the Origin of the Custom of Compressing the Feet; The Extent and Effects of the Practice; With an Anatomical Description of a Small Foot," *The Chinese Repository*, vol. 3, pp. 537-539, 1835.

53

communication with any bu the women-servants." Others state that the custom originated in the time of the woo tae, or 'five dynasties,' about A.D. 925. According to the native historian, quoted in Morrison's View of China, "it is not known when the small feet of females were introduced. It is said that the custom arose in the time of the five dynasties. Le Howchoo ordered his concubine, Yaou, to bind her feet with silk, and cause them to appear small, and in the shape of the new moon. From this, sprung the imitation of every other female."

In regard to the extent and effects of the practice, there is not the same degree of uncertainty. It prevails more or less throughout the whole empire, but only among the Chinese. The Tartar ladies do not yield to the cruel custom, but allow their feet to retain their natural form. In the largest towns and cities, and generally in the most fashionable parts of the country, a majority of the females have their feet compressed. In some places, as many as seven or eight in ten are tormented in this way; in other places, the number is not more than four or five in ten. The operation of compressing the feet is commenced in infancy; and so closely and constantly are the bandages applied, in the most successful cases, as to prevent almost entirely the growth and extension of the limb. Ladies of rank and taste, who are fashioned in this manner, are rendered quite unable to walk. The effects of this process are extremely painful. Children will often tear away the bandages in order to gain relief from the torture; but their temporary removal, it is said, greatly increase the pain by causing a violent revulsion of the blood to the feet. This violent compression of the limbs, moreover, is injurious to health, and renders the victim a cripple through life. In some cases the compression is very slight, and consequently the effect is less hurtful. It is no marvel that the Chinese ladies never dance; it is rather a matter of surprise that they can move at all on such ill shaped and distorted members; some of which, scarcely if at all, exceed two and a half inches in length. Those who can avoid it, seldom appear abroad except in sedans; (we speak of those in the neighborhood of Canton); but there are frequent cases, among the poorer classes, where the unhappy victims of this barbarous custom are compelled to walk on their little feet. Their gait appears exceedingly awkward to others, and must be painful to themselves. Generally, in attempting to walk any considerable distance, they find a stick, or the shoulder of a matron or servant girl, a necessary support. In walking, the body is bend forwards at a considerable inclination, in order to place the centre of gravity over the feet; and the great muscular exertion required for preserving the balance is evinced by the rapid motion of the arms, and the hobbling shortness of the steps.

The form of these 'golden lilies,' kin leën, as the Chinese call them, is accurately described in the following paper, from the *Transactions of the Royal Society of London*. It was written by Bransby Blake Cooper, esq., surgeon to Guy's hospital; and was communicated to the society by the secretary, P.M. Roget, M.D., March 5th, 1829.

"A specimen of a Chinese foot, the account of which I have the honor to lay before the Royal Society, was removed from the dead body of a female found floating in the river at Canton. On its arrival in England, it was presented to sir Astley Cooper, to whose kindness I am indebted for the opportunity of making this curious dissection. Without entering into an inquiry whether this singular construction, and as we should esteem it hideous deformity, of the Chinese female foot, had its origin in oriental jealousy, or was the result of an unnatural taste in beauty; I shall content myself with describing the remarkable deviations from the original structure, which it almost every-where presents."

READING 6

Han Yi, "Destroying the Family" (1907).

Written under the pseudonym Han Yi, this 1907 essay calls for the destruction of the family as an institution standing in the way of a social revolution.

Destroying the Family

Han Yi

All of society's accomplishments depends on people to achieve, while the multiplication of the human race depends on men and women. Thus if we want to pursue a social revolution, we must start with a sexual revolution—just as if we want to reestablish the Chinese nation, expelling the Manchus is the first step to the accomplishment of other tasks. ...Yet, whenever we speak of the sexual revolution, the masses doubt and obstruct us, which gives rise to problems. In bringing up this matter then we absolutely must make a plan that gets to the root of the problem. What is this plan? It is to destroy the family. The family is the origin of all evil. Because of the family, people become selfish. Because of the family, women are increasingly controlled by men. Because of the family, everything useless and harmful occurs (people now often say they are embroiled in family responsibilities while in fact they are all just making trouble for themselves, and so if there were no families, these trivial matters would instantly disappear). Because of the family, children—who belong to the world as a whole—are made the responsibility of a single woman (children should be raised publicly since they belong to the whole society, but with families the men always force the women to raise their children and use them to continue the ancestral sacrifices). These examples constitute irrefutable proof of the evils of the family. ... Moreover, from now on in a universal commonwealth, everyone will act freely, never again will they live and die without contact with one another as in olden times. The doctrine of human equality allows for neither forcing women to maintain the family nor having servants to maintain it. The difficulties of life are rooted in the family. When land belongs to everyone and the borders between here and there are eradicated, then there will be no doubt that the "family" itself definitely should be abolished. As long as the family exists, then debauched men will imprison women

Han Yi, "Destroying the Family," 1907.

in cages and force them to become their concubines and service their lust, or they will take the sons of others to be their own successors. If we abolish the family now, then such men will disappear. The destruction of the family will thus lead to the creation of public minded people in place of selfish people, and men will have no way to oppress women. Therefore, to open the curtain on the social revolution, we must start with the destruction of the family.

READING 7

Susan L. Mann, "Sexuality and the Other," in *Gender and Sexuality in Modern China* (Cambridge University Press, 2011), 169–185.

The excerpt from historian Susan Mann explains how European colonialism in China as well as China's "internal imperialism" used perceptions of difference to impose norms regarding gender and sexuality in the name of "civilization."

Sexuality and the Other

Susan L. Mann

The People's Government is really something

No longer do we comb up our hair but wear it in a bun
With our headdress removed, we are free and easy
With flowers in our hair, oh so pretty.
Local customs are really no good
The headdress and long vest, no sleeves for one's arms
In this new era we must change our style
Three bamboo sticks inside the headdress
A headscarf made from an array of colors
It's unattractive and must be reformed.

Propaganda folksong, Hui'an, Fujian (Sara Friedman 2006:259–260)

His clothing was crisply ironed and neat from top to bottom, and he'd applied lots of hair gel, too, so he looked like a brand-new, furled umbrella. Those eyes of his seemed like the epicenter of his body and all his energy emanated from there. A white man's eyes.

Wei Hui, *Shanghai Baby* (2001:29–30)

E ncountering an unfamiliar culture, the outsider looks for difference. Nowhere is difference more easily apprehended than in the arenas of gender and sexuality. In any cross-cultural encounter, gender roles and sexuality supply a medium for clarifying and symbolizing the essential cultural differences that separate "us" from "them." So sex—that most intimate of acts—is ironically one of the first things we think of when we imagine the remote

Susan L. Mann, "Sexuality and the Other", Gender and Sexuality in Modern Chinese History, pp. 169-185, 203-222. Copyright © 2011 by Cambridge University Press. Reprinted with permission

Other. Imperial expansion aimed at economic or political conquest therefore also, and inevitably, negotiates gender relations (Stoler 1991). In the history of Western colonialism, the gender models at the civilizing center were binary and heteronormative. Encountering Chinese culture, Europeans asked: What makes women women, and what makes men men, in this place? The civilizing projects of China's own late imperial government, and of China's contemporary Communist state, posed the same questions on the borderlands and in China's heartland itself. The effect of civilizing projects, in general, has been to masculinize the dominant metropole and feminize the colonized Other, as in Wei Hui's *Shanghai Baby*, quoted above. But gender bending and confusion can also arise. Who is liberated, who is modern, who is moral, who is perverse? Cross-cultural encounters also pose these questions and demand answers.

Consider the late imperial program to incorporate southwestern borderlands in Guizhou and Yunnan into the regular bureaucratic provincial administration, a civilizing project that lasted several centuries. Collecting intelligence on the subjects of this civilizing project, the Qing court commissioned albums of illustrated ethnographic reporting on each of the eighty-two non-Han peoples in Guizhou province. Laura Hostetler's analysis of these eighteenth-century albums shows that the illustrator, and the text, paid more attention to courtship and marriage than to anything else. For court officials drafting policies to bring those territories under direct administrative control, family relationships and gender roles were a focal point of concern (Deal and Hostetler 2006: xlii–xliv). In contemporary China, gendered strategies in minority areas have varied, depending on whether the government was trying to suppress or preserve ethnic identities. In Tibet and in Xinjiang, for example, where the Chinese government sought to suppress ethnic identity, the main targets of central government state policy were religious institutions and practices dominated by men—Llamaist monasteries, Muslim family law (Dautcher 2009, Makley 2007). By contrast, in the Miao homelands of the southwest, where ethnic identities were nurtured and protected, the government has made Miao women into cultural icons who preserve and perform ethnic difference (Schein 2000).

Whatever the policy or strategy, and whatever the colonial regime, sexuality is clearly judged a crucial arena for identifying, articulating, imagining, performing, or suppressing difference in any cross-cultural encounter. We can dramatize this point by comparing illustrations from three roughly contemporaneous civilizing projects: a British caricature of Lord Macartney's mission to the Qianlong Emperor's court in 1793 (Figure 7.1), a Chinese album painting of local customs in a minority area of China's southwest frontier (Figure 7.2), and a Chinese gazetteer woodcut print showing the customs of Taiwan's indigenous people (Figure 7.3).

The drawing depicted in Figure 7.1 by late-eighteenth-century British artist James Gillray (1756–1815), titled "The Reception of the Diplomatique & his Suite at the Court

FIGURE 7.1   James Gillray. "A caricature on Lord Macartney's Embassy to China." Hand-colored etching (s. 12 × 15 7/8 in. [31.7 × 40.2 cm.]). Published by H. Humphrey, London, September 14, 1792 (public domain). *Source:* John Merson, *Roads to Xanadu: East and West in the Making of the Modern World.* London: Weidenfeld and Nicolson, 1989, p. 145.

of Pekin,"[1] is a caricature of Lord Macartney's imagined reception at the court of Qianlong. It appeared in London in 1792, a week before Macartney departed on his mission. Lord Macartney, sent by King George with a formal request that China open its ports to British trade (a request that the Qianlong Emperor was to dismiss categorically), won fame for his alleged refusal to *ketou* (kneel and then fall prostrate in a ritual sequence) before the emperor, as required by Chinese imperial court etiquette. Gillray's drawing, however, lampoons the British attempt to engage the Chinese court in any level of diplomatic exchange. He depicts Macartney kneeling absurdly before a dissolute Qing emperor, who is drawn à la Turque, in a classic Orientalist pose. The emperor (Qianlong), reclining slothfully on cushions, wearing funny shoes, and smoking a water pipe, is palpably soft, weak, and foolish—a perfect foil for the cartoonist's Macartney. Gillray was convinced that the mission was an act of folly, and he wanted his audience to apprehend the ridiculousness of Macartney's obsequious bow. But Gillray, in his zeal to spoof Macartney's mission, unwittingly conveyed other civilizing subtexts. The Chinese emperor's pose as a decadent Oriental ruler also hints

---

1   I am indebted to Henrietta Harrison and Mark Elliott for assistance in identifying this cartoon.

FIGURE 7.2 "Hua (Flowery) Miao" (album leaf), dated sometime after 1797. *Source:* David M. Deal and Laura Hostetler, trans. *The Art of Ethnography: A Chinese "Miao Album."* Seattle: University of Washington Press, 2006, p. 26.

at his sex life. He must have a harem, because there are no women in sight. Women are shut up and cannot be viewed in public in a culture where they are reserved to serve the pleasure of men. And hovering behind the emperor we see a palace eunuch - a desexed man who reminds the viewer on another level that sexual indulgence (many women) is accompanied by sexual perversion (castration and paranoia about sexual access).

In the second illustration, depicted in Figure 7.2, we see a Han Chinese artist's depiction of courtship practices among the so-called Flowery Miao. The appended description begins with the following poem: "Dressing at dawn, she inserts a new wooden comb / And wraps colorful clothing around her body. / Blowing reeds, shaking bells—sound, movement, harmonize. / Strangers dance in moonlight. Young girls cherish springtime." Similar themes in other album leaves feature the casual sex customary among other Miao peoples, showing women ringing bells while men play reed flutes, men and women mingling while dancing around a pole or picnicking in the woods, and even (in one case) a new year festival in which women were carried off on the backs of their suitors. Most shocking to elite Han Chinese sensibilities were accounts of betrothal rituals that *followed* sexual intercourse or even the birth of a child, carefully detailed with ethnographic precision by the text's authors (Deal and Hosteder 2006:xliii-xliv).

Echoing the British interest in costume and civilization, Chinese travelers and officials who began the process of colonizing Taiwan in the eighteenth century took time to catalog both the dress and the work habits of indigenous peoples, with a focus on gender roles. The drawing depicted in Figure 7.3 conveys a doubly negative message, with a bare-breasted woman and a bare-chested man working side by side pounding rice. Emma Teng, who has studied these and similar texts, points out that such illustrations were confined to the so-called savage peoples who were least influenced by Han Chinese custom (Teng 2004:152–156). Other drawings show indigenous people whose customs more closely resembled the Han conventions in dividing men's and women's labor, by way of pointing to their relatively "civilized" condition.

In colonial encounters, then, sex and gender roles become a powerful proxy for who "we" or "they" *really* are: "we" are normal, "they" are perverse or exotic. In the Jesuit encounter with Chinese culture in the seventeenth century, for example, Jesuit observers were upset by the widespread casual sex between men that they encountered in the social lives of the Chinese literati with whom they consorted, and many Jesuits composed long tracts condemning "sodomy" in China, a kind of measure of immorality that they used for other purposes to promote and justify their civilizing mission (Hinsch 1990:1–2; Vitiello 2000:251–253). Then there are counterexamples in which the colonizer imagines the sexual world of the Other to be better than his own. The mid-twentieth-century Dutch sinologist Robert van Gulik, for instance, was charmed by what he viewed as the uninhibited sex lives of the "ancient Chinese," and he used his research on Chinese sexuality to criticize Victorian sexuality, publishing his monumental study of Chinese erotica to make the point (Furth 1994). Gulik was captivated by books advising Chinese men that because women had nothing to gladden their hearts but sexual intercourse (this was Gulik's understanding, at any rate): "it is the duty of every enlightened householder to have a thorough knowledge of the Art of the Bedchamber, so that he can give complete satisfaction to his wives and concubines every time he copulates with them" (Gulik 1951:107).

Gulik was also struck by the frank homoeroticism he found in Chinese prints and drawings, which he collected assiduously and studied with fascination. For Gulik, the message of the colonial encounter was that "we" are uptight, "they" are liberated.

Perhaps the most potent sexualized emblems of a civilizing project, which we have encountered in previous chapters, come from the Manchu conquest that established the Qing dynasty in 1644. During the first four decades of their rule, the Manchus embarked on a civilizing mission of their own, focused on the performance of male and female roles in the Han Chinese population. On one level, this was a move to make Han bodies signal submission to the Manchu conquest by requiring Han Chinese men to groom themselves like Manchu men and Han Chinese women like Manchu women. In a violent and exhaustive series of local campaigns, Han Chinese men were forced to abandon the topknot hairstyle that was the very essence of Han Chinese male identity, shave their foreheads, and grow a braid down the back - the Manchu style - signaling with their bodies their submission to Qing rule. (The late Frederic Wakeman, in a rhetorical coup, referred to this Manchu conquest policy as "tonsorial castration" [Wakeman 1985:1:649].) At the

FIGURE 73 "Pounding Rice," from the *Gazetteer of Zhuluo County* [Taiwan] (1717). *Source:* Emma Jinhua Teng, *Taiwan's Imagined Geography: Chinese Colonial Travel Writing and Pictures, 1683–1895.* Cambridge: Harvard University Press, 2004, p. 154. Teng notes that the author of this particular gazetteer was inclined to view the indigenous people's "savage customs" as benign examples of life in a primitive utopia (2004:74).

same time, the Manchus also banned footbinding among Chinese women because Manchu women never bound their feet. This policy they never managed to enforce, with complicated psychological consequences in the early Qing period ("men submit, women resist"). In that historical moment, bound feet became a marker of Han Chinese identity and resistance against foreign conquest, an emblem of Ming loyalism, and a sign of women's steadfast and superior moral strength (Mann 2002:437–439). A colonial encounter, in other words, can rapidly shift the meanings of customary practices and transform them into performances of cultural identity. What counts as "backward" or "conservative," after all, if the question is about civilization or barbarism?

Compounding the complexity of the Manchu conquest moment, as Mark Elliott has shown, was the Manchu concern to preserve a distinct cultural identity of their own, which led them to focus on certain gender issues within the Manchu population itself. As he puts it, the distinctive ideals for Manchu women in the Qing period tell us a lot "about the importance of women in the construction of ethnicity historically" (Elliott 1999:38). For the Qing court, for example, rewarding Manchu chaste widows alongside Han Chinese chaste widows signaled the court's willingness to let Manchu women embrace Han Chinese female virtues and to publicly recognize them for it. By contrast, the court never recognized Manchu men for the display of Han-style masculine virtue, especially in scholarship or in filiality. Instead, Manchu males were held to the old martial ideals of the Manchu Bannerman's "manly virtue" (*haha erdemu*): riding, shooting with bow and arrow, and living simply and unpretentiously (Elliott 1999:64). Similarly, Qing policy affecting Manchu women by no means aimed at their acculturation and assimilation into the Han population. On the contrary, like colonial regimes of Europe, the Manchus strictly controlled the marriage and fertility of Manchu women by requiring that they marry within the Banner system (Elliott 1999:69–71).

The gendered configuration of Manchu policies, carefully tailored to fit males and females of Manchu and Han populations, merely underscores the centrality of gender and sexuality in moments of conquest and colonial encounters. Still another example is the Qing practice of marriage exchange, in which imperial princesses were sent as consorts to live in Mongolia, especially Outer Mongolia, where their presence could serve a crucial diplomatic function (Rawski 1991:177–178, Rawski 1998:146- 152). By contrast with the strict rules limiting Han Chinese and Manchu intermarriage among commoners, imperial intermarriage across ethnic lines served as a tool for extending the multiethnic empire beyond the borders of China proper. Finally, we should take note of the Qing empire's other imperial civilizing missions, documented both in fiction and in travel accounts from the Qing period. As we have seen, travelers to Taiwan in the Qing period (who, following the rules of the Chinese family system, were almost entirely male) displayed a deep fascination with sexuality, both in representations of indigenous "savage women" who were accessible and promiscuous and in critiques of indigenous men, whom they criticized as lazy and dependent (Teng 2004). As C. Patterson Giersch has observed, "In both European and Qing empires, indigenous women were represented as symbols of sexual conquest whereas indigenous men were portrayed as weak and feminine" (Giersch 2006:75). Giersch, who studied Qing expansion into Yunnan province during the early nineteenth century, noticed that Han travelers dubbed one ethnic group the "Water Baiyi," a label associated with drawings of members of this group that featured a bare-breasted woman bathing in a stream in the company of a man (Giersch 2006:75). Both the public bathing and the scanty clothing triggered titillation and shock in a Han Chinese reader; the level of civilization of the Water Baiyi did not need further elaboration.

In the late-eighteenth-century Chinese novel *A Country Codger Puts His Words Out to Sun (Yesou puyan)*—encountered in Chapter 8—the Han Chinese protagonist travels to the southwest, where he predictably encounters sexual practices that he deems uncivilized and un-Confucian, highlighting the propriety of his own values (which some readers might have questioned in light of the pornographic content of the book). When his Miao informant (a "local wise man" [*tushenglao*]) protests that the Han Chinese "take so many precautions that the desires and longings men and women have for each other have no way to be let out" and defends "local customs" (permitting a wife to kiss and touch a male visitor to her home, sex between men and women without their parents' consent, and individual mate choice), the protagonist and others firmly disagree and dismiss the Miao informant's views as nonsense (McMahon 1988:46). The same novel elaborates the civilizing impact of Han Chinese culture on the Miao, not only as "reformed" gender relations (young couples start singing verses from the *Classic of Poetry* to one another) but also in a vignette featuring the hero's sexual encounter with a Miao girl who is "sterile" (a *shi nil*, or "stone woman"). His masculine *qi* and his *yang* energy not only awaken her sexual desire but even make her fertile by stimulating her menstrual period (see Martin Huang 2003:90). In this work of fiction, the grand civilizing mission of the "great man" (*da zhangfu*) once again casts the ethnic minorities as feminine and unlettered. In a final elegant touch, mentioned in Chapter 8, the author takes one of his Han heroes to Europe, where he embarks on a conversion program aimed at reforming sexual practices among certain members of Europe's royal families, who are taught how to time sexual intercourse according to the menstrual cycle rather than their own desires, to produce more sons (Martin Huang 2003:91).[2]

---

2   In early nineteenth-century novels, fears of European imperialism replaced the heroic Confucian expansionism so robustly captured in *Country Codger*, with syphilis and opium both cast as dread "foreign diseases" (Martin Huang 2003:90–93).

THE BOUND FOOT AS A MARKER OF THE OTHER

Western traders, missionaries, and diplomats were uniformly dismayed by what they viewed as the oppression of women in Asian cultures. Their sentiments were rooted in early-nineteenth-century values articulated by French utopian thinkers, especially Charles Fourier, who famously wrote: "As a general thesis: *Social progress ... occurs by virtue of the progress of women toward liberty, and social decline by virtue of decreases in the liberty of women*" (Leslie Goldstein 1982:100, italics original). The Chinese empire's decline, in other words, was clear to foreign observers the minute they saw women with bound feet. The bound foot was an uncontrovertible symbol of the oppression of Chinese women, which made it the emblem of the backwardness of the Chinese empire, and the ultimate sign of the uncivilized character of the Chinese people. In that guise, women's bound feet were also an inspiration and a justification for conquest (Zito 2006).

As Patricia Ebrey (1999) has pointed out, bound feet were not always regarded as an object of scorn or disgust by Western observers. Criticism sharpened in the nineteenth century, however, as observers shifted their focus from fashion and custom to pain and suffering, and to the oppression and control of females, especially female children. The rise of scientific medical views of the body, later bolstered by the new technology of the X-ray, revealed the extent of mutilation in footbinding and dramatized the resulting pain. This fed other concerns about child abuse fostered by the growing attention to childhood and childrearing in Euro-North American culture. All of this was ample fuel for the zeal that energized the colonial powers, as well as Christian missionaries and, ultimately, Chinese reformers at the end of the nineteenth century.

Current scholarship has been sharply revisionist in its account of the meanings of footbinding in the Chinese cultural context. Dorothy Ko (1997b), as we have seen, has stressed that bound feet stood for civility in late imperial times, part of the essential adornment reserved for the most advanced cultures, and that even the shaping of the foot itself was part of the styling of proper attire. In other words, far from representing a mutilation of the body, bound feet were considered part of the decoration of the body. In other work (2005), Ko has likened footbinding to a kind of cosmetic surgery whose appeal was enhanced by ordinary people's ordinary aspirations: the desire to be fashionable, to attract a good husband for a daughter, to be respectable, to be proper and refined, and to be correct and fit in. These are all reasons why a mother wanted to bind her daughter's feet. To be sure, young girls who were being prepared for work as courtesans or prostitutes had their feet bound with sexual or erotic appeal in mind, and in that sense, their bodies were marketed by pimps as commodities. But not so the vast majority of ordinary commoners. They were merely striving for respectability. So despite fantasies about the eroticism of bound feet, in cultural context they were viewed in much more complicated and even mundane ways. For example, the shoes embroidered to fit the feet were a display of a young

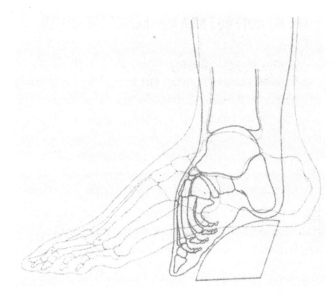

FIGURE 7.4   "A Bound Foot." *Source:* John K. Fairbank and Edwin O. Reischauer, *China: Tradition and Transformation.* Boston: Houghton Mifflin, 1978, p. 142.

woman's talent and creativity (Ko 2001). Moreover, the foot itself was always to be concealed, not only inside a shoe and bindings but also beneath a loose, long garment. In fact, concealment was the key to the erotic and aesthetic meanings of the bound foot, as shown in the very provocative drawing of a courtesan in Figure 14, above.

When foreigners insisted on X-rays to reveal the contortions that produced bound feet—when, in other words, the foot was no longer concealed, but open to view down to the bone—the "aura" and allure of concealment ended, and with it the mystique of fashion, status, and propriety that had attached itself to bound feet (see Figure 7.4). At the same time, loud cries condemning the weakness of Chinese women and the need to mobilize them for full participation in nation-building made footbinding appear backward as well as oppressive to patriotic reform-minded Chinese. Upper-class parents in droves refused to bind their daughters' feet, and within a few decades, bound feet had vanished from the urban elite, to be replaced by the pointy-toed heels preferred by Western female slaves to fashion. In the countryside where urban fashion and modern nationalist consciousness made no impact, it was left to the nationalists or, later, the Chinese Communists to finish off footbinding, sometimes with coercive measures.

In an age of Botox, breast implants, tattoos, and body piercing, we can readily see that there are more ways to understand footbinding than to condemn it as a sign of backwardness and women's oppression. That insight alerts us again to the powerful relationships that dictate taste and sex-gender performance in any culture. Reviewing the history of civilizing projects, in other words, makes us ask, what counts as backward or oppressive, and who gets to decide?

CHANGE IN THE TWENTIETH CENTURY

The relationship between gender, sexuality, and ethnicity in imperial China closely resembles the processes and practices familiar in colonial encounters everywhere. In the case of China's "internal colonialism," however, the civilizing process had its own particularly Chinese features. One of these, rooted in mid-Qing practice, was the universalizing impetus of Qing rule, which sought to hold everyone in the empire to the same standards of civilized conduct, including proper roles for men and women (Sommer 2000).[3] Like their Qing predecessors, twentieth-century officials had similar universalizing goals, and they were well aware of the extensive local variation in gender performance and sexual practice that challenged or flouted the rules and conventions of patrilineal kinship. Certain alternative marriage forms, some of which arguably favored the emotional and personal interests of women and their loved ones, were roundly opposed by the Republican and Communist governments in their zeal to promote "modern" marriage. A survey of local customs compiled in 1922 reveals astonishment in the researcher's account of the local customs in Shunde, the area near Canton where "delayed transfer marriage" thrived:

> When two women live together, although they cannot be like a man and a woman in every respect, in fact they do enjoy the pleasures of a man and a woman. Some say they use rubbing pressure, others say they use a clever mechanism [i.e., dildo]. These kinds of words are crude and difficult for highly educated men to discuss. Such couples will even select a female heir to inherit their property. Later this female heir will likewise sign a "golden lotus contract" like a daughter-in-law, just as if they had a blood relationship. Indeed but it is strange! (Hu Pu'an 1968:2:34)

Elite condescension quickly marginalized these local practices, which vanished from urban areas by the time of the 1949 Revolution. Delayed transfer marriage nonetheless survived into the 1970s in a few isolated communities, roundly scorned by residents of more economically developed areas (Siu 1990).

In urban China, where twentieth-century reformers and revolutionaries prevailed, the target of civilizing projects became the joint family system. In social Darwinist discourse, the joint family ruled by male elders represented an impediment to China's progress, which required the liberation of the energies of youth and women to build a strong nation. The civilized modern ideal, as we have seen, was the "small family"—a conjugal unit established through free mate choice in a neolocal marriage (Glosser 2003). The Republican government's promotion of the small family ideal

---

3   Chen Hongmou's eighteenth-century campaigns to promote chaste widowhood and eradicate matrilocal marriage and the levirate among non-Han peoples show how these policies energized an especially effective Qing official (Rowe 2001:312, 424–425).

was in part a response to long-term campaigns by reformist Christian missionaries, especially female missionaries, whose "imperial evangelism" (Hunter 1984) aimed to bring Chinese women, feet unbound, out of the home and into a public sphere where (among other things) missionaries' own Christian teachings might convert them. Many Christian missionaries noted that changing women's family roles posed new problems, because Chinese culture offered no moral guidelines for respectable women to follow once they left home. Luella Miner worried that Chinese women would need to "internalize conventions of control" in their new sphere and suggested that Western women might be able to teach them these new conventions. Like many other female missionaries at the turn of the century, Miner was worried about sex and adolescent girls (Hunter 1984:175). But this worry was conflated with another concern: missionary schools could not risk the taint of promiscuity. The result was that missionary schools delivered a heavy dose of moral support for marriage and compliant wives, and even unmarried female missionaries who prided themselves on their own independence found themselves instructing Chinese women to marry, have children, and retreat into domesticity.

Yet the speed with which urban Chinese women embraced new roles defied the concerns and correctives of missionary civilizing projects. Jane Hunter suggests that this flexible adaptation to new roles had historical and cultural roots of its own in China, where women were reared to behave appropriately *according to* the roles they were assigned. Hunter cites Mary Rankin's analysis of the path of the early-twentieth-century revolutionary Qiu Jin, whose short life took her through a dizzying sequence of disparate roles, from cloistered young lady to wife and mother, from there to studies in Japan, and finally, to revolutionary martyrdom: "A woman who succeeded in breaking away from family bonds and becoming a teacher, doctor, revolutionary, etc., was ... expected to act in accord with well-defined concepts of behavior. ... When a woman did enter one of these roles, she also assumed their normally male characteristics" (Rankin 1975:64, quoted in Hunter 1984:263).

Chinese reformers and foreign missionaries may have agreed on a model for a heteronormative nuclear family, but their interactions also produced confusion about gender roles, particularly about notions of masculinity and femininity. Mrinalini Sinha's work on colonial Bengal (1995:18–19 passim) has shown how the late-nineteenth-century ideal of the "manly Englishman" was constructed in opposition to an "effeminate Bengali *babu*." Hunter's study of American women missionaries in turn- of-the-century China points to a different kind of "gender confusion" around what were seen by Chinese as the "man-like" ways of American women, and the missionaries' corresponding perception of Chinese men as weak, effeminate, and not sexually threatening. To Chinese men, Hunter observes, American women appeared desexed ("neither one nor the other" [1984:214]), not only because of their free movement in public space but also because of their unbound feet, pale hair—especially grey hair—and long noses (1984:204–216). These observations about gender confusion resulting from colonial encounters and civilizing projects dramatize what many scholars have now discovered: that these are the richest areas—the most illuminating historical moments—for research on sexuality in history, cracking open identities that are erased or concealed, and defamiliarizing familiar evidence.

In its own civilizing project dedicated to "equality between men and women" (*nan nü ping deng*), the Maoist Chinese Communist government brought women fully into the productive labor force alongside men. Yet this civilizing project presumed a model of universal heterosexual marriage and reproduction that retained the household as the basic unit of residence and livelihood. Family production remained based on a division of labor by sex and age; patrilocal marriage and household production secured male rights to land and women. Similar goals pervaded state policy in minority areas. The case of Hui'an women (in the propaganda song that begins this chapter) shows the Chinese Communist government deciding vigorously what counts as backward. Tracing the history of government policies toward Hui'an women also shows that judgments about backwardness, as in the case of footbinding, are relative and malleable, subject to other political and cultural pressures. During the 1950s, for example, the women of Hui'an, Fujian, became the target of intense efforts to eliminate "feudal" conditions in the peripheral parts of China's eighteen provinces. What Hui'an women wore and how Hui'an women worked were cited as dramatic emblems of backward practices that hindered the building of a modern nation. A modern nation, in the Communists' view, had to mobilize women for productive economic activity outside the home. Women's rising economic power, so this argument went, would then also improve their status: another key goal of the modern state. The large and cumbersome headdress that served as a hallmark of the Hui'an woman of the southeast coast made an arresting symbol of feudalism: it was alien and exotic to most Han Chinese, and it was clearly an impediment to economic productivity outside the home and an embarrassment to modern personhood as envisioned by China's youthful women cadres.

As Sara Friedman observes, the Communist Party's attempts in the 1950s to eliminate traditional Hui'an women's headdresses, and its campaigns against female suicide in Hui'an, balanced "the state's commitment to women's liberation and its equally compelling support for rural men and patrilineal families." Those headdresses and the suicide pacts, along with the *dui pnua* (sisterhood) bonds they affirmed, undermined familial control. So in preventing young women from taking their own lives, the government was also stabilizing and reinforcing patrilineal families (Friedman 2006:84). The Communist reform agenda in Hui'an extended to other aspects of local women's culture as well. Women's collective suicide by drowning to resist marriage, for example, was a local "evil custom" celebrated in Hui'an songs and stories. This made good fodder for the Communist campaign against arranged marriage. Equally inviting as a "feudal" target was a form of Hui'an marriage in which the bride declined to move into her husband's home (the custom dubbed "extended natal residence marriage" or "delayed transfer marriage" by anthropologists). Although some scholars regard this practice as one that empowered brides, the Communists classified it as a problem for the heteronormative "modern" marriage form licensed by the government. Despite the fact that Hui'an people were officially classified as Han according to the ethnic categories drawn up in the early years of the People's Republic, such flamboyantly non-Han customs doubly stigmatized Hui'an women: Hui'an customs were both "feudal" (backward) and also "deviant" (departures from the Han patrilocal norm).

Yet all of this opposition and criticism vanished in the 1990s during the post-Mao reform era. Under the new reform policies, Hui'an women were suddenly called on to retrieve their traditional clothing from storage and revive the customs that displayed those exotic hats. The rationale for the policies was unapologetic: Han Chinese tourists loved exotic local customs, especially those involving women, and tourism was profitable. In other words, by making ethnic culture a commodity that tourists could purchase, the government also made female bodies in ethnic communities objects of new interest (Sara Friedman 2006). The Hui'an case shows how deeply questions of gender and sexuality figure in encounters with the Other, and how unstable gendered meanings can be in a volatile political environment.

Emma Teng has pointed out that Qing representations of aboriginal women emerge in new forms in modern-day tourism to Taiwan, with dance shows featuring indigenous girls, who also figure prominently as prostitutes in the Taiwan sex industry (Teng 2004:193). The rise of sex tourism in reform-era China has likewise situated minority women in frameworks of "internal Orientalism" (Schein 2000:100–131). Artists, photographers, journalists, ethnographers, officials, and tourists all flock to Guizhou province's Miao villages to see and capture images of women in ethnic (*minzu*) costume. These tourists and visitors are primarily male, and the messages they bring and take away vary from erotic fascination to paternalistic protectionism, all of it focused on Miao women, who are alternately portrayed as voluptuous and enticing or childlike and close to nature. In the ultimate commercialization of these tourist markets, local Han Chinese women dress up as Miao to earn the money that Miao women increasingly scorn (Hyde 2007).

What makes the Hui'an women's position different from that of the Miao women described by Louisa Schein is the fact that Hui'an women identify strongly as Han and are still more reluctant to act seductively and perform publicly to meet the demands of the tourist industry (Sara Friedman 2006:227–228). Moreover, in the post-Mao era, women who "wear the headscarf" are criticized from all sides: as "feudal" (i.e., close-minded and backward, and, perhaps, excessively modest) by women who do not, and as chaotic and disruptive in their sexual behavior by men (Sara Friedman 2006:238–243). Gendered images themselves, in other words, have a multivalent quality that eludes efforts by the contemporary government to control and contain sexual performance and its meanings. The instability and fluidity of these images are powerful challenges to government "civilizing" projects aimed at securing a stable heteronormative family system.

China's recent history of cross-cultural encounters underscores the salience of sexuality and gender in defining the Other. No wonder changes in gender roles and sexuality have been central to China's twentieth-century transformations. Given the depth and range of the central government's power since 1950, the contemporary state's intense commitment to heteronormative marriage and reproduction is now displayed in projects, like the one-child policy, whose efficacy late imperial Chinese rulers would have envied.

BIBLIOGRAPHY

Dautcher, Jay. 2009. *Down a Narrow Road: Identity and Masculinity in a Uyghur Community in Xinjiang China*. Cambridge: Harvard University Asia Center.

Deal, David and Laura Hostetler, trans. 2006. *The Art of Ethnography: A Chinese "Miao Album."* Seattle: University of Washington Press.

Ebrey, Patricia. 1999. "Gender and Sinology: Shifting Western Interpretations of Footbinding, 1300–1890." *Late Imperial China* 20, 1–34.

Elliott, Mark. 1999. "Manchu Widows and Ethnicity in Qing China," *Comparative Studies in Society and History* 41, 33–71.

Friedman, Sara. 2006. *Intimate Politics: Marriage, the Market, and State Power in Southeastern China*. Cambridge: Harvard University Asia Center.

Furth, Charlotte. 1994. "Rethinking van Gulik: Sexuality and Reproduction in Traditional Chinese Medicine," In *Engendering China*. Edited by Christina Gilmartin, Gail Hershatter, Lisa Rofel, and Tyrene White. Cambridge: Harvard University Press, 125–146.

Giersch, Patterson. 2006. *Asian Borderlands: The Transformation of Qing China's Yunnan Frontier*. Cambridge: Harvard University Press.

Glosser, Susan. 2003. Chinese Visions of Family and State, 1915–1953. Berkeley: University of California Press.

Goldstein, Leslie. 1982. "Early Feminist Themes in French Utopian Socialism: The St. Simonians and Fourier," *Journal of the History of Ideas* 43: 91–108.

Gulik, Robert Hans van. 1951. *Erotic Colour Prints in the Ming Period*, with an Essay on Chinese Sex Life from the Han to the Ch'ing Dynasty, B.C. 206-A.D. 1644. Tokyo: privately published in fifty copies.

Hinsch, Bret. 1990. *Passions of the Cut Sleeve: The Male Homosexual Tradition in China*. Berkeley: University of California Press.

Huang, Martin. 2003. "From caizi to yingxiong: Imagining Masculinities in Two Qing Novels, Yesou puyan and Sanfen meng quan zhuan," *Chinese Literature: Essays, Articles, Reviews* 25, 59–98.

Hunter, Jane. 1984. *The Gospel of Gentility: American Women Missionaries in Turn-of-the-Century China*. New Haven: Yale University Press.

Hyde, Sandra. 2007. Eating Spring Rice: The Cultural Politics of Aids in Southwest China. Berkeley: University of California Press.

Ko, Dorothy. 1997. "The Written Word and the Bound Foot: A History of the Courtesan's Aura," In *Writing Women in Late Imperial China*, Edited by Ellen Widmer and Kang-I Sun Chang. Palo Alto: Stanford University Press, 74–100.

Ko, Dorothy. 2001. *Every Step a Lotus: Shoes for Bound Feet*. Berkeley: University of California Press.

Ko, Dorothy. 2005. *Cinderella's Shoes: A Revisionist History of Footbinding*. Berkeley: University of California Press.

Makley, Charlene. 2007. *The Violence of Liberation: Gender and Tibetan Buddhist Revival in Post-Mao China*. Berkeley: University of California Press.

Mann, Susan. 2002. "Women, Families, and Gender Relations." In *The Cambridge History of China, Volume 9, Part One: The Ch'ing Dynasty until 1800*, Edited by Willard Peterson, New York: Cambridge University Press, 428–472.

McMahon, Keith. 1988. "A Case for Confucian Sexuality: The Eighteenth Century Novel Yesou Puyan," *Late Imperial China* 9, 32–55.

Rankin, Mary. 1975. "The Emergence of Women at the End of the Ch'ing: The Case of Ch'iu Chin." In *Women in Chinese Society*, edited by Margery Wolf and Roxane Witke. Palo Alto: Stanford University Press, 39–66.

Rawski, Evelyn. 1991. "Ch'ing Imperial Marriage and Problems of Rulership," In *Marriage and Inequality in Chinese Society*, edited by Rubie Watson and Patricia Ebrey. Berkeley: University of California Press, 170–203.

Rowe, William. 2003. *Saving the World: Chen Hongmou and Elite Consciousness in Eighteenth Century China*. Palo Alto: Stanford University Press.

Schein, Louisa. 2000. *Minority Rules: The Miao and the Feminine in China's Political Culture*. Durham: Duke University Press.

Sinha, Mrinalini. 1995. *Colonial Masculinity: The "Manly Englishman" and the "Effeminate Bengali" in the Late Nineteenth Century*. New York: Manchester University Press.

Siu, Helen. 1990. "Where Were the Women? Rethinking Marriage Resistance and Regional Culture in South China," *Late Imperial China* 11, 270–281.

Sommer, Matthew. 2000. *Sex, Law, and Society in Late Imperial China*. Palo Alto: Stanford University Press.

Stoler, Ann. 1991. *Carnal Knowledge and Imperial Power: Gender, Race, and Morality in Colonial Asia*. Berkeley: University of California Press.

Teng, Emma. 2004. *Taiwan's Imagined Geography: Chinese Colonial Travel Writing and Pictures, 1638–1895*. Cambridge: Harvard University Asia Center.

Vitiello, Giovanni. 2000. "Exemplary Sodomites: Chivalry and Love in Late Ming Culture," *Nan Nü: Men, Women, and Gender in Late Imperial China* 2, 207–257.

Wakeman, Frederic Jr. 1985. *The Great Enterprise: The Manchu Reconstruction of Imperial Order in Seventeenth Century China*. Berkeley: University of California Press.

Wei, Hui. 2001. *Shanghai Baby*, translated by Bruce Hume. New York: Pocket Books.

Zito, Angela. 2006. "Bound to be Represented: Fetishizing/Theorizing Footbinding," In *Embodied Modernities Corporeality, Representation, and Chinese Cultures*, edited by Larissa Heinrich and Fran Martin. Honolulu: University of Hawaii Press, 29–41.

PART III

RACE, SEX, AND GENDER IN EUROPE BEFORE THE TWENTIETH CENTURY

I deas of the complementary nature of human sexes in European thought are represented in this selection of sources. While *Aristotle's Masterpiece* and John Barclay's drawings highlight ideas of differences between the sexes, Wollstonecraft and the Women's Petition challenge differences in educational and political participation by pressing the case for equality.

READING 8

"Of Infants," *Aristotle's Masterpiece* (1680).

Aristotle's Masterpiece was a popular European sex manual written by an unknown author, not the ancient Greek philosopher Aristotle. In this excerpt, the author poses and answers questions regarding why children resemble their parents, among other things.

Aristotle's Masterpiece

Of Infants

W hy are some children altogether like the father, some like the mother, some to both, and some to neither?

If the seed of the father do wholly overcome that of the mother, the child doth wholly resemble the father; but if the mother's predominate, then it is like the mother; but if he be like neither, that doth happen for many causes; sometimes through the four qualities, sometimes through the influence of some heavenly constellation. Albertus gives an example, and saith, that there was on a time a good constellation for begetting hogs and a child was then begotten and brought forth, which had a face like a hog; and according to this divers sorts of monsters are brought forth.

Why are children oftener like the father than the mother?

That proceeds of imagination of the mother in the act of copulation, and therefore by reason of the strong imagination in the time of conception, the children get the disposition of the father; as appeared before of the queen which had her imagination on a blackamoor, and of an Ethiopian queen, which brought forth a white child, because her imagination was upon a white colour; as is seen in Jacob's skill in casting rods of divers colours into the water when his sheep went to ram.

Why doth children sometimes resemble more the grandfathers and great-grandfathers than their parents?

Because the virtue and force of the grandfather is grafted in the heart of the begetter, and it may be said that sometimes it doth proceed of

"Of Infants," *Aristotle's Masterpiece*, pp. 197-198, 1680.

the similitude of the nutriture, and then the child is formed by the similitude of the grandfather.

Why doth children, according to the common course and use of nature, come out of the mother's womb in the ninth month?

Because the child is then fully perfect, or else because some benign place doth reign, as Jupiter, who is a friend of nature; for according to astronomers, he is hot and moist; and therefore doth temper the malice and naughtiness of Saturn, which is cold and dry; and therefore for the most part children born in the ninth month are healthful.

Why do children born in the eighth month for the most part die quickly; and why are they called the children of the moon?

Because the moon is a cold planet, which has dominion over the child, and therefore doth bind it with its coldness, which is the cause of its death.

Why doth a child cry as soon as it is born?

Because of the sudden change from heat to cold, which cold doth hurt its tenderness. Another reason is, because the child's soft and tender body is wringed and put together, coming out of the narrow and straight passage of the matrix, and especially the brain being moist, and the head pressed and wrinkled together, is the cause that some humours do distil by the eyes which are the cause of tears and weeping. The divines say, it is for the transgression of our first fathers and original sin.

READING 9

Mary Wollstonecraft, *A Vindication of the Rights of Women* (1792). Introduction.

Mary Wollstonecraft (1759–1797) was an English writer and philosopher. She penned this defense of women's rights to education during the French Revolution when ideas of equality were being actively debated throughout Europe.

A Vindication of the Rights of Woman

Mary Wollstonecraft

INTRODUCTION.

TO
M. Talleyrand Perigord,
Late Bishop of Autun.

Sir:—
Having read with great pleasure a pamphlet, which you have lately published, on National Education, I dedicate this volume to you, the first dedication that I have ever written, to induce you to read it with attention; and, because I think that you will understand me, which I do not suppose many pert witlings will, who may ridicule the arguments they are unable to answer. But, sir, I carry my respect for your understanding still farther: so far, that I am confident you will not throw my work aside, and hastily conclude that I am in the wrong because you did not view the subject in the same light yourself. And pardon my frankness, but I must observe, that you treated it in too cursory a manner, contented to consider it as it had been considered formerly, when the rights of man, not to advert to woman, were trampled on as chimerical. I call upon you, therefore, now to weigh what I have advanced respecting the rights of woman, and national education; and I call with the firm tone of humanity. For my arguments, sir, are dictated by a disinterested spirit: I plead for my sex, not for myself. Independence I have long considered as the grand blessing of life, the basis of every virtue; and independence I will ever secure by contracting my wants, though I were to live on a barren heath.

It is, then, an affection for the whole human race that makes my pen dart rapidly along to support what I believe to be the cause of virtue: and the same motive leads me earnestly to wish to see woman placed

Mary Wolstoncraft, "Introduction," *A Vindication of the Rights of Women*, pp. 12-21, 1792.

in a station in which she would advance, instead of retarding, the progress of those glorious principles that give a substance to morality. My opinion, indeed, respecting the rights and duties of woman, seems to flow so naturally from these simple principles, that I think it scarcely possible, but that some of the enlarged minds who formed your admirable constitution, will coincide with me.

In France, there is undoubtedly a more general diffusion of knowledge than in any part of the European world, and I attribute it, in a great measure, to the social intercourse which has long subsisted between the sexes. It is true, I utter my sentiments with freedom, that in France the very essence of sensuality has been extracted to regale the voluptuary, and a kind of sentimental lust has prevailed, which, together with the system of duplicity that the whole tenor of their political and civil government taught, have given a sinister sort of sagacity to the French character, properly termed finesse; and a polish of manners that injures the substance, by hunting sincerity out of society. And, modesty, the fairest garb of virtue has been more grossly insulted in France than even in England, till their women have treated as PRUDISH that attention to decency which brutes instinctively observe.

Manners and morals are so nearly allied, that they have often been confounded; but, though the former should only be the natural reflection of the latter, yet, when various causes have produced factitious and corrupt manners, which are very early caught, morality becomes an empty name. The personal reserve, and sacred respect for cleanliness and delicacy in domestic life, which French women almost despise, are the graceful pillars of modesty; but, far from despising them, if the pure flame of patriotism have reached their bosoms, they should labour to improve the morals of their fellow-citizens, by teaching men, not only to respect modesty in women, but to acquire it themselves, as the only way to merit their esteem.

Contending for the rights of women, my main argument is built on this simple principle, that if she be not prepared by education to become the companion of man, she will stop the progress of knowledge, for truth must be common to all, or it will be inefficacious with respect to its influence on general practice. And how can woman be expected to co-operate, unless she know why she ought to be virtuous? Unless freedom strengthen her reason till she comprehend her duty, and see in what manner it is connected with her real good? If children are to be educated to understand the true principle of patriotism, their mother must be a patriot; and the love of mankind, from which an orderly train of virtues spring, can only be produced by considering the moral and civil interest of mankind; but the education and situation of woman, at present, shuts her out from such investigations.

In this work I have produced many arguments, which to me were conclusive, to prove, that the prevailing notion respecting a sexual character was subversive of morality, and I have contended, that to render the human body and mind more perfect, chastity must more universally prevail, and that chastity will never be respected in the male world till the person of a woman is not, as it were, idolized when little virtue or sense embellish it with the grand traces of mental beauty, or the interesting simplicity of affection.

Consider, Sir, dispassionately, these observations, for a glimpse of this truth seemed to open before you when you observed, "that to see one half of the human race excluded by the other from all participation of government, was a political phenomenon that, according to abstract principles, it was impossible to explain." If so, on what does your constitution rest? If the abstract rights of man will bear discussion and explanation, those of woman, by a parity of reasoning, will not shrink from the same test: though a different opinion prevails in this country, built on the very arguments which you use to justify the oppression of woman, prescription.

Consider, I address you as a legislator, whether, when men contend for their freedom, and to be allowed to judge for themselves, respecting their own happiness, it be not inconsistent and unjust to subjugate women, even though you firmly believe that you are acting in the manner best calculated to promote their happiness? Who made man the exclusive judge, if woman partake with him the gift of reason?

In this style, argue tyrants of every denomination from the weak king to the weak father of a family; they are all eager to crush reason; yet always assert that they usurp its throne only to be useful. Do you not act a similar part, when you FORCE all women, by denying them civil and political rights, to remain immured in their families groping in the dark? For surely, sir, you will not assert, that a duty can be binding which is not founded on reason? If, indeed, this be their destination, arguments may be drawn from reason; and thus augustly supported, the more understanding women acquire, the more they will be attached to their duty, comprehending it, for unless they comprehend it, unless their morals be fixed on the same immutable principles as those of man, no authority can make them discharge it in a virtuous manner. They may be convenient slaves, but slavery will have its constant effect, degrading the master and the abject dependent.

But, if women are to be excluded, without having a voice, from a participation of the natural rights of mankind, prove first, to ward off the charge of injustice and inconsistency, that they want reason, else this flaw in your NEW CONSTITUTION, the first constitution founded on reason, will ever show that man must, in some shape, act like a tyrant, and tyranny, in whatever part of society it rears its brazen front, will ever undermine morality.

I have repeatedly asserted, and produced what appeared to me irrefragable arguments drawn from matters of fact, to prove my assertion, that women cannot, by force, be confined to domestic concerns; for they will however ignorant, intermeddle with more weighty affairs, neglecting private duties only to disturb, by cunning tricks, the orderly plans of reason which rise above their comprehension.

Besides, whilst they are only made to acquire personal accomplishments, men will seek for pleasure in variety, and faithless husbands will make faithless wives; such ignorant beings, indeed, will be very excusable when, not taught to respect public good, nor allowed any civil right, they attempt to do themselves justice by retaliation.

The box of mischief thus opened in society, what is to preserve private virtue, the only security of public freedom and universal happiness?

Let there be then no coercion ESTABLISHED in society, and the common law of gravity prevailing, the sexes will fall into their proper places. And, now that more equitable laws are forming your citizens, marriage may become more sacred; your young men may choose wives from motives of affection, and your maidens allow love to root out vanity.

The father of a family will not then weaken his constitution and debase his senti-ments, by visiting the harlot, nor forget, in obeying the call of appetite, the purpose for which it was implanted; and the mother will not neglect her children to practise the arts of coquetry, when sense and modesty secure her the friendship of her husband.

But, till men become attentive to the duty of a father, it is vain to expect women to spend that time in their nursery which they, "wise in their generation," choose to spend at their glass; for this exertion of cunning is only an instinct of nature to enable them to obtain indirectly a little of that power of which they are unjustly denied a share; for, if women are not permitted to enjoy legitimate rights, they will render both men and themselves vicious, to obtain illicit privileges.

I wish, sir, to set some investigations of this kind afloat in France; and should they lead to a confirmation of my principles, when your constitution is revised, the rights of woman may be respected, if it be fully proved that reason calls for this respect, and loudly demands JUSTICE for one half of the human race.

I am, sir,
Yours respectfully,
M. W.

INTRODUCTION

After considering the historic page, and viewing the living world with anxious solicitude, the most melancholy emotions of sorrowful indignation have depressed my spirits, and I have sighed when obliged to confess, that either nature has made a great difference between man and man, or that the civilization, which has hitherto taken place in the world, has been very partial. I have turned over various books written on the subject of education, and patiently observed the conduct of parents and the management of schools; but what has been the result? a profound conviction, that the neglected education of my fellow creatures is the grand source of the misery I deplore; and that women in particular, are rendered weak and wretched by a variety of concurring causes, originating from one hasty conclusion. The conduct and manners of women, in fact, evidently prove, that their minds are not in a healthy state; for, like the flowers that are planted in too rich a soil, strength and usefulness are sacrificed to beauty; and the flaunting leaves, after having pleased a fastidious eye, fade, disregarded on the stalk, long before the season when they ought to have arrived at maturity. One cause of this barren blooming I attribute to a false system of education, gathered from the books written on this subject by men, who, considering females rather as women than human creatures, have been more anxious to make them alluring mistresses than rational wives; and the understanding of the sex has been so bubbled by this specious homage, that the civilized women of the present century, with a few exceptions, are only anxious to inspire love, when they ought to cherish a nobler ambition, and by their abilities and virtues exact respect.

In a treatise, therefore, on female rights and manners, the works which have been particularly written for their improvement must not be overlooked; especially when it is asserted, in direct terms, that the minds of women are enfeebled by false refinement; that the books of instruction, written by men of genius, have had the same tendency as more frivolous productions; and that, in the true style of Mahometanism, they are only considered as females, and not as a part of the human species, when improvable reason is allowed to be the dignified distinction, which raises men above the brute creation, and puts a natural sceptre in a feeble hand.

Yet, because I am a woman, I would not lead my readers to suppose, that I mean violently to agitate the contested question respecting the equality and inferiority of the sex; but as the subject lies in my way, and I cannot pass it over without subjecting the main tendency of my reasoning to misconstruction, I shall stop a moment to deliver, in a few words, my opinion. In the government of the physical world, it is observable that the female, in general, is inferior to the male. The male pursues, the female yields—this is the law of nature; and it does not appear to be suspended or abrogated in favour of woman. This physical superiority cannot be denied--and it is a noble prerogative! But not content with this natural pre-eminence, men endeavour to sink us still lower, merely to render us alluring objects for a moment; and women, intoxicated by the adoration which men, under the influence of their senses, pay them, do not seek to obtain a durable interest in their hearts, or to become the friends of the fellow creatures who find amusement in their society.

I am aware of an obvious inference: from every quarter have I heard exclamations against masculine women; but where are they to be found? If, by this appellation, men mean to inveigh against their ardour in hunting, shooting, and gaming, I shall most cordially join in the cry; but if it be, against the imitation of manly virtues, or, more properly speaking, the attainment of those talents and virtues, the exercise of which ennobles the human character, and which raise females in the scale of animal being, when they are comprehensively termed mankind—all those who view them with a philosophical eye must, I should think, wish with me, that they may every day grow more and more masculine.

This discussion naturally divides the subject. I shall first consider women in the grand light of human creatures, who, in common with men, are placed on this earth to unfold their faculties; and afterwards I shall more particularly point out their peculiar designation.

I wish also to steer clear of an error, which many respectable writers have fallen into; for the instruction which has hitherto been addressed to women, has rather been applicable to LADIES, if the little indirect advice, that is scattered through Sandford and Merton, be excepted; but, addressing my sex in a firmer tone, I pay particular attention to those in the middle class, because they appear to be in the most natural state. Perhaps the seeds of false refinement, immorality, and vanity have ever been shed by the great. Weak, artificial beings raised above the common wants and affections of their race, in a premature unnatural manner, undermine the very foundation of virtue, and spread corruption through the whole mass of society! As a class of mankind they have the strongest claim to pity! the education of the rich tends to render them vain and helpless, and the unfolding mind is not strengthened by the practice of those duties which dignify the human character. They only live to amuse themselves, and by the same law which in nature invariably produces certain effects, they soon only afford barren amusement.

But as I purpose taking a separate view of the different ranks of society, and of the moral character of women, in each, this hint is, for the present, sufficient; and I have only alluded to the subject, because it appears to me to be the very essence of an introduction to give a cursory account of the contents of the work it introduces.

My own sex, I hope, will excuse me, if I treat them like rational creatures, instead of flattering their FASCINATING graces, and viewing them as if they were in a state of perpetual childhood, unable to stand alone. I earnestly wish to point out in what true dignity and human happiness consists--I wish to persuade women to endeavour to acquire strength, both of mind and body, and to convince them, that the soft phrases, susceptibility of heart, delicacy of sentiment, and refinement of taste, are almost synonymous with epithets of weakness, and that those beings who are only the objects of pity and that kind of love, which has been termed its sister, will soon become objects of contempt.

Dismissing then those pretty feminine phrases, which the men condescendingly use to soften our slavish dependence, and despising that weak elegancy of mind, exquisite sensibility, and sweet docility of manners, supposed to be the sexual characteristics of the weaker vessel, I wish to show that elegance is inferior to virtue, that the first object of laudable ambition is to obtain a character as a human being, regardless of the distinction of sex; and that secondary views should be brought to this simple touchstone.

This is a rough sketch of my plan; and should I express my conviction with the energetic emotions that I feel whenever I think of the subject, the dictates of experience and reflection will be felt by some of my readers. Animated by this important object, I shall disdain to cull my phrases or polish my style--I aim at being useful, and sincerity will render me unaffected; for wishing rather to persuade by the force of my arguments, than dazzle by the elegance of my language, I shall not waste my time in rounding periods, nor in fabricating the turgid bombast of artificial feelings, which, coming from the head, never reach the heart. I shall be employed about things, not words! and, anxious to render my sex more respectable members of society, I shall try to avoid that flowery diction which has slided from essays into novels, and from novels into familiar letters and conversation.

These pretty nothings, these caricatures of the real beauty of sensibility, dropping glibly from the tongue, vitiate the taste, and create a kind of sickly delicacy that turns away from simple unadorned truth; and a deluge of false sentiments and over-stretched feelings, stifling the natural emotions of the heart, render the domestic pleasures insipid, that ought to sweeten the exercise of those severe duties, which educate a rational and immortal being for a nobler field of action.

The education of women has, of late, been more attended to than formerly; yet they are still reckoned a frivolous sex, and ridiculed or pitied by the writers who endeavour by satire or instruction to improve them. It is acknowledged that they spend many of the first years of their lives in acquiring a smattering of accomplishments: meanwhile, strength of body and mind are sacrificed to libertine notions of beauty, to the desire of establishing themselves, the only way women can rise in the world--by marriage. And this desire making mere animals of them, when they marry, they act as such children may be expected to act: they dress; they paint, and nickname God's creatures. Surely these weak beings are only fit for the seraglio! Can they govern a family, or take care of the poor babes whom they bring into the world?

If then it can be fairly deduced from the present conduct of the sex, from the prevalent fondness for pleasure, which takes place of ambition and those nobler passions that open and enlarge the soul; that the instruction which women have received has only tended, with the constitution of civil society, to render them insignificant objects of desire; mere propagators of fools! if it can be proved, that in aiming to accomplish them, without cultivating their understandings, they are taken out of their sphere of duties, and made ridiculous and useless when the short lived bloom of beauty is over[*1], I presume that RATIONAL men will excuse me for endeavouring to persuade them to become more masculine and respectable.

Indeed the word masculine is only a bugbear: there is little reason to fear that women will acquire too much courage or fortitude; for their apparent inferiority with respect to bodily strength, must render them, in some degree, dependent on men in the various relations of life; but why should it be increased by prejudices that give a sex to virtue, and confound simple truths with sensual reveries?

Women are, in fact, so much degraded by mistaken notions of female excellence, that I do not mean to add a paradox when I assert, that this artificial weakness produces a propensity to tyrannize, and gives birth to cunning, the natural opponent of strength, which leads them to play off those contemptible infantile airs that undermine esteem even whilst they excite desire. Do not foster these prejudices, and they will naturally fall into their subordinate, yet respectable station in life.

It seems scarcely necessary to say, that I now speak of the sex in general. Many individuals have more sense than their male relatives; and, as nothing preponderates where there is a constant struggle for an equilibrium, without it has naturally more gravity, some women govern their husbands without degrading themselves, because intellect will always govern.

---

1   A lively writer, I cannot recollect his name, asks what business women turned of forty have to do in the world.

READING 10

John Barclay, *A Series of Engravings Representing the Bones of the Human Skeleton* (1819), 140–144.

John Barclay (1758–1826) was a Scottish anatomist. He copied drawings of human skeletons to highlight differences between the sexes, and juxtaposed human skeletons with animal skeletons to emphasize distinctive sex differences.

A Series of Engravings Representing the Bones of the Human Skeleton

John Barclay

PLATE I—FROM ALBINUS

THE HORSE, FROM STUBBS

THE HEAD

A Frontal Bone
B Parietal Bone
C Temporal process of the Sphenoidal Bone
D Squamous portion of the Temporal Bone
E Mastoid process of the Temporal Bone
F Malar, or Cheek Bone
G Nasal Bones
H Superior Maxillary Bone
I Nasal process of the Maxillary Bone
K Inferior Maxillary Bone

NECK AND TRUNK

L Cervical Vertebrae, 7
M Dorsal Vertebrae, 12, connected with the Ribs
N Lumbar Vertebra?, 5
O Sacral Vertebrae, 5
   Coccygeal Vertebrae concealed
P First Bone of the Stermnn, articulated with the two Clavicles, with the first pair of Ribs, and with one half of the second pair
Q Second Bone of the Sternum, articulated with the remaining half of the second half of Ribs, with one half of the seventh pair, and with all the intermediate pairs
R Third Bone of the Sternum, articulated with one half of the seventh pair of Ribs
S The twelve Ribs on each side

John Barclay, *A Series of Engravings Representing the Bones of the Human Skeleton*, pp. 15-18, 21-24, 139-143, 1819.

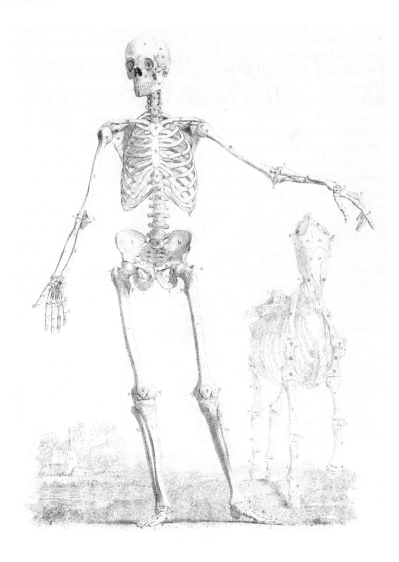

T The Cartilages of the first seven or true Ribs, articulated with the Sternum; the
   Cartilages of the five succeeding or false Ribs not extending so far

ATLANTAL EXTREMITIES
U The Clavicle
V The Scapula
X The Humerus
Y Proximal Extremity of the Humerus
Z Distal Extremity of the Humerus
a Radial Condyle of the Humerus
b Ulnar Condyle of the Humerus
c The Radius
d The Ulna

e The Carpus, 8 Bones

f The Metacarpus, 5 Bones

g The Digital Phalanxes, three in each Finger, and two in the thumb

SACRAL EXTREMITIES

h The Ilium

i The Ischium } the three forming the Os Innominatum

k The Pubis

l A part of the Ischiadic notch

m Foramen Obturatorium

n The Femur

o Its large Trochanter

p Its small Trochanter

q Its tibial Condyle

r Its fibnlar Condyle

s The Rotula, or Patella

t The Tibia

u The Fibula

v The Tarsus, 7 Bones

x The Metatarsus, 5 Bones

z The Digital Phalanxes, three in the small Toes, and two in the great Toe

PLATE II–FROM ALBINUS

THE HORSE, FROM STUBBS

THE HEAD.

A Frontal Bone

B Parietal Bone

C Mastoid process of the Temporal Bone

D Malar Bone

E Occipital Bone

F Inferior Maxillary Bone

NECK AND TRUNK

G Cervical Vertebras

H Dorsal Vertebrae

l Lumbar Vertebra;

K Sacral Vertebra?

L Coccygeal Vertebra*

M The Ribs

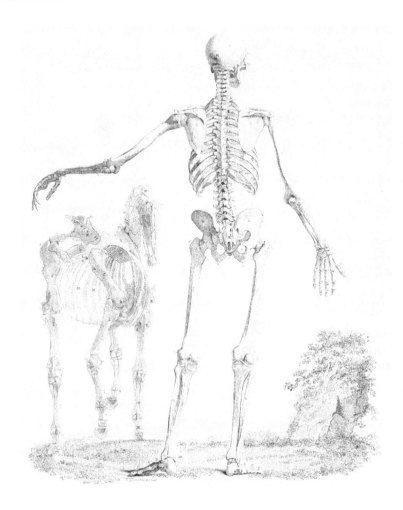

ATLANTAL EXTREMITIES

N Clavicle

O Scapula

P Its Spiuc

Q Its Acromion Process

R Humerus

S Radius

T Ulna

U Carpus

V Metacarpus

X Digital Phalanxes

SACRAL EXTREMITIES

a Ilium

b Ischium } forming the os Inominalum

c Pubis

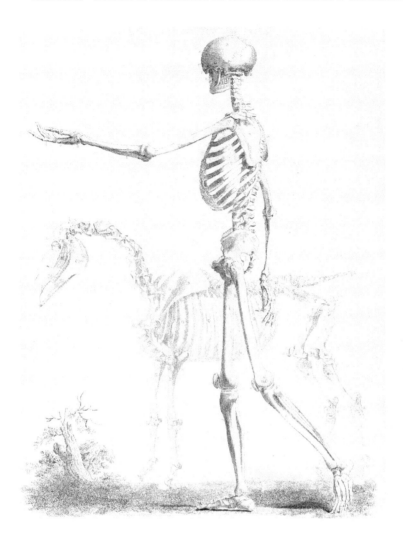

d Ischiadic Notch
e Foramen Obturatorium
f Femur
g Its large Trochanter
h Its small Trochanter
ɪ Its tibial Condyle
k Its fibular Condyle
l Tibia
m Malleolus Internus
n Fibula
o Malleolus Externus
p Tarsus
q Metatarsus
r Digital Phalanxes

PLATE III—FROM ALBINUS

THE HORSE, FROM STUBBS
THE HEAD.

A Frontal Bone

B Parietal Bone

C Temporal process of the Sphenoidal Bone

D Squamous portion of the Temporal Bone

E Mastoid process of the Temporal Bone

F Malar, or Cheek Bone

G Occipital Bone

H Superior Maxillary Bone

I Inferior Maxillary Bone

K Ramus of the Inferior Maxillary

NECK AND TRUNK

L Cervical Vertebra;

M Dorsal Vertebra*

N Lumbar Vertebra;

O Sacral Vertebra;

P Coccygeal Vertebra

Q Ribs

ATLANTAL EXTREMITIES

R Scapula

S Spine of the Scapula

T Acromion Process

U Humerus

V Proximal Extremity

X Distal Extremity

Y Radial Condyle

Z The Radius

a Tlie Ulna

b The Carpus

c The Metacarpus

d The Digital Phalanxes

SACRAL EXTREMITIES

e The Ilium

f The Ischium

g The Pubis
h Ischiadic Notch
I The Femur
k Proximal Extremity
l Tibial Condyle
m Fibular Condyle
n Rotula, or Patella
o Tibia
p Fibula
q Malleolus Interims
r Malleolus Externus
s Tarsus
t Metatarsus
u Digital Phalanxes

PLATE IV—THE FEMALE SKELETON, FROM SUE

THE OSTRICH, FROM CHESELDEN
THE HEAD.
A The Frontal Bone
B Parietal Bone
C Temporal process of the Sphenoidal Bone
D Squamous portion of the Temporal Bone
E Mastoid process of the Temporal Bone
F Malar, or Cheek Bone
G Superior Maxillary Bone
H Nasal process of the Superior Maxillary Bone
I Nasal Bones
K Inferior Maxillary Bone
L Ramus of the Inferior Maxillary Bone

NECK AND TRUNK.
M Cervical Vertebra
N Dorsal Vertebra?
O Lumbar Vertebrae
P Sacral Vertebra:
Q Coccygeal Vertebra'
R Ribs
S Sternum

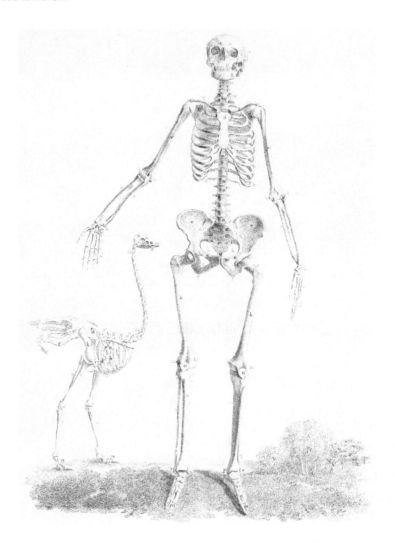

ATLANTAL EXTREMITIES

T Clavicle
U Scapula
V Humerus
X Its Radial Condyle
Y Its Ulnar Condyle
Z Radius
a Ulna
b Carpus
c Metacarpus
d Digital Phalanxes

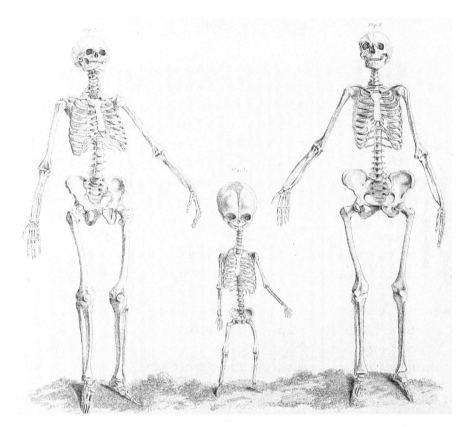

SACRAL EXTREMITIES

e Ilium

f Ischium

g Pubis

h Ischiadic Notch

1 Foramen Obturatorium

k Fernur

l Tibial Condyle

m Fibular Condyle

n Rotula, or Patella

o Tibia

p Malleolus Internus

q Fibula

r Malleolus Externus

s Tarsus

t Metatarsus

u Digital Phalanxes

PLATE XXXII—FROM SUE

Fig. 1. Is a view of the male skeleton; fig. 2. of the female skeleton; and fig. 3. of the size and form of a fœtal skeleton about the fourth month. The three are accurately copied from Sue, the second being only a repetition of that which has appeared in Plate IV. At my suggestion they have here been engraved on the same Plate, and represented in very nearly similar attitudes for the sake of comparison; these attitudes are also copied from Sue, for as to those which Soemmer-ring has given to his female skeleton, although they be more graceful and elegant, and suggested by men eminent in modelling, sculpture, and painting, they contribute nothing to the comparison which is here intended.[1] Besides, he has only drawn a comparison between the male and the female skeleton, while the third figure is here introduced to shew that many of those characters which he has described as peculiar to the female, are more obviously discernible in the fœtal skeleton. For instance, he observes, that the scull of the female is proportionally larger than that of the male, a character, surely, which is more discernible in the fœtal skeleton than in that of the female. He adds, that the frontal sinuses of the female are proportionally smaller, and that her glabella is less elevated; the observation, 1 believe, is correct, but it should be remembered, that the elevation of the glabella depends on the size of the frontal sinuses, and that it is less elevated in the fœtus, where there are no frontal sinuses, than in the adult or grown up female, where they are small.

Sue has represented the frontal bone of his foetal skeleton as divided into two similar halves. This appearance occasionally occurs in adult males, though not so Î frequently, Monro has remarked, as in adult females; at any rate, it is a regular and uniform appearance in; the fœtal skeleton. The foramina of the scull, continues Soemmerring, are, notwithstanding the size of the bones, proportionally smaller in the female skeleton than they are in the male, as, for instance, the two foramina optica. 1 am somewhat doubtful whether this remark be founded on widely extended observation, or only on a few particular cases; the size of foramina is not only proportioned to the size of the organs, which they have to transmit, but, at the same time, to the range of motion to which these are exposed. The following observations admit of less doubt, that the bones of the face, in the female skeleton, are smaller and smoother, the orifices of the nostrils less expanded, the forms of the jaws more elliptic, and the cavity of the mouth narrower and shorter. Yet if these be true with regard to the female, they are equally true with regard to the fœtus, where all the appearances to which they allude are more obviously striking. The size of the face depends much on the size of the jaws, now the jaws of the fœtus are formed only to hold twenty teeth, while those of a grown or adult female are elongated so as to hold thirty-two. The smoothness of the bones is affected chiefly by the actions of muscles,

---

1   Samuel Thomas soemmening. Tabula, Sceleti Feminine, junta descripciones *Trajecito ad Manum alud varrantrapy et Wenner*, 1787

but impressions by muscles are less perceptible on the bones of the fœtus than in those of the female. The elliptic appearance, in the form of the jaws, arises from the circumstance of their being less elongated backwards, and that elongation is proportionally less in the fœtal skeleton than it is in the female. As for the nostrils being less expanded, and the cavity of the mouth narrower and shorter, these are consequences of the smaller bones of which they are composed, and which also are proportionally smaller in the fœtus than they are in the grown or adult female. The remark, that the intervertebral cartilages are of a greater proportional depth in the female skeleton than they are in the male, may be true of the skeleton which he has depicted, which, he says, was that of a young female. The depth of these, to a certain extent, depends upon age, and upon the degree and continuance of the pressure to which they have; been previously exposed. It is always greatest, cseteris paribus, in early life when the fluids are abundant, and in old age, when these become scanty, it is so much diminished that the spine is bent forward ; it is also diminished in consequence of pressure, and therefore the body, which has been erect during the day, is shorter in the evening than it was in the morning, after lying for several hours in a posture where the pressure was removed. Be the depth, therefore, the effect of growth, or the want of pressure, these causes *f* operate more powerfully in the fœtal skeleton than in the grown or adult female, and the facts will be found to support the conclusion.

That the thorax of the female skeleton, in general, is proportionally less than that of the male, cannot be questioned. The thorax is expanded by habitually frequent and vigorous inspirations, and these occasioned by habitually frequent and vigorous exertions, to which the female is not in general so much accustomed, and the fœtus still less in proportion, having no occasion for any respiration while it lies *in utero*, and but little occasion for vigorous respiration for several months even after birth. The thorax, therefore, of the fœtal skeleton is not only proportionally smaller than that of the female, but is sometimes scarcely the size of the bead. Soemmerring adds, tliat the sternum of the female is proportionally shorter than that of the male; that her ribs lie in planes of inclination, which are somewhat different; that they form more acute angles with their sternal cartilages; that the shoulders slope more; and that there is a greater proportional distance between her last ribs and the crest of the Ilium. But all these appearances naturally result from thè smallness of the thorax, and from the unfrequency of full inspirations ; they are therefore more observable in the fœtal skeleton than in that of the female. As to his remark, that the cartilaginous parts of the ribs, compared with the ossified, are proportionally more extensive in the female than they are in the male; it may be observed, that, considering proportions, the same parts are still more extensive in the fœtal skeleton, where the ossification is only in its progress.

If the clavicles of the female be less curved, and her atlantal extremities proportionally smaller than those of the male, it should be recollected that the curves of the clavicles are somewhat increased by the more vigorous actions of the muscles, and, consequently, are proportionally less in the fœtus than they are in the female; that the smallness of her atlantal extremities keeps them more in proportion to the size of the thorax, and, besides that, their size must depend, in some measure, upon the nature of the employment to which they are habituated. It is well known that not only the strength, but the bulk of a hand, accustomed to frequent and hard labour, are considerably different from what they would have been, had the owner led an easy sedentary life.

That the feet of the female are proportionally smaller than those of the male, is an observation that, with few exceptions, is confirmed by experience. Yet this is not a character peculiar to the female, as not only the feet, but even the whole sacral extremities are proportionally smaller in the fœtal skeleton than they are in the female. During the time that the fœtus is *in utero,* the head, from its greater specific gravity, is the part most dependent in the liquor amnii; hence the impulse of the heart, which sends the blood to it, and the two atlantal extremities is partly increased by the force of gravitation. On the contrary, after birth, when the body is erect, the same force operates against the impulse to the head, co-operating with that which sends the blood to the sacral extremities. The effects of such a gravitating force are frequently perceived in the cedematous swellings of the legs, counteracting the return of the venous blood and lymphatic fluids during the day, when the legs are perpendicular, or nearly perpendicular to the horizon, but permitting their return, during the night, on assuming the horizontal position, so that the swellings are generally found diminished towards morning, and increased towards evening. Nay, it is not improbable, that this gravitating force, by acting in favour of the sacral extremities, in consequence of the change which takes place at birth, may be partly the cause why these grow in length and in thickness proportionally faster than the two atlantal, and ultimately arrive at a larger size.

In his Appendix to his Treatise on the Bones, Monro has mentioned several characters of the female skeleton, which he supposes to result as much from a difference of habits, as a difference of sex; but, be the cause, or causes, what they may, that produce these changes, it certainly appears, that the female skeleton, in all the parts hitherto compared, does, in form and structure, deviate less than that of the male from those characters which were originally common to both. It is in the pelvis, and pelvis alone, that we perceive the strongly-marked and peculiar characters of the female skeleton. It is there that we cease to trace the analogies between its proportions and those of the fœtus; or, in other words, it is there that, in deviating from those characters which at one time were common to both, we regularly find it deviating farther than that of male—the pelvis of the fœtus being always proportionally the smallest of the three, and that of the female proportionally the largest. In attempting to account for these marked distinctions, the anatomist seldom pursues his inquiries into the nature of the primary cause, which plans the structure, and directs the processes of its organization. Confining his researches to objects of sense, he is generally satisfied with describing phenomena in the order of succession in which they appear, and supposes his explanation complete when he ascertains the visible means employed by the primary and invisible cause. In tracing these means, he observes the dependant posture of the head in the liquor amnii; sees the blood ascending in the arteries towards the pelvis, in opposition to the force of gravitation, and the same accelerated by the same force, as it descends inits return through the veins and lymphatics; he sees likewise the greatest portion of that blood which, after birth, flows towards the pelvis, diverted at this period into the two umbilical arteries, and the viscera of the abdomen pressing atlantad towards the diaphragm, instead of sacrad, toward the pelvis. From these appearances he is led irresistibly to the conclusion—that the cavity of the pelvis, in these circumstances, cannot have the same means of expansion that it has afterwards, when the umbilical arteries are closed, and when, in consequence of this change of structure, and the change of position, the blood is impelled to it with greater force and in greater quantity, and, at the same time, the abdominal viscera made to descend with a pressure from above, and a pressure outwards in every direction. At birth, therefore, the pelvis of the foetus must always be proportionally small, though at this period, and for some time after, very little difference is to be observed between male and female in this part of their osseous structure. This difference becomes only striking when they are approaching to the age of puberty. It is then that the female begins to exhibit a new phenomenon peculiar to her sex. It is then that in her, the blood begins to flow in a greater proportional quantity towards the pelvis than in the male; nay, in such a quantity as to exceed the demands of nourishment, and to require that the superabundance be regularly evacuated by a monthly discharge, a superabundance which, during her pregnancy, is reserved as necessary for the nourishment of her offspring. By this determination of her circulating fluids, the Os sacrum becomes broader and less bent, forwards; her Ossa Ilia are expanded outwards; the angle under the symphysis pubis is enlarged; and the distance between the tuberosities of the Ischia considerably increased, while the Os coccyx and sacral extremities, from this diversion of blood to the pelvis, increase not so fast, nor arrive at the same proportional size as in the skeleton of the male adult.

After these remarks on the forms and structures of the human skeleton, which relate to the differences of age and sex, I have only to add, that certain forms of the face and head, different from any that are known to occur in the male, the female, or the fœtal skeleton, are, as Camper has shewn, regularly observed in those seulptured figures which the ancients formed to represent their imaginary deities. In the singular design of these uncommon artificial forms, it evidently appears, that the artists had something more in their view than the mere difference of what Camper has denominated the facial angle. The part called the Face has many resemblances to that of the fœtus, and therefore is found proportionally small compared with the part which is named the Cranium. The two jaws seem also to be formed like those of the fœtus, as if destined to hold only twenty teeth instead of thirty-two, but at the same time with such a depth and quantity of bone as are only to be found in the full vigour and meridian of life; the forehead, too, as well as the jaws, presents a combination equally uncommon; a fœtal form of the frontal bone, with two sinuses and a glabella proportionally elevated ; a combination that leads to a feature which, to the eye of the anatomist, is strikingly peculiar; a nose raised from the small receding bones of the face to the same elevation as the glabella; a nose of such size, prominence, and strength, as irresistibly to suggest an idea very different from what we are apt to form in looking at the small, the slightly prominent, and the feeble nose continued from the flat glabella of the fœtus. By methods such as these, the effects certainly of much previous observation and reflection, the ancient sculptors, by artificial, yet harmonious combinations of those characters which indicate youth, with those which express the vigour of manhood, and the dignity of age, and by carefully excluding whatever implied debility in the one, or decay in the other, have produced forms which, though not natural, are admirably calculated to dazzle the eye, to captivate the fancy, and engage the feelings, before the judgment, which is tardy in its processes, has time to operate. Besides, these forms were not intended to be those merely of ordinary men; for, though meant to be human, they were also meant to be something more—the representations of heroes or of gods, of whom men were supposed to be resemblances; though resemblances as unlike as an ape is to a man.

READING 11

Women's Petition to the National Assembly (1789).

Written sometime after the 1789 women's march on Versailles during the French Revolution, this petition appealed to the National Assembly to address a range of inequalities.

Women's Petition to the National Assembly

Translated by Karen Offen

NOSSEIGNEURS,

It is altogether astonishing that, having gone so far along the path of reforms, and having cut down (as the illustrious d'Alembert once put it), a very large part of the forest of prejudices, you would leave standing the oldest and most general of all abuses, the one which excludes the most beautiful and most lovable half of the inhabitants of this vast kingdom from positions, dignities, honors, and especially from the right to sit amongst you.

What! you have generously decreed equality of rights for all individuals; you have made the humble inhabitant of the hovel march alongside the princes and lords of the earth. Thanks to your paternal solicitude the poor villager is no longer obliged to grovel before the proud seigneur of his parish; the unfortunate vassal can halt in his tracks the impetuous boar that piteously ravaged his crops; the timid soldier dares to complain when he is run down by the splendid coach of the superb publican; the modest priest can sit down in ease at the table of his most illustrious and most reverend superior; . . . the black African will no longer find himself compared to a stupid animal which, goaded by the prod of a fierce driver, irrigates our furrows with his sweat and blood. Talent, disengaged from the sorrowful confines of ignoble birth, can be developed with confidence, and he who possesses it will no longer bit forced to bow and scrape to get the support of an imbecile protector, to burn incense to an ignorant Creseus and to "monseigneur" a goat. At last, thanks to your good influence, a serene day will break above our heads, a new people, a people of citizens, wise and happy, will raise itself on the ruins of a barbarous people, and the stupified earth will witness the birth upon its very bosom of this golden age, this time of good fortune that until now only existed in the fabulous descriptions of the poets.

Ah! our masters! will we then be the only ones for whom the iron age will forever exist . . . ? Will we be the only ones who will not participate in this astonishing regeneration that will renew the face of France and revive its youthfulness like that of the eagle?

You have broken the scepter of despotism, you have pronounced the beautiful axiom [that] . . . the French are a free people. Yet still you allow thirteen million slaves shamefully to wear the irons of thirteen million despots! You have devined the true equality of rights—and you still unjustly withhold them from the sweetest and most interesting half among you! . . .

Finally, you have decreed that the path to dignities and honors should be open without prejudice to all talents; yet you continue to throw up insurmountable barriers to our own! Can you think, then, that nature, this mother who is so generous to all her children, has been stingy to us, and that she only grants her graces and favors to our pitiless tyrants? Open the great book of the past and see what illustrious women have done in all ages, the honor of their provinces, the glory of our sex, and judge what we would be capable of, if your blind presumption, your masculine aristocracy, did not incessantly chain down our courage, our wisdom, and our talents. [Here follows six pages on women's contributions: Ed.]

Ah! our masters; do not henceforth leave in ignominious darkness these qualities, which are so glorious for us and of such great interest to the nation. Dare this very day to alter in our favor the old injustices of your sex; give us the possibility to work like you and with you for the glory and happiness of the French people, and if, as we hope, you consent to share your empire with us, we will no longer owe this precious advantage to our attractiveness; and your own susceptibility to it, but solely to your justice, to our talents, and to the sacredness of your laws.

Wherefore, we depose the following proposal for a decree that we believe has bearing on the subject:

PROPOSAL FOR A DECREE

The National Assembly, wishing to reform the greatest and most universal of abuses, and to repair the wrongs of a six-thousand-year long injustice, has decreed and decrees as follows:

1. All the privileges of the male sex are entirely and irrevocably abolished throughout France;
2. The feminine sex will always enjoy the same liberty, advantages, rights, and honors as does the masculine sex;
3. The masculine gender (genre) will no longer be regarded, even grammatically, as the more noble genre, given that all genders, all sexes, and all beings should be and are equally noble;

4. That no one will henceforth insert in acts, contracts, obligations, etc., this clause, so common but so insulting for women: That the wife is authorized by her husband before those present, because in the household both parties should enjoy the same power and authority;

5. That wearing breeches will no longer be the exclusive prerogative of the male sex, but each sex will have the right to wear them in turn;

6. When a soldier has, out of cowardice, compromised French honor, he will no longer be degraded as is the present custom, by making him wear women's clothing; but as the two sexes are and must be equally honorable in the eyes of humanity, he will henceforth be punished by declaring his gender to be neuter.

7. All persons of the feminine sex must be admitted without exception to the district and departmental assemblies, elevated to municipal responsibilities and even as deputies to the National Assembly, when they fulfill the requirements set forth in the electoral laws. They will have both consultative and deliberative voices . . . ;

8. They can also be appointed as Magistrates. There is no better way to reconcile the public with the courts of justice than to seat beauty and to see the graces presiding there;

9. The same applies to all positions, compensations, and military dignities. In this way the French will be truly invincible, when their courage is inspired by the joint themes of glory and love; we do not even make exception for the staff of a marshal of France; so that justice can be rendered equally, we order this instrument to be passed alternatively between men and women;

10. Nor do we hesitate to open the sanctuary to the feminine sex, which has so long rightly been referred to as the devoted sex. But since the piety of the faithful has noticeably diminished, said sex promises and obligates itself, when it mounts the chair of truth, to moderate its zeal and not make excessive demands on the attention of the audience.

PART IV

VICTORIAN NORMS

The Victorian period encompassed the latter half of the nineteenth century and marks the peak of the British Empire. In this section, Victorian efforts to regulate sex, gender, and sexuality are represented in Richard Burton's translation of the *Kama Sutra* from India, William Stead's attacks on prostitution as a social ill, and Richard Krafft-Ebbing's medical handbook on "deviant" sexuality. Michel Foucault's introduction to *The History of Sexuality* roots twentieth-century attitudes toward sexuality in the norms of the Victorian era.

READING 12

"About the Kinds of Women Resorted to by the Citizens, and of Friends, and Messengers," *The Kama Sutra of Vātsyāyana* (1884). Translated by Richard F. Burton.

Vātsyāyana was a second-century BCE philosopher from what is now India. He wrote the Kama Sutra as a book of practical advice on sex and marriage. In this excerpt, he describes the kinds of relationships with different women that were deemed acceptable.

About the Kinds of Women Resorted to by the Citizens, and of Friends and Messengers

Translated by Richard F. Burton

When Kama is practised by men of the four castes according to the rules of the Holy Writ (i.e. by lawful marriage) with virgins of their own caste, it then becomes a means of acquiring lawful progeny and good fame, and it is not also opposed to the customs of the world. On the contrary the practice of Kama with women of the higher castes, and with those previously enjoyed by others, even though they be of the same caste, is prohibited. But the practice of Kama with women of the lower castes, with women excommunicated from their own caste, with public women, and with women twice married,[1] is neither enjoined nor prohibited. The object of practising Kama with such women is pleasure only.

Nayikas,[2] therefore, are of three kinds, viz. maids, women twice married, and public women. Gonikaputra has expressed an opinion that there is a fourth kind of Nayika, viz. a woman who is resorted to on some special occasion even though she be previously married to another. These special occasions are when a man thinks thus:

This woman is self-willed, and has been previously enjoyed by many others besides myself. I may, therefore, safely resort to her as to a public woman though she belongs to a higher caste than mine, and, in so doing, I shall not be violating the ordinances of Dharma.

---

1   This term does not apply to a widow, but to a woman who has probably left her husband, and is living with some other person as a married woman, maritalement, as they say in France.

2   Any woman fit to be enjoyed without sin. The object of the enjoyment of women is twofold, viz. pleasure and progeny. Any woman who can be enjoyed without sin for the purpose of accomplishing either the one or the other of these two objects is a Nayika. The fourth kind of Nayika which Vatsya admits further on is neither enjoyed for pleasure or for progeny, but merely for accomplishing some special purpose in hand. The word Nayika is retained as a technical term throughout.

"About the Kinds of Women Resorted to by the Citizens, and of Friends, and

Messengers," *The Kama Sutra of Vatsyayana*, trans. Richard F. Burton, 1883..

117

Or thus:

This is a twice-married woman and has been enjoyed by others before me; there is, therefore, no objection to my resorting to her.

Or thus:

This woman has gained the heart of her great and powerful husband, and exercises a mastery over him, who is a friend of my enemy; if, therefore, she becomes united with me she will cause her husband to abandon my enemy.

Or thus:

This woman will turn the mind of her husband, who is very powerful, in my favour, he being at present disaffected towards me, and intent on doing me some harm.

Or thus:

By making this woman my friend I shall gain the object of some friend of mine, or shall be able to effect the ruin of some enemy, or shall accomplish some other difficult purpose.

Or thus:

By being united with this woman, I shall kill her husband, and so obtain his vast riches which I covet.

Or thus:

The union of this woman with me is not attended with any danger, and will bring me wealth, of which, on account of my poverty and inability to support myself, I am very much in need. I shall therefore obtain her vast riches in this way without any difficulty.

Or thus:

This woman loves me ardently, and knows all my weak points; if therefore, I am unwilling to be united with her, she will make my faults public, and thus tarnish my character and reputation. Or she will bring some gross accusation against me, of which it may be hard to clear myself, and I shall be ruined. Or perhaps she will detach from me her husband who is powerful, and yet under her control, and will unite him to my enemy, or will herself join the latter.

Or thus:

The husband of this woman has violated the chastity of my wives, I shall therefore return that injury by seducing his wives.

Or thus:

By the help of this woman I shall kill an enemy of the king, who has taken shelter with her, and whom I am ordered by the king to destroy.

Or thus:

The woman whom I love is under the control of this woman. I shall, through the influence of the latter, be able to get at the former.

Or thus:

This woman will bring to me a maid, who possesses wealth and beauty, but who is hard to get at, and under the control of another.

Or lastly thus:

My enemy is a friend of this woman's husband, I shall therefore cause her to join him, and will thus create an enmity between her husband and him.

For these and similar other reasons the wives of other men may be resorted to, but it must be distinctly understood that is only allowed for special reasons, and not for mere carnal desire.

Charayana thinks that under these circumstances there is also a fifth kind of Nayika, viz. a woman who is kept by a minister, or who repairs to him occasionally; or a widow who accomplishes the purpose of a man with the person to whom she resorts.

Suvarnanabha adds that a woman who passes the life of an ascetic and in the condition of a widow may be considered as a sixth kind of Nayika.

Ghotakamukha says that the daughter of a public woman, and a female servant, who are still virgins, form a seventh kind of Nayika.

Gonardiya puts forth his doctrine that any woman born of good family, after she has come of age, is an eighth kind of Nayika.

But these four latter kinds of Nayikas do not differ much from the first four kinds of them, as there is no separate object in resorting to them. Therefore, Vatsyayana is of opinion that there are only four kinds of Nayikas, i.e. the maid, the twice-married woman, the public woman, and the woman resorted to for a special purpose.

The following women are not to be enjoyed:

- A leper
- A lunatic
- A woman turned out of caste
- A woman who reveals secrets
- A woman who publicly expresses desire for sexual intercourse
- A woman who is extremely white
- A woman who is extremely black
- A bad-smelling woman
- A woman who is a near relation
- A woman who is a female friend
- A woman who leads the life of an ascetic
- And, lastly the wife of a relation, of a friend, of a learned Brahman, and of the king

The followers of Babhravya say that any woman who has been enjoyed by five men is a fit and proper person to be enjoyed. But Gonikaputra is of opinion that even when this is the case, the wives of a relation, of a learned Brahman and of a king should be excepted.

READING 13

W. T. Stead, *The Maiden Tribute of Modern Babylon* (1885), Excerpts.

William T. Stead (1849–1912) was an English newspaper editor. In this excerpt from his newspaper, *The Pall Mall Gazette*, he launches his campaign against prostitution in London.

The Maiden Tribute of Modern Babylon I

The Report of our Secret Commission

W. T. Stead

In ancient times, if we may believe the myths of Hellas, Athens, after a disastrous campaign, was compelled by her conqueror to send once every nine years a tribute to Crete of seven youths and seven maidens. The doomed fourteen, who were selected by lot amid the lamentations of the citizens, returned no more. The vessel that bore them to Crete unfurled black sails as the symbol of despair, and on arrival her passengers were flung into the famous Labyrinth of Daedalus, there to wander about blindly until such time as they were devoured by the Minotaur, a frightful monster, half man, half bull, the foul product of an unnatural lust. "The labyrinth was as large as a town and had countless courts and galleries. Those who entered it could never find their way out again. If they hurried from one to another of the numberless rooms looking for the entrance door, it was all in vain. They only became more hopelessly lost in the bewildering labyrinth, until at last they were devoured by the Minotaur."

Twice at each ninth year the Athenians paid the maiden tribute to King Minos, lamenting sorely the dire necessity of bowing to his iron law. When the third tribute came to be exacted, the distress of the city of the Violet Crown was insupportable. From the King's palace to the peasant's hamlet, everywhere were heard cries and groans and the choking sob of despair, until the whole air seemed to vibrate with the sorrow of an unutterable anguish. Then it was that the hero Theseus volunteered to be offered up among those who drew the black balls from the brazen urn of destiny, and the story of his self-sacrifice, his victory, and his triumphant return, is among the most familiar of the tales which since the childhood of the world have kindled the imagination and fired the heart of the human race. The labyrinth was cunningly wrought like a house;

W.T. Stead, "The Maiden Tribute of Modern Babylon I: the Report of our Secret Commission"," *The Pall Mall Gazette*, July 6, 1885.

says Ovid, with many rooms and winding passages, that so the shameful creature of lust whose abode it was to be should be far removed from sight.

Destinat hunc Minos thalamis removere pudorem,

Multiplicique domo, caecisque includere tectis.

Daedalus ingenio fabra celeberrimus artis

Ponit opus: turbatque notas, et lumina flexura

Ducit in errorera variarum ambage viarum.

And what happened to the victims—the young men and maidens—who were there interned, no one could surely tell. Some say that they were done to death; others that they lived in servile employments to old age. But in this alone do all the stories agree, that those who were once caught in the coils could never retrace their steps, so "inextricable" were the paths, so "blind" the footsteps, so "innumerable" the ways of wrong-doing. On the southern wall of the porch of the cathedral at Lucca there is a slightly traced piece of sculpture, representing the Cretan labyrinth, "out of which," says the legend written in straggling letters at the side, "nobody could get who was inside":–

Hie quern credicus edit Dedalus est laberinthus

De quo nullus vadere quirit qui fuit intus.

The fact that the Athenians should have taken so bitterly to heart the paltry maiden tribute that once in nine years they had to pay to the Minotaur seems incredible, almost inconceivable. This very night in London, and every night, year in and year out, not seven maidens only, but many times seven, selected almost as much by chance as those who in the Athenian market-place drew lots as to which should be flung into the Cretan labyrinth, will be offered up as the Maiden Tribute of Modern Babylon. Maidens they were when this morning dawned, but tonight their ruin will be accomplished, and tomorrow they will find themselves within the portals of the maze of London brotheldom. Within that labyrinth wander, like lost souls, the vast host of London prostitutes, whose numbers no man can compute, but who are probably not much below 50,000 strong. Many, no doubt, who venture but a little way within the maze make their escape. But multitudes are swept irresistibly on and on to be destroyed in due season, to give place to others, who also will share their doom.

The maw of the London Minotaur is insatiable, and none that go into the secret recesses of his lair return again. After some years' dolorous wandering in this palace of despair—for "hope of rest to solace there is none, nor e'en of milder pang," save the poisonous anodyne of drink—most of those ensnared to night will perish, some of them in horrible torture. Yet, so far from this great city being convulsed with woe,

London cares for none of these things, and the cultured man of the world, the heir of all the ages, the ultimate product of a long series of civilizations and religions, will shrug his shoulders in scorn at the folly of any one who ventures in public print to raise even the mildest protest against a horror a thousand times more horrible than that which, in the youth of the world, haunted like a nightmare the imagination of mankind. Nevertheless, I have not yet lost faith in the heart and conscience of the English folk, the sturdy innate chivalry and right thinking of our common people; and although I am no vain dreamer of Utopias peopled solely by Sir Galahads and vestal virgins, I am not without hope that there may be some check placed upon this vast tribute of maidens, unwitting or unwilling, which is nightly levied in London by the vices of the rich upon the necessities of the poor.

London's lust annually uses up many thousands of women, who are literally killed and made away with—living sacrifices slain in the service of vice. That may be inevitable, and with that I have nothing to do. But I do ask that those doomed to the house of evil fame shall not be trapped into it unwillingly, and that none shall be beguiled into the chamber of death before they are of an age to read the inscription above the portal—"All hope abandon ye who enter here." If the daughters of the people must be served up as dainty morsels to minister to the passions of the rich, let them at least attain an age when they can understand the nature of the sacrifice which they are asked to make. And if we must cast maidens—not seven, but seven times seven—nightly into the jaws of vice, let us at least see to it that they assent to their own immolation, and are not unwilling sacrifices procured by force and fraud.

That is surely not too much to ask from the dissolute rich. Even considerations of self-interest might lead our rulers to assent to so modest a demand. For the hour of Democracy has struck, and there is no wrong which a man resents like this. If it has not been resented hitherto, it is not because it was not felt. The Roman Republic was founded by the rape of Lucrece, but Lucrece was a member of one of the governing families. A similar offence placed Spain under the domination of the Moors, but there again the victim of Royal licence was the daughter of a Count. But the fathers and brothers whose daughters and sisters are purchased like slaves, not for labour, but for lust, are now at last enrolled among the governing classes—a circumstance full of hope for the nation, but by no means without menace for a class. Many of the French Revolutionists were dissolute enough, but nothing gave such an edge to the guillotine as the memory of the *Parc aux Cerfs*; and even in our time the horrors that attended the suppression of the Commune were largely due to the despair of the femme vengeresse. Hence, unless the levying of the maiden-tribute in London is shorn of its worst abuses—at present, as I shall show, flourishing unchecked—resentment, which might be appeased by reform, may hereafter be the virus of a social revolution. It is the one explosive which is strong enough to wreck the Throne.

READING 14

Richard Krafft-Ebbing, *Psychopathia Sexualis* (1886), 409–419.

Richard Krafft-Ebbing (1840–1902) was a German psychiatrist. In this passage from his landmark reference work on sexuality, he discusses physical, mental, and legal dimensions of male homosexuality.

Psychopathia Sexualis

Richard Freiherr von Krafft-Ebing

" Nevertheless, in spite of everything, it will happen that I betray myself by some expression of feminine feeling, either in sexual matters, when I say that I feel so and so, expressing what a man without the female feeling cannot know; or when I accidentally betray that female attire is my talent. Before women, of course, this does not amount to anything; for a woman is greatly flattered when a man understands something of her matters; but this must not be displayed to my own wife. How frightened I once was when my wife said to a friend that I had great taste in ladies' dress! How a haughty, stylish lady was astonished when, as she was about to make a great error in the education of her little daughter, I described to her in writing and verbally all the feminine feelings! To be sure, I lied to her, saying that my knowledge had been gleaned from letters. But her confidence in me is as great as ever; and the child, who was on the road to insanity, is rational and happy. She had confessed all the feminine inclinations as sins; now she knows what, as a girl, she must bear and control by will and religion; and she feels that she is human. Both ladies would laugh heartily if they knew that I had only drawn on my own sad experience. I must also add that I now have a finer sense of temperature, and, besides, a sense of the elasticity of the skin and tension of the intestines, etc., in patients, that was unknown to me before; that in operations and autopsies, poisonous fluids more readily penetrate my (uninjured) skin. Every autopsy causes me pain; examination of a prostitute, or a woman having a discharge, a cancerous odor, or the like, is actually repugnant to me. In all respects I am now under the influence of antipathy and sympathy, from the sense of colour to my judgment of a person. Women usually see in each other the periodical sexual disposition; and, therefore, a lady wears a veil, if she is not always accustomed to wear one, and usually she perfumes herself, even though it be only with handkerchief or gloves; for her olfactory sense in relation to her own sex is intense. Odours have an incredible effect on the female organism; thus, for example, the odours of violets and roses quiet me, while others disgust me; and with Yling-Ylang I cannot contain myself for sexual excitement. Contact with a woman seems homogeneous to me; coitus with my wife seems possible to me because she is somewhat masculine, and has a firm skin; and yet it is more an *amor lesbicus.*

"Besides, I always feel passive. Often at night, when I cannot sleep for excitement, it is finally accomplished, if I have my thighs apart, like a woman having intercourse with a man (i.e., he can sleep in that position) or if I lie on my side; but an arm or the bedclothing must not touch the breasts, or there is no sleep; and there must be no pressure on the abdomen. I sleep best in a chemise and night-robe, and with gloves on; for my hands easily get cold. I am also comfortable in female drawers and petticoats, because they do not touch the genitals. I liked female dresses best when crinolines were worn. Female dresses do not annoy the feminine-feeling man; for he, like every woman, feels them as belonging to his person, and not as something foreign.

"My dearest associate is a lady suffering with neurasthenia, who, since her last confinement, feels like a man, but who, since I explained these feelings to her, abstains from intercourse as much as possible, a thing I, as a husband, dare not do. She, by her example, helps me to endure my condition. She has a most perfect memory of the female feelings, and has often given me good advice. Were she a man and I a young girl I should seek to win her; for her I should be glad to endure the fate of a woman. But her present appearance is quite different from what it formerly was. She is a very elegantly dressed gentleman, notwithstanding bosom and hair; she also speaks quickly and concisely, and no longer takes pleasure in the things that please me. She has a kind of melancholy dissatisfaction with the world, but she bears her fate worthily and with resignation, finding her comfort only in religion and the fulfilment of her duty. At the time of the menses, she almost dies. She no longer likes female society and conversation, and has no liking for delicacies.

"A youthful friend felt like a girl from the very first, and had inclinations towards the male sex. His sister had the opposite condition; and when the uterus demanded its right, and she saw herself as a loving woman in spite of her masculinity, she cut the matter short, and committed suicide by drowning.

"Since complete effemination, the principal changes I have observed in myself are:—

1. "The constant feeling of being a woman from top to toe.
2. "The constant feeling of having female genitals.
3. "The periodicity of the monthly menstruation.
4. "The regular occurrence of female desire, though not directed to any particular man.
5. The passive female feeling in coitus.
6. "After that, the feeling of impregnation.
7. "The female feeling in thought of coitus.

8. "At the sight of women, the feeling of being of their kind, and the feminine interest in them.
9. "At the sight of men, the feminine interest in them.
10. "At the sight of children, the same feeling.
11. "The changed disposition and much greater patience.
12. "The final resignation to my fate, for which I have nothing to thank but positive religion; without it I should have long ago committed suicide.

"To be a man and to be compelled to feel that every woman either has intercourse or desires it. This is hard to endure."

The foregoing autobiography, scientifically so important, was accompanied by the following no less interesting letter:—

"*Sir,*—I must next beg your indulgence for troubling you with my communication. I lost all control, and thought of myself only as a monster before which I myself shuddered. Then your work gave me courage again; and I determined to go to the bottom of the matter, and examine my past life, let the result be what it might. It seemed a duty of gratitude to you to tell you the result of my recollection and observation, since I had not seen any description by you of an analogous case; and, finally, I also thought it might perhaps interest you to learn, from the pen of a physician, how such a worthless human, or masculine, being thinks and feels under the weight of the imperative idea of being a woman.

"It is not perfect; but I no longer have the strength to reflect more upon it, and have no desire to go into the matter more deeply. Much is repeated; but I beg you to remember that any mask may be allowed to fall off, particularly when it is not voluntarily worn, but enforced.

"After reading your work, I hope that, if I fulfil my duties as physician, citizen, father and husband, I may still count myself among human beings who do not deserve merely to be despised.

"Finally, I wished to lay the result of my recollection and reflection before you, in order to show that one thinking and feeling like a woman can still be a physician. I consider it a great injustice to debar woman from Medicine. A woman, through her feeling, is prone to many ailments which, in spite of all skill in diagnosis, remain obscure to a man; at least, in the diseases of women and children. If I could have my way, I should have every physician live the life of a woman for three months; then he would have a better understanding and more consideration in matters affecting the half of humanity from which he comes; then he would learn to value the greatness of woman, and appreciate the difficulty of her lot."

Remarks: The badly tainted patient was originally psycho-sexually abnormal, in that, in character and in the sexual act, he felt as a female. The abnormal feeling remained purely a psychical anomaly until three years ago, when, owing to severe neurasthenia, it received overmastering support in imperative bodily sensations of a sexual change, which now dominate consciousness. Then, to the patient's horror, he felt bodily like a woman; and, under the impulse of his imperative feminine sensations, he experienced a complete transformation of his former masculine feeling, thought and will; in fact, of his whole sexual life, in the sense of eviration. At the same time, his "ego" was able to control these abnormal psycho-physical manifestations, and prevent descent to *paranoia,* a remarkable example of imperative feelings and ideas on the basis of neurotic taint, which is of great value for a comprehension of the manner in which the psycho-sexual transformation may be accomplished. In 1893, three years later, this unhappy colleague sent me a new account of his present state. This corresponded essentially with the former. His physical and psychical feelings were absolutely those of a woman; but his intellectual powers were intact, and he was thus saved from *paranoia.*

A counterpart to this case, which is of clinical and psychological moment, is that of a lady as given in:—

CASE 130. Mrs. X., daughter of a high official. Her mother died of nervous disease. The father was untainted, and died from pneumonia at a good old age. Her brothers and sisters had inferior psychopathic dispositions; one brother was of abnormal character, and very neurasthenic.

As a girl Mrs. X. had decided inclinations for boys' sports. So long as she wore short dresses she used to rove about the fields and woods in the freest manner, and climbed the most dangerous rocks and cliffs. She had no taste for dresses and finery. Once, when they gave her a dress made in boys' fashion, she was highly delighted; and when at school they dressed her up in boys' clothes on the occasion of some theatrical performance, she was filled with bliss.

Otherwise nothing betrayed her homosexual inclinations. Up to her marriage (at the age of twenty-one) she could not recall to mind a single instance in which she felt herself drawn to persons of her own sex. Men were equally indifferent to her. When matured she had many admirers. This flattered her greatly. However, she claimed that the difference of the sexes never entered her mind; she was only influenced by the difference in the dress.

When attending the first and only ball she felt interest only in intellectual conversation, but not in dancing or the dancers.

At the age of eighteen the menses set in without difficulty. She always looked upon menstruation as an unnecessary and bothersome function. Her engagement with a man who, though good and rich, yet possessed not the slightest knowledge of woman's nature, was a matter of utter indifference to her. She had neither sympathy for nor antipathy against matrimony. Her connubial duties were at first painful to her, later on simply loathsome. She never experienced sexual pleasure, but became the mother of six children. When her husband began to observe *coitus interruptus,* on account of the prolific consequences, her religious and moral sentiments were hurt. Mrs. X. grew more and more neurasthenic, peevish and unhappy.

She suffered from prolapsed uterus and vaginal erosions and became anaemic. Gynecological treatment and visits to watering-places procured but slight improvements.

At the age of thirty-six she had an apoplectic stroke, which confined her to bed for two years, with heavy neurasthenic ailments (insomnia, pressure in the head, palpitation of the heart, psychical depression, feelings of lost physical and mental power, bordering even on insanity, etc.). During this long illness a peculiar change of her psychical and physical feelings took place.

The small talk of the ladies visiting her about love, toilet, finery, fashions, domestic and servants' affairs disgusted her. She felt mortified at being a woman. She could not even make up her mind again to look in the mirror. She loathed combing her hair and making her toilet. Much to the surprise of her own people her hitherto soft and decidedly feminine features assumed a strongly masculine character, so much so that she gave the impression of being a man clad in female garb. She complained to her trusted physician that her periods had stopped,—in fact, she had nothing to do with such functions. When they recurred again she felt ill-tempered, and found the odor of the menstrual flow most nauseating, but definitely refused the use of perfumes, which affected her in a similar unpleasant manner.

But in other ways she felt that a peculiar change had come over her entire being. She had athletic spells, and great desire for gymnastic exercises. At times she felt as if she were just twenty. She was startled,—when her neurasthenic brain allowed of thought at all,—at the flight and novelty of her thoughts, at her quick and precise method of arriving at conclusions and forming opinions, at the curt and short way of expressing herself, and her novel choice of words not always becoming to a lady. Even an inclination to use curse words and oaths was noticeable in this otherwise so pious and correct woman.

She reproached herself bitterly, and grieved because she had lost her femininity, and scandalized her friends by her thoughts, sentiments, and actions.

She also perceived a change in her body. She was horrified to notice her breasts disappearing, that her pelvis grew smaller and narrower, the bones became more massive, and her skin rougher and harder.

She refused to wear any more a lady's night-dress or a lady's cap, and put away her bracelets, earrings and fans. Her maid and her dress-maker noticed a different odour coming from her person; her voice also grew deeper, rougher, and quite masculine.

When the patient was finally able to leave her bed, the female gait had altered, feminine gestures and movments in her female attire were forced, and she could no longer bear to wear a veil over her face. Her former period of life spent as a woman seemed strange to her, as if it did not belong to her existence at all; she could play no longer the *rôle* of woman.

She assumed more and more the character of a man. She experienced strange feelings in her abdomen; and complained to the physician attending her that she could feel no longer the internal organs of generation, that her body was closed up, the region of her genitals enlarged, and often had the sensation of possessing a penis and scrotum. She showed, also, unmistakable symptoms of male *libido*. All these observations affected her deeply, filled her with horror, and depressed her so much that an attack of insanity was apprehended. But by incessant efforts and kind advice the family physician finally succeeded in calming the patient and piloting her safely over this dangerous point. Little by little she gained her equilibrium in this novel, strange and morbid physic-psychical form. She took pains in performing her duties as house-wife and mother. It was interesting to observe the truly manly firmness of will which she developed, but her former softness of character had vanished. She assumed the *rôle* of the man in her house, a circumstance which led to many dissensions and mis-understandings. She became an enigma which her husband was unable to solve.

She complained to her physician that at times a "bestial masculine *libido*" threat-ened to overcome her, which made her despondent. Marital intercourse with the husband appeared to her most repulsive—in fact, impossible. Periodically the patient experienced feminine emotions, but they became scarcer and weaker as time went by. At such periods she became conscious again of her female genitals and breasts, but these episodes affected her painfully, and she felt that such a "second transmutation" would be unbearable, and would drive her to insanity.

She now became reconciled to her change of sex, brought about by her severe illness, and bore her fate with resignation, finding much support in her religious convictions.

What affected her most keenly was the fact that, like an actress, she must move in a strange sphere—*i.e.,* in that of a woman (Status Pareses," Sept., 1892).

READING 15

Michel Foucault, "We 'Other Victorians,'" in
The History of Sexuality, Volume 1 (1976), 3–13.

Michel Foucault (1926–1984) was a French philosopher and historian of sexuality. This excerpt from the beginning of his influential book *The History of Sexuality* grounds contemporary approaches to the history of sexuality in the legacies of Victorian ideas of sex, gender, and sexuality.

We "Other Victorians"

Michel Foucault

For a long time, the story goes, we supported a Victorian regime, and we continue to be dominated by it even today. Thus the image of the imperial prude is emblazoned on our restrained, mute, and hypocritical sexuality.

At the beginning of the seventeenth century a certain frankness was still common, it would seem. Sexual practices had little need of secrecy; words were said without undue reticence, and things were done without too much concealment; one had a tolerant familiarity with the illicit. Codes regulating the coarse, the obscene, and the indecent were quite lax compared to those of the nineteenth century. It was a time of direct gestures, shameless discourse, and open transgressions, when anatomies were shown and intermingled at will, and knowing children hung about amid the laughter of adults: it was a period when bodies "made a display of themselves."

But twilight soon fell upon this bright day, followed by the monotonous nights of the Victorian bourgeoisie. Sexuality was carefully confined; it moved into the home. The conjugal family took custody of it and absorbed it into the serious function of reproduction. On the subject of sex, silence became the rule. The legitimate and procreative couple laid down the law. The couple imposed itself as model, enforced the norm, safeguarded the truth, and reserved the right to speak while retaining the principle of secrecy. A single locus of sexuality was acknowledged in social space as well as at the heart of every household, but it was a utilitarian and fertile one: the parents' bedroom. The rest had only to remain vague; proper demeanor avoided contact with other bodies, and verbal decency sanitized one's speech. And sterile behavior carried the taint of abnormality; if it insisted on making itself too visible, it would be designated accordingly and would have to pay the penalty.

Nothing that was not ordered in terms of generation or transfigured by it could expect sanction or protection. Nor did it merit a hearing. It would be driven out, denied, and reduced to silence. Not only did it not exist, it had no right to exist and would be made to disappear upon its least manifestation—whether in acts or in words. Everyone knew, for example, that children had no sex, which was why they were forbidden to talk about it, why one closed one's eyes and stopped one's ears whenever they came to show evidence to the contrary, and why a general and studied silence was imposed. These are the characteristic features attributed to repression, which serve to distinguish it from the prohibitions maintained by penal law: repression operated as a sentence to disappear, but also as an injunction to silence, an affirmation of nonexistence, and, by implication, an admission that there was nothing to say about such things, nothing to see, and nothing to know. Such was the hypocrisy of our bourgeois societies with its halting logic. It was forced to make a few concessions, however. If it was truly necessary to make room for illegitimate sexualities, it was reasoned, let them take their infernal mischief elsewhere: to a place where they could be reintegrated, if not in the circuits of production, at least in those of profit. The brothel and the mental hospital would be those places of tolerance: the prostitute, the client, and the pimp, together with the psychiatrist and his hysteric—those "other Victorians," as Steven Marcus would say—seem to have surreptitiously transferred the pleasures that are unspoken into the order of things that are counted. Words and gestures, quietly authorized, could be exchanged there at the going rate. Only in those places would untrammeled sex have a right to (safely insularized) forms of reality, and only to clandestine, circumscribed, and coded types of discourse. Everywhere else, modern puritanism imposed its triple edict of taboo, nonexistence, and silence.

But have we not liberated ourselves from those two long centuries in which the history of sexuality must be seen first of all as the chronicle of an increasing repression? Only to a slight extent, we are told. Perhaps some progress was made by Freud; but with such circumspection, such medical prudence, a scientific guarantee of innocuousness, and so many precautions in order to contain everything, with no fear of "overflow," in that safest and most discrete of spaces, between the couch and discourse: yet another round of whispering on a bed. And could things have been otherwise? We are informed that if repression has indeed been the fundamental link between power, knowledge, and sexuality since the classical age, it stands to reason that we will not be able to free ourselves from it except at a considerable cost: nothing less than a transgression of laws, a lifting of prohibitions, an irruption of speech, a reinstating of pleasure within reality, and a whole new economy in the mechanisms of power will be required. For the least glimmer of truth is conditioned by politics. Hence, one cannot hope to obtain the desired results simply from a medical practice, nor from a theoretical discourse, however rigorously pursued. Thus, one denounces Freud's conformism, the normalizing functions of psychoanalysis, the obvious timidity underlying Reich's vehemence, and all the effects of integration ensured by the "science" of sex and the barely equivocal practices of sexology.

This discourse on modern sexual repression holds up well, owing no doubt to how easy it is to uphold. A solemn historical and political guarantee protects it. By placing the advent of the age of repression in the seventeenth century, after hundreds of years of open spaces and free expression, one adjusts it to coincide with the development of capitalism: it becomes an integral part of the bourgeois order. The minor chronicle of sex and its trials is transposed into the ceremonious history of the modes of production; its trifling aspect fades from view. A principle of explanation emerges after the fact: if sex is so rigorously repressed, this is because it is incompatible with a general and intensive work imperative. At a time when labor capacity was being systematically exploited, how could this capacity be allowed to dissipate itself in pleasurable pursuits, except in those—reduced to a minimum—that enabled it to reproduce itself? Sex and its effects are perhaps not so easily deciphered; on the other hand, their repression, thus reconstructed, is easily analyzed. And the sexual cause—the demand for sexual freedom, but also for the knowledge to be gained from sex and the right to speak about it—becomes legitimately associated with the honor of a political cause: sex too is placed on the agenda for the future. A suspicious mind might wonder if taking so many precautions in order to give the history of sex such an impressive filiation does not bear traces of the same old prudishness: as if those valorizing correlations were necessary before such a discourse could be formulated or accepted.

But there may be another reason that makes it so gratifying for us to define the relationship between sex and power in terms of repression: something that one might call the speaker's benefit. If sex is repressed, that is, condemned to prohibition, nonexistence, and silence, then the mere fact that one is speaking about it has the appearance of a deliberate transgression. A person who holds forth in such language places himself to a certain extent outside the reach of power; he upsets established law; he somehow anticipates the coming freedom. This explains the solemnity with which one speaks of sex nowadays. When they had to allude to it, the first demographers and psychiatrists of the nineteenth century thought it advisable to excuse themselves for asking their readers to dwell on matters so trivial and base. But for decades now, we have found it difficult to speak on the subject without striking a different pose: we are conscious of defying established power, our tone of voice shows that we know we are being subversive, and we ardently conjure away the present and appeal to the future, whose day will be hastened by the contribution we believe we are making. Something that smacks of revolt, of promised freedom, of the coming age of a different law, slips easily into this discourse on sexual oppression. Some of the ancient functions of prophecy are reactivated therein. Tomorrow sex will be good again. Because this repression is affirmed, one can discreetly bring into coexistence concepts which the fear of ridicule or the bitterness of history prevents most of us from putting side by side: revolution and happiness; or revolution and a different body, one that is newer and more beautiful; or indeed, revolution and pleasure. What sustains our eagerness to speak of sex in terms of repression is doubtless this opportunity to speak out against the powers that be, to utter truths and promise bliss, to link together enlightenment, liberation, and manifold pleasures; to pronounce a discourse that combines the fervor of knowledge, the determination to change the laws, and the longing for the garden of earthly delights. This is perhaps what also explains the market value attributed not only to what is said about sexual repression, but also to the mere fact of lending an ear to those who would eliminate the effects of repression. Ours is, after all, the only civilization in which officials are paid to listen to all and sundry impart the secrets of their sex: as if the urge to talk about it, and the interest one hopes to arouse by doing so, have far surpassed the possibilities of being heard, so that some individuals have even offered their ears for hire.

But it appears to me that the essential thing is not this economic factor, but rather the existence in our era of a discourse in which sex, the revelation of truth, the overturning of global laws, the proclamation of a new day to come, and the promise of a certain felicity are linked together. Today it is sex that serves as a support for the ancient form—so familiar and important in the West—of preaching. A great sexual sermon—which has had its subtle theologians and its popular voices—has swept through our societies over the last decades; it has chastised the old order, denounced hypocrisy, and praised the rights of the immediate and the real; it has made people dream of a New City. The Franciscans are called to mind. And we might wonder how it is possible that the lyricism and religiosity that long accompanied the revolutionary project have, in Western industrial societies, been largely carried over to sex.

The notion of repressed sex is not, therefore, only a theoretical matter. The affirmation of a sexuality that has never been more rigorously subjugated than during the age of the hypocritical, bustling, and responsible bourgeoisie is coupled with the grandiloquence of a discourse purporting to reveal the truth about sex, modify its economy within reality, subvert the law that governs it, and change its future. The statement of oppression and the form of the sermon refer back to one another; they are mutually reinforcing. To say that sex is not repressed, or rather that the relationship between sex and power is not characterized by repression, is to risk falling into a sterile paradox. It not only runs counter to a well-accepted argument, it goes against the whole economy and all the discursive "interests" that underlie this argument.

This is the point at which I would like to situate the series of historical analyses that will follow, the present volume being at the same time an introduction and a first attempt at an overview: it surveys a few historically significant points and outlines certain theoretical problems. Briefly, my aim is to examine the case of a society which has been loudly castigating itself for its hypocrisy for more than a century, which speaks verbosely of its own silence, takes great pains to relate in detail the things it does not say, denounces the powers it exercises, and promises to liberate itself from the very laws that have made it function. I would like to explore not only these discourses but also the will that sustains them and the strategic intention that supports them. The question I would like to pose is not, Why are we repressed? but rather, Why do we say, with so much passion and so much resentment against our most recent past, against our present, and against ourselves, that we are repressed? By what spiral did we come to affirm that sex is negated? What led us to show, ostentatiously, that sex is something we hide, to say it is something we silence? And we do all this by formulating the matter in the most explicit terms, by trying to reveal it in its most naked reality, by affirming it in the positivity of its power and its effects. It is certainly legitimate to ask why sex was associated with sin for such a long time—although it would remain to be discovered how this association was formed, and one would have to be careful not to state in a summary and hasty fashion that sex was "condemned"—but we must also ask why we burden ourselves today with so much guilt for having once made sex a sin. What paths have brought us to the point where we are "at fault" with respect to our own sex? And how have we come to be a civilization so peculiar as to tell itself that, through an abuse of power which has not ended, it has long "sinned" against sex? How does one account for the displacement which, while claiming to free us from the sinful nature of sex, taxes us with a great historical wrong which consists precisely in imagining that nature to be blameworthy and in drawing disastrous consequences from that belief?

It will be said that if so many people today affirm this repression, the reason is that it is historically evident. And if they speak of it so abundantly, as they have for such a long time now, this is because repression is so firmly anchored, having solid roots and reasons, and weighs so heavily on sex that more than one denunciation will be required in order to free ourselves from it; the job will be a long one. All the longer, no doubt, as it is in the nature of power—particularly the kind of power that operates in our society—to be repressive, and to be especially careful in repressing useless energies, the intensity of pleasures, and irregular modes of behavior. We must not be surprised, then, if the effects of liberation vis-à-vis this repressive power are so slow to manifest themselves; the effort to speak freely about sex and accept it in its reality is so alien to a historical sequence that has gone unbroken for a thousand years now, and so inimical to the intrinsic mechanisms of power, that it is bound to make little headway for a long time before succeeding in its mission.

One can raise three serious doubts concerning what I shall term the "repressive hypothesis." First doubt: Is sexual repression truly an established historical fact? Is what first comes into view—and consequently permits one to advance an initial hypothesis—really the accentuation or even the establishment of a regime of sexual repression beginning in the seventeenth century? This is a properly historical question. Second doubt: Do the workings of power, and in particular those mechanisms that are brought into play in societies such as ours, really belong primarily to the category of repression? Are prohibition, censorship, and denial truly the forms through which power is exercised in a general way, if not in every society, most certainly in our own? This is a historico-theoretical question. A third and final doubt: Did the critical discourse that addresses itself to repression come to act as a roadblock to a power mechanism that had operated unchallenged up to that point, or is it not in fact part of the same historical network as the thing it denounces (and doubtless misrepresents) by calling it "repression"? Was there really a historical rupture between the age of repression and the critical analysis of repression? This is a historicopolitical question. My purpose in introducing these three doubts is not merely to construct counterarguments that are symmetrical and contrary to those outlined above; it is not a matter of saying that sexuality, far from being repressed in capitalist and bourgeois societies, has on the contrary benefitted from a regime of unchanging liberty; nor is it a matter of saying that power in societies such as ours is more tolerant than repressive, and that the critique of repression, while it may give itself airs of a rupture with the past, actually forms part of a much older process and, depending on how one chooses to understand this process, will appear either as a new episode in the lessening of prohibitions, or as a more devious and discreet form of power.

The doubts I would like to oppose to the repressive hypothesis are aimed less at showing it to be mistaken than at putting it back within a general economy of discourses on sex in modern societies since the seventeenth century. Why has sexuality been so widely discussed, and what has been said about it? What were the effects of power generated by what was said? What are the links between these discourses, these effects of power, and the pleasures that were invested by them? What knowledge (*savoir*) was formed as a result of this linkage? The object, in short, is to define the regime of power-knowledge-pleasure that sustains the discourse on human sexuality in our part of the world. The central issue, then (at least in the first instance), is not to determine whether one says yes or no to sex, whether one formulates prohibitions or permissions, whether one asserts its importance or denies its effects, or whether one refines the words one uses to designate it; but to account for the fact that it is spoken about, to discover who does the speaking, the positions and viewpoints from which they speak, the institutions which prompt people to speak about it and which store and distribute the things that are said. What is at issue, briefly, is the over-all "discursive fact," the way in which sex is "put into discourse." Hence, too, my main concern will be to locate the forms of power, the channels it takes, and the discourses it permeates in order to reach the most tenuous and individual modes of behavior, the paths that give it access to the rare or scarcely perceivable forms of desire, how it penetrates and controls everyday pleasure—all this entailing effects that may be those of refusal, blockage, and invalidation, but also incitement and intensification: in short, the "polymorphous techniques of power." And finally, the essential aim will not be to determine whether these discursive productions and these effects of power lead one to formulate the truth about sex, or on the contrary falsehoods designed to conceal that truth, but rather to bring out the "will to knowledge" that serves as both their support and their instrument.

Let there be no misunderstanding: I do not claim that sex has not been prohibited or barred or masked or misapprehended since the classical age; nor do I even assert that it has suffered these things any less from that period on than before. I do not maintain that the prohibition of sex is a ruse; but it is a ruse to make prohibition into the basic and constitutive element from which one would be able to write the history of what has been said concerning sex starting from the modern epoch. All these negative elements—defenses, censorships, denials—which the repressive hypothesis groups together in one great central mechanism destined to say no, are doubtless only component parts that have a local and tactical role to play in a transformation into discourse, a technology of power, and a will to knowledge that are far from being reducible to the former.

In short, I would like to disengage my analysis from the privileges generally accorded the economy of scarcity and the principles of rarefaction, to search instead for instances of discursive production (which also administer silences, to be sure), of the production of power (which sometimes have the function of prohibiting), of the propagation of knowledge (which often cause mistaken beliefs or systematic misconceptions to circulate); I would like to write the history of these instances and their transformations. A first survey made from this viewpoint seems to indicate that since the end of the sixteenth century, the "putting into discourse of sex," far from undergoing a process of restriction, on the contrary has been subjected to a mechanism of increasing incitement; that the techniques of power exercised over sex have not obeyed a principle of rigorous selection, but rather one of dissemination and implantation of polymorphous sexualities; and that the will to knowledge has not come to a halt in the face of a taboo that must not be lifted, but has persisted in constituting—despite many mistakes, of course—a science of sexuality. It is these movements that I will now attempt to bring into focus in a schematic way, bypassing as it were the repressive hypothesis and the facts of interdiction or exclusion it invokes, and starting from certain historical facts that serve as guidelines for research.

PART V

"NEW WOMEN"

By the 1920s, women around the world were claiming independence from traditional gender norms with new ideas regarding marriage, relationships, appearance, and political action. This section begins with Clarke's and Roosevelt's calls against women's education and for motherhood. Raichō Hiratsuka, Huda Shaarawi, and Lola Landau offer new visions for women from Japan, Egypt, and Germany, respectively, each advocating for female education. Vicki Ruiz's essay describes the tension between tradition and modernity for American Latina women during this time period.

READING 16

Edward Clarke, *Sex in Education* (1873), Excerpt.

Edward Clarke (1820–1877) was an American physician. In this excerpt he makes a medical case against women's education in the United States.

Sex in Education, or A Fair Chance for the Girls

Edward H. Clarke

This case needs very little comment: its teachings are obvious. Miss D—went to college in good physical condition. During the four years of her college life, her parents and the college faculty required her to get what is properly called an education. Nature required her, during the same period, to build and put in working order a large and complicated reproductive mechanism, a matter that is popularly ignored—shoved out of sight like a disgrace. She naturally obeyed the requirements of the faculty, which she could seem rather than the requirements of the mechanism within her, that she could not see. Subjected to the college regimen, she worked four years in getting a liberal education. Her way of work was sustained and continuous, and out of harmony with the rhythmical periodicy of the female organization. The stream of vital and constructive force evolved within her was turned steadily to the brain, and away from the ovaries and their accessories. The result of this sort of education was, that these last-mentioned organs, deprived of sufficient opportunity and nutriment, first began to perform their functions with pain, a warning of error that was unheeded; then to cease to grow; next, to set up once a month a grumbling torture that made life miserable; and, lastly, the brain and the whole nervous system, disturbed, in obedience to the law, that, if one member suffers, all the members suffer, became neuralgic and hysterical. And so Miss D—spent the next few years succeeding her graduation in conflict with dysmenorrehea, headache, neuralgia, and hysteria. Her parents marveled at her ill health; and she furnished another test for the repeated sermon on the delicacy of American girls.

Edward H. Clarke, Sex in Education: Or, A Fair Chance for Girls, pp. 83-85, 1873.

READING 17

Theodore Roosevelt, "On Motherhood" (1905).

Theodore Roosevelt (1858–1919) was president of the United States of America from 1901 to 1909. In this speech, he used his "bully pulpit" to argue that women had a duty to the nation to reproduce.

On Motherhood

Theodore Roosevelt

A speech given by President Roosevelt in Washington on March 13, 1905, before the National Congress of Mothers.

In our modern industrial civilization there are many and grave dangers to counterbalance the splendors and the triumphs. It is not a good thing to see cities grow at disproportionate speed relatively to the country; for the small land owners, the men who own their little homes, and therefore to a very large extent the men who till farms, the men of the soil, have hitherto made the foundation of lasting national life in every State; and, if the foundation becomes either too weak or too narrow, the superstructure, no matter how attractive, is in imminent danger of falling.

But far more important than the question of the occupation of our citizens is the question of how their family life is conducted. No matter what that occupation may be, as long as there is a real home and as long as those who make up that home do their duty to one another, to their neighbors and to the State, it is of minor consequence whether the man's trade is plied in the country or in the city, whether it calls for the work of the hands or for the work of the head.

No piled-up wealth, no splendor of material growth, no brilliance of artistic development, will permanently avail any people unless its home life is healthy, unless the average man possesses honesty, courage, common sense, and decency, unless he works hard and is willing at need to fight hard; and unless the average woman is a good wife, a good mother, able and willing to perform the first and greatest duty of womanhood, able and willing to bear, and to bring up as they should be brought up, healthy children, sound in body, mind, and character, and numerous enough so that the race shall increase and not decrease.

There are certain old truths which will be true as long as this world endures, and which no amount of progress can alter. One of these is

Theodore Roosevelt, "On American Motherhood," 1905.

the truth that the primary duty of the husband is to be the home-maker, the bread-winner for his wife and children, and that the primary duty of the woman is to be the helpmate, the housewife, and mother. The woman should have ample educational advantages; but save in exceptional cases the man must be, and she need not be, and generally ought not to be, trained for a lifelong career as the family breadwinner; and, therefore, after a certain point, the training of the two must normally be different because the duties of the two are normally different. This does not mean inequality of function, but it does mean that normally there must be dissimilarity of function. On the whole, I think the duty of the woman the more important, the more difficult, and the more honorable of the two; on the whole I respect the woman who does her duty even more than I respect the man who does his.

No ordinary work done by a man is either as hard or as responsible as the work of a woman who is bringing up a family of small children; for upon her time and strength demands are made not only every hour of the day but often every hour of the night. She may have to get up night after night to take care of a sick child, and yet must by day continue to do all her household duties as well; and if the family means are scant she must usually enjoy even her rare holidays taking her whole brood of children with her. The birth pangs make all men the debtors of all women. Above all our sympathy and regard are due to the struggling wives among those whom Abraham Lincoln called the plain people, and whom he so loved and trusted; for the lives of these women are often led on the lonely heights of quiet, self-sacrificing heroism.

Just as the happiest and most honorable and most useful task that can be set any man is to earn enough for the support of his wife and family, for the bringing up and starting in life of his children, so the most important, the most honorable and desir-able task which can be set any woman is to be a good and wise mother in a home marked by self-respect and mutual forbearance, by willingness to perform duty, and by refusal to sink into self-indulgence or avoid that which entails effort and self-sac-rifice. Of course there are exceptional men and exceptional women who can do and ought to do much more than this, who can lead and ought to lead great careers of outside usefulness in addition to—not as substitutes for—their home work; but I am not speaking of exceptions; I am speaking of the primary duties, I am speaking of the average citizens, the average men and women who make up the nation.

Inasmuch as I am speaking to an assemblage of mothers, I shall have nothing what-ever to say in praise of an easy life. Yours is the work which is never ended. No mother has an easy time, the most mothers have very hard times; and yet what true mother would barter her experience of joy and sorrow in exchange for a life of cold selfish-ness, which insists upon perpetual amusement and the avoidance of care, and which often finds its fit dwelling place in some flat designed to furnish with the least possible expenditure of effort the maximum of comfort and of luxury, but in which there is literally no place for children?

The woman who is a good wife, a good mother, is entitled to our respect as is no one else; but she is entitled to it only because, and so long as, she is worthy of it. Effort and self-sacrifice are the law of worthy life for the man as for the woman; tho neither the effort nor the self-sacrifice may be the same for the one as for the other. I do not in the least believe in the patient Griselda type of woman, in the woman who submits to gross and long continued ill treatment, any more than I believe in a man who tamely submits to wrongful aggression. No wrong-doing is so abhorrent as wrong-doing by a man toward the wife and the children who should arouse every tender feeling in his nature. Selfishness toward them, lack of tenderness toward them, lack of consideration for them, above all, brutality in any form toward them, should arouse the heartiest scorn and indignation in every upright soul.

I believe in the woman keeping her self-respect just as I believe in the man doing so. I believe in her rights just as much as I believe in the man's, and indeed a little more; and I regard marriage as a partnership, in which each partner is in honor bound to think of the rights of the other as well as of his or her own. But I think that the duties are even more important than the rights; and in the long run I think that the reward is ampler and greater for duty well done, than for the insistence upon individual rights, necessary tho this, too, must often be. Your duty is hard, your responsibility great; but greatest of all is your reward. I do not pity you in the least. On the contrary, I feel respect and admiration for you.

Into the woman's keeping is committed the destiny of the generations to come after us. In bringing up your children you mothers must remember that while it is essential to be loving and tender it is no less essential to be wise and firm. Foolishness and affection must not be treated as interchangeable terms; and besides training your sons and daughters in the softer and milder virtues, you must seek to give them those stern and hardy qualities which in after life they will surely need. Some children will go wrong in spite of the best training; and some will go right even when their surroundings are most unfortunate; nevertheless an immense amount depends upon the family training. If you mothers through weakness bring up your sons to be selfish and to think only of themselves, you will be responsible for much sadness among the women who are to be their wives in the future. If you let your daughters grow up idle, perhaps under the mistaken impression that as you yourselves have had to work hard they shall know only enjoyment, you are preparing them to be useless to others and burdens to themselves. Teach boys and girls alike that they are not to look forward to live spent in avoiding difficulties, but to lives spent in overcoming difficulties. Teach them that work, for themselves and also for others, is not a curse but a blessing; seek to make them happy, to make them enjoy life, but seek also to make them face life with the steadfast resolution to wrest success from labor and adversity, and to do their whole duty before God and to man. Surely she who can thus train her sons and her daughters is thrice fortunate among women.

There are many good people who are denied the supreme blessing of children, and for these we have the respect and sympathy always due to those who, from no fault of their own, are denied any of the other great blessings of life. But the man or woman who deliberately forego these blessings, whether from viciousness, coldness, shallow-heartedness, self-indulgence, or mere failure to appreciate aright the difference between the all-important and the unimportant,—why, such a creature merits contempt as hearty as any visited upon the soldier who runs away in battle, or upon the man who refuses to work for the support of those dependent upon him, and who tho able-bodied is yet content to eat in idleness the bread which others provide.

The existence of women of this type forms one of the most unpleasant and unwholesome features of modern life. If any one is so dim of vision as to fail to see what a thoroughly unlovely creature such a woman is I wish they would read Judge Robert Grant's novel "Unleavened Bread," ponder seriously the character of Selma, and think of the fate that would surely overcome any nation which developed its average and typical woman along such lines. Unfortunately it would be untrue to say that this type exists only in American novels. That it also exists in American life is made unpleasantly evident by the statistics as to the dwindling families in some localities. It is made evident in equally sinister fashion by the census statistics as to divorce, which are fairly appalling; for easy divorce is now as it ever has been, a bane to any nation, a curse to society, a menace to the home, an incitement to married unhappiness and to immorality, an evil thing for men and a still more hideous evil for women. These unpleasant tendencies in our American life are made evident by articles such as those which I actually read not long ago in a certain paper, where a clergyman was quoted, seemingly with approval, as expressing the general American attitude when he said that the ambition of any save a very rich man should be to rear two children only, so as to give his children an opportunity "to taste a few of the good things of life."

This man, whose profession and calling should have made him a moral teacher, actually set before others the ideal, not of training children to do their duty, not of sending them forth with stout hearts and ready minds to win triumphs for themselves and their country, not of allowing them the opportunity, and giving them the privilege of making their own place in the world, but, forsooth, of keeping the number of children so limited that they might "taste a few good things!" The way to give a child a fair chance in life is not to bring it up in luxury, but to see that it has the kind of training that will give it strength of character. Even apart from the vital question of national life, and regarding only the individual interest of the children themselves, happiness in the true sense is a hundredfold more apt to come to any given member of a healthy family of healthy-minded children, well brought up, well educated, but taught that they must shift up, well educated, but taught that they must shift for themselves, must win their own way, and by their own exertions make their own positions of usefulness, than it is apt to come to those whose parents themselves have acted on and have trained their children to act on, the selfish and sordid theory that the whole end of life is to "taste a few good things."

The intelligence of the remark is on a par with its morality; for the most rudimentary mental process would have shown the speaker that if the average family in which there are children contained but two children the nation as a whole would decrease in population so rapidly that in two or three generations it would very deservedly be on the point of extinction, so that the people who had acted on this base and selfish doctrine would be giving place to others with braver and more robust ideals. Nor would such a result be in any way regrettable; for a race that practised such doctrine—that is, a race that practised race suicide—would thereby conclusively show that it was unfit to exist, and that it had better give place to people who had not forgotten the primary laws of their being.

To sum up, then, the whole matter is simple enough. If either a race or an individual prefers the pleasure of more effortless ease, of self-indulgence, to the infinitely deeper, the infinitely higher pleasures that come to those who know the toil and the weariness, but also the joy, of hard duty well done, why, that race or that individual must inevitably in the end pay the penalty of leading a life both vapid and ignoble. No man and no woman really worthy of the name can care for the life spent solely or chiefly in the avoidance of risk and trouble and labor. Save in exceptional cases the prizes worth having in life must be paid for, and the life worth living must be a life of work for a worthy end, and ordinarily of work more for others than for one's self.

The woman's task is not easy—no task worth doing is easy—but in doing it, and when she has done it, there shall come to her the highest and holiest joy known to mankind; and having done it, she shall have the reward prophesied in Scripture; for her husband and her children, yes, and all people who realize that her work lies at the foundation of all national happiness and greatness, shall rise up and call her blessed.

READING 18

Raichō Hiratsuka, "Restoring Women's Talents" (1911).

Raichō Hiratsuka (1886–1971) was a writer and feminist activist in Japan. This excerpt was used to launch her literary journal, *Seitō*, where she called for women's liberation in Japan.

Liberation of Women

Raichō Hiratsuka

R estoring Women's Talents, 1911[1] In the beginning, woman was the
sun and a true being. Now woman is the moon. She lives through
others and shines through the light of others. Her countenance is pale,
like a patient.

We must now restore the sun, which has been hidden from us.

"Let the hidden talent, our hidden sun, reemerge!" This has been
our continuous outcry directed inwardly to ourselves. It represents our
insatiable longings, our final instinctive feelings encompassing our
total beings, unifying all our different sentiments....

Freedom and Liberation! Oftentimes we have heard the term
"liberation of women." But what does it mean? Are we not seriously
misunderstanding the term freedom or liberation? Even if we call
the problem liberation of women, are there not many other issues
involved? Assuming that women are freed from external oppression, liberated from constraint, given the so-called higher education,
employed in various occupations, given the right to vote, and provided
an opportunity to be independent from the protection of their parents and husbands, and to be freed from the little confinement of their
homes, can all of these be called liberation of women? They may provide proper surroundings and opportunities to let us fulfill the true
goal of liberation. Yet they remain merely the means and do not represent our goals or ideals.

However, I am unlike many intellectuals in Japan who suggest
that higher education is not necessary for women. Men and women
are endowed by nature to have equal faculties. Therefore, it is odd to

---

1 Hiratsuka Raichō, "*Genshi, Josei wa Taiyō de Atta*" (In the Beginning Woman
Was the Sun), in *Seitō*, first issue, September 1911, reproduced in the *Chūō Koron*,
November 1965, pp. 354–57.

Raichō Hiratsuka, "Restoring Women's Talents," Seito, vol. 1, 1911.

153

assume that one of the sexes requires education while the other does not. This may be tolerated in a given country and in a given age, but it is fundamentally a very unsound proposition.

I bemoan the fact that there is only one private college for women in Japan and that there is no tolerance on man's part to permit entrance of women into many universities maintained for men. However, what benefit is there when the intellectual level of women becomes similar to that of men? Men seek knowledge to escape from their lack of wisdom and lack of enlightenment. They want to free themselves.... Yet multifarious thoughts can darken true wisdom and lead men away from nature. Men who live by playing with knowledge may be called scholars, but they can never be men of wisdom. Nay, on the contrary, they are almost like blind men, who lack the perception to see the things in front of their eyes as what they are....

Now what is the true liberation that I am seeking? It is none other than to provide an opportunity for women to develop fully their hidden talents and hidden abilities. We must remove all barriers that stand in the way of women's development, whether they be external oppression or lack of knowledge. And above and beyond these factors, we must realize that we are the masters in possession of great talents, for we are the bodies that enshrine the great talents....

READING 19

Huda Shaarawi, *Harem Years: The Memoirs of an Egyptian Feminist, 1879–1924* (The Feminist Press, 1987), 112–137, 146-147.

Huda Shaarawi (1879–1947) founded the Egyptian Feminist Union. In this excerpt from her autobiography, she describes her involvement as a woman and a feminist with the Egyptian nationalist movement.

Harem Years
Huda Shaarawi

EPILOGUE

The final years in Huda's memoirs, from 1919 to 1924, were highly charged. Both women and men fought for national liberation. It was up to women to initiate the fight for their own liberation. This epilogue tells the story of women's dual struggle as reflected in Huda's memoirs.

Huda and other upper-class women had been living through a period of change and confrontation, as her account reveals, themselves still hidden by the discretion and distancing harem convention required. When the Egyptian nation under imperialist oppression rose up to take matters into its own hands, the only way to achieve independence, all Egyptians participated. Upper-class women ignored harem convention, and so did men, in the fight for national liberation. Women's unprecedented acts were welcomed and justified by national needs.

Egyptians demanded independence at the end of the First World War. In 1919, after they had been denied the chance to discuss their demands in London, they formed the Wafd to voice their demands on home soil. They no sooner did this under the leadership of Saad Zaghlul than the British arrested him and other Wafdist leaders and deported them to the Seychelles. Huda's husband, the treasurer of the Wafd, was not among those deported, and was left in charge. The next day, March 9th, the first of many demonstrations broke out in Cairo and soon spread to other cities and towns throughout the country. All classes rose up. Huda and other upper-class women— anywhere from one hundred and fifty to three hundred according to witnesses—poured out of their harems, clad in veils, on to the streets

Huda Shaarawi, from Harem Years: The Memoirs of an Egyptian Feminist, ed. and

trans. Margot Badran, pp. 112-137, 146-147. Copyright © 1987 by The Feminist Press.

Reprinted with permission.

to demonstrate.[1]

Huda has vivid recall of this historic moment.[2]

> We women held our first demonstration on 16 March to protest the repressive acts and intimidation practised by the British authority. In compliance with the orders of the authority we announced our plans to demonstrate in advance but were refused permission. We began to telephone this news to each other, only to read in *al-Muqattam* that the demonstration had received official sanction. We got on the telephone again, telling as many women as possible that we would proceed according to schedule the following morning. Had we been able to contact more than a limited number of women, virtually all the women of Cairo would have taken part in the demonstration.
>
> On the morning of 16 March, I sent placards to the house of the wife of Ahmad Bey Abu Usbaa, bearing slogans in Arabic and French painted in white on a background of black—the colour of mourning. Some of the slogans read, 'Long Live the Supporters of Justice and Freedom', others said 'Down with Oppressors and Tyrants' and 'Down with Occupation'.
>
> We assembled according to plan at the Garden City Park, where we left our carriages. Having agreed upon our route and carefully instructed the young women assigned to carry the flags and placards in front, we set out in columns towards the legation of the United States and intended to proceed from there to the legations of Italy and France. However, when we reached Qasr al-Aini Street, I observed that the young women in front were deviating from the original plan and had begun to head in the direction of *Bait al-Umma* (The House of the Nation), as Saad Zaghlul's house was called. I asked my friend Wagida Khulusi[3] to find out why we were going toward Saad Pasha's house and she returned saying that the women had decided it was a better route. According to our first plan we were to have ended our demonstration there. Reluctantly I went along with this change. No sooner were we approaching Zaghlul's house than British troops surrounded us. They blocked the streets with machine guns, forcing us to stop along with the students who had formed columns on both sides of us.
>
> I was determined the demonstration should resume. When I advanced, a British soldier stepped toward me pointing his gun, but I made my way past him. As one of the women tried to pull me back, I shouted in a loud voice, 'Let me die so Egypt shall have an Edith Cavell' (an English nurse shot and killed by the Germans during the First World War, who became an instant martyr). Continuing in the direction of the soldiers, I called upon the women to follow. A pair of arms grabbed me and the voice of Regina Khayyat[4] rang in my ears. 'This is madness. Do you want to risk the lives of the students? It will happen if the British raise a hand against you.'

FIGURE 19.1   Saad Zaghlul Pasha, National Leader.

At the thought of our unarmed sons doing battle against the weaponry of British troops, and of the Egyptian losses sure to occur, I came to my senses and stopped still. We stood still for three hours while the sun blazed down on us. The students meanwhile continued to encourage us, saying that the heat of the day would soon abate. Some of the students departed for the legations of the United States, France, and Italy, announcing that the British had surrounded the women in front of Saad Pasha's house. I did not care if I suffered sunstroke—the blame would fall upon the tyrannical British authority—but we stood up to the heat and suffered no harm. The British also brought out Egyptian soldiers armed with sticks.

What these troops were commanded to do is recounted by the man who gave them their orders, the British commandant of the Cairo police, Russell Pasha. 'At a given signal I closed the cordon and the ladies found their way opposed by a formidable line of Egyptian conscript police who had been previously warned that they were not to use violence but to stand still ... considerable licence was given them by their officers to practise their ready peasant wit on the smart ladies who confronted them.'[5]

When the men began to taunt their compatriots as Huda tells it,

FIGURE 19.2   A school girl, surrounded by other students, on the balcony of 'The House of the Nation', Saad Zaghlul's house, during the revolution, encourages the crowds below.

The women rebuked the soldiers. Some were moved to the point of tears. Eventually Russell Pasha arrived. 'You have conducted your demonstration in defiance of orders. Now that you have done what you set out to do you are requested to return home.' I answered, 'We read in *al-Muqattam* yesterday that the authorities had granted permission for the demonstration. Why do you now stand in our way?' He replied that permission had not been granted and the news was false. Yielding in the face of force, we made our way to our carriages. After departing from the scene we called on some of the foreign legations to inform them of events and to register protest against the Protectorate (imposed by the British in 1914) and martial law. We received courtesy but nothing more. Before returning home we promised to hold another demonstration.[6]

Russell Pasha, in a letter to his father, described the women's demonstration in a condescending tone. 'My next problem was a demonstration by the native ladies of Cairo. This rather frightened me as if it came to pass it was bound to collect a big crowd and my orders were to stop it. Stopping a procession means force and any force you use on women puts you in the wrong. Well, they assembled in motor cars, etc. got out and started to walk in a procession ... I let them get a little way and then blocked them in with police supported by troops and there the dear things had to remain for an hour and a half in the hot sun with nothing to sit on except the curb stone.'[7]

FIGURE 19.3   Women's demonstration in Cairo 1919 National Revolution.

The nationalist movement brought husbands and wives who normally led more separate existences in the divided harem world into closer contact as Huda's memoirs indicate. She tells us that this was the moment of greatest collaboration between herself and her husband. At a time when streets were full of angry demonstrators and armed troops and there were constant arrests and deportations, women had thrown themselves into the movement, and men needed their help. Huda says, 'My husband kept me informed of events so that I could fill the vacuum if he were imprisoned or exiled.'

Huda, who up to then had lived a life removed from national politics, threw herself into political activism. Following a demonstration in which some Egyptians were shot she wrote her first letter of protest to Lady Brunyate, an American by birth and longtime friend, the wife of Sir William Brunyate, the judicial and financial adviser to the Egyptian government.

> During these sad times I should like to remind you of the conversations we had last summer at my house in Ramleh. You assured me that Britain had taken part in the war to do service to the cause of justice and humanity, to protect the freedom of oppressed peoples and safeguard their rights. Would you kindly tell me if you remain convinced of this today? May I ask what you think when your government accords itself the right to impose martial law in time of peace and banishes people from their own land when they ask for nothing but the right to live in freedom in their own country and to be hospitable to all?

FIGURE 19.4   Women sewed crescents and crosses on green cloth to proclaim the solidarity of Muslims and Christians,

Before sending the letter, Huda showed it to her husband. He, in turn, showed it to the Wafd, who applauded it. The letter was never answered. Huda says, 'I thought she might have some influence and at the very least I expected her to answer my letter. Instead, she broadcast her dismay to our mutual friends and acquaintances.'

In April, Saad Zaghlul and his companions were released from detention by the British and the Wafd was allowed to go abroad for negotiations. The next day, Huda and women of different classes formed part of a huge demonstration headed by cabinet ministers including members of the Legislative Assembly, army officers, religious scholars, judges, lawyers, doctors, government employees and workers and students. 'Upper-class women rode in carriages and women of the lower class rode in carts. As the women's carriages passed in front of one of the large hotels some soldiers tried to grab an Egyptian flag from the hand of the wife of Ratib Pasha and in the process struck her arm. Unable to get the flag, they hit her carriage with their bayonets. Foreigners cheered her from the hotel terrace.'

The uprising continued,

The women continued to support the Wafd and at the same time gave encouragement to the people. We consoled relatives of students and others injured by British bullets, visited the wounded, and did what we could to assist the poor and needy among them. In the working class quarters women went to their windows and balconies to applaud their men in displays of national solidarity. Sometimes soldiers fired at the houses, killing and wounding women. Some were hit by bullets that pierced the walls of their houses. The death of Shafiqa bint Muhammad, the first woman killed by a British bullet, caused widespread grief. Egyptians of all classes followed her funeral procession. It became the focus of intense national mourning.[8] Events like these, coming one after the other, did not please the British. They disregarded the solemnity of funeral processions, often scattering the mourners and precipitating bloody confrontations. We women began to compile a list of the dead and wounded. Among the women I remember Shafiqa bint Muhammad, Aisha bint Umar, Fahima Riyad, Hamida bint Khalil, and Najiyya Said Ismail—all from the working classes.

Not only did women of all classes rise up together but women of different religions worked closely together. Huda remarks on the solidarity of the various religions in Egypt which would not allow the colonial power to ignite sectarian strife. She says, 'The British claimed our national movement was a revolt of the Muslim majority against religious minorities. This slander aroused the anger of the Copts and other religious groups. Egyptians showed their solidarity by meeting together in mosques, churches, and synagogues. *Shaikhs* walked arm in arm with priests and rabbis.'

Growing increasingly alarmed the British pressured the Wafd to stop the strikes that had meanwhile been organized. Leaders of the Wafd were summoned to a meeting with the British authority. At that moment came the first hint that women might soon take over crucial roles from men. When leaders of the Wafd assembled at the Shaarawi house before proceeding together to a meeting with the British, Huda relates, 'My husband gave me an envelope saying, "If we are arrested please give this money to the wife of Saad Pasha. She may need it in our absence." From the window I watched him and the others leave, some with grim smiles and others with heads bent.'

At the meeting the British forced the Wafd to issue an appeal to end the strikes. Huda says,

The Wafd composed an appeal trying not to compromise their nationalism. When they reached the street an anxious crowd welcomed them. When the appeal for a resumption of order was published the following day, it had no effect because everyone knew that the Wafd had been forced to issue it. The strike not only continued but spread, until virtually all civil servants and workers were involved. The British authority pressured the government to threaten to fire the civil servants if they persisted, and urged them to return to their jobs. They refused, however, and called for the downfall of the government. Rushdi Pasha, the prime minister, then summoned senior government officials in a futile attempt to persuade them to support the government's directive.

Huda and other women, for the first but not last time, also asked for the resignation of the government. The prime minister at the time, Husain Rushdi, was the husband of Huda's late friend and mentor, Eugénie Le Brun. Huda records in her memoirs that when the prime minister received the women's letter he sighed, 'The women want my resignation as well.' He resigned that day. Huda notes, 'The prime minister resigned after receiving an ultimatum from the British and so it served as another form of protest.'

Huda and other women helped keep the strikes alive. Segregation of sex and class broke down as harem women stationed themselves at the doors to government offices urging men not to return to work. 'Women took off their jewellery and offered it to government workers with the plea, "If you want money take this but do not hinder our cause by going back to work under British threat."' She goes on to say, 'Unfortunately, many went back to work and signed papers apologizing for their absence. As I watched the strikers return I was sad yet I could excuse it to some extent since the men had been without salaries, for most their sole income, for a long time.' She adds, 'However, even personal hardship did not prevent more acts of revolt and strikes on the part of all classes.'

The women stepped up their political activities. At the end of 1919 when the Milner Mission arrived in Egypt to investigate the revolution the women mounted another demonstration. Huda recalls, 'We women demonstrated against the Milner Mission, As we drove past the headquarters of the Protectorate we were accosted by British soldiers who jumped on the steps of our carriages taunting and hitting us. In the mêlée a woman's veil was torn from her.' Soon afterwards, the women convened in the Cathedral of Saint Mark. They drafted a resolution 'in the name of the women of Egypt' to send to the British authority protesting that the Milner Mission was out to preserve the British occupation of Egypt. They sent another communication .protesting their own maltreatment during the demonstration.[9]

Within a month the women met at the Cathedral once again. Over a thousand women of all classes were reported to have attended. Here Egyptian women for the first time formed a political body. They called it the Wafdist Women's Central Committee to support the Wafd, at the time not yet a year old. Huda was elected president.[10]

The end of 1920 was a period of strained unity between women and men Wafdists, a strain precipitated by the men's neglect. In October, Wafdist male leaders who had finally managed to get to London for talks, returned with proposed terms for independence to present to the people. The proposal was shown to numerous male groups and

FIGURE 19.5   Huda at age forty-four. This is one of the first photographs of an unveiled Egyptian woman to appear in local newspapers.

organizations but not to the Wafdist Women's Central Committee, who in the words of Huda, 'had worked hard alongside the Wafd in the nationalist movement.' The women took matters into their own hands and got a copy of the proposal themselves. They found the terms inadequate, and published their views in the press.[11] The members of the Wafdist Women's Central Committee also sent a sharp letter to the head of the Wafd. Huda says, 'We criticized the delegates from the Wafd for disregarding our rights and our very existence by neglecting to solicit our views.' Huda signed the letter the Wafdist Women's Central Committee sent to Saad Zaghlul on 12 December. It read:

> We are surprised and shocked by the way we have been treated recently, in contrast to previous treatment and certainly contrary to what we expect from you. You supported us when we created our Committee. Your congratulatory telegrams expressed the finest hopes and most noble sentiments. What makes us all the more indignant is that by

FIGURE 19.6   Safiyya Zaghlul appears unveiled in London in 1921 with Saad Zaghlul and other members of the Wafd during negotiations for independence. In Egypt, Safiyya still veiled while the men discarded their tophats for tarbushes. (See other photograph of Saad Zaghlul p.114)

disregarding us the Wafd has caused foreigners to disparage the renaissance of women. They claim that our participation in the nationalist movement was merely a ploy to dupe civilized nations into believing in the advancement of Egypt and its ability to govern itself. Our women's renaissance is above that as you well know. At this moment when the future of Egypt is about to be decided, it is unjust that the Wafd, which stands for the rights of Egypt and struggles for its liberation, should deny half the nation its role in that liberation.

The women got a letter of apology from Zaghlul.

There was not only strained unity between women and men Wafdists but strains within male Wafdist ranks. While Wafdist leaders were conferring abroad relations between Huda's husband and Saad Zaghlul deteriorated. Huda displayed considerable political skill in managing to act independently as a Wafdist yet showing loyalty towards her husband. This is illustrated on the occasion of Zaghlul's return to Egypt in April 1921, when Huda as president of the Wafdist Women's

Central Committee went to welcome the president of the Wafd while Ali Shaarawi remained at home.

Huda recounts the incident:

> I was among the delegation of women who went to greet Saad and his wife at their house. We found great crowds of women and men congregating in the two tents, one for women and one for men erected next to the house (segregation was still in force). I felt uncomfortable about being there while my husband, who was instrumental in helping the Wafd gain the trust of the nation, remained at home, neglected by the people. As those thoughts ran through my head, I heard the voice of Sayyid Agha calling to me, 'Saad Pasha is inquiring, "Where is the *raisa* (president), where is the *raisa?*"' However, I preferred to remain on the sidelines, owing to my awkward position. Saad Pasha made his way out through the lines of women (men in elevated positions were permitted by etiquette formally to visit women or to receive formal visits from women), looking from side to side asking, 'Where is the *raisa?* I. wish to offer my thanks.' I congratulated him on his safe return. Afterwards, I asked Sharifa Hanim Riyad and the other women of the Committee to stand in for me and to excuse my departure. They understood my position. The same day, Saad Pasha came to our house and thanked me again for welcoming him, but he did not ask for my husband, which upset me. However, I was glad the following day when he returned and shook hands with Shaarawi Pasha.

Another incident also reveals Huda's political adroitness. When she and other Wafdist women learned that Saad Zaghlul had planned angry demonstrations against the Egyptian prime minister, Adli Yakan, returning to Egypt from abortive negotiations in London, they went to Zaghlul's house to dissuade him. Huda absented herself while the other women talked with Zaghlul because of renewed discord between her husband and the president of the Wafd. She remained in another room with Safiyya Zaghlul, Saad's wife. Huda says, 'When Saad Pasha noticed I was not with the women he insisted on coming to greet me.' While the harem system prevailed, if women and men communicated under ordinary circumstances they did so through a barrier. Huda confides, 'I allowed him to greet me from behind a screen,' Keeping her distance, Huda used the harem screen politically. She continues:

> He thanked me for the services I had rendered in strengthening the Wafd and said he wished to reward me. Each of us, I responded, acts out of a sense of duty toward the nation in the hour of need. I have done nothing to deserve thanks or reward. He answered, 'How can that be? You have served the movement. How can I reward you for it?' I seized the moment and said, 'Since you insist upon rewarding me I shall make

a request.' He replied, 'With pleasure, what is your wish?' I said, 'Receive Adli Pasha with honour and respect, the way he received you when you returned to Egypt. Stop the plans for the insulting demonstrations being prepared for his welcome.' He remained silent for a moment, and then answered, 'By God, if it were up to me, alone, I would do it to please you, but even if I were to agree to your request the others would not.' I asked who refused him when he wanted something. At that point, Safi-yya Hanim[12] rushed toward him saying, 'If you place your hand in Adli's I swear by God, I shall cease to be your wife after what Adli has done.' Saad said to me, 'Did you hear Madame?' 'Yes,' I responded.

When Adli returned to Egypt he was, indeed, badly received and subsequently resigned.

At the end of the year (1921) Huda and other Wafdist women moved to centre stage when Zaghlul was deported after increased political agitation. The Wafdist Women's Central Committee, putting aside their disagreement with Zaghlul, closed ranks and protested in a letter to the British High Commissioner on 25 December signed by Huda Shaarawi. 'You cannot silence the voice of the nation by stifling the voice of the person who speaks for the nation. There are millions who will speak out for liberty and denounce injustice. We shall not cease our vehement protest against the arbitrary and tyrannical measures you take against us—deeds that excite the wrath of the people.'[13]

The women now resorted to new militant tactics. In January 1922 Huda opened her house to a mass meeting of women. They passed resolutions calling for an end to martial law, the abolition of the Protectorate, and opposing the formation of a cabinet while the president of the Wafd was in exile. They forwarded these to the British government. The women also voted for an economic boycott against the British. This involved refusing to buy British goods and withdrawing money from British banks. At the same time the women would campaign to buy Egyptian goods and support Bank Misr, the new Egyptian bank.[14] Although the women used their own private space, the harem, to decide their political moves as meetings were banned, British intelligence penetrated this private world. Copies of discussions of the boycott at a second meeting at Huda's house in the Public Records Office in London attest to this.[15]

The women used their own networks to execute their economic boycott. Women under Islamic law inherit money and property in their own name and in principle may dispose of it as they wish: women, responsible for running households and looking after families, played major roles in consumption. Through their links with middle-class women active in new associations in Cairo and provincial towns, Huda and her friends were able to reach a broad section of the population.[16] The Wafd sent a letter to the women saying, 'We shall never forget your great service when you quickly rose to action with the boycott. It was one of the most powerful weapons in our struggle.' Later, when he was back in Egypt, Zaghlul himself commended the women's boycott.[17]

During the detention and exile of the Wafd leaders, Huda and other women assumed important roles in communications. They kept news flowing between the exiled nationalists and the Egyptian people: they were often a link between the men and the British: they played delicate diplomatic roles connected with the release of the Wafdists, dealt with finances, and monitored the health of the detainees. At the same time, the women kept up the morale of the movement and maintained a stream of political protest. It is not easy to exaggerate the bravery of the women at a time when massive numbers of British troops were in the country, martial law was in effect, meetings were banned, and the press and letters censored.[18]

In the midst of all this the British issued a unilateral declaration of Egyptian independence considerably modified by four Reserved Points. This meant, among other things, the continued stationing of British troops in the country, and left the question of the future fate of the relationship between Egypt and the Sudan in the hands of the British. The women and men of the Wafd opposed these conditions.

In February 1922, Ali Shaarawi died. A widow in mourning, Huda remained at the head of the Wafdist women. She told them at a meeting not long afterwards,

> Neither illness, grief, nor fear of censure can prevent me from shouldering my duty with you in the continuing fight for our national rights. I have vowed to you and to myself to struggle until the end of my life to rescue our beloved country from occupation and. oppression. I shall always honour the trust you have placed in me. Let it never be said that there was a woman in Egypt who failed, for personal reasons, to perform

FIGURE 19.7 Nabawiyya Musa, Huda, and Saiza Nabarawi attending an International Feminist Meeting in Rome in 1923.

Success to the new women
of Egypt!
Carrie Chapman Catt
171 Madison Ave
New York
Rome, May 19, 1923

FIGURE 19.8 Carrie Chapman Catt, president of the International Alliance of Women, wishes Egyptian sisters success.

her duty to the nation. I would rather die than bring shame upon myself and my sisters. I will remain by your side and at your head through good and bad times, with hope in the future while we defend the rights of our beloved country. Neither repeated hardships, nor the heavy-handedness of our present government will lessen my will nor deter me from fighting for the full independence of my country.

On this occasion she scorned 'the merely verbal independence of Egypt. Tharwat Pasha (who formed a government on 1 March) now boasts about the independence the imperialists hail as a magnanimous gift. It is no more than a right only partially restored to its owners. We women consider it merely a move to paralyse our national movement and mute our passions. ' She continued:

The burden of proof is not upon us. The leader of our national renaissance, Saad Zaghlul Pasha, and other members of the Wafd, are suffering the pain of exile in the Seychelles. Their only guilt was to have demanded independence. Here in Egypt military courts pass judgement on the lives of our sons. Censorship of the press gags our mouths. The prisons are filled with our best men. Special laws are enacted to prevent us from congregating. All this persists despite the conditions Tharwat Pasha laid down for forming a new government, which included the abolition of martial law and of the restrictions upon the freedom of the press and freedom of speech, the return of those in exile, and freeing those detained at home. Such is the subterfuge of our enemy, to trap us in the net of eternal enslavement. I am not implying our ministers were deliberate partners to this, because I refuse, like every other Egyptian, to say there is a single disloyal Egyptian, but I must affirm that the majority of our national demands would have been met if Tharwat Pasha had not agreed to form a government. I think he acted out of naïve trust in the British and faintheartedness.

Ladies, the leaders of our enemy have sensed this weakness in some of our political leaders. They have used these persons as a shield, from behind which they shoot arrows of deceit and cunning. However, the British have failed to reckon with our weapon, the weapon that cannot fail to miss the target, one we have already employed, the lethal weapon of the boycott. Let us aim it again at the face of our enemy and swear not to let it drop until Saad returns and we achieve all our demands. Long live the boycott! Long live unity! Long live Saad and his companions! Long live total independence! Long live the will of Egyptian women![19]

For a good year Huda and the other Wafdist women kept up their political activities on all fronts.

1923 was a crucial year for Huda and other women. On the fourth anniversary of the day they had emerged from their harems and marched veiled in the streets, Huda led some of these same women in founding the Egyptian Feminist Union. She was elected president. Less than a fortnight later Egyptian women hailed a victory when Saad Zaghlul was released. In April the new constitution declared: 'All Egyptians are equal before the law. They enjoy equally civil and political rights and are equally charged with public duties and responsibilities without destination of race, language, or religion.' The constitution was not the work of the Wafdists, who scorned the new government charged with writing it, but it seemed to augur well for women. Hope died, however, after just three weeks when the new electoral law granted suffrage to men only. Since the law was the work of the government both Wafdist women and men scorned, the Wafd could not be implicated. Soon after the women had left their seclusion for the arena of public political protest, male leaders of the Wafd had agreed to work for the liberation of women after independence, according to a conversation recorded in Saad Zaghlul's diary.[20] They had yet to show their hand.

In May, Huda led a delegation of three from the Egyptian Feminist Union to a meeting of the International Alliance of Women in Rome. Just going to the meeting was itself a victory for Huda, as well as for Saiza Nabarawi, a young woman in her twenties, the daughter of a late friend of Huda (Adila Nabarawi recalled earlier in the memoirs), and Nabawiyya Musa, a teacher from Alexandria. Three years earlier Huda had formed a delegation from the Wafdist Women's Central Committee to attend the

Alliance meeting in Geneva but the women were prevented by their husbands from going. While some might argue that times were better in 1923, it is worth noting that the new delegation was composed of a widow and two single women. It was upon their return from this feminist conference that Huda and Saiza took off their veils in the dramatic incident recounted in the beginning of the Introduction.

Huda refused to sacrifice women's liberation for male political purposes. An episode in the summer of 1923 is telling: she was sailing to Egypt on the same boat that carried Saad Zaghlul, accompanied by his wife, home from exile. Huda's veil now simply covered her head; her face was free. Observing this, Saad asked Huda to help his wife arrange her veil the same way. At Alexandria, Safiyya Zaghlul stood ready to disembark with her face uncovered. When men of the Wafd came aboard to welcome the returning hero and saw Safiyya they said the people would never accept it. She left the boat veiled. Huda, the president of the Wafdist women's Central Committee, left unveiled.[21]

The Wafdt came to power in January 1924. They had gained an overwhelming majority in the Chamber of Deputies and soon after Zaghlul formed a government. The inauguration of Parliament was a landmark and a celebration of national achievement. However, women were barred from the occasion, except as wives of ministers and other high officials. At that moment they had either to go forward or backwards. The day Parliament opened the women were at the gates with pickets. The Wafdist Women's Central Committee and the Egyptian Feminist Union had written nationalist and feminist demands on placards which young girls from the workshops of the Society of the New Women paraded back and forth. The two women's organizations printed a list of thirty-two nationalist and feminist demands and distributed them to Members of Parliament and government officials.

Nevertheless, it was Huda's radical nationalism, not her feminism, which led to her separation from the Wafd. In 1924 the central issue in the relations between Egypt and Britain was the Sudan which had been one of the four Reserved Points in the declaration of independence. Since the late nineteenth century the Sudan had been under the joint rule of the Anglo-Egyptian Condominium but now Britain wished to remove Egypt. The Wafdist government was conciliatory but the Wafdist women adamantly opposed it and called for another anti-British boycott. Six days later on the anniversary of the founding of the Wafd, Huda, the president of the Wafdist Women's Central Committee, was not invited to attend. She protested to Zaghlul, who replied with a face-saving excuse and an apology. Huda had been given a signal and a second chance to march in line with the male Wafd leadership.

Within a week the British sirdar of the Egyptian army and governor-general of the Sudan was killed in Cairo. The British issued a stinging seven-point ultimatum to Egypt. The Women's Boycott Committee telegrammed Zaghlul to refuse the ultimatum. The Egyptian government, however, accepted the first four points requiring an apology, suppression of political demonstrations, a fine and criminal investigation. Huda communicated her disapproval to Zaghlul. In an open letter to the newspaper,

Al-Akhbar, she said: 'Since you have failed while in public office to fulfil your mandate by positive action, I ask you not to be an obstacle in your country's struggle for liberation ... I ask you to step down.'[22]

Afterwards Huda resigned as president of the Wafdist Women's Central Committee. From that moment she continued her nationalist activity within the framework of the Egyptian Feminist Union. A final passage in her memoirs captures her sentiments.

> Exceptional women appear at certain moments in history and are moved by special forces. Men view these women as supernatural beings and their deeds as miracles. Indeed, women are bright stars whose light penetrates dark clouds. They rise in times of trouble when the wills of men are tried. In moments of danger, when women emerge by their side, men utter no protest. Yet women's great acts and endless sacrifices do not change men's views of women. Through their arrogance, men refuse to see the capabilities of women. Faced with contradiction, they prefer to raise women above the ordinary human plane instead of placing them on a level equal to their own. Men have singled out women of

FIGURE 19.9   Delegates Saiza and Huda, at Rome, 1923.

outstanding merit and put them on a pedestal to avoid recognizing the capabilities of all women. Women have felt this in their souls. Their dignity and self-esteem have been deeply touched. Women reflected on how they might elevate their status and worth in the eyes of men. They decided that the path lay in participating with men in public affairs. When they saw the way blocked, women rose up to demand their liberation, claiming their social, economic, and political rights. Their leap forward was greeted with ridicule and blame, but that did not weaken their will. Their resolve led to a struggle that would have ended in war, if men had not come to acknowledge the rights of women.

From 1923 until her death at sixty-eight in 1947, Huda Shaarawi led a feminist movement in Egypt. All but one of the other ten initial members of the Egyptian Feminist

FIGURE 19.10   Girls from 'The New Women Society' demanding women's rights at the opening of the New Egyptian Parliament in 1924.

Union were women from the world of the upper-class harem.

The transition of Huda and other feminist pioneers was fraught with contradictions. While active in feminist and nationalist politics and participating in international feminist meetings abroad, the women in their everyday life continued to face restrictions. Removing the veil signalled the end of the harem system but the actual process was piecemeal, slow and painstaking. Old conventions had to be overcome by individual acts rather than formal demands. Saiza Nabarawi, the editor of *L'Egyptienne (The Egyptian Woman),* the journal of the Feminist Union, told me some stories about breaking with precedent such as the time Huda and she attended their first party where men were present (the other women were all foreigners). It occurred at the Legation of the United States. Egyptian men showed surprise but nothing more serious resulted.

The same year (1925), Huda helped start the Club of the Women's Union, a cultural centre for upper-class women and a successor to the Intellectual Association of Egyptian Women which she had also helped create a decade earlier. Later Huda, remarking to women about the distance they had come, told them how she and the other women had flaunted convention when they acquired premises for the first association. It had been unheard of in 1914 for women to have a meeting place outside the privacy of the harem. She went on to say that they did not dare call the first association a *club* 'because our traditions would not have allowed it.'[23] The women had to know when to act but no to be too explicit about it. In the early 1930s, the Feminist Union moved into its imposing new headquarters in the centre of Cairo. It soon became known as 'The House of the Woman'. The Feminist Union wanted to carve this on the façade of the

FIGURE 19.11   Women meeting in Huda's house to plan for the boycott of British goods in 1924.

FIGURE 19.12   Huda at the door to her Cairo house wearing the *Nishan al-Kamal*, the highest state decoration of Egypt for services rendered to the country (taken in 1945, two years before her death).

building but public objection was so strong that the matter was dropped.[24] Stories like these reveal how difficult it was for women to put the harem years behind them.

But Huda would not be daunted. She was a powerful and charismatic leader. Before the end of the 1920s the Egyptian Feminist Union had, under her direction, grown to some two hundred and fifty members and had attracted middle-class as well as upper-class women. However, staunch activists with sustained commitment like Huda remained relatively few. Huda gave generously of her large fortune to finance the movement. The Feminist Union itself also raised money. The women's funds supported two monthly journals (in French and Arabic), a clinic and dispensary for poor women and children, craft workshops for poor girls, and childcare facilities for working mothers. Financial independence was essential to the longevity and success of the movement.

For Huda, who herself had been married at thirteen, a priority was to have a minimum marriage age set by law. This was achieved during the first year of the movement. The Feminist Union also fought for other changes in family law: within the framework of Islamic law they argued for such things as controls on men's easy access to divorce and a restriction of polygamy. There was no success on either front but their educational demands fared better. In 1924, the first secondary school for girls opened in Shubra (it produced some second-generation feminists) and before the decade had ended the first women had entered the Egyptian university. They were required to sit in the front row in class—a vestige of segregation.

In the 1930s, the feminists focused on work for women in the new textile factories and retail shops and in the expanding educational, health and legal professions. When young women working in Cairo pastry shops took complaints of exploitation directly to Huda herself, she pressured the Labour Office to hire a woman inspector to investigate women's working conditions. In the second half of the 1930s the feminists stepped up the campaign for women's suffrage. In France for a feminist meeting one summer, Huda and other Egyptian feminists even campaigned on behalf of French women who also lacked political rights. Huda also endeavoured to broaden the base of the feminist movement in the second half of the 1930s by reaching out to women in the rural areas. She tried to promote a branch of the Feminist Union in Minya but met with limited response from both local women and Cairo feminists. More successful was the new youth group of the Feminist Union which Hawa Idris headed.

Huda was known not only in Egypt and in the international feminist community—through ties with the International Alliance of Women of which she became a vice-president—but also in other Arab countries. In the late 1930s, when political crises mounted in Palestine, Arab women contacted Huda for help. She took political action and collected funds to send to Palestine. At the same time she organized a conference of Arab women in Cairo to deal with the Palestinian situation. The women's collective nationalist activity led to collective Arab feminism in a manner reminiscent of Egyptian women's earlier move from nationalist to feminist activism. Huda organized a second conference of Arab women in Cairo in 1944, where the women formed the Arab Feminist Union and elected Huda president.

Through her feminism Huda had taken charge of her life and had broken through barriers dividing gender and class upheld by the old harem system. Within the upper class, barriers between women and men had diminished and in the context of feminist struggle class boundaries between women lessened. Towards the end of her life, the state awarded Huda Shaarawi its highest decoration. Yet it withheld from her political rights. It was a symbol of the contradictions with which she and other women had to live.

NOTES

1   For a historian's account of the women's demonstration see Abd alRahman al-Rafii, *Thaura Sana 1919* (The 1919 Revolution), Cairo, 1946, 2 vols, vol. 1, pp. 137–40; for interviews fifty years later with women who participated in the events of 1919 see Naila Alluba, Muhammad Rifaat, et al., 'Thaura 1919 Rafaat al-Hijab wa alYashmak an Wajh al-Mara al-Misriyya' (The 1919 Revolution Lifted the Veil and Yashmak from the Face of the Egyptian Woman), *al-Musawwar*, 7 March 1969.

2   Everything by Huda Shaarawi, unless otherwise indicated, comes from her memoirs.

3   Wagida Khulusi became a founding member of the Egyptian Feminist Union.

4   Regina Khayyat was also a founder of the Egyptian Feminist Union.

5   Thomas Russell, Egyptian Service, London, 1949, pp. 46–7.

6   The next women's demonstration took place on 20 March 1919, see al-Rafii, op. cit., pp. 194–5.

7   Letter from Thomas Russell to his father, est. date, 1 April 1919, in Russell Papers, Middle East Centre, St Antony's College, Oxford.

8   For an account of the funeral of the 28-year-old widow whose coffin was wrapped in the Egyptian flag, see Ahmad Shafiq, Hauliyyat Misr al-Siyasiyya (Political Chronicles of Egypt), Cairo, 1926, 1st ed., vol. 1, pp. 260,-1.

9   Milner Papers at New College, Oxford, Box 164, vol. 12(c), no. 12, communication, 12/12/19 from Women of Egypt, St Mark's Cathedral and no. 56, communication 8/1/20 from Ladies Committee of Egyptian Delegation, St Mark's Cathedral.

10 According to Saad Zaghlul's secretary, the idea to form the Wafdist Women's Central Committee was Zaghlul's but he himself never makes this claim; see Muhammad Ibrahim al-Jaziri, Saad Zaghlul: Dhikriyyat Tarikhiyya Tarifa (Saad Zaghlul: Interesting Historical Memoirs), Cairo, n.d., pp. 207–8.

11 For other reactions see Afaf Lutfi al-Sayyid Marsot, Egypt's Liberal Experiment 1922–1936, Berkeley, 1977, p. 53, who says, 'Public reaction was distinctly cool ...'; and Jacques Berque, Egypt: Imperialism and Revolution, trans. J. Stewart, London, 1972, who relates, 'Lawyers first: these supported the Wafd's attitude. The Legislative Council accepted almost unanimously. Religious and spiritual leaders also approved, with only a few reservations. Members of the judiciary, of provincial councils, of municipal authorities all gave their support; only the Watani party dissented, pointing out the all too real risk of a swindle ... ,'p. 320.

12 Safiyya Hanim, the wife of Saad Zaghlul was born in 1876 in Cairo. Her father, Mustafa Pasha Fahrni, was three times prime minister. She was raised in an upper-class harem, given an education at home and in 1896 at the age of twenty, old for the times, married Saad Zaghlul, a talented middle-class lawyer at the National Court of Appeals. Safiyya devoted herself totally to her husband's career. During periods of his exile, when not sharing it with him, she stood in as his surrogate in Egypt. For more about her, see Fina Gued Vidal, Safia Zaghlul, Cairo, n.d.

13 Huda Shaarawi to Allenby, High Commissioner, 25 December 1921, Political Views and Activities of Egyptian Women, Consular and Embassy Archives File 14083, Foreign Office 141, Box 511, Public Records Office, London.

14 According to the private papers of Huda Shaarawi, she herself bought 250 shares. Her brother, Umar Sultan, had been among those who had helped capitalize the bank at its foundation. See Eric Davis, *Challenging Colonialism: Bank Misr and Egyptian Industrialization, 1920–1941*, Princeton, 1983.

15 'Decision of the Women's Central Committee of the Delegation', Cairo, 7 February 1922 (meeting held on 3 February 1922), Political Views and Activities of Egyptian Women, Consular and Embassy Archives, File 14083, Foreign Office 141, Box 511, Public Records Office, London.

16 Among the women's associations were the Society of the New Woman, the Society of the Renaissance of the Egyptian Woman, and the Society of Mothers of the Future in Cairo, and the Women's Union of Minya, the Women's Union in Asyut, and the Society of Union and Progress in Tanta.

17 Letter from Wasif Ghali on behalf of the Egyptian Wafd to Huda Shaarawi in Majmuaa al-Khutab Alati Ulqiyat fi Ijtima al-Sayyidat al Misriyyat bi Dar al-Marhum Husain Basha Abu Usha Yaum al-Jumaa 5 Mayu 1922 (Collection of speeches given at the Egyptian women's meeting at the house of the late Husain Pasha Abu Usha on Friday, 5 May 1922), pp. 27–8. Muhammad Ibrahim al-Jaziri, op. cit., pp. 103–6.

18 Safiyya Zaghlul issued communiques to the public to help keep the nationalist cause alive. She also kept attention focused on her husband as the leader of the nationalist struggle. She had a great appeal among Egyptians who called her Umm al-Masriyyin (colloquial transliteration), Mother of Egyptians. Louise Majorelle Ghali, the French wife of Wafdist leader, Wasif Ghali, was among the women active in maintaining communications with the exiled Wafdists who included her husband. Documents in the Ghali family private papers were made available to me by Mirit Ghali.

19 Speech of the president in Majmuaa al-khutab ... (see note 17), pp. 6–10.

20 Saad Zaghlul, Mudhakirrat (Memoirs), National Archives, the Citadel, Cairo, notebook 39 (9 June 1920–7 June 1921), entry for 24 November 1920, p. 2380. Reference provided by Abd al-Khaliq Lashin.

21 Personal communication by Saiza Nabarawi.

22 Al-Akhbar, 24 November 1924.

23 Huda Shaarawi, 'Kalima al-Sayyida al-Jalila Huda Hanim Shaarawi,' (The lecture of her excellency, Huda Shaarawi) al-Misriyya, 15 February 1937, p. 13.

24 Personal communication from Saiza Nabarawi, Cairo, 13 March 1972; Myriam Harrey, 'La femme orientale et son destin: l'Egyptienne,' *Journal de la femme*, Paris, 21 July 1934 (interview with Saiza Nabarawi).

READING 20

Lola Landau, *The Companionate Marriage* (1929).

Lola Landau (1892–1990) was a German writer. In this article from a magazine aimed at educated, middle-class readers, she advocates social reformer Ben Lindsey's (1927) vision of companionate marriage.

The Companionate Marriage

Lola Landau

Marriage, as the cell of collective life, has always possessed a social significance that raises it far above the happiness of two individuals or the purely expedient consideration of protecting the interests of descendants. That is how marriage as a model in miniature of human community acquired its ethical idea. It became the primal basis of the larger cellular structure and the source of fruitful and constructive forces.

[. . .]

By the end of the previous century the bourgeois marriage had evolved into an economic institution; the family had become a small trust with the earnings and operation of capital. The magnetic attraction of monetary accumulation, however, led increasingly to marriage for money, which suppressed its original sense of ethical community.

While a hypocritical social morality artificially maintained the old forms and symbols, they had long since rigidified into dead formulas. Venerable words like fidelity, home, and family lost their incantatory power since their content had become merely apparent. Meanwhile, however, the elemental life force of youth pressed onward under the thin veneer of convention, rooting out new paths for itself. Unnoticed, a mighty revolution in ways of life had already been completed in reality when people first began to discuss openly the crisis in marriage.

At the center of these fermenting forces is the woman of our day. As an autonomous person economically and intellectually independent from the man, the new woman shattered the old morality. The compulsory celibacy of the young woman and the indissolubility of marriage were invalidated by the straightforward reality of life. The independent woman of today, just as much as the man, assumes for herself the right to a love life before marriage, the more so since marital togetherness for the woman can signify nothing but a faint future possibility given the current numerical deficiency of men.

In this way, the psychological attitude of women toward marriage changed fundamentally. Women no longer wait for marriage, frequently not even desiring such a tie for themselves, which they fear might hinder their free development. While in previous times the life of a young woman was little more than a period of preparation for marriage, which she then took on as a full-time occupation, the woman of today is scarcely capable of accepting marriage as her life's work. Back then household activities and the never-ending work of motherhood taxed a woman's energies to the utmost. Today there is some relief to be had in the private household from modern conveniences, and birth control, a matter of utter economic necessity, either shelters women from motherhood or interrupts it with long breaks. Certainly, by being able to prevent conception, the woman has escaped from the slavery of her own body; but at the same time she is deprived of the elemental happiness of fulfilled tranquility. The woman—whose natural maternal energies, through no fault of her own, have to lay fallow today, who, just like the man is forced at an early age into the work-a-day grind—searches for a substitute experience of her vitality and finds it in fruitful employment, usually outside the home. The occupational independence thus gained signifies as well a looser psychological tie to the man. The home is no longer the fortified garden of profound and happy rest. Family life is also subject to the effects of the transformation; it is already being replaced, in part, by the self-tutelage of the young, by group life that takes the children out of their parents' house.

Who would want to deny that this reorganization unsettles certain essential emotional values, that it silences a kind of gentle atmospheric music! But development marches to a relentless beat. No wishful romanticism can force woman back to her earlier way of being. The bourgeois woman has also become a worker. Her face, too, is chiseled by the hard mechanism of our time; she too is subject to the depersonalization and leveling of our age. And she too will slowly have to assume the shape of the new female personality in order to stand beside the man as an equal and complementary companion.

If, however, the man of today continues to seek the woman of yesterday, his creature, the pliant helpmate, he will be bitterly disappointed not to find her anymore.

Marriage and its value as the cell of community is threatened with crisis. For new ideas of marriage have not yet caught on. What is permitted today? Nearly everything. But what is truly good? What is bad? The warning signals of inhibition no longer function. Everywhere, however, one notes the confusion, the aimlessness, a tortured seeking, and in between, the impotent smile of flippancy.

In his book, *Companionate Marriage,* Ben Lindsey, the American juvenile-court judge, has attempted to save marriage from this chaos by lending it a new form. As impossible as it is simply to transpose his reform proposals into our European conditions, he nevertheless offers fruitful suggestions from his socially critical point of view. Lindsey would like to introduce, alongside permanent marriage, the companionate marriage as a second legal form of marriage. Companionate marriage in his sense denotes the lawful tie between two young people who, in the first years, use birth control to avoid having children, so that they can check carefully whether their respective characters will match harmoniously in the long run.

If the first rush of love has passed and the young people have been disappointed in their expectations, then the companionate marriage can be dissolved quite easily. All that is required for divorce is a simple, mutual agreement. Nor is there any obligation of support, since they have no responsibility for children and the wife has continued in her occupation. If, however, the two people live happily with each other, then after a certain trial period they can change their companionate marriage into a family marriage and fulfill their desires for children.

[. . .]

The marriage of the future will perhaps be the companionate marriage, but in a much broader sense than Lindsey's. It will mean not only a childless trial marriage for young people but the ever-maturing challenge to live a full life. It will reestablish in another form its original idea of community and grow into a fruitful cell in the overall cellular state. It will unite the woman, with her informed views and matured heart, to the man as a comrade, and two free personalities will march along the same path toward a great goal, allowing the uniform beat of their steps to blend into a single rhythm.

READING 21

Vicki Ruiz, "The Flapper and the Chaperone," in *From Out of the Shadows: Mexican Women in Twentieth Century America* (Oxford University Press, 1998), 12–26.

In this excerpt, historian Vicki Ruiz describes early twentieth-century generational tensions among Latina women in the United States as they navigated between traditional expectations for women and new ideals of the new woman and the flapper.

The Flapper and the Chaperone

Vicki L. Ruiz

I n grappling with Mexican-American women's consciousness and agency, oral history offers avenue for exploring teenage expectations and preserving a historical memory of attitudes and feelings. In addition to archival research, the recollections of seventeen women serve as the basis for my reconstruction of adolescent aspirations and experiences (or dreams and routines).[1] The women themselves are fairly homogeneous in terms of nativity, class, residence, and family structure. With two exceptions, they are U.S. citizens by birth and attended southwestern schools. All the interviewees were born between 1908 and 1926.[2] Although three came from families once considered middle class in Mexico, most can be considered working class in the United States. Their fathers' typical occupations included farm worker, miner, day laborer, and railroad hand. These women usually characterized their mothers as homemakers, although several remembered that their mothers took seasonal jobs in area factories and fields. The most economically privileged woman in the sample, Ruby Estrada, helped out in her family-owned hardware and furniture store. She is also the only interviewee who attended college.[3] It should be noted that seven of the seventeen narrators married Euro-Americans. Although intermarriage was uncommon, these oral histories give us insight into the lives of those who negotiated across cultures in a deeply personal way and who felt the impact of acculturation most keenly. Rich in emotion and detail, these interviews reveal women's conscious decision-making in the production of culture. In creating their own cultural spaces, the interwar generation challenged the trappings of familial oligarchy.

Chicano social scientists have generally portrayed women as "the 'glue' that keeps the Chicano family together" as well as the guardians of traditional culture.[4] Whether one accepts this premise or not, within families, young women, perhaps more than their brothers, were

Vicki L. Ruiz, "Selection from "The Flapper and the Chaperone"," *Seeking Common Ground: Multidisciplinary Studies of Immigrant Women in the United States*, pp. 141-157, 189-194. Copyright © 1992 by ABC-CLIO. Reprinted with permission.

expected to uphold certain standards. Parents, therefore, often assumed what they perceived as their unquestionable prerogative to regulate the actions and attitudes of their adolescent daughters. Teenagers, on the other hand, did not always acquiesce in the boundaries set down for them by their elders. Intergenerational tension flared along several fronts.

Like U.S. teenagers, in general, the first area of disagreement between an adolescent and her family would be over her personal appearance. As reflected in F. Scott Fitzgerald's "Bernice Bobs Her Hair," the length of a young woman's tresses was a hot issue spanning class, region, and ethnic lines. During the 1920s, a woman's decision "to bob or not bob" her hair assumed classic proportions within Mexican families. After considerable pleading, Belen Martinez Mason was permitted to cut her hair, though she soon regretted the decision. "Oh, I cried for a month."[5] Differing opinions over fashions often caused ill feelings. One Mexican American woman recalled that as a young girl, her mother dressed her "like a nun" and she could wear "no make-up, no cream, no nothing" on her face. Swimwear, bloomers, and short skirts also became sources of controversy. Some teenagers left home in one outfit and changed into another at school. Once Maria Fierro arrived home in her bloomers. Her father inquired, "Where have you been dressed like that, like a clown?" "I told him the truth," Fierro explained "He whipped me anyway.... So from then on whenever I went to the track meet, I used to change my bloomers so that he wouldn't see that I had gone again."[6] The impact of flapper styles on the Mexican community was clearly expressed in the following verse taken from a corrido appropriately entitled "Las Pelonas" [The BobbedHaired Girls]:

Red Banannas [sic]

I detest,

And now the flappers

Use them for their dress.

The girls of San Antonio

Are lazy at the *metate*.

They want to walk out bobbed-haired,

With straw hats on.

The harvesting is finished,

So is the cotton;

The flappers stroll out now

For a good time.[7]

With similar sarcasm, another popular ballad chastised Mexican women for apply-ing makeup so heavily as to resemble a piñata.[8]

The use of cosmetics, however, cannot be blamed entirely on Madison Avenue ad campaigns. The innumerable barrio beauty pageants, sponsored by *mutualistas*, patriotic societies, churches, the Mexican Chamber of Commerce, newspapers, and even progressive labor unions, encouraged young women to accentuate their physi-cal attributes. Carefully chaperoned, many teenagers did participate in community contests from La Reina de Cinco de Mayo to Orange Queen. They modeled evening gowns, rode on parade floats, and sold raffle tickets.[9] Carmen Bernal Escobar remem-bered one incident where, as a contestant, she had to sell raffle tickets. Every ticket she sold counted as a vote for her in the pageant. Naturally the winner would be the woman who had accumulated the most votes. When her brother offered to buy $25 worth of votes [her mother would not think of letting her peddle the tickets at work or in the neighborhood], Escobar, on a pragmatic note, asked him to give her the money so that she could buy a coat she had spotted while window-shopping.[10]

The commercialization of personal grooming made additional inroads into the Mexican community with the appearance of barrio beauty parlors, Working as a beautician conferred a certain degree of status—"a nice, clean job"—in comparison to factory or domestic work. As one woman related:

> I always wanted to be a beauty operator. I loved makeup; I loved to dress up and fix up. I used to set my sisters' hair. So I had that in the back of my mind for a long time, and my mom pushed the fact that she wanted me to have a profession—seeing that I wasn't thinking of getting married.[11]

While further research is needed, one can speculate that neighborhood beauty shops reinforced women's networks and became places where they could relax, exchange *chimse* (gossip), and enjoy the company of other women.

During the 1920s, the ethic of consumption became inextricably linked to making it in America.[12] The message of affluence attainable through hard work and a bit of luck was reinforced in English and Spanish-language publications. Mexican barrios were not immune from the burgeoning consumer culture. The society pages of the influential Los Angeles-based *La Opinion,* for example, featured advice columns, horoscopes, and celebrity gossip. Advertisements for makeup, clothing, even femi-nine hygiene products reminded teenagers of an awaiting world of consumption.[13] One week after its inaugural issue in 1926, *La Opinion* featured a Spanish translation of Louella Parsons' nationally syndicated gossip column. Advertisements not only hawked products but offered instructions for behavior. As historian Roberto Trevino related in his recent study of Tejano newspapers, "The point remains that the Spanish-language press conveyed symbolic American norms and models to a potentially assimilable readership."[14]

Advertisements aimed at women promised status and affection if the proper bleaching cream, hair coloring, and cosmetics were purchased. Or, as one company boldly claimed, "Those with lighter, more healthy skin tones will become much more successful in business love, and society."[15] A print ad [in English] for Camay Soap carried by *Hispano America* in 1932 reminded women readers that "Life Is a Beauty Contest."[16] Flapper fashions and celebrity testimonials further fused the connections between gendered identity and consumer culture. Another promotion encouraged readers to "SIGA LAS ESTRELLAS" (FOLLOW THE STARS) and use Max Factor cosmetics. It is important to keep in mind that Spanish-language newspapers filtered to their readers not only the iconography of U.S. popular culture, but also their perceptions of gender relations within that culture. For example, an advertisement for Godefroy's "Larieuse" hair coloring featured an attractive woman in profile smiling at the tiny man cupped in the palm of her hand. The diminutive male figure is shown on bended knee with his hands outstretched in total adoration. Does this hair coloring promotion found in the February 8, 1938, issue of *La Opinion* relay the impression that by using this Anglo product Mexican women will exert the same degree of power over their men as their Anglo peers supposedly plied?[17]

These visual representations raise all sorts of speculation as to their meaning, specifically with regard to the social construction of gender. I cannot identify the designers of these layouts, but the architects are less important than the subtle and not-so-subtle messages codified within their text. Mexican women interpreted these visual representations in a myriad of ways. Some ignored them, some redefined their messages, and other internalized them. The popularity of bleaching creams offers a poignant testament to color consciousness in Mexican communities, a historical consciousness accentuated by Americanization through education and popular culture.[18]

Reflecting the coalescence of Mexican and U.S. cultures, Spanish-language publications promoted pride in Latino theater and music while at the same time celebrated the icons of Americanization and consumption. Because of its proximity to Hollywood, *La Opinion* ran contests in which the lucky winner would receive a screen test. On the one hand, *La Opinion* nurtured the dreams of "success" through entertainment and consumption while, on the other, the newspaper railed against the deportations and repatriations of the 1930s.[19] Sparked by manufactured fantasies and clinging to youthful hopes, many Mexican women teenagers avidly read celebrity gossip columns, attended Saturday matinees, cruised Hollywood and Vine, and nurtured their visions of stardom. A handful of Latina actresses, especially Dolores del Rio and Lupe Velez, whetted these aspirations and served as public role models of the "American dream." As a *La Opinión* article on Lupe Vele idealistically claimed, "Art has neither nationalities nor borders."[20]

In her essay "City Lights: Immigrant Women and the Rise of the Movies," Elizabeth Ewen has argued that during the early decades of the twentieth century, "The social authority of the media of mass culture replaced older forms of family authority and behavior." Ewen further explained that the "authority of this new culture organized itself around the premise of freedom from customary bonds as a way of turning peoples attention to the consumer market place as a source of self-definition."[21] Yet Mexican women had choices (though certainly circumscribed by economic considerations) about what elements to embrace and which to ignore. As Ceorge Lipsitz reminds us in *Time Passages,* "Hegemony is not just imposed on society from the top; it is struggled for from below, and no terrain is a more important part of that struggle than popular culture."[22] Mexican-American women teenagers also positioned themselves within the cultural messages they gleaned from English and Spanish-language publications, afternoon matinees, and popular radio programs. Their shifting conceptions of acceptable heterosocial behavior, including their desire "to date," heightened existing generational tensions between parents and daughters.[23]

Obviously, the most serious point of contention between an adolescent daughter and her Mexican parents regarded her behavior toward young men. In both cities and rural towns, close chaperonage was a way of life. Recalling the supervisory role played by her "old maid" aunt, Maria Fierro laughingly explained, "She'd check up on us all the time. I used to get so mad at her." Ruby Estrada recalled that in her small southern Arizona community, "all the mothers" escorted their daughters to the local dances. Estradas mother was no exception when it came to chaperoning her daughters. "She went especially for us. She'd just sit there and take care of our coats and watch us." Even talking to male peers in broad daylight could be grounds for discipline.[24] Adele Hernandez Milligan, a resident of Los Angeles for over fifty years, elaborated:

> I remember the first time that I walked home with a boy from school. Anyway, my mother saw me and she was mad. I must have been sixteen or seventeen. She slapped my face because I was walking home with a boy.[25]

Describing this familial protectiveness, one social scientist remarked that the "supervision of the Mexican parent is so strict as to be obnoxious."[26]

Faced with this type of situation, young women had three options: they could accept the rules set down for them; they could rebel; or they could find ways to compromise or circumvent traditional standards. "I was *never* allowed to go out by myself in the evening; it just was not done," related Carmen Bernal Escobar. In rural communities, where restrictions were perhaps even more stringent, "nice" teenagers could not even swim with male peers. According to Ruby Estrada, "We were ladies and wouldn't go swimming out there with a bunch of boys." Yet many seemed to accept these limits with equanimity. Remembering her mother as her chaperone, Lucy Acosta insisted, "I could care less as long I danced." "It wasn't devastating at all," echoed Ruby Estrada. "We took it in stride. We never thought of it as cruel or mean.... It was taken for granted that that's the way it was."[27] In Sonora, Arizona, like other small towns, relatives and neighbors kept close watch over adolescent women and quickly reported any suspected indiscretions. "They were always spying on you," Estrada remarked. Women in cities had a distinct advantage over their rural peers in that they could venture miles from their neighborhood into the anonymity of dance halls, amusement parks, and other forms of commercialized leisure. With carnival rides and the Cinderella Ballroom, the Nu-Pike amusement park of Long Beach proved a popular hangout for Mexican youth in Los Angeles.[28] It was more difficult to abide by traditional norms when excitement loomed just on the other side of the streetcar line.

Some women openly rebelled. They moved out of their family homes and into apartments. Considering themselves freewheeling single women, they could go out with men unsupervised as was the practice among their Anglo peers. Others challenged parental and cultural standards even further by living with their boyfriends. In his field notes, University of California economist Paul Taylor recorded an incident in which a young woman had moved in with her Anglo boyfriend after he had convinced her that such arrangements were common among Americans. "This terrible freedom in the United States," one Mexicana lamented. "I do not have to worry because I have no daughters, but the poor *señoras* with many girls, they worry."[29]

Those teenagers who did not wish to defy their parents openly would "sneak out" of the house to meet their dates or attend dances with female friends. Whether meeting someone at a drugstore, roller rink, or theater, this practice involved the invention of elaborate stories to mask traditionally inappropriate behavior.[30] In other words, they lied. In his study of Tuscon's Mexican community, Thomas Sheridan related the following saga of Jacinta Pérez de Valdez:

> As she and her sisters grew older, they used to sneak out of the house to go to the Riverside Ball Room. One time a friend of their father saw them there and said, "Listen, Felipe, don't you know your daughters are hanging around the Riverside?" Furious, their father threw a coat over his longjohns and stormed into the dance hall, not even stopping to tie his shoes.... Doña Jacinta recalled. "He entered by one door and we left by another. We had to walk hack home along the railroad tracks in our high heels. I think we left those heels on the rails." She added that when their father returned, "We were all lying in bed like little angels."[31]

A more subtle form of rebellion was early marriage. By marrying at fifteen or sixteen, these women sought to escape parental supervision; yet it could be argued that, for many of these child brides, they exchanged one form of supervision for another in addition to the responsibilities of child-rearing.[32] In her 1933 ethnography, Clara Smith related the gripping testimony of one teenage bride:

> You see, my father and mother wouldn't let us get married.... Mother made me stay with her all the time. She always goes to church every morning at seven-thirty as she did in Mexico. I said I was sick. She went with my brothers and we just ran away and got married at the court.... They were strict with my sister, too. That's why she took poison and died."[33]

One can only speculate on the psychic pressures and external circumstances that would drive a young woman to take her own life.

Elopement occurred frequently since many parents believed that no one was good enough for their daughters. "I didn't want to elope ... so this was the next best thing to a wedding," recalled María Ybarra as she described how the justice of the peace performed the ceremony in her parents' home. "Neither my Dad or my Mom liked my husband. Nobody liked him," she continued. "My husband used to run around a lot. After we got married, he did settle down, but my parents didn't know that then."[34] One fifteen year old locked her grandmother in the outhouse so she could elope with her boyfriend. Indeed, when he first approached her at a San Joaquin Valley migrant camp asking if he could be her *novio,* she supposedly replied, "No, but I'll marry you." Lupe was just that desperate to escape familial supervision.[35]

If acquiescence, apartment living, early marriage, or elopement were out of the question, what other tactics did teenagers devise? The third alternative sometimes involved quite a bit of creativity on the part of young women as they sought to circumvent traditional chaperonage. Alicia Mendeola Shelit recalled that one of her older brothers would accompany her to dances ostensibly as a chaperone. "But then my oldest brother would always have a blind date for me." Carmen Bernal Escobar was permitted to entertain her boyfriends at home, but only under the supervision of her brother or mother. The practice of "going out with the girls," though not accepted until the 1940s, was fairly common. Several Mexican-American women, often related, would escort one another to an event (such as a dance), socialize with the men in attendance, and then walk home together. In the sample of seventeen interviews, daughters negotiated their activities with their parents. Older siblings and extended kin appeared in the background as either chaperones or accomplices. Although unwed teenage mothers were not unknown in Mexican barrios, families expected adolescent women to conform to strict standards of behavior.[36]

As can be expected, many teenage women knew little about sex other than what they picked up from friends, romance magazines, and the local theater. As Mary Luna remembered, "I thought that if somebody kissed you, you could get pregnant." In *Singing for My Echo,* New Mexico native Gregorita Rodríguez confided that on her wedding night, she knelt down and said her rosary until her husband gently asked, "Gregorita, *mi esposa,* are you afraid of me?" At times this naiveté persisted beyond the wedding. "It took four days for my husband to touch me," one woman revealed. "I slept with dress and all. We were both greenhorns, I guess."[37]

Of course, some young women did lead more adventurous lives. A male interviewer employed by Mexican anthropologist Manuel Gamio recalled his "relations" with a woman met at a Los Angeles dance hall. Although born in Hermosillo, Elisa "Elsie" Morales considered herself Spanish. She helped support her family by dancing with strangers. Even though she lived at home and her mother and brother attempted to monitor her actions, she managed to meet the interviewer at a "hot pillow" hotel. To prevent pregnancy, she relied on contraceptive douches provided by "an American doctor." Although Morales realized her mother would not approve of her behavior, she noted that "she [her mother] is from Mexico ... I am from there also but I was brought up in the United States, we think about things differently." Just as Morales rationalized her actions as "American," the interviewer perceived her within a similar, though certainly less favorable, definition of Americanization. "She seemed very coarse to me. That is, she dealt with one in the American way." Popular corridos, such as "El Enganchado" and "Las Pelonas," also touched on the theme of the corrupting influence of U.S. ways on Mexican women.[38] If there were rewards for women who escaped parental boundaries, there were also sanctions for those who crossed established lines.[39]

Women who had children out of wedlock seemed to be treated by their parents in one of two ways—as pariahs or prodigal daughters. Erminia Ruiz recalled the experiences of two girlhood friends:

> It was a disgrace to the whole family. The whole family suffered and ... her mother said she didn't want her home. She could not bring the baby home and she was not welcome at home.... She had no place to go.... And then I had another friend. She was also pregnant and the mother actually went to court to try to get him to marry her.... He hurried and married someone else but then he had to give child support.[40]

In another instance, Carmen and her baby were accepted by her family. She was, however, expected to work in the fields to support her infant. Her parents kept a watchful eye on her activities. When Diego, a young Mexicano immigrant, asked Carmen out to dinner, her baby became her chaperone. "[My mother] said to take the baby with you. She was so smart so I wouldn't go any farther than the restaurant. At first, I was ashamed but [he] said, "Bring him so he can eat." Before Carmen accepted Diego's proposal of marriage, she asked him for his family's address in Mexico so she could make sure he was not already married. "I told him I wouldn't answer him until I got an answer." Diego's mother replied that her son was single, but had a girlfriend waiting for him. Carmen and Diego have been married for over fifty years.[41]

Carmen's story illustrates the resiliency and resourcefulness of Mexican-American women. Her behavior during her courtship with Diego demonstrates shrewdness and independence. Once burned, she would be nobody's *pendeja* (fool).

Yet autonomy on the part of young women was hard to win in a world where pregnant, unmarried teenagers served as community "examples" of what might happen to you or your daughter if appropriate measures were not taken. As an elderly Mexicana remarked, "Your reputation was everything."[42] In this sense, the chaperone not only protected the young woman's position in the community, but that of the entire family.

Chaperonage thus exacerbated conflict not only between generations but within individuals as well. In gaily recounting tales of ditching the *dueña* or sneaking down the stairwell, the laughter of the interviewees fails to hide the painful memories of breaking away from familial expectations. Their words resonate with the dilemma of reconciling their search for autonomy with their desire for parental affirmation.

It is important to note that every informant who challenged or circumvented chaperonage held a fulltime job, as either a factory or service worker. In contrast, most woman who accepted constant supervision did not work for wages. Perhaps because they labored for long hours, for little pay, and frequently under hazardous conditions, factory and service workers were determined to exercise some control over their leisure time. Indeed, Douglas Monroy has argued that outside employment "facilitated greater freedom of activity and more assertiveness in the family for Mexicanas."[43]

It may also be significant that none of the employed teenagers had attended high school. They entered the labor market directly after or even before the completion of the eighth grade. Like many female factory workers in the United States, most Mexican operatives were young, unmarried daughters whose wage labor was essential to the economic survival of their families. As members of a "family wage economy," they relinquished all or part of their wages to their elders, According to a 1933 University of California study, of the Mexican families surveyed with working children, the children's monetary contributions constituted 35 percent of total household income.[44] Cognizant of their earning power, they resented the lack of personal autonomy.

Delicate negotiations ensued as both parents and daughters struggled over questions of leisure activities and discretionary income. Could a young woman retain a portion of her wages for her own use? If elders demanded every penny, daughters might be more inclined to splurge on a new outfit or other personal item on their way home from work or, even more extreme, they might choose to move out, taking their paychecks with them. Recognizing their dependence on their children's income, some parents compromised. Their concessions, however, generally took the form of allocating spending money rather than relaxing traditional supervision. Still, women's earning power could be an important bargaining chip.[45]

On one level, many teenagers were devoted to their parents as evident (at least, in part) by their employment in hazardous, low-paying jobs, For example, Julia Luna Mount recalled her first day at a Los Angeles cannery:

> I didn't have money for gloves so I peeled chiles all day long by hand. After work, my hands were red, swollen, and I was on fire! On the streetcar going home, I could hardly hold on my hands hurt so much. The minute I got home, I soaked my hands in a pan of cold water. My father saw how I was suffering and he said, *"Mi hija,* you don't have to go back there tomorrow," and I didn't.[46]

On the other hand, adolescents rebelled against what they perceived as an embarrassingly old-fashioned intrusion into their private lives. When chastised by her aunt for dancing too close to her partner, Alma Araiza García would retort, "I am not going to get pregnant just by leaning on his cheek, okay?"[47] They wanted the right to choose their own companions and to use their own judgment.

Chaperonage triggered deep-seated tensions over autonomy and self-determination. "Whose life is it anyway?" was a recurring question with no satisfactory answer. Many women wanted their parents to consider them dutiful daughters, but they also desired degrees of freedom. While ethnographies provide scintillating tales of teenage rebellion, the voices of the interviewees do not. Their stories reflect the experiences of those adolescents who struggled with boundaries. How can one retain one's "good name" while experiencing the joys of youth? How can one be both a good daughter and an independent woman?

To complete the picture, we also have to consider the perspective of Mexican immigrant parents who encountered a youth culture very different from that of their generation. For them, courtship had occurred in the plaza; young women and men promenaded under the watchful eyes of town elders, an atmosphere in which an exchange of meaningful glances could well portend engagement. One can understand their consternation as they watched their daughters apply cosmetics and adopt the apparel advertised in fashion magazines. In other words, "If she dresses like a flapper, will she then act like one?" Seeds of suspicion reaffirmed the penchant for traditional supervision.

Parents could not completely cloister their children from the temptations of "modern" society, but chaperonage provided a way of monitoring their activities. It was an attempt to mold young women into sheltered young matrons. But one cannot regard the presence of *la dueña* as simply an old world tradition on a collision course with twentieth-century life. The regulation of daughters involved more than a conflict between peasant ways and modern ideas. Chaperonage was both an actual and symbolic assertion of familial oligarchy. A family's reputation was linked to the purity' of women. As reiterated in a Catholic catechism, if a young woman became a "faded lily," she and her family would suffer dire consequences.[48] Since family honor rested, to some degree, on the preservation of female chastity (or *vergüenza*), women were to be controlled for the collective good, with older relatives assuming unquestioned responsibility in this regard. Mexican women coming of age during the 1920s and 1930s were not the first to challenge the authority of elders. Ramón Gutiérrez in his pathbreaking scholarship on colonial New Mexico uncovered numerous instances of women who tried to exercise some autonomy over their sexuality.[49] The Mexican-American generation, however, had a potent ally unavailable to their foremothers—consumer culture.

United States consumerism did not bring about the disintegration of familial oligarchy, but it did serve as a catalyst for change. The ideology of control was shaken by consumer culture and the heterosocial world of urban youth. As previously indicated, chaperonage proved much easier to enforce in a small town. Ruby Estrada described how a young woman would get the third degree if caught with a potential boyfriend alone. "And they [the elders] would say what are [you] doing there all alone.... Yeah, what were you up to or if you weren't up to no good, why should you be talking to that boy?"[50]

In contrast, parents in the barrios of major cities fought a losing battle against urban anonymity and commercialized leisure. The Catholic Church was quick to point out the "dangerous amusement" inherent in dancing, theater-going, dressing fashionably, and reading pulp fiction. Under the section, "The Enemy in the Ballroom," a Catholic advice book warned of the hidden temptations of dance. "I know that some persons can indulge in it without harm; but sometimes even the coldest temperaments are heated by it."[51] Therefore, the author offered the following rules:

> (1) If you know nothing at all … about dancing do not trouble yourself to learn (2) Be watchful … and see that your pleasure in dancing does not grow Into a passion… (3) Never frequent fairs, picnics, carnivals, or public dancing halls where Heaven only knows what sorts of people congregate. (4) Dance only at private parties where your father or mother is present.[52]

Pious pronouncements such as these had little impact on those adolescents who cherished the opportunity to look and act like vamps and flappers.

Attempting to regulate the social life of young parishioners, barrio priests organized gender-segregated teen groups. In Los Angeles, Juventud Católica Feminina Mexicana (JCFM) had over fifty chapters. In her autobiography *Hoyt Street,* Marry Helen Ponce remembered the group as one organized for "nice" girls with the navy blue uniform as its most appealing feature. The local chapter fell apart during World War II as young women rushed off to do their patriotic duly at "canteens," preferring to keep company with "lonely soldiers" than to sitting "in a stuffy church while an elderly priest espoused the virtues of a pure life." Too young for the USO, Ponce enjoyed going to *"las vistas,"* usually singing cowboy movies shown in the church hall after Sunday evening rosary.[53]

Priests endeavored to provide wholesome entertainment, showing films approved by the Legion of Decency. Movies in parish halls also served other purposes. The cut-rate features, like church *jamaicas,* raised money for local activities and offered a social space for parishioners. In an era of segregated theatres, church halls tendered an environment where Mexicanos and their children could enjoy inexpensive entertainment and sit wherever they pleased.[54] Even within the fishbowl of church-sponsored functions, romance could blossom. In Riverside, Frederico Buriel kept going to the movies held every Sunday night at Our Lady of Guadalupe Shrine so he could chat with the pretty ticket seller, Eusebia Vásque'z. Theirs, however, was not a teenage courtship. When they married, she was thirty-seven, he forty-three.[55]

Parents could also rely on Catholic practices in the home to test the mettle of prospective suitors. When Fermín Montiel came to call on Livia León in Rillito, Arizona, her parents instructed him to join them as they knelt to recite the family rosary. In Livia s words: "It was a real education for him to be told it was rosary time."[56]

As a manifestation of familial oligarchy, chaperonage crossed denominational lines, Protestant teens, too, yearned for more freedom of movement. "I was beginning to think that the Baptist church was a little too Mexican, too much restriction," remembered

Rose Escheverria Mulligan. Indeed, she longed to join her Catholic peers who regularly attended church-sponsored dances—"I noticed they were having a good time."[57]

As mentioned earlier, popular culture offered an alternative vision to parental and church expectations complete with its own aura of legitimacy. While going out with a man alone violated Mexican community norms, such behavior seemed perfectly appropriate outside the barrio. Certainly Mexican-American women noticed the less confined lifestyles of their Anglo co-workers who did not live at home and who went out on dates unchaperoned. Some wage-earning teenagers rented apartments, at times even moving in with Anglo peers. Both English and Spanish-language media promoted a freer heterosocial environment. Radios, magazines, and movies held out images of neckers and petters, hedonistic flappers bent on a good time. From Middletown to East Los Angeles, teenagers across class and ethnicity sought to emulate the funseeking icons of a burgeoning consumer society.[58]

Even the Spanish-language press fanned youthful passions. On May 9, 1927, *La Opinion* ran an article entitled, "How do you kiss?" Informing readers that "el beso no es un arte sino una ciencia ' [kissing is not an art but rather a science], this short piece outlined the three components of a kiss: quality, quantity, and topography. The modern kiss, furthermore, should last three minutes.[59] Though certainly shocking older Mexicanos, such titillating fare catered to a youth market. *La Opinion,* in many respects, reflected the coalescence of Mexican and American cultures. While promoting pride in Latino theater and music, its society pages also celebrated the icons of Americanization and mass consumption.

Mexican-American women were not caught between two worlds. They navigated across multiple terrains at home, at work, and at play. They engaged in cultural coalescence. The Mexican- American generation selected, retained, borrowed, and created their own cultural forms. Or as one woman informed anthropologist Ruth luck, "Fusion is what we want—the best of both ways."[60] These children of immigrants may have been captivated by consumerism, but few would attain its promises of affluence. Race and gender prejudice as well as socioeconomic segmentation constrained the possibilities of choice.

The adult lives of the seventeen narrators profiled in this chapter give a sense of these boundaries. Most continued in the labor force, combining wage work with household responsibilities. I heir occupations varied from assembling airplanes at McDonnell-Douglas to selling clothes at K-Mart.[61] Seven of the seventeen married Euro-American men, yet, their economic status did not differ substantially from those who chose Mexican partners.[62] With varying degrees of financial security, the majority of the narrators are working-class retirees whose lives do not exemplify rags to riches mobility, but rather upward movement within the working class, Although painfully aware of prejudice and discrimination, many people of their generation placed faith in themselves and faith in the system. In 1959, Margaret Clark asserted that the second-generation residents of Sal si Puedes [a northern California barrio] "dream and work toward the day when Mexican Americans will become fully integrated into American society' at large."[63] Perhaps, as part of that faith, they rebelled against chaperonage.

Indeed, what seems most striking is that the struggle over chaperonage occurred against a background of persistent discrimination. During the early 1930s, Mexicans were routinely rounded up and deported and even when deportations diminished, segregation remained. Historian Albert Camarillo has demonstrated that in Los Angeles restrictive real estate covenants and segregated schools increased dramatically between 1920 and 1950. The proportion of Los Angeles area municipalities with covenants prohibiting Mexicans and other people of color from purchasing residences in certain neighborhoods climbed from 20 percent in 1920 to 80 percent in 1946. Many restaurants, theaters, and public swimming pools discriminated against their Spanish-surnamed clientele. In southern California, for example, Mexicans could swim at the public plunges only one day out of the week (just before they drained the pool).[64] Small town merchants frequently refused to admit Spanish-speaking people into their places of business. "White Trade Only" signs served as bitter reminders of their second-class citizen ship.[65]

NOTES

1   I would like to introduce these women by grouping them geographically. Maria Fierro, Rose Escheverria Mulligan, Adele Hernindez Milligan, Beatrice Morales Clifton, Mary Luna, Alicia Mendeola Shelit, Carmen Bernal Escobar, Belen Martinez Mason, and Julia Luna Mount grew up in Los Angeles. Lucy Acosta and Alma Araiza Garcia came of age in El Paso and Erminia Ruiz in Denver. Representing the rural experience are Maria Arredondo, and Jesusita Torres (California), Maria Ybarra (Texas), and Ruby Estrada (Arizona). As a teenager, Eusebia Buriel moved with her family from Silvis, Illinois, to Riverside, California. Note: Of the seventeen full-blown life histories, nine are housed in university archives, seven as part of the Rosie the Riveter collection at California State University, Long Beach. I appreciate the generosity and longstanding support of Sherna Gluck who has given me permission to use excerpts from the Rosie interviews. This sample also does not include oral interviews found in published sources.

2   The age breakdowns for the fourteen interviewees are as follows: nine were born between 1908 and 1919 and eight between 1920 and 1926. This sample includes some who were chaperoned during the 1920s and others who were chaperoned during the thirties and forties. As a result, the sample does not a represent a precise generational grouping, but instead gives a sense of the pervasiveness and persistence of unremitting supervision.

3   Estrada interview, pp. 2, 15, 17, 19. Note: Most families were nuclear, rather than extended, although kin usually (but not always) resided nearby. Carmen Bernal Escobar and Alma Araiza Garcia grew up in single-parent households with extended kin present, Carmen reared by her mother, Alma by her father.

4   George J. Sinchez, "'Go After the Women': Americanization and the Mexican Immigrant Woman 1915–1929," in *Unequal Sisters: A Multicultural Reader in U.S. Women's History*, 2nd ed., eds. Vicki L. Ruiz and Ellen Carol DuBois (New York: Routledge, 1994), p. 285.

5   F. Scott Fitzgerald, *Flappers and Philosophers* (London: W. Collins Sons and Co., Ltd., 1922), pp. 209–46; Emory S. Bogardus, *The Mexican in the United States* (Los Angeles: University of Southern California Press, 1934), p. 741; Martfnez Mason interview, p. 44. During the 1920s, Mexican parents were not atypical in voicing their concerns over the attitudes and appearance of their "flapper adolescents." A general atmosphere of tension between youth and their elders existed-a generation gap that cut across class, race, ethnicity, and region. See Paula Fass, *The Damned and the Beautiful: American Youth in the 1920's* (New York: Oxford University Press, 1977).

6   Interview with Alicia Mendeola Shelit, Volume 37 of *Rosie the Riveter*, p. 18; Paul S. Taylor, *Mexican Labor in the United States, Volume II* (Berkeley: University of California Press, 1932), pp. 199–200; Interview with Maria Fierro, Volume 12 of *Rosie the Riveter*, p. 10. Changing clothes at school is not peculiar to our mothers and grandmothers. As a high school student in the early 1970s, I was not allowed to wear the fashionable micro-mini skirts. But I bought one anyway. I left home in a full dirndl skirt with a flowing peasant blouse, but once I arrived at school, I would untie the skirt (which I would then dump in my locker) to reveal the mini-skirt I had worn underneath.

7   Manuel Gamio, *Mexican Immigration to the United States* (Chicago: University of Chicago Press, 1930; rpt. Arno Press, 1969), p. 89. The verse taken from "Las Pelonas" in the original Spanish follows: Los patios colorados/Los tengo aborrecidos/Ya hora las pelonas/Los usan de vestidos/Las muchachas de S. Antonio/Son flojas pa'l metate/Quieren andar pelonas/Con sombreros de petate/Se acabaron las pizcas/Se acabó el algodón/Ya andan las pelonas/De puro vacilón.

8   Taylor, *Mexican Labor*, Vol. II, pp. vi–vii.

9   Rodolfo F. Acufia, *Community Under Siege: A Chronicle of Chicanos East of the Los Angeles River, 1945–1975* (Los Angeles: UCLA Chicano Studies Publications, 1984), pp. 278, 407–408, 413–14, 418, 422; FTA News, May 1, 1945; interview with Carmen Bernal Escobar, June 15, 1986, conducted by the author. For an example of the promotion of a beauty pageant, see issues of *La Opinion*, June-July 1927.

10   Escobar interview, 1986.

11   Sherna B. Gluck, *Rosie the Riveter Revisited: Women, The War and Social Change* (Boston: Twayne Publishers, 1987), pp. 81, 85.

12   The best elaboration of this phenomenon can be found in Roland Marchand, *Advertising the American Dream: Making Way for Modernity, 1920–1940* (Berkeley: University of California Press, 1985).

13   For examples, see *La Opinion*, September 26, 1926; May 14, 1927; June 5, 1927; September 9, 1929; January 15, 1933; January 29, 1938. Lorena Chambers is currently

writing a dissertation focusing on the gendered representations of the body in Chicano cultural narratives. I thank her for our wonderful discussions.

14 Vicki L. Ruiz, "'Star Struck': Acculturation, Adolescence, and Mexican American Women, 1920–1940" in *Small Worlds: Children and Adolescents in America*, eds. Elliot West and Paula Petrik (Lawrence: University of Kansas Press, 1992): 61–80; Roberto R. Trevifo, "Prensa YPatria: The Spanish-Language Press and the Biculturation of the Tejano Middle Class, 1920–1940," *The Western Historical Quarterly*, Vol. 22 (November 1991): 460.

15 *La Opinion*, September 29, 1929.

16 Hispano-America, July 2, 1932. Gracias a Gabriela Arredondo for sharing this advertisement with me, one she included in her seminar paper, "'Equality' for All: Americanization of Mexican Immigrant Women in Los Angeles and San Francisco Through Newspaper Advertising, 1927–1935" (M.A. seminar paper, San Francisco State University, 1991).

17 *La Opinion*, June 5, 1927; *La Opinion*, February 8, 1938.

18 Richard A. Garcia, *Rise of the Mexican American Middle Class: San Antonio, 1929–1941* (College Station: Texas A&M Press, 1991), pp. 118–19; Trevifio, "Prensa Y Patria," pp. 459–60.

19 For examples, see *La Opinion*, September 23, 1926; *La Opinion*, September 24 1926; *La Opinion*, September 27, 1926; *La Opinion*, September 30, 1926; *La Opinion*, June 4, 1927; *La Opinion*, February 27, 1931; and *La Opinion*, August 17, 1931.

20 For an elaboration of this theme, see Ruiz, "'Star Struck.'" The quote is taken from *La Opinion*, March 2, 1927.

21 Ewen and Ewen, *Channels of Desire*, pp. 95–96.

22 Lipsitz, *Time Passages*, p. 16.

23 The struggles young Mexican-American women faced just to talk freely with men and attend the movies unchaperoned stand in stark contrast to their Euro-American peers who had passed first base and were headed toward greater liberties, like having a drink in a bar without tainting their reputations. See Mary Murphy, "Bootlegging Mothers and Drinking Daughters: Gender and Prohibition in Butte, Montana," *American Quarterly*, 46:2 (June 1994): 174–94.

24 Martinez Mason interview, pp. 29–30; Ybarra interview; Escobar interview; Fierro interview, p. 15; Estrada interview, pp. 11–12; interview with Erminia Ruiz, July 30, 1990, conducted by the author; Ruiz interview, 1993, conducted by the author; interview with Alma Araiza Garcia, March 27, 1993, conducted by the author. Chaperonage was also common in Italian immigrant communities. Indeed, many of the same conflicts between parents and daughters had surfaced a generation earlier among Italian families on the East Coast, although in some communities chaperonage persisted into the 1920s. See Kathy Peiss, *Cheap Amusements: Working Women and Leisure in Turn-of-the Century New York* (Philadelphia: Temple University Press, 1986), pp. 69–70, 152.

25 Interview with Adele Hernindez Milligan, Volume 26 of *Rosie the Riveter*, p. 17.

26 Evangeline Hymer, "A Study of the Social Attitudes of Adult Mexican Immigrants in Los Angeles and Vicinity: 1923" (M.A. thesis, University of Southern California, 1924; rpt. San Francisco: R and E Research Associates, 1971), pp. 24–25. Other ethnographies that deal with intergenerational tension include Helen Douglas, "The Conflict of Cultures in First Generation Mexicans in Santa Ana, California" (M.A. thesis, University of Southern California, 1928) and Clara Gertrude Smith, "The Development of the Mexican People in the Community of Watts" (M.A. thesis, University of Southern California, 1933).

27 Escobar interview, 1986; Estrada interview, pp. 11, 13; interview no. 653 with Lucy Acosta conducted by Mario T. Garcia, October 28, 1982 (on file at the Institute of Oral History, University of Texas, El Paso), p. 17. I wish to thank Rebecca Craver, coordinator of the Institute of Oral History, for permission to use excerpts from the Acosta interview.

28 Estrada interview, p. 12; Shelit interview, p. 9; Antonio Rios-Bustamante and Pedro Castillo, *An Illustrated History of Mexican Los Angeles, 1781–1985* (Los Angeles: Chicano Studies Research Center, UCLA, 1986), p. 153.

29 Paul S. Taylor, "Women in Industry," field notes for his book, *Mexican Labor in the Unites States, 1927–1930*, Bancroft Library, University of California, 1 box; Richard G. Thurston, "Urbanization and Sociocultural Change in a Mexican-American Enclave" (Ph.D. dissertation, University of California, Los Ange les, 1957; rpt. R and E Research Associates, 1974), p. 118; Bogardus, *The Mexican*, pp. 28–29, 57–58. Note: Paul S. Taylor's two-volume study, Mexican Labor in the United States, is considered the classic ethnography on Mexican Americans during the interwar period. A synthesis of his field notes, "Women in Industry," has been published. See Taylor, "Mexican Women in Los Angeles Industry in 1928," *Aztlán*, 11 (Spring 1980): 99–131.

30 Martinez Mason interview p. 30; Ruiz interviews (1990, 1993); Thomas Sheridan, *Los Tucsonenses* (Tucson: University of Arizona Press, 1986), pp. 131–32.

31 Sheridan, *Los Tucsonenses*, loc. cit.

32 Interview with Beatrice Morales Clifton, Volume 8 of *Rosie the Riveter*, pp. 14–15.

33 Smith, "The Development of the Mexican People," p. 47.

34 Ybarra interview. Ethnographies by Smith, Thurston, and Douglas refer to elopement as a manifestation of generational tension.

35 Discussion following my presentation of "The Flapper and the Chaperone" at the Riverside Municipal Museum, May 28, 1995. Comment provided by Rose Medina, co-curator with Vincent Moses of the museum's special exhibition: "Nuestros Antepasados: Riverside's Mexican American Community, 1917–1950."

36 Shelit interview, pp. 9, 24, 30; Ruiz interviews (1990, 1993); Escobar interview; Garcia interview; Martinez Mason interview p. 30; Hernandez Milligan interview, pp. 27–28; interview with Maria Arredondo, March 19, 1986, conducted by Carolyn Arredondo; Taylor notes.

37 Interview with Julia Luna Mount, November 17, 1983, by the author; Fierro interview, p. 18; Luna interview, p. 29; Ruiz interview (1993); Gregorita Rodriguez, *Singing for My Echo* (Santa Fe: Cota Editions, 1987), p. 52; Martinez Mason interview, p. 62.

38 "Elisa Morales," interview by Luis Recinos, April 16, 1927, Biographies and Case Histories II folder, Manuel Gamio Field Notes, Bancroft Library, University of California; Taylor, *Mexican Labor*, Vol. II, pp. vi–vii; Gamio, *Mexican Immigration*, p. 89. The corrido "El Enganchado" in Volume two of Mexican Labor offers an intriguing glimpse into attitudes toward women and Americanization.

39 Ruth Alexander in her study of wayward girls in New York City makes an important point about this balancing of boundaries among teenagers. Using a variety of strategies, the great majority of adolescent girls and young women must have negotiated America's urban terrain in relative safety, enjoying and inventing a sexualized lifestyle while acknowledging the limits of their freedom and acting to protect themselves from social stigma or state action. [Ruth Alexander, "'The Only Thing I Wanted Was Freedom': Wayward Girls in New York, 1900–1930," in *Small Worlds*, p. 294.]

40 Ruiz interview (1993).

41 Carmen and Diego are pseudonyms used to ensure the privacy of the family. Carmen's oral interview is in the author's possession.

42 Discussion following my presentation, of "The Flapper and the Chaperone," May 28, 1995. Comment provided by B.V. Meyer.

43 Douglas Monroy, "An Essay on Understanding the Work Experiences of Mexicans in Southern California, 1900–1939," *Aztlán*, 12 (Spring 1981): 70. Note: Feminist historians have also documented this push for autonomy among the daughters of European immigrants. In particular, see Peiss, *Cheap Amusements*, Glenn, *Daughters of the Shtetl*, E. Ewen, *Immigrant Women*; and Alexander, "The Only Thing I Wanted Was Freedom." See also Meyerowitz, *Women Adrift*.

44 Heller Committee for Research in Social Economics of the University of California and Constantine Panuzio, *How Mexicans Earn and Live, University of California Publications in Economics, XIII, No. 1, Cost of Living Studies V* (Berkeley: University of California, 1933), pp. 11, 14, 17; Taylor notes; Luna Mount interview; Ruiz interviews (1990, 1993); Shelit interview, p. 9. For further delineation of the family wage economy, see Louise A. Tilly and Joan W. Scott, *Women, Work, and Family* (New York: Holt, Rinehart, and Winston, 1978).

45 These observations are drawn from my reading of the seventeen oral interviews and the literature on European immigrant women.

46 Luna Mount interview.

47 Garcia interview.

48 Rev. F. X. Lasance, *The Catholic Girl's Guide and Sunday Missal* (New York: Benziger Brothers, 1905), Esther Perez Papers, Cassiano-P&rez Collection, Daughters of the Republic of Texas Library at the Alamo, San Antonio, Texas, pp. 279–80. I have a

1946 reprint edition passed down to me by my older sister who had received it from our mother.

49 Gutierrez, "Honor, Ideology," pp. 88–93, 95–98.

50 Estrada interview, p. 12. Focusing on the daughters of European immigrants, Elizabeth Ewen has written that "the appropriation of an urban adolescent culture" served as "a wedge against patriarchal forms of social control." This holds true, to some degree, for the women profiled here. But, for Mexican Americans, the underlying ideological assumption was familial oligarchy rather than patriarchy. See Ewen and Ewen, *Channels of Desire*, p. 95.

51 Lasance, *Catholic Girl's Guide*, pp. 249–75. [Quote is on p. 270.]

52 Ibid., p. 271.

53 George J. Sanchez, *Becoming Mexican American: Ethnicity, Culture, and Identity in Chicano Los Angeles, 1900–1945* (New York: Oxford University Press, 1993), p. 167; Mary Helen Ponce, *Hoyt Street* (Albuquerque: University of New Mexico Press, 1993), pp. 258, 266–71. [Quote is taken from p. 258.] "Las vistas" is slang for the movies.

54 Ponce, *Hoyt Street*, p. 266; Margo McBane, "Tale of Two Cities: A Comparative Study of the Citrus Heartlands of Santa Paula and LaVerne" (unpublished paper courtesy of the author), pp. 15–16. Discussion following my presentation of "The Flapper and the Chaperone," May 28, 1995. Comment provided by Rose Medina. Jamaicas are church bazaars or festivals.

55 Interview with Eusebia Buriel, January 16, 1995, conducted by the author; interview with Ray Buriel, December 21, 1994, conducted by the author.

56 Patricia Preciado Martin, *Songs My Mother Sang to Me* (Tucson: University of Arizona Press, 1992), pp. 19–20.

57 Interview with Rose Escheverria Mulligan, Volume 27 of *Rosie the Riveter*, p. 24.

58 Taylor notes; Monroy, "An Essay on Understanding," p. 70; Rosalinda Gonzalez, "Chicanas and Mexican Immigrant Families 1920–1940: Women's Subordination and Economic Exploitation," in *Decades of Discontent: The Women's Movement, 1920–1940*, eds. Lois Scharf and Joan M. Jensen (Westport, Conn.: Greenwood Press, 1983), p. 72; Vicki L. Ruiz, *Cannery Women, Cannery Lives: Mexican Women, Unionization, and the California Food Processing Industry, 1930–1950* (Albuquerque: University of New Mexico Press, 1987), pp. 10–12, 17–18; Ruiz interview (1990); John D'Emilio and Estelle B. Freedman, *Intimate Matters: A History of Sexuality in America* (New York: Harper & Row, 1988), pp. 233–35, 239–41. Note: *Intimate Matters* provides a thought-provoking analysis of sexual liberalism during the interwar period.

PART VI

INVENTING SEXOLOGY

The scientific study of sex began in the nineteenth century. By the twentieth century, sexology was enrolled in arguments for and against sexual rights. Magnus Hirschfeld's Scientific Humanitarian Committee used science to advocate for tolerance for what was called homosexuality. Sigmund Freud offered a new psychological explanation for homosexuality, while popular accounts, such as Radclyffe Hall's novel, were met with censorship. The use of gender ideals to oppose rights to political self-determination are evident in Katherine Mayo's depiction of women in India and Gandhi's response. Veronika Fuechtner brings together European traditions of sexology with Indian political and scientific movements in her essay on Magnus Hirschfeld's trip to India.

READING 22

The Scientific Humanitarian Committee,
"The Social Problem of Sexual Inversion" (1903).

Founded in Berlin in 1897 by German sexologist Magnus Hirschfeld
(1868–1935), the Scientific Humanitarian Committee advocated for
LGBT rights. This is a translation of a pamphlet intended to educate
the public with regard to "intermediate sexes."

The Social Problem of Sexual Inversion

WHAT IS KNOWN OF THE INTERMEDIATE SEX

Everyone interested in public affairs must have heard of the recent petition, signed by a number of the best-known and most distinguished
men in Germany, and having for its object the repeal of a penal law
aimed at a not inconsiderable class of persons who, otherwise normal,
are peculiarly constituted as regards their sexual tendencies—a class
of persons whose nature and peculiarities have, until comparatively
recent years, escaped scientific enquiry.

The object of this pamphlet is to enlighten the thoughtful public
on the subject of this "Intermediate sex," in the hope of removing
·a widespread prejudice and inducing a sane judgment. We are following, in so doing, the private advice which Dr. M. Hirschfeld, the
president of the "Humanitarian-Science" committee, received from
an important quarter: "Try to enlighten public opinion, so that the
action of the Government in dealing with these clauses may not
be misunderstood."

Whoever reads these pages conscientiously and without prejudice
cannot fail to see that their object is not the advocacy of any form of
vice, but the removal of a form of injustice which presses heavily upon
a certain type of human being.

May this little pamphlet help to render unnecessary the fear
expressed by Ernst von Wtldenbruch, one of the earliest signatories to
the petition. He wrote as follows: "I hasten to reply to your request for
my signature. It is a serious request, for I cannot disguise from myself
that the signatories to your petition for the repeal of these penalties
will expose themselves to the danger of slander and misrepresentation
from the stupid and evil-minded. Nevertheless, it seems to me impossible not to comply with your request."

The Scientific Humanitarian Committee, *The Social Problem of Sexual Inversion,*

trans. British Society for the Study of Sexual Psychology, 1903.

Everyone should be aware that the physical and mental characteristics which are considered essentially masculine are found, occasionally, in woman; and that the essentially feminine characteristics are found, occasionally, in men. There are, for instance, men with a feminine pelvis, with a feminine formation of breast and vocal organs, with feminine growth of hair and lack of beard, with the delicate skin and rounded figure which are characteristically womanly. Hence, one comes across men whose manners and movements are womanly; whose handwriting resembles a woman's, who have the tastes and mental outlook of a woman, who number among their traits a womanly modesty and gentleness.

There are even men—though this is rarer—whose resemblance to women is actually organic.

In the same way, we find women who, in body as well as in mind, bear the stamp of masculinity. Still more frequent are the "intermediates" of both sexes; that is to say, persons in whom the exchange of characteristics, though dearly marked, is by no means complete.

This exchange of characteristics is not only found amongst humans of every race; it is common also to the animal kingdom, in every species of animal where the division into sexes exists. It is to be traced to the fact that the sexes arose from a common origin by a varying process of growth—a process which sometimes fails to reach the average and sometimes overshoots it.

Of this the simplest proof is that each human being carries about with him for as long as he lives certain traces of the sex to which he does not belong. Such traces, to give one example among many, are to be found in the survival on the breast of a man, of the nipple, a purely feminine organ.

Sexual desire which has its root not, as is commonly supposed, in the external organs, but in the brain, is either masculine—and therefore aroused by a woman—or feminine and aroused by a man. Should it, however—in the same way as other characteristics—have undergone this process of exchange, and be, though implanted in a masculine body, essentially feminine in character, it will be impossible for such a man, however masculine in other respects, not to be attracted to his own sex rather than the other. In the same way, a woman in whom the sexual tendency is masculine will feel the impulse of love towards those of her own sex.

Nor must it be supposed that any organic operation on such persons can change or exterminate this attraction. To do so effectually it would be necessary to remove the seat of the instinct, that is to say the brain.

In scientific parlance such persons are described as homosexual, popularly they are known by other terms; in Roman days a man of this type was called *homo mollis*. By some scientists the name "urning" or "uranian" has been employed.

God, or Nature, has brought into being not only normal men and women but uranians; and Professor O. Schulze has rightly declared that it is really too ridiculous to imagine that the processes of nature can be abolished, or even appreciably restrained, by pen and paper enactments. All parents ought to realize that one of their own children may possibly be a uranian—and understand, further, that the penal clause in question (paragraph 175) may chance to threaten their nearest and dearest. Amongst those who have openly opposed the repeal of the law is a clergyman who is quite unaware of the fact—of which we have absolute proof—that one of his sons is a uranian.

About 750 headmasters and teachers in the higher schools have signed the petition; and one of them, who had recently lost a son, accompanied *his* signature with the following words:

"Even at the time of the Krupp case, I was still in ignorance of the facts we are now considering, and I believed in the necessity of retaining clause 175. It was only after the death of a promising lad—a lad whose mind was set on the best and highest, and who was driven to suicide by his discovery of his own tendencies—that my eyes were opened to the truth. A father, who has known what it is to suffer, thanks your Society for its work in the cause of Humanity."

There is many a mother who fails to understand why her boy, in spite of so much that she knows to be good in him, seems to have no pleasure in life and one day makes an end of himself; or who wonders why it is that her daughter turns from one suitor after another. Often enough such parents would grasp the situation had they only learnt what we are here trying to teach them; and, being possessed of such knowledge, they would take it into account in settling questions of education, profession and marriage. They would realize that, for these particular children, marriage and the founding of a family would be a sin against nature—a torment to themselves and a danger to their descendants, who are especially liable to nervous and mental trouble.

There are certain primitive races who shew far more understanding and justice than we do in their treatment of uranians, who reserve for them certain callings as for example, the care of the sick.

The public ought not to be ignorant that the number of the in-born homosexuals (in Germany probably between half a million and a million) if insignificant in comparison with the number of the normal, is yet far too formidable for any State to attempt to get rid of by confinement in prisons, asylums or institutions; nor is it possible for any State to render practical the alternatives of suicide, wholesale emigration, or the suppression of one of the strongest natural impulses—an impulse concerning whose workings the world of science is by no means in agreement.

There are uranians in the highest as in the lowest ranks of society; among the roughest as among the most cultured, in capitals as in villages, among the most moral as among the most vicious.

Anyone who has studied the problem knows that, in a thousand uranians, hardly one is suspected; in fifty thousand hardly one detected; and knows, further, that Bebel was right when he said in the Reichstag (Jan. 13, 1898): "If the offences against paragraph 175—offences committed by thousands of persons from the highest to the lowest—were really brought to light, there would be a scandal such as the world has never known."

It ought to be understood that the attraction towards those of the same sex is not, as is commonly believed, the result of satiety, self-abuse, evil example, viciousness, or fear of propagation; Dr. Hirschfeld, in his observation of more than 1800 cases, has failed to establish any of these causes. On the contrary, in most cases, efforts have been made to overcome the desire. *Its* victims know the dangers to which they are exposed, the disgrace that threatens them; but the tendency is stronger than the will.

Professor von Krafft-Ebing, of Vienna, the greatest authority on the subject, says: "At times the homo-sexual passion is so strong that it is impossible to control it." It may be added that there is much popular misconception as to the manner in which this desire attains its fulfillment.

But even those in whom the desire produces no active results feel the existing law as a burden and a reproach, since it strikes at the finest side of them, their capacity for love. Love for a member of the same sex can be just as pure and noble as love for a member of the other—the only difference between the two sentiments being one of direction, and not of kind. Like normal love, it can be an inspiration; there are numerous examples of great men of whose tendencies there cannot be the slightest doubt—for instance, Socrates, Michelangelo, Frederick the Great, Hans Andersen. The verses written by Frederick the Great to "Cesarion": as he called the young Count Kaiserlingk, give documentary evidence of this fact as regards himself.

Every normal being should try to imagine himself in the position of a uranian, a difficult but not an unprofitable task. His inner life resembles that of a man unjustly condemned, a man who does penance for a crime that he has not committed; he knows that he is guiltless of his own desires, that nature has played a trick on him and that, try as he may, he cannot think or feel except as she has ordered. This unhappy plight, which he has had no hand in bringing about, is the cause of contempt and loathing in the minds of those of his fellow men who fail to grasp that his nature is not theirs.

The authors of paragraph 175 assumed—and its administrators and people in general assume likewise—that the persons at whom it is aimed are men like them-selves who, of their own free will, divert their natural desires towards women into unnatural desires towards men. They cannot see that the uranian is as strongly drawn towards his own sex as those who sit in judgment on him are drawn towards the other; that, to him, intercourse with women is unnatural, and that he is forced, whether he will or not, to feel the attraction which draws him to men. The same argument applies, of course, where the uranian is a woman.

The uranian is all too often unhappy, not merely on account of his passion itself, but because of the persecution, the social condemnation and loss of honour which threaten him for an impulse which the normal man can obey without reproach.

It is this lack of understanding which fills him with bitterness. One has only to think of the scorn which would be heaped on a lad, who, without attempting to act upon them should put his feelings into words.

No, this clause to which we object does not protect the natural and inborn instincts. It attacks them; for the law fails to recognise what Nature has already done. If the law is to stand, we must declare Nature herself unnatural. It is impossible that we shall continue to brand as criminals, men and women who often blend in their characters the best traits of the two sexes.

As it is impossible to extirpate the Intermediate sex, society and the State must do their best to tolerate it. As a matter of fact, that is what they have to do now, since only a comparatively small number of uranians are removed by suicide or by imprisonment in gaols, hospitals or asylums.

We are attributing to the Law a power it does not possess when we imagine that it can have any real influence upon an instinct implanted by Nature. Penalties cannot suppress that instinct, immunity from penalty cannot produce it; the repeal of a law against it does not increase it; the existence of a law against it does not diminish it. Bavaria and Hanover where, from the War of Liberation to the introduction of the Imperial Penal Code (1815–73) the offence was not illegal, afford absolute proof of this statement.

The idea that an entire people can be enervated by the existence of the homosexual temperament is an idea without foundation. Such temperaments have existed amongst primitive nations and were frequent, not only in Greece and Rome, but in other countries as well during their rise to power as during their decay.

On the contrary, the uranian, unfitted though he be to found a family, can, after his own fashion, be of service to the community—has, in spite of his unfortunate position, often been of service. He should not be regarded as an anti-social being: he should have his place alloted to him. And, since we require a young woman to protect herself from seduction, we can certainly require the same of a young man, without enacting special legislation for his protection.

Every uranian owes a duty to himself: self-realisation is his right, of that which has come to him by birth he must make the best. To that which he feels to be honourable he must give honourable form, and seek for its honourable recognition from the State. He should not be ashamed of his promptings, but should devote his energies to ennobling them and to directing them as far as possible to the service of his kind.

But if he owes so much to others, the State and society owe him a like recognition in return. They must not deny in blind prejudice that those natural and inborn feelings can be put to social use, so as to be recognized and honoured.

But if society refuses to recognise the uranian, how can he be rightly placed, or attain to the full stature of his nature?

We repeat expressly that we disclaim any desire to dispute the precepts of the Christian moral law; that is an ideal of which all men, however normal, fall short. What we *do* desire to fight is the practice of stamping as criminals and visiting with legal penalties, one section alone, which upon its own lines of advance has not yet attained to the ideal.

READING 23

Sigmund Freud, "The Sexual Aberrations" (1905),
in *Three Essays on the Theory of Sexuality*
(Martino Fine Books, 2011), 1–12.

Sigmund Freud (1856–1939) was an Austrian neurologist who founded
psychoanalysis as a method of therapy. In this passage, he explains his
views on the origins of "sexual inversions," or homosexuality.

The Sexual Aberrations

Sigmund Freud

The fact[1] of sexual need in man and animal is expressed in biology by the assumption of a "sexual impulse." This impulse is made analogous to the impulse of taking nourishment, and to hunger. The sexual expression corresponding to hunger not being found colloquially, science uses the expression " libido."[2]

Popular conception assumes very different ideas concerning the nature and qualities of this sexual impulse. It is supposed to be absent during childhood and to commence about the time of and in connection with the maturing process of puberty; it is supposed that it manifests itself in irresistible attractions exerted by one sex upon the other, and that its aim is sexual union or at least such actions as would lead to union.

But we have every reason to see in these assumptions a very untrustworthy picture of reality. On closer examination they are found to abound in errors, inaccuracies and hasty conclusions.

If we introduce two terms and call the person from whom the sexual attraction emanates the sexual object, and the action towards which the impulse strives the sexual aim, then the scientifically examined experience shows us many deviations in reference to both sexual object and sexual aim, the relations of which to the accepted standard require thorough investigation.

---

1   The facts contained in the first "Contribution" have been gathered from the familiar publications of Krafft-Ebing, Moll, Moebius, Havelock Ellis, Schrenk-Notzing, Löwenfeld, Eulenberg, J. Bloch, and M. Hirschfeld, and from the later works published in the "Jahrbuch für sexuelle Zwischenstufen." As these publications also mention the other literature bearing on this subject I may forbear giving detailed references.

The conclusions reached through the investigation of sexual inverts are all based on the reports of J. Sadger and on my own experience.

2   For general use the word "libido" is best translated by "craving." (Prof. James J.. Putnam, *Journal of Abnormal Psychology*, Vol. IV, 6.)

Sigmund Freud, "The Sexual Aberrations," *Three Contributions to the Sexual Theory,* trans. A.A. Brill, pp. 1-12, 1910.

DEVIATION IN REFERENCE TO THE SEXUAL OBJECT

The popular theory of the sexual impulse corresponds closely to the poetic fable of dividing the person into two halves—man and woman—who strive to become reunited through love. It is therefore very surprising to hear that there are men for whom the sexual object is not woman but man, and that there are women for whom it is not man but woman. Such persons are called contrary sexuals, or better, inverts; that is, these form the actualities of inversion. They exist in very considerable numbers, although their definite ascertainment is subject to difficulties.'[3]

INVERSION
THE BEHAVIOR OF INVERTS
The above-mentioned persons behave in many ways quite differently.

(a) They are absolutely inverted; *i. e.*, their sexual object must be always of the same sex, while the opposite sex can never be to them an object of sexual longing, but leaves them indifferent or may even evoke sexual repugnance. As men they are unable, on account of this repugnance, to perform the normal sexual act or miss all pleasure in its performance. (b) They are amphigenously inverted (psychosexually hermaphroditic) ; *i. e.*, their sexual object may belong indifferently to either the same or to the other sex. The inversion lacks the character of exclusiveness. (c) They are occasionally inverted; i. *e.*, under certain external conditions, chief among which are the inaccessibility of the normal sexual object and imitation, they are able to take as the sexual object a person of the same sex and thus find sexual gratification.

The inverted also manifest a manifold behavior in their judgment about the peculiarities of their sexual impulse. Some take the inversion as a matter of course, just as the normal looking at his libido does, firmly demanding the same rights as the normal. Others, however, strive against the fact of their inversion and perceive in it a morbid compulsion.[4]

Other variations concern the relations of time. The characteristics of the inversion in any individual may date back as far as his memory goes, or they may become manifest to him at a definite period before or after puberty.[5] The character is either retained throughout life, or it occasionally recedes or represents an episode on the road to normal development. A periodical fluctuation between the normal and the

---

3   For the difficulties entailed in the attempt to ascertain the proportional number of inverts compare the work of M. Hirschfeld in the *Jahrbuch für sexuelle Zwischenstufen*, 1904.

4   Such a striving against the compulsion to inversion favors cures by suggestion or psychoanalysis.

5   Many have justly emphasized the fact that the autobiographic statements of inverts, as to the time of the appearance of their tendency to inversion, are untrustworthy as they may have repressed from memory any evidences of heterosexual feelings.
Psychoanalysis has confirmed this suspicion in all cases of inversion accessible, and has decidedly changed their anamnesis by filling up the infantile amnesias.

inverted sexual object has also been observed. Of special interest are those cases in which the libido changes, taking on the character of inversion after a painful experience with the normal sexual object.

These different categories of variation generally exist independently of one another. In the most extreme cases it can regularly be assumed that the inversion has existed at all times and that the person feels contented with his peculiar state.

Many authors will hesitate to gather into a unit all the cases enumerated here and will prefer to emphasize the exceptional rather than the customary groups, a view which corresponds with their preferred judgment of inversions. But no matter what divisions may be set up, it cannot be overlooked that all transitions are abundantly met with, so that as it were, the formation of series forcibly obtrudes itself.

CONCEPTION OF INVERSION

The first attention bestowed upon inversion gave rise to the conception that it was a congenital sign of nervous degeneration. This harmonized with the fact that doctors first met it among the nervous, or among persons giving such an impression. There are two elements which should be considered independently in this conception: the congenitality, and the degeneration.

DEGENERATION

This term *degeneration* is open to the objections which may be urged against the promiscuous use of this word in general. It has in fact become customary to designate all morbid manifestations not of traumatic or infectious origin as degenerative. Indeed, Magnan's classification of degenerates makes it conceivable that the highest general configuration of nervous accomplishment need not exclude the application of the concept of degeneration. Under the circumstances it is a question what use and what new content the meaning of "degeneration" still possesses. It would seem more appropriate not to speak of degeneration: (i) Where there are not many marked deviations from the normal; (2) where the capabilities and the capacity to exist do not in general appear markedly impaired.[6]

That the inverted are not degenerates in this qualified sense can be seen from the following facts:

1. The inversion is found among persons who otherwise show no marked deviation from the normal.

---

6   With what reserve the diagnosis of degeneration should be made and what slight practical significance can be attributed to it can be gathered from the discussions of Moebius (*Ueber Entartung; Grenzfragen des Nerven- und Seelenlebens*, No. Ill, 1900). He says: "If we review the wide sphere of degeneration upon which we have here turned some light we can conclude without further ado that it is really of little value to diagnose degeneration."

2.   It is found also among persons whose capabilities are not disturbed, who on the contrary are distinguished by especially high intellectual development and ethical culture.[7]

3.   If one disregards the patients of one's own practice and strives to comprehend a wider field of experience, he will in two directions encounter facts which will prevent him from assuming inversions as a degenerative sign.

(a) It must be considered that inversion was a frequent manifestation among the ancient nations at the height of their culture. It was an institution endowed with important functions. (b) It is found to be unusually prevalent among savages and primitive races, whereas the term degeneration is generally limited to higher civilization (I. Bloch). Even among the most civilized nations of Europe, climate and race have a most powerful influence on the distribution of, and attitude toward, inversion.[8]

INNATENESS

Only for the first and most extreme class of inverts, as can be imagined, has innateness been claimed, and this from their own assurance that at no time in their life has their sexual impulse followed a different course. The fact of the existence of two other classes, especially of the third, speaks against the assumption of its being congenital. Hence, the propensity of those holding this view to separate the group of absolute inverts from the others results in the abandonment of the general conception of inversion. Accordingly in a number of cases the inversion would be of a congenital character, while in others it might originate from other causes.

In contradistinction to this conception is that which assumes inversion to be an acquired character of the sexual impulse. It is based on the following facts, (1) In many inverts (even absolute ones) an early effective sexual impression can be demonstrated, as a result of which the homosexual inclination developed. (2) In many others outer favoring and inhibiting influences of life can be demonstrated, which in earlier or later life led to a fixation of the inversion—among which are exclusive relations with the same sex, companionship in war, detention in prison, dangers of hetero-sexual intercourse, celibacy, sexual weakness, etc. (3) Hypnotic suggestion may remove the inversion, which would be surprising in that of a congenital character.

In view of all this, the existence of congenital inversion can certainly be questioned. The objection may be made to it that a more accurate examination of those claimed to be congenitally inverted will probably show a determination of the direction of the libido by a definite experience of early childhood, which has not, indeed, been retained in the conscious memory of the person, but which can he brought back to

---

7   We must agree with the spokesman of "Uranism" that some of the most prominent men known have been inverts and perhaps absolute inverts.

8   In the conception of inversion the pathological features have been separated from the anthropological. For this credit is due to J. Bloch (*Beiträge zur Ätiologie der Psychopathia Sexualis, 2 Teile*, 1902—3) who has also brought into prominence the existence of inversion in the old civilized nations.

memory by proper influences (Havelock Ellis). According to that author inversion can be designated only as a frequent variation of the sexual desire which may be determined by a number of external circumstances of life.

The apparent certainty thus reached is, however, overthrown by the retort that manifestly there are many persons who have experienced even in their early youth those very sexual influences, such as seduction, mutual onanism, without becoming inverts, or without constantly remaining so. Hence, one is forced to assume that the alternative between congenital and acquired inversion is either incomplete or does not cover the circumstances present in inversions.

EXPLANATION OF INVERSION

The nature of inversion is explained by neither the assumption that it is congenital or that it is acquired. In the first case, we need to be told what there is in it of the congenital, unless we are satisfied with the roughest explanation, namely, that a person brings along a congenital sexual desire connected with a definite sexual object. In the second case it is a question whether the manifold accidental influences suffice to explain the acquisition unless there is something in the individual to meet them half way. The negation of this last factor is inadmissible according to our former conclusions.

THE RELATION OF BISEXUALITY

Since the time of Frank Lydston, Kieman, and Chevalier, a new stream of thought has been introduced for the explanation of the possibility of sexual inversion. This contains a new contradiction to the popular belief which assumes that a human being is either a man or a woman. Science shows cases in which the sexual characteristic appears blurred and thus the sexual distinction is made difficult, especially on an anatomical basis. The genitals of such persons unite the male and female characteristics (hermaphroditism). In rare cases both parts of the sexual apparatus are well developed (true hermaphroditism), but usually both are stunted.[9]

The importance of these abnormalities lies in the fact that they unexpectedly facilitate the understanding of the normal formation. A certain degree of anatomical hermaphroditism really belongs to the normal. In no normally formed male or female are traces of the apparatus of the other sex lacking; these either continue functionless as rudimentary organs, or they are transformed for the purpose of assuming other functions.

The conception which we gather from this long known anatomical fact is the original predisposition to bisexuality, which in the course of development has changed to monosexuality, leaving slight remnants of the stunted sex.

---

9 Compare the last detailed discussion of somatic hermaphroditism (Taruffi, *Hermaphroditismus und Zeugungunfähigkeit*, German edit, by R. Teuscher, 1903), and the works of Neugebauer in many volumes of the *Jahrbuch für sexuelle Zwischenstufen*.

It was natural to transfer this conception to the psychic sphere and to conceive the inversion in its aberrations as an expression of psychic hermaphroditism. In order to bring the question to a decision, it was only necessary to have one other circumstance, viz., a regular concurrence of the inversion with the psychic and somatic signs of hermaphroditism.

But the expectation thus formed was not realized. The relations between the assumed psychical and the demonstrable anatomical androgyny should never be conceived as being so close. There is frequently found in the inverted a diminution of the sexual impulse (H. Ellis) and a slight anatomical stunting of the organs. This, however, is found frequently but by no means regularly or preponderately. Thus we must recognize that inversion and somatic hermaphroditism are totally independent of each other.

Great value has also been placed on the so-called secondary and tertiary sex characteristics, and their aggregate occurrence in the inverted has been emphasized (H. Ellis). There is much truth in this but it should not be forgotten that the secondary and tertiary sex characteristics very frequently manifest themselves in the other sex, thus indicating androgyny without, however, involving changes in the sexual object in the sense of an inversion.

Psychic hermaphroditism would gain in substantiality if parallel with the inversion of the sexual object there should be at least a change in the other psychic qualities, such as in the impulses and distinguishing traits characteristic of the other sex. But such inversion of character can be expected with some regularity only in inverted women; in men the most perfect psychic manliness may be united with the inversion. If one firmly adheres to the hypothesis of a psychic hermaphroditism, one must add that in certain spheres its manifestations allow the recognition of only a very slight contrary determination. The same also holds true in the somatic androgyny. According to Halban, the appearance of individual stunted organs and secondary sex character are quite independent of each other.[10]

A spokesman of the masculine inverts stated the bisexual theory in its crudest form in the following words: "It is a female brain in a male body." But we do not know the characteristics of a "female brain." The substitution of the anatomical for the psychological is as frivolous as it is unjustified. The attempted explanation by v. Krafft-Ebing seems to be more precisely formulated than that of Ulrich but does not essentially differ from it. v. Krafft-Ebing thinks that the bisexual predisposition gives to the individual male and female brain cells as well as somatic sexual organs. These centers develop first towards puberty mostly under the influence of the independent sex glands. We can, however, say the same of the male and female " centers " as of the male and female brains; and moreover, we do not even know whether we can assume for the sexual functions separate brain locations (" centers ") such as we may assume for language.

After this discussion, two thoughts, as it were, remain; first, that a bisexual

---

10   J. Halban, "Die Entstehung der Geschlechts Charaktere," *Arch, für Gynäkologie*, Bd. 70, 1903. See also there the literature on the subject.

predisposition is to be presumed for the inversion also, only we do not know wherein it exists beyond the anatomical formations; and, second, that we are dealing with disturbances which are experienced by the sexual impulse during its development.[11]

THE SEXUAL OBJECT OF INVERTS

The theory of psychic hermaphroditism presupposed that the sexual object of the inverted is the reverse of the normal. The inverted man, like the woman, succumbs to the charms emanating from manly qualities of body and mind; he feels himself like a woman and seeks a man.

But however true this may be for a great number of inverts it by no means indicates the general character of inversion. There is no doubt that a great part of the male inverted have retained the psychic character of virility, that proportionately they show but little the secondary characters of the other sex, and that they really look for real feminine psychic features in their sexual object If that were not so it would be incomprehensible why masculine prostitution, in offering itself to inverts, copies in all its exterior, to-day as in antiquity, the dress and attitudes of woman. This imitation would otherwise be an insult to the ideal of the inverts. Among the Greeks, where the most manly men were found among inverts, it is quite obvious that it was not the masculine character of the boy which kindled the love of man, but it was his physical resemblance to a woman as well as his feminine psychic qualities, such as shyness, demureness, and the need of instruction and help. As soon as the boy himself became a man he ceased to be a sexual object for men and in turn became a lover of boys. The sexual object in this case as in many others is therefore not of the like sex, but it unites both sex characters, a compromise between the impulses striving for the man and for the woman, but firmly conditioned by the masculinity of body (the genitals).[12]

---

11   According to a report in Vol. 6 of the *Jahrbuch f. sexuelle Zwischenstufen*, E. Gley is supposed to have been the first to mention bisexuality as an explanation of inversion. He published a paper (Les Abérrations de l'instinct Sexuel) in the *Revue Philosophique* as early as January, 1884. It is moreover noteworthy that the majority of authors who trace the inversion to bisexuality assume this factor not only for the inverts but also for those who have developed normally, and justly interpret the inversion as a result of a disturbance in development. Among these authors are Chevalier (*Inversion Sexuelle*, 1893), and v. Krafft-Ebing ("Zur Erklärung der konträren Sexualempfindung," *Jahrbücher f. Psychiatrie u. Nervenheilkunde*, XII) who states that there are a number of observations "from which at least the virtual and continued existence of this second center (of the underlying sex) results." A Dr. Arduin (Die Frauenfrage and die sexueOen Zwischenstufen, 2d vol. of the *Jahrbach f. sexuelle Zwischenstufen*, 1900) states that "in every man there exist male and female elements." See also the same Jahrbuch, Bd. I, 1899 ("Die objektive Diagnose der Homosexualitat" by M. Hirschfeld, pp. 8–9). In the determination of sex, as far as heterosexual persons are concerned some are disproportionately more strongly developed than others. G. Herman is firm in his belief " that in every woman there are male, and in every man there are female germs and qualities" (*Genesis, das Gesetz der Zeugung, 9 Bd., Libido und Manie*, 1903). As recently as 1906 has W. Fliess (*Der Ablauf des Lebens*) claimed ownership of the idea of bisexuality (in the sense of double sex).

12   Although psychoanalysis has not yet given us a full explanation for the origin of inversion, it has revealed the psychic mechanism of its genesis and has essentially enriched the problems in question.

The conditions in the woman are more definite; here the active inverts, with special frequency, show the somatic and psychic characters of man and desire femininity in their sexual object; though even here greater variation will be found on more intimate investigation.

THE SEXUAL AIM OF INVERTS

The important fact to bear in mind is that no uniformity of the sexual aim can be attributed to inversion. Intercourse per anum in men by no means goes with inversion; masturbation is just as frequently the exclusive aim; and the limitation of the sexual aim to mere effusion of feelings is here even more frequent than in hetero-sexual love. In women, too, the sexual aims of the inverted are manifold, among which contact with the mucous membrane of the mouth seems to be preferred.

CONCLUSION

Though from the material on hand we are by no means in a position satisfactorily to explain the origin of inversion, we can say that through this investigation we have obtained an insight which can become of greater significance to us than the solution of the above problem. Our attention is called to the fact that we have assumed a too close connection between the sexual impulse and the sexual object. The experience gained from the so called abnormal cases teaches us that there exists between the sexual impulse and the sexual object a connection which we are in danger of overlooking in the uniformity of normal states where the impulse seems to bring with it the object. We are thus instructed to fix our attention upon this connection between the impulse and the object. The sexual impulse is probably entirely independent of its object and does not depend on the stimuli of the same for its origin.

In all the cases examined we have ascertained that the later inverts go through in their childhood a phase of very intense but short-lived fixation on the woman (usually on the mother) and after overcoming it they identify themselves with the woman and take themselves as the sexual object; that is, following narcissism they look for young men resembling themselves; in person who shall love them as their mother has loved them. We have, moreover, frequently found that alleged inverts are by no means; indifferent to the charms of women, but the excitation evoked by the woman is always transferred to a male object. They thus repeat through life the mechanism which gave origin to their inversion. Their obsessive striving for the man proves to be determined by their restless flight from the woman. It must be remembered, however, that until now only one type of inversion has been subjected to psychoanalysis, viz., that of persons with a general stunted sexual activity, the remnant of which manifested itself as inversion. The problem of inversion is very complex and embraces many diverse types of sexual activity and development. Notionally it should be strictly distinguished whether the inversion reverses the sex character of the object or of the subject.

READING 24

Radclyffe Hall, *The Well of Loneliness* (1928), Chapter 19.

Radclyffe Hall (1880–1943) was an English author. In this excerpt from her best-known novel, she depicts a lesbian relationship that resulted in an obscenity trial and the banning of this book in England.

The Well of Loneliness

Radclyffe Hall

CHAPTER NINETEEN

Through the long years of life that followed after, bringing with them their dreams and disillusions, their joys and sorrows, their fulfilments and frustrations, Stephen was never to forget this summer when she fell quite simply and naturally in love, in accordance with the dictates of her nature.

To her there seemed nothing strange or unholy in the love that she felt for Angela Crossby. To her it seemed an inevitable thing, as much a part of herself as her breathing; and yet it appeared transcendent of self, and she looked up and onwards towards her love—for the eyes of the young are drawn to the stars, and the spirit of youth is seldom earth-bound.

She loved deeply, far more deeply than many a one who could fearlessly proclaim himself a lover. Since this is a hard and sad truth for the telling; those whom nature has sacrificed to her ends—her mysterious ends that often lie hidden—are sometimes endowed with a vast will to loving, with an endless capacity for suffering also, which must go hand in hand with their love.

But at first Stephen's eyes were drawn to the stars, and she saw only gleam upon gleam of glory. Her physical passion for Angela Crossby had aroused a strange response in her spirit, so that side by side with every hot impulse that led her at times beyond her own understanding, there would come an impulse not of the body; a fine, selfless thing of great beauty and courage—she would gladly have given her body over to torment, have laid down her life if need be, for the sake of this woman whom she loved. And so blinded was she by those gleams of glory which the stars fling into the eyes of young lovers, that she saw perfection where none existed; saw a patient endurance that was purely fictitious, and conceived of a loyalty far beyond the limits of Angela's nature.

All that Angela gave seemed the gift of love; all that Angela withheld seemed withheld out of honour: 'If only I were free,' she was always saying, 'but I can't deceive Ralph, you know I can't, Stephen—he's ill.' Then Stephen would feel abashed and ashamed before so much pity and honour.

She would humble herself to the very dust, as one who was altogether unworthy: 'I'm a beast, forgive me; I'm all, all wrong—I'm mad sometimes these days—yes, of course, there's Ralph.'

But the thought of Ralph would be past all bearing, so that she must reach out for Angela's hand. Then, as likely as not, they would draw together and start kissing, and Stephen would be utterly undone by those painful and terribly sterile kisses.

'God!' she would mutter, 'I want to get away!'

At which Angela might weep: 'Don't leave me, Stephen! I'm so lonely—why can't you understand that I'm only trying to be decent to Ralph?' So Stephen would stay on for an hour, for two hours, and the next day would find her once more at The Grange, because Angela was feeling so lonely.

For Angela could never quite let the girl go. She herself would be rather bewildered at moments—she did not love Stephen, she was quite sure of that, and yet the very strangeness of it all was an attraction. Stephen was becoming a kind of strong drug, a kind of anodyne against boredom. And then Angela knew her own power to subdue; she could play with fire yet remain unscathed by it. She had only to cry long and bitterly enough for Stephen to grow pitiful and consequently gentle.

'Stephen, don't hurt me—I'm awfully frightened when you're like this—you simply terrify me, Stephen! Is it my fault that I married Ralph before I met you? Be good to me, Stephen!' And then would come tears, so that Stephen must hold her as though she were a child, very tenderly, rocking her backwards and forwards.

They took to driving as far as the hills, taking Tony with them; he liked hunting the rabbits—and while he leapt wildly about in the air to land on nothing more vital than herbage, they would sit very close to each other and watch him. Stephen knew many places where lovers might sit like this, unashamed, among those charitable hills. There were times when a numbness descended upon her as they sat there, and if Angela kissed her cheek lightly, she would not respond, would not even look round, but would just go on staring at Tony. Yet at other times she felt queerly uplifted, and turning to the woman who leant against her shoulder, she said suddenly one day:

'Nothing matters up here. You and I are so small, we're smaller than Tony—our love's nothing but a drop in some vast sea of love—it's rather consoling—don't you think so, beloved?'

But Angela shook her head: 'No, my Stephen; I'm not fond of vast seas, I'm of the earth earthy,' and then: 'Kiss me, Stephen.' So Stephen must kiss her many times, for the hot blood of youth stirs quickly, and the mystical sea became Angela's lips that so eagerly gave and took kisses.

But when they got back to The Grange that evening, Ralph was there—he was hanging about in the hall. He said: 'Had a nice afternoon, you two women? Been motoring Angela round the hills, Stephen, or what?'

He had taken to calling her Stephen, but his voice just now sounded sharp with suspicion as his rather weak eyes peered at Angela, so that for her sake Stephen must lie, and lie well—nor would this be the first time either.

'Yes, thanks,' she lied calmly, 'we went over to Tewkesbury and had another look at the abbey. We had tea in the town. I'm sorry we're so late, the carburettor choked, I couldn't get it right at first, my car needs a good overhauling.'

Lies, always lies! She was growing proficient at the glib kind of lying that pacified Ralph, or at all events left him with nothing to say, nonplussed and at a distinct disadvantage. She was suddenly seized with a kind of horror, she felt physically sick at what she was doing, Her head swam and she caught the jamb of the door for support—at that moment she remembered her father.

2

Two days later as they sat alone in the garden at Morton, Stephen turned to Angela abruptly: 'I can't go on like this, it's vile—it's beastly, it's soiling us both—can't you see that?'

Angela was startled: 'What on earth do you mean?'

'You and me—and then Ralph. I tell you it's beastly—I want you to leave him and come away with me.'

'Are you mad?'

'No, I'm sane. It's the only decent thing, it's the only clean thing; we'll go anywhere you like, to Paris, to Egypt, or back to the States. For your sake I'm ready to give up my home. Do you hear I'm ready to give up even Morton. But I can't go on lying about you to Ralph, I want him to know how much I adore you—I want the whole world to know how I adore you. Ralph doesn't understand the first rudiments of loving, he's a nagging, mean-minded cur of a man, but there's one thing that even he has a right to, and that's the truth. I'm done with these lies—I shall tell him the truth and so will you, Angela; and after we've told him we'll go away, and we'll live quite openly together, you and I, which is what we owe to ourselves and our love.'

Angela stared at her, white and aghast: 'You are mad,' she said slowly, 'you're raving mad. Tell him what? Have I let you become my lover? You know that I've always been faithful to Ralph; you know perfectly well that there's nothing to tell him, beyond a few rather schoolgirlish kisses. Can I help it if you're—what you obviously are? Oh, no, my dear, you're not going to tell Ralph. You're not going to let all hell loose around me just because you want to save your own pride by pretending to Ralph that you've been my lover. If you're willing to give up your home I'm not willing to sacrifice mine, understand that, please. Ralph's not much of a man, but he's better than nothing, and I've managed him so far without any trouble. The great thing with him is to blaze a false trail, that distracts his mind, it works like a charm. He'll follow any trail that I want him to follow—you leave him to me, I know my own husband a darned sight better than you do, Stephen, and I won't have you interfering in my home.' She was terribly frightened, too frightened to choose her words to consider their effect upon Stephen, to consider anyone but Angela Crossby who stood in such dire and imminent peril. So she said yet again, only now she spoke loudly: 'I won't have you interfering in my home!'

Then Stephen turned on her, white with passion: 'You—you—' she stuttered, 'you're unspeakably cruel. You know how you make me suffer and suffer because I love you the way I do; and because you like the way I love you, you drag the love out of me day after day—Can't you understand that I love you so much that I'd give up Morton? Anything I'd give up—I'd give up the whole world. Angela, listen; I'd take care of you always. Angela, I'm rich—I'd take care of you always. Why won't you trust me? Answer me—why? Don't you think me fit to be trusted?'

She spoke wildly, scarcely knowing what she said; she only knew that she needed this woman with a need so intense, that worthy or unworthy, Angela was all that counted at that moment. And now she stood up, very tall, very strong, yet a little grotesque in her pitiful passion, so that looking at her Angela trembled—there was something rather terrible about her. All that was heavy in her face sprang into view, the strong line of the jaw, the square massive brow, the eyebrows too thick and too wide for beauty; she was like some curious, primitive thing conceived in a turbulent age of transition.

'Angela, come very far away—anywhere, only come with me soon—tomorrow.'

Then Angela forced herself to think quickly, and she said just five words: 'Could you marry me, Stephen?'

She did not look at the girl as she said it—that she could not do, perhaps out of something that, for her, was the nearest she would ever come to pity. There ensued a long, almost breathless silence, while Angela waited with her eyes turned away. A leaf dropped, and she heard its minute, soft falling, heard the creak of the branch that had let fall its leaf as a breeze passed over the garden.

Then the silence was broken by a quiet, dull voice, that sounded to her like the voice of a stranger: 'No—' it said very slowly, 'no—I couldn't marry you, Angela.' And when Angela at last gained the courage to look up, she found that she was sitting there alone.

READING 25

Katherine Mayo, *Mother India* (1927).

Katherine Mayo (1867–1940) was an American writer who advocated white, Anglo-Saxon Protestant superiority. Her book *Mother India* argued against Indian independence from British rule. In this excerpt, she offers a depiction of the suffering of Indian women as a reason why British rule was necessary.

Mother India

Katherine Mayo

CHAPTER I - THE ARGUMENT

The area we know as India is nearly half as large as the United States. Its population is three times greater than ours. Its import and export trade—as yet but the germ of the possible—amounted, in the year 1924–25, to about two and a half billion dollars.[1] And Bombay is but three weeks' journey from New York.

Under present conditions of human activity, whereby, whether we will or no, the roads that join us to every part of the world continually shorten and multiply, it would appear that some knowledge of main facts concerning so big and today so near a neighbor should be a part of our intelligence and our self-protection.

But what does the average American actually know about India? That Mr. Gandhi lives there; also tigers. His further ideas, if such he has, resolve themselves into more or less hazy notions more or less unconsciously absorbed from professional propagandists out of one camp or another; from religious or mystical sources; or from tales and travel-books, novels and verses, having India as their scene.

It was dissatisfaction with this status that sent me to India, to see what a volunteer unsubsidized, uncommitted, and unattached, could observe of common things in daily human life.

Leaving untouched the realms of religion, of politics, and of the arts, I would confine my inquiry to such workaday ground as public health and its contributing factors. I would try to determine, for example, what situation would confront a public health official charged with the duty of stopping an epidemic of cholera or of plague; what elements

---

1 Review of the Trade of India In 1924–25, Department of Commercial Intelligence and Statistics, Calcutta, 1926, p. 51.

Katherine Mayo, "The Argument," *Mother India,* ed. Mrinalini Sinha, pp. 75-80.

would work for and against a campaign against hookworm; or what forces would help or hinder a governmental effort to lower infant mortality, to better living conditions, or to raise educational levels, supposing such work to be required.

None of these points could well be wrapped in "eastern mystery," and all concern the whole family of nations in the same way that the sanitary practices of John Smith of 23 Main Street concern Peter Jones at the other end of the block.

Therefore, in early October, 1925, I went to London, called at India Office, and, a complete stranger, stated my plan.

"What would you like us to do for you?" asked the gentlemen who received me.

"Nothing," I answered, "except to believe what I say. A foreign stranger prying about India, not studying ancient architecture, not seeking philosophers or poets, not even hunting big game, and commissioned by no one, anywhere, may seem a queer figure. Especially if that stranger develops an acute tendency to ask questions. I should like it to be accepted that I am neither an idle busybody nor a political agent, but merely an ordinary American citizen seeking test facts to lay before my own people."

To such Indians as I met, whether then or later, I made the same statement. In the period that followed, the introductions that both gave me, coupled with the untiring courtesy and helpfulness alike of Indians and of British, official or private, all over India, made possible a survey more thorough than could have been accomplished in five times the time without such aid.

"But whatever you do, be careful not to generalize," the British urged. "In this huge country little or nothing is everywhere true. Madras and Peshawar, Bombay and Calcutta—attribute the things of one of these to any one of the others, and you are out of court."

Those journeys I made, plus many another up and down and across the land. Everywhere I talked with health officers, both Indian and British, of all degrees, going out with them into their respective fields, city or rural, to observe their tasks and their ways of handling them. I visited hospitals of many sorts and localities, talked at length with the doctors, and studied conditions and cases. I made long sorties in the open country from the North-West Frontier to Madras, sometimes accompanying a district commissioner on his tours of checkered duty, sometimes "sitting in" at village councils of peasants, or at Indian municipal board meetings, or at court sessions with their luminous parade of life. I went with English nurses into bazaars and courtyards and inner chambers and over city roofs, visiting where need called. I saw, as well, the homes of the rich. I studied the handling of confinements, the care of children and of the sick, the care and protection of food, and the values placed upon cleanliness. I noted the personal habits of various castes and grades, in travel or at home, in daily life. I visited agricultural stations and cattle-farms, and looked into the general management of cattle and crops. I investigated the animal sanctuaries provided by Indian piety. I saw the schools, and discussed with teachers and pupils their aims and experience. The sittings of the various legislatures, all-India and provincial, repaid attendance by the light they shed upon the mind-quality of the elements represented.

I sought and found private opportunity to question eminent Indians—princes, politicians, administrators, religious leaders; and the frankness of their talk, as to the mental and physical status and conditions of the peoples of India, thrown out upon the background of my personal observation, proved an asset of the first value.

And just this excellent Indian frankness finally led me to think that, after all, there are perhaps certain points on which—south, north, east and west—you *can* generalize about India. Still more: that you can generalize about the only matters in which we of the busy West will, to a man, see our own concern.

John Smith of 23 Main Street may care little enough about the ancestry of Peter Jones, and still less about his religion, his philosophy, or his views on art. But if Peter cultivates habits of living and ways of thinking that make him a physical menace not only to himself and his family, but to all the rest of the block, then practical John will want details.

"Why," ask modern Indian thinkers, "why, after all the long years of British rule, are we still marked among the peoples of the world for our ignorance, our poverty, and our monstrous death rate? By what right are light and bread and life denied?"

"What this country suffers from is want of initiative, want of enterprise, and want of hard, sustained work," mourns Sir Chimanlal Setalvad.[2] "We rightly charge the English rulers for our helplessness and lack of initiative and originality," says Mr. Gandhi.[3]

Other public men demand:

"Why are our enthusiasms so sterile? Why are our mutual pledges, our self-dedications to brotherhood and the cause of liberty so soon spent and forgotten? Why is our manhood itself so brief? Why do we tire so soon and die so young?" Only to answer themselves with the cry: "Our spiritual part is wounded and bleeding. Our very souls are poisoned by the shadow of the arrogant stranger, blotting out our sun. Nothing can be done—nothing, anywhere, but to mount the political platform and faithfully denounce our tyrant until he takes his flight. When Britain has abdicated and gone, then, and not till then, free men breathing free air, may we turn our minds to the lesser needs of our dear Mother India."

Now it is precisely at this point, and in a spirit of hearty sympathy with the suffering peoples, that I venture my main generality. It is this:

The British administration of India, be it good, bad, or indifferent, has nothing whatever to do with the conditions above indicated. Inertia, helplessness, lack of initiative and originality, lack of staying power and of sustained loyalties, sterility of enthusiasm, weakness of life-vigor itself—all are traits that truly characterize the Indian not only of today, but of long-past history. All, furthermore, will continue to characterize him, in increasing degree, until he admits their causes and with his

---

2   Legislative Assembly Debates, 1923, Vol. VI, No. 6, p. 396

3   *Young India*, March 25, 1926, p. 112. This is Mr. Gandhi's weekly publication from which much hereinafter will be quoted

own two hands uproots them. His soul and body are indeed chained in slavery. But he himself wields and hugs his chains and with violence defends them. No agency but a new spirit within his own breast can set him free. And his arraignments of outside elements, past, present, or to come, serve only to deceive his own mind and to put off the day of his deliverance.

Take a girl child twelve years old, a pitiful physical specimen in bone and blood, illiterate, ignorant, without any sort of training in habits of health. Force motherhood upon her at the earliest possible moment. Rear her weakling son in intensive vicious practices that drain his small vitality day by day. Give him no outlet in sports. Give him habits that make him, by the time he is thirty years of age, a decrepit and querulous old wreck—and will you ask what has sapped the energy of his manhood?

Take a huge population, mainly rural, illiterate and loving its illiteracy. Try to give it primary education without employing any of its women as teachers—because if you do employ them you invite the ruin of each woman that you so expose. Will you ask why that people's education proceeds slowly?

Take bodies and minds bred and built on the lines thus indicated. Will you ask why the death rate is high and the people poor?

Whether British or Russians or Japanese sit in the seat of the highest; whether the native princes divide the land, reviving old days of princely dominance; or whether some autonomy more complete than that now existing be set up, the only power that can hasten the pace of Indian development toward freedom, beyond the pace it is traveling today, is the power of the men of India, wasting no more time in talk, recriminations, and shiftings of blame, but facing and attacking, with the best resolution they can muster, the task that awaits them in their own bodies and souls.

This subject has not, I believe, been presented in common print. The Indian does not confront it in its entirety; he knows its component parts, but avoids the embarrassment of assembling them or of drawing their essential inferences. The traveler in India misses it, having no occasion to delve below the picturesque surface into living things as they are. The British official will especially avoid it—will deprecate its handling by others. His own daily labors, since the Reforms of 1919, hinge upon persuasion rather than upon command; therefore his hopes of success, like his orders from above, impose the policy of the gentle word. Outside agencies working for the moral welfare of the Indian seem often to have adopted the method of encouraging their beneficiary to dwell on his own merits and to harp upon others' shortcomings, rather than to face his faults and conquer them. And so, in the midst of an agreement of silence or flattery, you find a sick man growing daily weaker, dying, body and brain, of a disease that only himself can cure, and with no one, anywhere, enough his friend to hold the mirror up and show him plainly what is killing him.

In shouldering this task myself, I am fully aware of the resentments I shall incur: of the accusations of muck-raking; of injustice; of material-mindedness; of lack of sympathy; of falsehood perhaps; perhaps of prurience. But the fact of having seen conditions and their bearings, and of being in a position to present them, would seem to deprive one of the right to indulge a personal reluctance to incur consequences.

Here, in the beginning of this book, therefore, stands the kernel of what seems to me the most important factor in the life and future of one-eighth of the human race. In the pages to come will be found an attempt to widen the picture, stretching into other fields and touching upon other aspects of Indian life. But in no field, in no aspect, can that life escape the influences of its inception.

READING 26

M. K. Gandhi, "Drain Inspector's Report,"
Young India, September 15, 1927.

Mahatma Gandhi (1869–1948) was a leader in India's movement for
independence. His essay "Drain Inspector's Report" is his response to
Katherine Mayo's *Mother India*.

"Drain Inspector's Report"

Mahatma Gandhi

S everal correspondents have sent me cuttings containing reviews of, or protests against, Miss Mayo's "Mother India." A few have in addition asked me to give my own opinion on it. An enraged correspondent from London asks me to give him answers to several questions that he has framed upon the authoress's reference to me. Miss Mayo has herself favored me with a copy of her book.

I would certainly not have made time, especially when I have only limited energy and caution has been enjoined upon me by medical friends against overwork, to read the book during my tour. But these letters made it obligatory on me to read the book at once.

The book is cleverly and powerfully written. The carefully chosen quotations give it the appearance of a truthful book. But the impression it leaves on my mind is, that it is the report of a drain inspector sent out with the one purpose of opening and examining the drains of the country to be reported upon, or to give a graphic description of the stench exuded by the opened drains. If Miss Mayo had confessed that she had gone to India merely to open out and examine the drains of India, there would perhaps be little to complain about her compilation. But she says in effect with a certain amount of triumph, "The drains are India." True, in the concluding chapter there is a caution. But her caution is cleverly made to enforce her sweeping condemnation. I feel that no one who has any knowledge of India can possibly accept her terrible accusations against the thought and the life of the people of this unhappy country.

The book is without doubt untruthful, be the facts stated ever so truthful. If I open out and describe with punctilious care all the stench exuded from the drains of London and say, "Behold London," my facts will be incapable of challenge, but my judgment will be rightly condemned as a travesty of truth. Miss Mayo's book is nothing better, nothing else.

M.K. Gandhi, "Drain-Inspector's Report," *Young India.* Copyright © 1927 by

Navajivan Trust. Reprinted with permission.

The authoress says she was dissatisfied with the literature she read about India, and so she came to India "to see what a volunteer unsubsidized, uncommitted and unattached could observe of common things in daily human life."

After having read the book with great attention, I regret to say that I find it difficult to accept this claim. Unsubsidized she may be. Uncommitted and unattached she certainly fails to show herself in any page. We in India are accustomed to interested publications patronized—"patronized" is accepted as an elegant synonym for "subsidized"—by the Government. We have become used to understanding from pre-British days that the art (perfected by the British) of government includes the harnessing of the secret services of men learned and reported to be honest and honorable for shadowing suspects and for writing up the virtues of the Government of the day as if the certificate had come from disinterested quarters. I hope that Miss Mayo will not take offense if she comes under the shadow of such suspicion. It may be some conosolation to her to know that even some of the best English friends of India have been so suspected.

But ruling out of consideration the suspicion, it remains to be seen why she has written this untruthful book. It is doubly untruthful. It is untruthful in that she condemns a whole nation, or in her words, "the peoples of India" (she will not have us as one nation) practically without any reservation as to their sanitation, morals, religion, etc. It is also untruthful because she claims for the British Government merits which cannot be sustained and which many an honest British officer would blush to see the Government credited with.

If she is not subsidized Miss Mayo is an avowed Indophobe and Anglophile, refusing to see anything good about Indians and anything bad about the British and their rule. She does not *Rive* one an elevated idea of Western standard of judgment. Though she represents a class of sensational writers in the West, it is a class that, I flatter myself with the belief, is on the wane. There is a growing body of Americans who hate anything sensational, smart or crooked. But the pity of it is that there are still thousands in the West who delight in "shilling shockers." Nor are all the authoress's quotations or isolated facts truthfully stated. I propose to pick up those I have personal knowledge of. The book bristles with quotations torn from their contexts and with extracts which have been authoritatively challenged.

The authoress has violated all sense of propriety by associating the Poet's (Rabindranath Tagore's) name with child-marriage. The Poet has indeed referred to early marriage as not an undesirable institution. But there is a world of difference between child-marriage and early marriage. If she had taken the trouble of making the acquaintance of the free and freedom-loving girls and women of Shantiniketan, she would have known the poet's meaning of early marriage.

She has done me the honor of quoting me frequently in support of her argument. Any person who collects extracts from a reformer's diary, tears them from their context, and proceeds to condemn, on the strength of these, the people in whose midst the reformer has worked would get no hearing from sane and unbiased readers or hearers. But in her hurry to see everything Indian in a bad light, she has not only taken liberty with my writings, but she has not thought it necessary even to verify through me certain things ascribed by her or others to me. In fact she has combined in her own person what we understand in India as the judicial and executive officer. She is both the prosecutor and the judge. She has described the visit to me, and informed her readers that there are always with me two "secretaries" who write down every word I say.

I know that this is not a wilful perversion of facts. Nevertheless the statement is not true. I beg to inform her that I have no one near me who has been appointed or is expected to write down every word that I say. I have by me a coworker called Mahadev Desai who is striving to out-Boswell Boswell and does, whenever he is near me, take down whatever he considers to be wisdom dropping from my lips. I can't repel his advances, even if I would, for the relationship between us is, like the Hindu marriage, indissoluble. But the real crime committed against me is described by her at pages 387–388. She ascribes to the Poet "a fervent declaration that Ayurvedic science surpasses anything that the West can offer." (she has this time no quotation to back her statement.) Then she quotes my opinion that hospitals are institutions for propagating sin, and then distorts out of all recognition a sacred incident, honorable to the British surgeons and, I hope, to myself. I must ask the reader to excuse me for giving the full quotation from the book.

> As he happened to be in the prison at the time, a British surgeon of the Indian Medical Service came straightway to see him. "Mr. Gandhi," said the surgeon, as the incident was then reported. "I am sorry to tell you that you have appendicitis. If you were my patient. I should operate at once. But you will probably prefer to call in our Ayurvedic physician."
>
> Mr. Gandhi proved otherwise minded.
>
> "I should prefer not to operate," pursued the surgeon, "because in case the outcome should be unfortunate, all your friends will lay it as a charge of malicious intent against us whose duty is to care for you."
>
> "If you will only consent to operate," pleaded Mr. Gandhi, "I will call in my friends, now, and explain to them that you do so at my request."
>
> "So Mr. Gandhi wilfully went to an 'institutution for propagating sin,' was operated upon by one of the 'worst of all,' an officer of the Indian Medical Service and was attentively nursed through convalenscence by an English Sister whom he is understood to have thought after all rather a 'useful sort of person'."

This is a travesty of truth. I shall confine myself to correcting only what is libelous and not the other inaccuracies. There was no question here of calling in any Ayurvedic physician. Col. Maddock who performed the operation had the right, if he had so chosen, to perform the operation without a reference to me, and even in spite of me. But he and Surgeon-General Hooton showed a delicate consideration to me, and asked me whether I would wait for my own doctors who were known to them and who were also trained in the Western medicine and surgical science. I would not be behind-hand in returning their courtesy and consideration, and I immediately told them that they could perform the operation without waiting for my doctors to whom they had telegraphed, and that I would gladly give them a note for their protection in the event of the operation miscarrying. I endeavored to show that I had no distrust either in their ability or their good faith. It was to me a happy opportunity of demonstrating my personal goodwill.

READING 27

Veronika Fuechtner, "Indians, Jews, and Sex: Magnus Hirschfeld and Indian Sexology," in *Imagining Germany Imagining Asia* (Camden House, 2013), 111–130.

Reprinted in its entirety, this essay by historian Veronika Fuechtner describes the world tour of German sexologist Magnus Hirschfeld (1868–1935). Fuechtner uses the relationship between Hirschfeld and Indian sexologists as a way of approaching issues of political and social autonomy from Europe in India at the time.

Indians, Jews, and Sex

Magnus Hirschfeld and Indian Sexology

Veronika Fuechtner

The world tour of German-Jewish sexologist Magnus Hirschfeld stands in the midst of a series of fundamental transitions in the early 1930s: the transition between the world of Weimar Germany and the world of fascism and exile, the transition between the colonial and the postcolonial world, and the transition between sexology and eugenics as dominantly European-based new sciences to globalizing sciences that find their centers and protagonists in non-European societies. In this article I will focus on Hirschfeld's visit to India in 1931, where these transitions play out most visibly. Using Hirschfeld's own account of his world travel, the contemporary Indian press coverage, and other archival materials, I argue that Hirschfeld's account of Indian sexology presents a complicated reaction against the rise of fascism and an implicit rejection of fascist ideas of race and eugenics on the eve of Hirschfeld's exile from Germany. I also explore Hirschfeld's identification with the Indian independence movement and the connection he draws between his liberal-humanist view of sexual autonomy and the anti-colonial fight for political autonomy. In his encounter with India, Hirschfeld also reconceptualizes the science of sexology and his own role within it in complicated and at times contradictory ways. While Hirschfeld presents himself as a "sage from the West" and largely does not engage the main proponents of contemporary Indian sexology, he posits India as the birthplace of sexology and the *Kamasutra* as its original text. I argue that the way in which Hirschfeld's writing affirms either global universalism or cultural and national difference in sexological matters depends on what could be described as the implied racial politics of such an affirmation. Therefore, on the one hand Hirschfeld's text explicitly challenges the ideology of racial hierarchies. On the other hand, the text's "sexological Orientalism" subtly reinforces notions of racial inferiority in regard

Veronika Fuechtner, "Indians, Jews, and Sex: Magnus Hirschfeld and Indian Sexology," *Imagining Germany Imagining Asia: Essays in Asian-German Studies*, ed. Veronika Fuechtner and Mary Rhiel, pp. 111-130. Copyright © 2013 by Boydell & Brewer. Reprinted with permission.

to blackness and constructs the Jew as "white." It becomes clear that Hirschfeld's text represents as much a construction of Indian as of German politics, history, and culture. Hirschfeld's cosmopolitan outlook into what comes to stand for the future of a globalizing sexology is coupled with a premonition of the destruction of the world of Weimar Germany and a distinctly nostalgic sense of his loss of home.[1]

HIRSCHFELD'S PASSAGE TO INDIA

In November 1930 Magnus Hirschfeld left his work at the Institute for Sexual Science in Berlin to begin a lecture tour around the world, giving, as he wrote, 176 lectures in 500 days. This tour led him among others to the United States, Japan, China, the Philippines, Indonesia, India, and the Middle East. His world journey stands between his most productive time at the Institute for Sexual Science in Berlin during the Weimar Republic and his exile from fascism. While this transition period in his life marks the beginning of the destruction of his work in Germany, it also marks his connection with sexology as a global scientific movement, which will come to supersede the National Socialist attempt to eradicate it completely. Hirschfeld's world journey was also significant, since in China he met Li Shiu Tong, nicknamed Tao Li, who became his travel companion for the remainder of the journey, and his student and life companion for the last years of his life.

In April 1932, after more than a year of travel, Hirschfeld arrived in Vienna, where he decided not to return to Germany. He had been the victim of violent fascist attacks since the beginnings of the Weimar Republic and was receiving new threats. He settled briefly in Switzerland, where *Die Weltreise eines Sexualforschers* was published in early 1933. (An English translation was published in the United States in 1935 as *Men and Women: The World Journey of a Sexologist*.) A few months after the publication, Hirschfeld moved on to Paris, where sitting in a movie theater he had to watch a newsreel showing the destruction of his life's work, the library of his Institute being burned by a National Socialist mob. Two years later he died in exile in Southern France on his sixty-seventh birthday.[2]

Hirschfeld's own account of his journey through India in *The World Journey of a Sexologist* is an important, however not entirely reliable, source, but his trip can also be traced in Indian newspapers.[3] According to *The World Journey of a Sexologist*, Hirschfeld and Tao Li spent about eight and a half weeks in India between late September and mid-November 1931. They took a luxury train from Colombo to Madras to Calcutta, traveled on to Darjeeling, Patna, Benares, Delhi, Lahore, Agra, and Jaipur, and finally ended their trip in Bombay. There Hirschfeld was diagnosed with malaria, which he claimed to have contracted near the Taj Mahal. Instead of travelling on to Karachi as planned, Hirschfeld and Tao Li decided to take an ocean liner toward Port Said and then to make their way to Cairo from there. On 19 November 1931 they embarked on the S.S. Pilsna and left India.

During his time in India, Hirschfeld lectured incessantly. The audiences for his lectures ranged from medical associations to women's clubs. They were Indian, British, or both and hailed mostly from the scientific community or the educated elites. Depending on the composition of his audience, Hirschfeld adjusted his lectures. The titles ranged from closed lectures, such as "Sex Pathology" for the doctors of the Calcutta branch of the Indian Medical Association, or "Homosexuality, Inborn or Acquired?" at the Indian Psychoanalytic Society, to the open question-and-answer format of "Love, Sex and Marriage" at the Calcutta YMCA or the Taj Hotel in Bombay. The newspaper coverage indicates clearly that his lectures met with much interest. A reader of the *Bombay Chronicle* complained in a letter to the editor that the times of Hirschfeld's lectures should be rearranged, so that "as large a number of persons as possible [could] take advantage of them." He continues:

> In this connexion I think the evening time of seven o'clock on week days and any time on Sundays will be found convenient to most. In view of the fact that problems like those of sexual reforms and Birth-Control are little or hardly discussed in this city or rather country of ours, it will be no small gain to us, if we are enabled to drink deep into the cup of this branch of human knowledge by the good office of this eminent authority of Germany.[4]

This quote is pertinent to this context for two particular reasons. First, it documents the fact that there was great interest in issues of sexual reproduction and reform in the educated Indian middle-class (based on his name, the letter writer was in all likelihood a native speaker of Gujarati). Second, it documents the vocabulary of fetishization of the German medical profession in connection with the widespread belief in the educated Indian middle-class that science would be the basis of national progress, modernization, and possibly independence. While I will mostly be addressing the exoticization of the "Indian" in this paper, this exoticization also correlates with totemic constructions of whiteness in relation to science (by Indian, British, or German sources).

Contemporary press coverage gives us a glimpse into how Hirschfeld structured his lectures in India: he usually started out with a history of the Institute for Sexual Science and the World League for Sexual Reform, then he described the work of sexology as a scientific battle for enlightenment and a necessity for humanity, and finally he presented case studies and numbers on the topic of choice. Hirschfeld's lecture at the Grant Medical College in Bombay is described as follows:

> Dr. Hirschfeld began by explaining the various aspects of sexology. It was not only a medical science, he added, but a very important social science as well. A time had come when they had to give this science its due place in the human knowledge. Ignorance and the world traditions in this respect had brought about disasters under which the present day humanity was suffering. The doctor then explained various forms

of homo-sexuality and how they were practiced. The slides that were exhibited on the magic lantern were deeply instructive. They were the rarest cases of abnormalities of the sexual impulse.[5]

Besides elucidating the structure of Hirschfeld's presentation and the emphasis on sexology as part of a universal scientific project, the quote also visualizes the double-bind that Hirschfeld found himself in. In public professional settings, he showed slides of patients (and in some cases friends) as examples of what we would distinguish today as a wide spectrum of sexual physiologies, sexual orientations, and gender identities, but what at that point was conceived of as sexual abnormality. In private, Hirschfeld was living as a gay man. The magic lantern Hirschfeld was operating was revealing at least as much as it was concealing. Clearly, this was something that could not be articulated publicly at that time, neither in India nor in Germany, and speaking as a self-interested advocate would have undermined Hirschfeld's status as a scientist and the credibility of sexology as a scientific discipline. But it certainly informed the way in which Hirschfeld framed his scientific work as a humanitarian project and as a fight for social justice, and the way in which he at times quite fervently and emotionally connected to the Indian independence movement.

INDIA AS THE BATTLEGROUND FOR POLITICAL AND SEXUAL AUTONOMY

Hirschfeld and Tao Li arrived in India at a politically turbulent time. The second London roundtable conference, during which conditions for India's self-rule were to be negotiated, provided the backdrop to their trip and dominated newspaper coverage. The vision of the Indian National Congress, represented by Gandhi, who called for complete independence, and that of the British government, who offered a dominion status, proved incompatible. For Hirschfeld, clearly the call for sexual enlightenment and autonomy connected with the anti-colonial struggle. Hirschfeld met many of the leaders of the Indian Independence Movement, including Jawaharlal Nehru, whom he had already met in Germany, and whom he presciently described as possibly the first president of a decolonized India, an "überhealthy freedom fighter" (in contrast to Gandhi's "uptight Yogi nature").[6] Hirschfeld's wording reveals his dual perspective on the people he encounters—he sees them as objects of study and uses eugenic categories to describe them, but also as inspirational figures for his own humanitarian cause. When Nehru's wife, Kamala Nehru, saw Hirschfeld off, Hirschfeld unfolded the tri-color flag of the independence movement and waved it out of the train window. The *Bombay Chronicle* notes with amazement that Hirschfeld did the same when he embarked to leave India:

> "My best wishes to India and to Bombay," said the doctor. And finally, the Doctor drew out of his bag a tri-coloured flag and displayed it saying:

"See, I am taking your flag as a souvenir." We do not know if the doctor took along with the flag an account of the story of how India fought and is fighting for the flag and also photographs of some of the men, women, boys and girls who last year were belaboured with lathis [sticks] by the police for honoring the flag and for refusing to surrender it.[7]

Hirschfeld's political gesture signals solidarity with the Indian independence movement, but it is also addressed to the German public. In the context of the rise of fascism and the persecution of sexology as Jewish science, Hirschfeld shows what come to be his colors and models peaceful resistance against political violence.

Throughout *The World Journey of a Sexologist* Hirschfeld does not miss any opportunity to characterize the Indian intellectual elite as competent to take political matters into their own hands and to decry the injustice of their imprisonment. For the scientist Hirschfeld, colonial rule is not just a political wrong but "unnatural," a "biological absurdity" (*WS*, 231). Not only does he comment on many aspects of how colonialism damages Indian political life, for example, in the manipulation of Muslim-Hindu tensions or the British support of regional potentates, but Hirschfeld also describes what we would conceive of as a "colonial gaze" today and denounces the European construction of the "primitive" (*WS*, 12).

He especially takes issue with the 1927 book *Mother India* by the American historian Katherine Mayo. This book argued that the root of India's problems and specifically the repression of women lay in the sexual organization of Hindu society.[8] Mayo's study championed the idea of an Indian masculinity weakened by sexual excess. Hirschfeld counters that it would be difficult to speak of purely Indian sexual practices, given India's long history of British colonial rule. He also questions the validity of Mayo's data, but first and foremost her approach: "For me as a sexual scientist, there is no question that anybody who is set on uncovering similarly baffling sexual facts, even if they may be different in specific details, can collect and publish them in regard to any country" (*WS*, 208). For Hirschfeld, what is moral, *sittlich*, always stands in relationship to local customs, to *Sitte*. These categories are in flux. Ultimately though, they are expressions of the same universal sexual drives, and thus the Indian nose ring fulfills the same sexually enticing function as the European earring (*WS*, 198). In this instance, Hirschfeld rejects the category of the exotic altogether. He does, however, reinstate it in other instances, and I will return to these contradictions shortly.

INDIAN SEXOLOGY AND HIRSCHFELD'S CONSTRUCTION OF INDIAN SEXOLOGY

Hirschfeld's stay in India has to be put in the context of the globalization of sexology. He was not the only European sexologist to take an interest in India or to be received there. Havelock Ellis corresponded with Indian colleagues and cited Indian case studies. The American sexologist Margaret Sanger came to India in 1937 and famously debated Gandhi on the idea of "love sex," which Gandhi, who championed and practiced abstinence, of course rejected.[9] The globalization of sexology also included a lucrative global marketing of sexual tonics or aphrodisiacs. At the time when Hirschfeld visited India, German products such as *Okasa, Dibil, Viriline, Fertiline* and the very promising sounding *Casanova Cream* were already being marketed there with much success. Hirschfeld's world journey was also a very pragmatic business trip, designed to expand the market share for his own products, which were also sold in India. During his time in Bombay he successfully negotiated an exclusive sales agreement with the Modern Pharmaceuticals Company for the import and distribution of his own brand, *Titus Pearls.*[10]

In his book, Hirschfeld describes his journey throughout India as a mission of sorts and stylizes himself as a wise man from the Occident ("Weiser aus dem Abendland"), to whom the impotent men and sterile women of India flock for advice and possibly healing (WS, 219). This self-stylization presents a reversal of the image of the three kings from the Orient ("Drei Könige aus dem Morgenland"), who travel to the birthplace of Jesus. As Hirschfeld frequently points out throughout his account, he is traveling to the birthplace of sexology. To underscore the mythical quality of his journey and his impact, Hirschfeld frequently quotes from his travel diary, featuring such inscriptions as the following by an anonymous ardent fan: "My meeting with Dr. Magnus Hirschfeld I consider to be the greatest event of my life" (WS, 271). This rhetoric emphasizes the transformative power of Hirschfeld's appearances and presents Hirschfeld as the embodiment of a messianic science. And the sense of totemic whiteness I have mentioned earlier is implicitly imagined and cultivated on both sides.

In accordance with this self-stylization, Hirschfeld deplores what he perceives as the Indian backwardness in sexual matters and the lack of education. He conducts medical exams and consultations in all the cities where he lectures, and is occasionally presented with what he describes as medical curiosities by his Indian colleagues, for example, a pair of Siamese twins or a child bride.

This image of Hirschfeld in India is significant, as it is evocative of Hirschfeld's double-bind, which I mentioned earlier in the context of his slide lectures. Hirschfeld is clearly distinguished from his object of study by his white suit (evoking the color of the medical profession) and by his gaze onto the young girl from above. While Hirschfeld models the scientific gaze for the viewer in this image, however, he is also positioned on the same level as the young girl and her baby and unlike in the other photos in the volume, where the gaze of those being photographed back toward the viewer constitutes the relationship of observation, neither looks at the camera. The caption emphasizes that it is the author who is speaking with the girl, which betrays a general anxiety around separating the scientist from his object of study, but also foregrounds that Hirschfeld is to be seen as the ambassador of a different kind of science, a science based on empathy and advocacy.

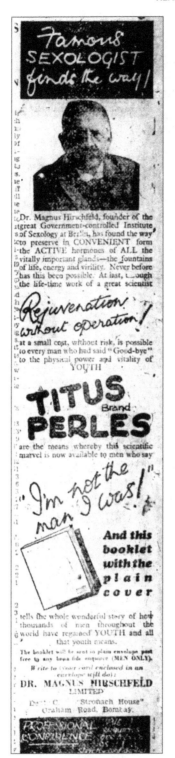

FIGURE 27.1 Advertisement for Hirschfeld's *Titus Pearls* in the *Bombay Chronicle,* March 1, 1931.

Verfasser spricht mit 13jähriger Mutter
(Kinderehe)

FIGURE 27.2   Author speaking with 13-year-old mother (child marriage). From Magnus Hirschfeld, *Die Weltreise eines Sexualforschers* (Brugg: Bözberg Verlag, 1933), 28.

In other instances not only the case studies Hirschfeld was presented with, such as the child bride, became artifacts in the book, but also the Indian scientists themselves. One example is Hirschfeld's account of his interaction with the founder of the Indian Psychoanalytic Society, Girindrashekhar Bose.

By his own account, Bose was, after Freud, the "second self-analyzed analyst in the history of psychoanalysis." He founded the Indian Psychoanalytic Society in 1921. It was the first Psychoanalytic Association outside Europe or the United States. Bose also corresponded with Freud for more than twenty years. In his work, he attempted to develop a specifically Indian brand of psychoanalysis, departing from the model of the psychoanalyst as a teacher, a guru. Most importantly, in contrast to Freud, he posited that the structure of the psyche varies across different cultures.[11]

In his book, Hirschfeld does not engage with Bose on a theoretical level, although they shared a lot of interests, given that Hirschfeld himself had been a member of the Berlin Psychoanalytic Association in its early days. Instead, Hirschfeld praises Bose mainly for one thing, namely his ability to produce an uncannily accurate drawing of Freud without ever having seen him. It functions as a kind of "native" magic trick. Furthermore, while Bose entertains Hirschfeld and other guests, he finds out that his mother passed away. Hirschfeld is highly impressed, but also somewhat uncomfortable, with the stoic manner in which Bose carries on the conversation. While Hirschfeld presents Bose as a man of Western science on the surface, he also depicts a form of intuitive, "native" knowledge and difference in

Girindrashekhar Bose
Professor für Experimental-Psychologie an der Universität Calcutta

FIGURE 27.3   Girindrashekhar Bose, Professor of Experimental Psychology at the University of Calcutta. From Magnus Hirschfeld, *Die Weltreise eines Sexualforschers* (Brugg: Bözberg Verlag, 1933), 24.

affect that stands in contrast to the European culture of scientific rationality and a German sense of appropriate emotion management. The image of Bose reflects this tension: he is portrayed in Indian dress, and in contrast to the other portraits of scientists in this book, his full body is visible for evaluation, his hands are folded, and he sits in a relaxed manner.

Interestingly, only some of the Indian scientists Hirschfeld encounters become encased as exhibit pieces in his ethnographic narrative, and it seems that they are the ones who are closest to him in their research interest. While Hirschfeld frequently points out the contemporary contributions of India's scientific elite, he does not engage with contemporary Indian sexology, its proponents, and their arguments. Instead, he develops an alternative account of ancient Indian sexology that establishes India as the birthplace of sexology. Hirschfeld quotes one of his own talks in Patna as follows: "Sex and love are as old as mankind, but the science of sex and love, sexology, is the youngest of all sciences. Of course we must not forget to remark that in India already 2300 years ago there existed a real science of sex" (*WS*, 238).

The first sexological study worldwide, Hirschfeld continues, was the *Kamasutra*. He subsequently develops a narrative of an autonomous Indian scientific sexology that consists of a mix of religious practices, bits of folklore, ethnography, and art history. These rather tenuous claims serve to posit India as a place of origin of sexology (as I will elaborate, a common trope of the time). According to Hirschfeld, the boom of Indian sexology 2300 years ago was followed by a rather long period of stagnation. Now, in the twentieth century, India is ready to experience a sexological renaissance, in which Hirschfeld will play a vital role as a catalyst (*WS*, 5, 239).

As we have also seen earlier, on the one hand Hirschfeld's text clearly buys into the vision of bringing Western-style scientific progress and modernization to India. On the other hand, however, the idea of India as the birthplace of sexology also explicitly serves to emphasize the autonomy of the contemporary Indian scientific community, its independence from "Western science." However, Hirschfeld expresses discomfort with what he perceives as uniquely Indian in this scientific community: a combination of religious mysticism and science. His book thus renders Indian sexology into a type of "native" science. One could say with Foucault, whose work reflects some of the assumptions and contradictions I have outlined in regard to Hirschfeld, that Hirschfeld presents an "ars erotica" as a "scientia sexualis."[12]

In order to understand how Hirschfeld's text engages or, one could argue, fails to engage contemporary Indian sexology, I would like to take a closer look at the Indian sexology of the time. As historians such as Sanjam Ahluwalia and Douglas Haynes, and the anthropologist Sanjay Shrivastava have demonstrated, the late 1920s and early 1930s experienced a strong birth control movement and the emergence of the scientifically framed disciplines of sexology and eugenics in India that is intrinsically connected with the nationalist movement. The popularity of these disciplines and their language of population control at this time also tied in with the emergence of a strong middle class, the migration of a large population of single male workers to the cities, and rising concerns about reproduction among the lower classes and minorities. Indian sexologists like N. S. Phadke or A. P. Pillay renegotiated notions of male or female sexuality.[13]

Phadke sought to connect what he saw as ancient thought with the framework of a scientific sexology. He was foremost a eugenicist and described population design as a tenet of an Aryan culture of physiological purity and fitness. This idea of eugenics also has socially progressive aspects for the time, in so far as it questioned the taboo of inter-caste marriage. If the genes were right, an untouchable and a Brahmin could and should marry.

In contrast, Pillay was foremost a sex reformer and much influenced by the American sexologist Margaret Sanger and by the British sexologist Havelock Ellis. He saw sexual pleasure as a universal right. That meant that women were equally as entitled as men to experience pleasure; therefore Pillay saw the education of women as a crucial factor in a general sexual education. Pillay's vision of gender equality had its limits, though, in the language of control and efficiency that was applied to the female body.

The advertising for Phadke's 1927 work *Sex Problem in India* in Indian newspapers shows the extent to which sexology had become part of public discussions of the English-speaking population in urban environments. The fact that the American sexologist Margaret Sanger introduced Phadke's work also points to the global traffic of sexological knowledge. And lastly, the connection this ad draws between "modern scientific knowledge" and "ancient Indian wisdom" in Phadke's work illuminates that Hirschfeld's construction of a specifically Indian form of science was a rhetoric that was at least in part shared by Indian sexologists.

While Phadke and Pillay's visions were politically explicitly anti-colonial, they did operate with the colonial-scientific categories of "degeneration" or "nerve exhaustion."[14] And maybe it is this heritage that Hirschfeld himself had turned away from at an earlier point in his scientific trajectory that led him to ignore the two most prominent sexologists in India. And that led him instead to develop an alternative narrative of ancient Indian sexology. It might not be too far-fetched to read Hirschfeld's Sanskritic and art-historic account as an answer to Phadke's Aryan eugenics. To Hirschfeld in 1931, there was much more at stake than the science of sexology in establishing other accounts of origin that did not lead back to an idealized Aryan past based on exclusionary population control. The Indian sexologists whom Hirschfeld identifies as the ancient founders of sexology are, among others, "Gonikaputra, who seems to have been the son of a prostitute, [and] Dattaka, who was himself a psychosexual hermaphrodite, or, as we call it to-day, an intersexual (or intermediate) type; as it is said of him that he could experience both: the male and female sort of sexual emotion"(*WS*, 238). In Hirschfeld's vision, these Indian founders of sexology derived their knowledge from a position that would be marginalized in his time, but was integrated and revered in this mythical Indian past. It is noteworthy that Hirschfeld presents Dattaka, this in both senses "other" founder of sexology, as a figure who occupies a male and female position simultaneously, not unlike the position he conceived for himself in private. One might also say that Hirschfeld construes throughout his writing a different type of Aryan past, based on heterogeneity and worldliness. For example, Hirschfeld writes in another instance that his favorite depiction of the Hindu God Shiva is the one that shows him as a dancer of the worlds ("Weltentänzer") rather than the one that shows him as the God of destruction and purification (*WS*, 242). In a significant aside, Hirschfeld situates the origin of the Shiva cult in Central Asia rather than in Western Asia, as some of the contemporary theories on Indo-Europeanism and the Aryan race would have it (*WS*, 243).

As becomes clear in these passages, Hirschfeld's vision of ancient India as the birthplace of sexology could be read as contemporary political commentary. First on the narratives of origin within Indian sexology and second on politically charged European conceptions of Aryanism. But third and maybe most significantly, Hirschfeld's narrative also has to be seen in the context of the attacks on sexology as a Jewish

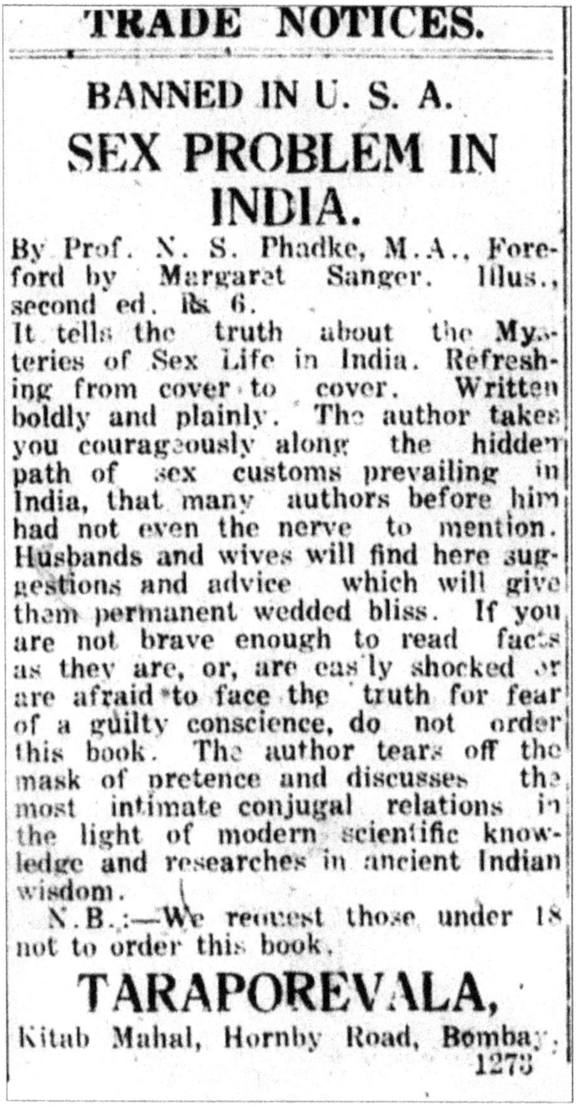

TRADE NOTICES.

BANNED IN U. S. A.

SEX PROBLEM IN INDIA.

By Prof. N. S. Phadke, M.A., Foreford by Margaret Sanger. Illus., second ed. Rs 6.

It tells the truth about the Mysteries of Sex Life in India. Refreshing from cover to cover. Written boldly and plainly. The author takes you courageously along the hidden path of sex customs prevailing in India, that many authors before him had not even the nerve to mention. Husbands and wives will find here suggestions and advice which will give them permanent wedded bliss. If you are not brave enough to read facts as they are, or, are easily shocked or are afraid to face the truth for fear of a guilty conscience, do not order this book. The author tears off the mask of pretence and discusses the most intimate conjugal relations in the light of modern scientific knowledge and researches in ancient Indian wisdom.

N.B.:—We request those under 18 not to order this book.

TARAPOREVALA,

Kitab Mahal, Hornby Road, Bombay.
1279

FIGURE 274 Book advertising for Phadke's *Sex Problem in India* in *Times of India*, January 19, 1931.

science corrupted by early twentieth-century decadence.[15] In Hirschfeld's account, sexology becomes an ancient science, located in the historical and geographical space that is frequently claimed as Aryan, but mobilized by Hirschfeld as a socially and culturally heterogeneous space. Hirschfeld comes to India at a moment when sexology is on the verge of destruction in Germany but booming in India. *The World Journey of a Sexologist* was published outside Germany in 1933, but it created for a German audience the concept that the science of sexology can not be eradicated because of its ancient roots and its global reach.

HIRSCHFELD'S SELECTIVE AFFINITIES

For his German readers, Hirschfeld emphasizes the place of sexology as a German science by positioning it within a long German scientific tradition, but also by describing this tradition as part what he very overtly construes as a global scientific community. In *World Journey of a Sexologist* Hirschfeld depicts at great length a community of world travelers in the name of science ("Weltenwanderer"), German scientists in exile or Indian scientists who have spent time in Germany, in the case of J. N. Ghosh even at the Institute for Sexual Science (*WS*, 235). This worldwide community also exists on a historical axis—for example, at the moment when Hirschfeld proudly announces on Java that he is following in the footsteps of the evolutionary biologist Ernst Haeckel (*WS*, 187). The text therefore positions Hirschfeld as part of a geographically and historically wide-ranging scientific past and present and further bolsters his status as a scientist, especially for his German readership.

Hirschfeld also extensively references the German cultural canon, further engaging his German readers. In the German cultural imagination, India was conceived of as an exotic, yet at the same time very familiar place and culture. The romanticist Friedrich Schlegel famously formulated that ancient India was "the source of all languages, all thought, and all poetry of the human spirit; everything, everything stems from India without exception."[16] Throughout the nineteenth century India was described as a place of origin linguistically with the Sanskrit language and literature, and racially with the idea of the Aryan.[17] Well into the twentieth century these perceived affinities factored into the formation of strange alliances—for example, between the Indian independence movement leader Subhas Chandra Bose and the National Socialists, who sponsored Bose's work toward an Indo-German Axis in 1940s Berlin.[18] In contrast, Hirschfeld's text construes a different kind of Indo-German axis, namely the sense of a common scientific project and the sense of cultural familiarity.

In fact Hirschfeld takes great care to create familiarity with India in his travel descriptions: the mountains of Darjeeling evoke St. Moritz, the Parsis are the Indian *Hugenotten*, Buddhism is India's Protestantism, and the Bombay seashore reminds him of his native Kolberg. India seems so familiar, so related, that Hirschfeld feels compelled to remind the reader that in the First World War India actually fought against the German Reich (*WS*, 217). He refers to a broad cultural canon on writings about India, presuming the reader's knowledge of these texts. For example, Hirschfeld implicitly takes on Hegel's comparison of India and China in regard to the function of the state, and postulates instead religion as the central comparative category.[19] In a similar vein, Hirschfeld also quite smugly corrects Goethe, whose depiction of temple dancers he deems too romanticizing (*WS*, 204). Hirschfeld's text also implicitly engages other India travel narratives of the time (such as Waldemar Bonsels's 1916 *Indienfahrt*). Most significantly in this regard, Hirschfeld's title *The World Journey of a Sexologist* and its emphasis of a distinct professional perspective clearly refers to Hermann Count Keyserling's highly influential 1919 *Travel Diary of a Philosopher*.[20] In contrast to Hirschfeld, Keyserling had championed a version of *Völkerpsychologie* that was based on a distinctly European ideal of universality. For Keyserling, the idea of racial purity was linked to biological survival and what he described as different levels of aristocracy of spirit, or spiritual caste, but not (or not yet) to blood. Hirschfeld's allusion to Keyserling in the title of his book is meaningful, since it is this very idea of Indian race and nobility that Hirschfeld questions. He does so explicitly when quoting Friedrich Rückert's 1839 epic poem *Brahmin Stories*. Rückert describes a noble love between husband and wife as the reason for the practice of *sati*, widow burnings. In turn, Hirschfeld accuses Rückert of idealizing what he sees as a primarily socio-economic and religious issue. Hirschfeld's rejection of the noble Indian relates to his rejection of the concept of the Aryan altogether, which also expresses itself in his construction of Indian sexology, as I argued earlier.

HIRSCHFELD'S RACES

As we have seen, Hirschfeld rejects the concept of the Aryan on several levels and seeks to emancipate sexual typology and sexology from race. However, this narrative can be temporarily suspended, and Hirschfeld subtly or in some cases not so subtly reinstates the exotic and the racially other. He closes his chapter on India by expressing the hope that Europe may learn from a free India as much as a free India may learn from Europe. But he also expresses the fear that India's original power, "Urkraft," and original spirit, "Urgeist," may be crushed by Euro-American sexual prudishness and repression (*WS*, 282). In this instance, Hirschfeld subscribes to the idea of a vital, healthy, native sexuality, which needs to be protected from the destructive forces of Western civilization. Hirschfeld's universalist position defines itself in opposition to the colonial liberalism of the British, but it is not free of its vocabulary and pitfalls—for example, when Hirschfeld talks about the "brown people's aptitude for education" (*WS*, 159; Bildungsfähigkeit).

But the inconsistency in asserting the primacy of culture in one instance and at the same time asserting the primacy of race in another in *The World Journey of a Sexologist* is of special significance when it comes to Hirschfeld's discussions of Jews. In his descriptions of Eastern European Jews in Palestine Hirschfeld asserts the primacy of culture and forcefully counters the stereotype of the Eastern European Jew as eternally unassimilated. The ghetto Jew is a product of history, writes Hirschfeld; he will be unrecognizable after a few years. There are no characterological differences between Eastern European Jews and others, let alone other Jews. Culture, education, and environment are the decisive factors: "Life shapes the dough" (*WS*, 359; Das Leben knetet den Teig).

His encounter with South-Indian Jews in the same book reads very differently. The text characterizes them as "black Jews" and finds them "strange" (*WS*, 278; merkwürdig). In this instance he claims that these South-Indian tribes must have adopted

Judaism many centuries ago and argues against the possibility of racial mixture with Jewish settlers in India. Here Hirschfeld seems to assert the primacy of race over the primacy of culture, and a notion of racial superiority and significant racial difference finds its way into the text. These South-Indian Jews look like the straight black haired "Indian type," Hirschfeld observes. His language subtly distinguishes between these "black" or "colored" Jews and the "dark-skinned" North-African Jews. The anxiety seems to evolve around delineating Jews from blacks.

This dynamic becomes especially apparent at another point in the book, when Hirschfeld describes an Egyptian wedding. The men of the wedding party are entertained by a "negroe from Sudan," a servant, a clown of sorts, who performs a belly dance in drag and encourages the young men to imitate him (WS, 296). Hirschfeld observes that his feminized gestures and facial expressions are "both grotesque and graceful, as this is so common in blacks." Early on in his book Hirschfeld had postulated that the sexual type always trumps the racial type. In this scene, however, the gender drag is deemphasized in favor of what is understood as some sort of racial drag that crosses the assumed racial boundaries between North Africa and sub-Saharan Africa. While Hirschfeld's text for the most part refrains from what Edward Said has described as classic orientalist imagery, this imagery, the belly dance, ironically reemerges in racial drag. Blackness clearly seems to present the limit of Hirschfeld's universalist vision.

I have argued that Hirschfeld's description of India in *The World Journey of a Sexologist* is to be read not only as sexual ethnography, which is what the book claims to be, but also as a direct response to National Socialist racial ideology, in the way the text references German-language culture, discusses the Indian independence movement, and construes or engages with eugenic and sexological knowledge. Hirschfeld dedicates his book to the science of eugenics, but it is a very different eugenics that he has in mind, namely one that sees racial mixture as a necessity and in some instances even an ideal and idealized occurrence. It is true, Hirschfeld's sexology and eugenics still carry with them remnants of the discourse on degeneration and primitivity present in late nineteenth- and early twentieth-century medical literature. And his wish to create a "better and happier humanity" via eugenic control might sound rather dystopian, and not only to ears attuned to Foucault. But his book still presents an effort to rethink eugenic selection on the eve of state-sponsored euthanasia.

It seems strange in hindsight that in 1920s Germany eugenics was not only associated with institutions such as the Institute for Sexual Science but also other progressive and emancipatory movements of the Weimar Republic, such as Wilhelm Reich's psychoanalytically inspired Sexpol movement. Only more recently has the scholarship on Hirschfeld explored the issue of whether the rhetoric of population control and physiological and psychological fitness for procreation was as much part of Hirschfeld's project as the recognition of everybody's uniquely composed sexual persona and the fight for the decriminalization of homosexuality or abortion.[21] I would argue even more broadly that the theoretical framework of disciplines such as sexology and psychoanalysis, which became defined in the early twentieth century, is intrinsically connected to contemporary notions of racial affinity and difference. While these scientists believe in a humanist liberalism as a basis for their scientific enterprise, this liberalism is also tested and fractured in the need to respond to racial prejudice from within their disciplinary history—as seen especially in medical science—or from outside—for example, the political pressures and threats of National Socialist racial ideology.

The contradictions and stereotypes I have laid out in regard to Hirschfeld's book obviously also abound in other ethnographic texts, and not only those of Hirschfeld's time. But for many reasons Hirschfeld's account of embracing the world while losing his homeland is also liberating and touching. While enacting power relations, Hirschfeld's ethnography still unfolds a counter-hegemonic potential. Despite the fact that the text indulges in self-aggrandizing prose, images of exotic excess, and tantalizing sex stories, and despite the fact that it presents Indian scientists as artifacts (as I have mentioned for Bose's case) along with wooden medical dolls, uncommented pages of sexological questionnaires, or Indian temples—despite all this, the book presents an interesting attempt at polyvocality. Hirschfeld also integrates voices of dissent into his text—for example, the observation by Professor P. Nath Kathju that unfortunately Hirschfeld also sees sexual symbolism in lots of places where he really should not and where it was not intended (*WS*, 257). This attempt at polyvocality, while not consistent or always successful, seems at least to be a textual proposition ahead of its time and anticipates the ethnographic collages of the early 1980s.[22] As the historian James Clifford has noted, "one can not escape dichotomizing, restructuring, textualizing in the making of interpretative statements about other cultures."[23] And Hirschfeld's prose is in many instances humorous and charming in its combination of an utterly provincial outlook (for example, when Hirschfeld rants about these silly Tibetan prayer flags that obstruct the beautiful view), with the farsighted stance of a cosmopolitan traveler who deems the exotic a question of perspective and to whom, as he exclaims time and again, the world is so very, very small.

NOTES

1   This article benefitted from the discussions of its preliminary stages in various settings. I especially want to thank Ute Frevert, Robert Tobin, and Veronika Lipphardt for giving me the opportunity to present on my work at the Max Planck Institute for Human Development, NEMLA, and the Max Planck Institute for the History of Science. I also thank the Boston group of Women in German for their feedback. A short-term fellowship at the Max Planck Institute for the History of Science in Berlin helped me complete this article. I am also very grateful to Manan Ahmed, Darcy Buerkle, Ralf Dose, Doug Haynes, Rainer Herrn, Rich Kremer, and Nikhil Rao for their generous encouragement, shared work, multiple readings and invaluable feedback. My two research assistants, Maia Pfeffer and Danielle Smith, worked

patiently through many microfiche rolls of newspapers and contributed greatly to this research. I also owe thanks to Hazen Allen from the Dartmouth Library, who managed to track down material that I didn't think was possible to get.

2   Manfred Herzer, *Magnus Hirschfeld: Leben und Werk eines jüdischen, schwulen und sozialistischen Sexologen* (Frankfurt am Main: Campus Verlag, 1992), 144, 230. For another comprehensive account of Hirschfeld's life, based on meticulous archival research, see Ralf Dose, *Magnus Hirschfeld: Deutscher—Jude—Weltbürger* (Berlin: Hentrich & Hentrich, 2005). Elena Mancini's English-language intellectual biography is primarily focused on reclaiming Hirschfeld as an early champion of contemporary sexual and gender rights, and provides a good sense of Hirschfeld's overall trajectory and historical context. Elena Mancini, *Magnus Hirschfeld and the Quest for Sexual Freedom: A History of the First International Sexual Freedom Movement* (New York: Palgrave Macmillan, 2010). The following two edited volumes present some of the most important recent scholarship on Hirschfeld: Andreas Seeck, ed., *Durch Wissenschaft zur Gerechtigkeit? Textsammlung zur kritischen Rezeption des Schaffens von Magnus Hirschfeld* (Berlin: LIT Verlag, 2003); Elke-Vera Kotowski and Julius H. Schoeps, eds., *Magnus Hirschfeld: Ein Leben im Spannungsfeld von Wissenschaft, Politik und Gesellschaft*, Sifria Wissenschaftliche Bibliothek 8 (Berlin: be.bra Wissenschaft, 2004). The journal *Mitteilungen der Magnus-Hirschfeld-Gesellschaft* provides a sense of the most current research.

3   For this article I have relied on available English-language newspapers, but an analysis of Indian newspapers in other languages such as Bengali would yield more insight into Hirschfeld's audiences and the reception of his work.

4   Letter by Nanalal N. Talaty, *Bombay Chronicle*, 17 Nov. 1931, 4.

5   *Bombay Chronicle*, 16 Nov. 1931, 7.

6   Magnus Hirschfeld, *Die Weltreise eines Sexualforschers* (Brugg: Bözberg Verlag, 1933), 250. I have relied on the German edition and retranslated the quotes to maintain some of the meaning that gets lost in the following historical translation: Magnus Hirschfeld, *Men and Women: The World Journey of a Sexologist* (New York: G. P. Putnam's Sons, 1935). Further references to this work are given in the text using the abbreviation *WS* and the page number. Like many of Hirschfeld's works, parts of this work have been republished under different titles, such as Magnus Hirschfeld, *Curious Sex Customs in the Far East* (New York: Grosset & Dunlap, 1935).

7   *Bombay Chronicle*, 21 Nov. 1931. There is evidence that the Institute for Sexual Science in Berlin was connected to the Indian independence movement well before Hirschfeld's trip to India, and the circles of sexology and international political activism overlapped considerably. According to Ralf Dose the Indian communist Manabendra Nath Roy stayed with the communist activist and publisher Willi Münzenberg, who had a flat at the institute (conversation with Ralf Dose on 20 August 2012).

8   Katherine Mayo argued that the principles of egocentricity and materialism disguised as spiritualism were carried to an extreme in India and represented

"a spotlight toward the end of the road" for the West. Katherine Mayo, *Mother India* (New York: Harcourt Brace, 1927). Selections of the book were edited and commented on by Mrinalini Sinha for the University of Michigan Press in 2000. Mrinalini Sinha, ed., *Mother India: Selections from the Controversial 1927 Text* (Ann Arbor: University of Michigan Press, 2000).

9   Douglas Haynes, "Selling Masculinity: Advertisements for Sex Tonics and the Making of Modern Conjugality in Western India, 1900–1945," *South Asia* 35, no. 4 (2012): 820.

10 This fact was conveyed to me by Hirschfeld scholar Ralf Dose, who reconstructed and documented Hirschfeld's business activities in India from sources at the Landesarchiv Berlin (A Rep 250–02-00/162). In regard to the context for the marketing of aphrodisiacs on the Indian market, see Haynes, "Selling Masculinity," and for the wider context of discourses of sex and sexuality in colonial India see Sanjam Ahluwalia, *Reproductive Restraints: Birth Control in India, 1877–1947* (Champaign: University of Illinois Press, 2008); Charu Gupta, *Sexuality, Obscenity, Community: Women, Muslims and the Hindu Public in Colonial India* (New York: Palgrave, 2002); Sarah Hodges, *Contraception, Colonialism and Commerce: Birth Control in South India, 1920–40* (Burlington, VT: Ashgate, 2008); Mrinalini Sinha, *Colonial Masculinity: The "Manly Englishman" and the "Effeminate Bengali" in the Late Nineteenth Century* (Manchester: Manchester University Press, 1995); Deepa Sreenivas, *Sculpting a Middle Class: History, Masculinity and the Amar Chitra Katha in India* (New York: Routledge, 2010); Sanjay Srivastava, "Introduction: Semen, History, Desire and Theory" and "Non-Gandhian Sexuality, Commodity Cultures and a 'Happy Married Life,'" in *Sexual Sites, Seminal Attitudes*, ed. Sanjay Srivastava (New Delhi: Sage Publications, 2004), 11–48 and 342–90; and Sanjay Srivastava, *Passionate Modernity: Sexuality, Class and Consumption in India* (New Delhi: Routledge, 2007).

11 See Christiane Hartnack, *Psychoanalysis in Colonial India* (Oxford: Oxford University Press, 2001); C. V. Ramana, "On the Early History and Development of Psychoanalysis in India," *Journal of the American Psychoanalytic Association* 12 (1964): 110–34; Tarun Chandra Sinha, "Development of Psychoanalysis in India," *International Journal of Psychoanalysis* (1966): 427–39.

12 Michel Foucault, *The History of Sexuality*, vol.1, *An Introduction* (New York: Vintage Books, 1990), 57.

13 Haynes, "Selling Masculinity," 822.

14 A. P. Pillay, *Disorders of Sex and Reproduction; Aetiology, Diagnosis and Treatment* (London: H. K. Lewis, 1948), 116 and 176–77. See also A. P. Pillay, *The Art of Love and Sane Sex Living* (Bombay: Taraporevala, 1940).

15 One of many examples is the 1929 front-page article in the National Socialist propaganda paper *Der Stürmer*, which describes Hirschfeld as an "apostle of sodomy" and as a propagator of intercourse with children. *Der Stürmer* 7, no. 8 (1929). An image of the article is available on the permanent online exhibit of the Magnus-Hirschfeld Society in Berlin: http://www.hirschfeld.in-berlin.de (accessed 16 Dec. 2012).

16 Edgar Lohner, ed., *Ludwig Tieck und die Brüder Schlegel: Briefe* (Munich: Winkler Verlag, 1972), 135.

17 Sara Eigen and Mark Joseph Larrimore, eds., *The German Invention of Race* (Albany: State University of New York Press, 2006), 168. See also Tuska Benes, *In Babel's Shadow: Language, Philology, and Nation in Nineteenth Century Germany* (Detroit: Wayne State University Press, 2008); Suzanne Marchand, *German Orientalism in the Age of Empire: Religion, Race, and Scholarship* (New York: Cambridge University Press, 2009); Léon Poliakov, *The Aryan Myth: A History of Racist & Nationalistic Ideas in Europe* (New York: Barnes & Noble, 1996).

18 Marshall J. Getz, *Subhas Chandra Bose: A Biography* (Jefferson, NC: McFarland, 2002), 3.

19 "In China sind Philosophie und Wissenschaft zugleich Religion, in Indien ist Religion zugleich Philosophie und Wissenschaft." Hirschfeld, *Weltreise eines Sexualforschers*, 273. Hegel writes in his *Lectures on the Philosophy of History* that while China may be regarded as nothing else but a state, Hindu political existence presents us with a people but no state.

20 Introducing a recent new edition of Hirschfeld's book, the writer Hans Christoph Buch points out this relationship and draws the comparison with Keyserling's and Hanns Heinz Ewers's travel narratives. Buch points out how much less prejudiced Hirschfeld's account and politics seem in hindsight. Magnus Hirschfeld, *Weltreise eines Sexualforschers im Jahre 1931/32* (Frankfurt: Eichborn Verlag, 2006), 20.

21 See especially Rainer Herrn, "Phantom Rasse: Ein Hirngespinst als Weltgefahr. Anmerkungen zu einem Aufsatz Magnus Hirschfelds," in *Durch Wissenschaft zur Gerechtigkeit? Textsammlung zur kritischen Rezeption des Schaffens von Magnus Hirschfeld*, ed. Andreas Seek (Münster: LIT, 2003), 111–24; Atina Grossmann, "Magnus Hirschfeld, Sexualreform und die Neue Frau. Das Institut für Sexualwissenschaft und Weimar Berlin," in *Der Sexualreformer Magnus Hirschfeld: Ein Leben im Spannungsfeld von Wissenschaft, Politik und Gesellschaft*, ed. Elke-Vera Kotowski and Julius H. Schoeps (Berlin: Bebra, 2004), 201–16.

22 James Clifford, *The Predicament of Culture: Twentieth-Century Ethnography, Literature, and Art* (Cambridge, MA: Harvard University Press, 1988), 15.

23 Clifford, *The Predicament of Culture*, 261.

PART VII

WAR AND ITS AFTERMATH

The forced sexual slavery of "comfort women" described by Maria Rosa Henson marks one of the ways in which the violence of the Second World War was gendered and sexualized. In the postwar period, Alfred Kinsey's studies of male and female sexuality brought the range of sexual behavior into public discussion in an unprecedented manner. Vernon Rosario's essay contextualizes the efforts of Kinsey and others to scientifically study sex, sexuality, and sexual response.

READING 28

Maria Rosa Henson, *Comfort Woman: A Filipina's Story of Prostitution and Slavery under the Japanese Military* (Rowman & Littlefield, 1999), Excerpt.

Maria Rosa Henson (1927–1997) was a Filipina woman. In this excerpt she describes part of her experience as a "comfort woman" for the occupying Japanese military during World War II.

Comfort Woman

A Filipina's Story of Prostitution and Slavery under the Japanese Military

Maria Rosa Hanson

One morning in April 1943, I was asked by my Huk comrades to collect some sacks of dried corn from the nearby town of Magalang. I went with two others in a cart pulled by a carabao. One comrade sat with me in the cart, the other rode on the carabao's back. It was the height of the dry season. The day was very hot.

We loaded the sacks of corn into the cart and made our way back to our barrio. As we approached the Japanese checkpoint near the town hospital of Angeles, the man beside me whispered, 'Be careful, there are some guns and ammunition hidden in the sacks of corn." I froze. I did not know till then that what we were sitting on were guns. I became very nervous, fearing that if the Japanese soldiers discovered the weapons, we would all get killed.

I got off the cart and showed the sentry our passes. At that time, everyone in the barrio needed to have a pass to show that he or she lived there. The sentry looked at the sacks of corn, touching here and pressing there without saying anything.

Finally, he allowed us to pass, but after we had gone thirty meters from the checkpoint he whistled and signaled us to return. We looked at each other and turned pale. If he emptied the sack, he would surely find the guns and kill us instantly. The soldier raised his hands and signaled that I was the only one to come back, and my companions were allowed to go.

I walked to the checkpoint, thinking the guns were safe but I would be in danger. I thought that maybe they would rape me. The guard led me at gunpoint to the second floor of the building that used to be the town hospital. It had been turned into the Japanese headquarters and garrison. I saw six other women there. I was given a small room with a bamboo bed. The room had no door, only a curtain. Japanese soldiers kept watch in the hall outside. That night, nothing happened to me.

The following day was hell. Without warning, a Japanese soldier entered my room and pointed his bayonet at my chest. I thought he was going kill me, but he used his bayonet to slash my dress and tear it open. I was too frightened to scream. And then he raped me. When he was done, other soldiers came into my room, and they took turns raping me.

Twelve soldiers raped me in quick succession, after which I was given half an hour to rest. Then twelve more soldiers followed. They all lined up outside the room waiting for their turn. I bled so much and was in such pain, I could not even stand up. The next morning, I was too weak to get up. A woman brought me a cup of tea and breakfast of rice and dried fish. I wanted to ask her some questions, but the guard in the hall outside stopped us from saying anything to each other.

I could not eat. I felt much pain, and my vagina was swollen. I cried and cried, calling my mother. I could not resist the soldiers because they might kill me. So what else could I do? Every day, from two in the afternoon to ten in the evening, the soldiers lined up outside my room and the rooms of the six other women there. I did not even have time to wash after each assault. At the end of the day, I just closed my eyes and cried.

READING 29

Alfred Kinsey, "Homosexual Responses and
Contacts," *Sexual Behavior in the Human Female*
(1953) (Indiana University Press, 1998), 446–501.

Alfred Kinsey (1894–1956) was an American biologist and sex researcher.
His books *Sexual Behavior in the Human Male* (1948) and *Sexual Behavior
in the Human Female* (1953) became known as the Kinsey Reports. In
this excerpt, he describes the results of his research on female homosexuality in the United States.

Homosexual Responses and Contacts

By Alfred Kinsey

The classification of sexual behavior as masturbatory, heterosexual, or homosexual is based upon the nature of the stimulus which initiates the behavior. The present chapter, dealing with the homosexual behavior of the females in our sample, records the sexual responses which they had made to other females, and the overt contacts which they had had with other females in the course of their sexual histories.

The term homosexual comes from the Greek prefix *homo*, referring to the sameness of the individuals involved, and not from the Latin word *homo* which means man. It contrasts with the term heterosexual which refers to responses or contacts between individuals of different (*hetero*) sexes.

While the term homosexual is quite regularly applied by clinicians and by the public at large to relations between males, there is a growing tendency to refer to sexual relationships between females as *lesbian* or *sapphic*. Both of these terms reflect the homosexual history of Sappho who lived on the Isle of Lesbos in ancient Greece. While there is some advantage in having a terminology which distinguishes homosexual relations which occur between females from those which occur between males, there is a distinct disadvantage in using a terminology which suggests that there are fundamental differences between the homosexual responses and activities of females and of males.

PHYSIOLOGIC AND PSYCHOLOGIC BASES

It cannot be too frequently emphasized that the behavior of any animal must depend upon the nature of the stimulus which it meets, its anatomic and physiologic capacities, and its background of previous experience. Unless it has been conditioned by previous experience, an

Alfred C. Kinsey, Wardell B. Pomeroy, Clyde E. Martin, and Paul H. Gebhard, "Homosexual Responses and Contacts," *Sexual Behavior in the Human Female*, pp. 446-501. Copyright © 1998 by Indiana University Press. Reprinted with permission.

animal should respond identically to identical stimuli, whether they emanate from some part of its own body, from another individual of the same sex, or from an individual of the opposite sex.

The classification of sexual behavior as masturbatory, heterosexual, or homosexual is, therefore, unfortunate if it suggests that three different types of responses are involved, or suggests that only different types of persons seek out or accept each kind of sexual activity. There is nothing known in the anatomy or physiology of sexual response and orgasm which distinguishes masturbatory, heterosexual, or homosexual reactions (Chapters 14–15). The terms are of value only because they describe the source of the sexual stimulation, and they should not be taken as descriptions of the individuals who respond to the various stimuli. It would clarify our thinking if the terms could be dropped completely out of our vocabulary, for then socio-sexual behavior could be described as activity between a female and a male, or between two females, or between two males, and this would constitute a more objective record of the fact. For the present, however, we shall have to use the term homosexual in something of its standard meaning, except that we shall use it primarily to describe sexual *relationships,* and shall prefer not to use it to describe the *individuals* who were involved in those relationships.

The inherent physiologic capacity of an animal to respond to any sufficient stimulus seems, then, the basic explanation of the fact that some individuals respond to stimuli originating in other individuals of their own sex—and it appears to indicate that every individual could so respond if the opportunity offered and one were not conditioned against making such responses. There is no need of hypothesizing peculiar hormonal factors that make certain individuals especially liable to engage in homosexual activity, and we know of no data which prove the existence of such hormonal factors (p. 758). There are no sufficient data to show that specific hereditary factors are involved. Theories of childhood attachments to one or the other parent, theories of fixation at some infantile level of sexual development, interpretations of homosexuality as neurotic or psychopathic behavior or moral degeneracy, and other philosophic interpretations are not supported by scientific research, and are contrary to the specific data on our series of female and male histories. The data indicate that the factors leading to homosexual behavior are (1) the basic physiologic capacity of every mammal to respond to any sufficient stimulus; (2) the accident which leads an individual into his or her first sexual experience with a person of the same sex; (3) the conditioning effects of such experience; and (4) the indirect but powerful conditioning which the opinions of other persons and the social codes may have on an individual's decision to accept or reject this type of sexual contact.[1]

---

1 Various factors which have been supposed to cause or contribute to female homosexual activity are the following: *Fear of pregnancy or venereal disease:* Talmey 1910:149. Krafft-Ebing 1922:397. Norton 1949:62. Cory 1951:88. *Heterosexual trauma or disappointment:* Havelock Ellis 1915(2) :323. Stekel 1922:292–305. Krafft-Ebing 1922:397–398. Marañón 1932:20. Caufeynon 1934:31. Hutton 1937:1S9. Kahn 1939:268. Beauvoir 1952:418. *Sated with males:* Bloch 1908:546–547. Krafft-Ebing 1922:398. Moreck

MAMMALIAN BACKGROUND

The impression that infra-human mammals more or less confine themselves to heterosexual activities is a distortion of the fact which appears to have originated in a man-made philosophy, rather than in specific observations of mammalian behavior. Biologists and psychologists who have accepted the doctrine that the only natural function of sex is reproduction have simply ignored the existence of sexual activity which is not reproductive. They have assumed that heterosexual responses are a part of an animal's innate, "instinctive" equipment, and that all other types of sexual activity represent "perversions" of the "normal instincts." Such interpretations are, however, mystical. They do not originate in our knowledge of the physiology of sexual response (Chapter 15), and can be maintained only if one assumes that sexual function is in some fashion divorced from the physiologic processes which control other functions of the animal body. It may be true that heterosexual contacts outnumber homosexual contacts in most species of mammals, but it would be hard to demonstrate that this depends upon the "normality" of heterosexual responses, and the "abnormality" of homosexual responses.

In actuality, sexual contacts between individuals of the same sex are known to occur in practically every species of mammal which has been extensively studied. In many species, homosexual contacts may occur with considerable frequency, although never as frequently as heterosexual contacts. Heterosexual contacts occur more frequently because they are facilitated (1) by the greater submissiveness of the female and the greater aggressiveness of the male, and this seems to be a prime factor in

---

1929:286. *Society's heterosexual taboos:* Hutton 1937:139–140. Henry 1941(2): 1026. English and Pearson 1945:378. Strain 1948:179. *Seeing parents in coitus:* Farnham 1951–108. *Seduction by older females:* Moll 1912:314. Havelock Ellis 1915 (2):322. Moreck 1929:302. English and Pearson 1945:378. Norton 1949:62. Farnham 1951:167. *Masturbation which leads to homosexuality:* Havelock Ellis 1915(2) :277. Krafft-Ebing 1922:286. *Thsfactor is also mentioned for males by:* Taylor 1933:63, and Remplein 1950:246–247. *Endocrine imbalance:* Havelock Ellis 1915 (2): 316. Lipschütz 1924:371. S. Kahn 1937:135. Hvman 1946(3): 2491. Negri 1949:197. *Penis envy and castration complex:* Chideckel 1935:14. Brody 1943:56. Deutsch 1944:347. Fenichel 1945:338. Freud 1950 (5):257. *Father-fixation or hatred toward mother:* Blanchard and Manasses 1930:104, 106. Hesnard 1933:208–209. S. Kahn 1937:20. Bergler 1943:48. Fenichel 1945:338–339. *Mother-fixation:* S. Kahn 1937:20. Deutsch 1944: 347–348. Fenichel 1945:338. Farnham 1951:169. *A continuation of a childhood "bisexual" phase, or a fixation at, or a regression to, an early adolescent stage of psychosexual development:* Moil 1912:60–61, 125. Havelock Ellis 1915(2):309–310. Stekel 1922:39. Marañon 1929:172–174. Blanchard and Manasses 1930:104. Hesnard 1933:188. Freud 1933:177–178. Hamilton in Robinson 1936:336, 341. S. Kahn 1937:18–19. Deutsch 1944:330–331. Sadler 1944:91. English and Pearson 1945:379. Negri 1949:203–204. Hutton in Neville-Rolfe 1950:429. London and Caprio 1950:635. Famham 1951:166, 175. Kallmann 1952:295. Brody 1943:58 (adds that a homosexual would be neurotic even in a society which accepted homosexuality). *A defense against' or a flight from incestuous desires:* Hamilton in Robinson 1936:341. Farnham 1951:175. *Constitutional, congenital, or inherited traits or tendencies:* Parke 1906:320. Bloch 1908:489. Carpenter 1908:55. Moll 1912:125, 130; 1931:234. Havelock Ellis 1915(2):308–311, 317. Krafft-Ebing 1922:285, 288. Kelly 1930:132–133, 220. Robinson 1931:280–231. Freud 1933:178. Potter 1933: 151. Caufeynon 1934:34. Hirschfeld in Robinson 1936:326. S. Kahn 1937:89. Henry 1941(2):1023–1026. Sadler 1944:106. Hirschfeld 1944:281. Thornton 1946:94. Negri 1949:163, 187. Benvenuti 1950:168. Kallmann 1952:295 (in a study of twins).

determining the roles which the two sexes play in heterosexual relationships; (2) by the more or less similar levels of aggressiveness between individuals of the same sex, which may account for the fact that not all animals will submit to being mounted by individuals of their own sex; (3) by the greater ease of intromission into the female vagina and the greater difficulty of penetrating the male anus; (4) by the lack of intromission when contacts occur between two females, and the consequent lack of those satisfactions which intromission may bring in a heterosexual relationship; (5) by olfactory and other anatomic and physiologic characteristics which differentiate the sexes in certain mammalian species; (6) by the psychologic conditioning which is provided by the more frequently successful heterosexual contacts.

Homosexual contacts in infra-human species of mammals occur among both females and males. Homosexual contacts between females have been observed in such widely separated species as rats, mice, hamsters, guinea pigs, rabbits, porcupines, marten, cattle, antelope, goats, horses, pigs, lions, sheep, monkeys, and chimpanzees.[2] The homosexual contacts between these infra-human females are apparently never completed in the sense that they reach orgasm, but it is not certain how often infra-human females ever reach orgasm in any type of sexual relationship. On the other hand, sexual contacts between males of the lower mammalian species do proceed to the point of orgasm, at least for the male that mounts another male.[3]

In some species the homosexual contacts between females may occur as frequently as the homosexual contacts between males.[4] Every farmer who has raised cattle knows, for instance, that cows quite regularly mount cows. He may be less familiar with the fact that bulls mount bulls, but this is because cows are commonly kept together while bulls are not so often kept together in the same pasture.

It is generally believed that females of the infra-human species of mammals are sexually responsive only during the so-called periods of heat, or what is technically referred to as the estrus period. This, however, is not strictly so. The chief effect of

---

2 We have observed homosexual behavior in male monkeys, male dogs, bulls, cows, male and female rats, male porcupines, and male and female guinea pigs. Homosexual activities in other animals are noted by: Karseh 1900:128–129 (female antelope, male and female goat, ram. stallion). Féré 1904:78 (male donkey). Havelock Ellis 1910(1):165 (male elephant, male hyena). Hamilton 1914:307 (female monkey). Bingham 1928:126–127 (female chimpanzee). Marshall and Hammond 1944:89 (doe rabbit). Reed 1946:200 (male bat). Beach 1947a:41 (female cat). Beach 1948:36 (male mouse). Beach in Hoch and Zubin 1949:63–64 (female marten, female porcupine, male lion, male rabbit). Gantt in Wolff 1950:1036 (male cat). Ford and Beach 1951:139 (male porpoise), 141 (lioness, mare, sow, ewe, female hamster, female mouse, female dog). Snadie, verbal communication (male porcupine, male raccoon).

3 Ejaculation resulting from homosexual contact between males of lower mammalian species has been noted in: Karsch 1900:129 (ram and goat). Kempf 1917:134–135 (monkey). Moll 1931:17 (dog). Beach 1948:36 (mouse), Ford and Beach 1951:139 (rat). Brookfield Zoo, verbal communication (baboon), We have observed such ejaculation in the bull.

4 For the sub-primates, Beach 1947a:40 states that "the occurrence of masculine sexual responses in female animals is more common than is the appearance of feminine behavior in males." Ford and Beach 1951: 143 note, however, that in the class Mammalia taken as a whole, homosexual behavior among males is more frequent than homosexual behavior among females.

estrus seems to be the preparation of the animal to accept the approaches of another animal which tries to mount it. The cows that are mounted in the pasture are those that are in estrus, but the cows that do the mounting are in most instances individuals which are not in estrus (p. 737).[5]

Whether sexual relationships among the infra-human species are heterosexual or homosexual appears to depend on the nature of the immediate circumstances and the availability of a partner of one or the other sex. It depends to a lesser degree upon the animal's previous experience, but no other mammalian species is so affected by its experience as the human animal may be. There is, however, some suggestion, but as yet an insufficient record, that the males among the lower mammalian species are more likely than the females to become conditioned to exclusively homosexual behavior; but even then such exclusive behavior appears to be rare.[6]

The mammalian record thus confirms our statement that any animal which is not too strongly conditioned by some special sort of experience is capable of responding to any adequate stimulus. This is what we find in the more uninhibited segments of our own human species, and this is what we find among young children who are not too rigorously restrained in their early sex play. Exclusive preferences and patterns of behavior, heterosexual or homosexual, come only with experience, or as a result of social pressures which tend to force an individual into an exclusive pattern of one or the other sort. Psychologists and psychiatrists, reflecting the mores of the culture in which they have been raised, have spent a good deal of time trying to explain the origins of homosexual activity; but considering the physiology of sexual response and the mammalian backgrounds of human behavior, it is not so difficult to explain why a human animal does a particular thing sexually. It is more difficult to explain why each and every individual is not involved in every type of sexual activity.

ANTHROPOLOGIC BACKGROUND

In the course of human history, distinctions between the acceptability of heterosexual and of homosexual activities have not been confined to our European and American cultures. Most cultures are less acceptant of homosexual, and more

---

5   Two situations may be involved: (1) the estrual female may be receptive to being mounted and often attempts to elicit such mounting (see Beach in Hoch and Zubin 1949:64; Rice and Andrews 1951:151). (2) If she is not mounted the estrual female may mount another animal of the same or opposite sex. For the latter, see: Beach 1948:66–68 (cow, sow, rabbit, cat, shrew). Ford and Beach 1951:141–142 (rabbit, sow, mare, cow, guinea pig).

6   Exclusive, although usually temporary male homosexuality is noted in: Hamilton 1914:307–308 (monkey). Beach in Hoch and Zubin 1949:64–65 (lion). Ford and Beach 1951:136, 139 (baboon and porpoise). Shadle, verbal communication (porcupine). No exclusively homosexual patterns have been reported for female mammals.

acceptant of heterosexual contacts. There are some which are not particularly disturbed over male homosexual activity, and some which expect and openly condone such behavior among young males before marriage and even to some degree after marriage; but there are no cultures in which homosexual activity among males seems to be more acceptable than heterosexual activity.[7] It is probable that in some Moslem, Buddhist, and other areas male homosexual contacts occur more frequently than they do in our European or American cultures, and in certain age groups they may occur more frequently than heterosexual contacts; but heterosexual relationships are, at least overtly, more acceptable even in those cultures.

Records of male homosexual activity are also common enough among more primitive human groups, but there are fewer records of homosexual activity among females in primitive groups. We find some sixty pre-literate societies from which some female homosexual activity has been reported, but the majority of the reports imply that such activity is rare. There appears to be only one pre-literate group, namely the Mohave Indians of our Southwest, for whom there are records of exclusively homosexual patterns among females. That same group is the only one for which there are reports that female homosexual activity is openly sanctioned.[8] For ten or a dozen groups, there are records of female transvestites—*i.e.*, anatomic females who dress and assume the position of the male in their social organization—but transvestism and homosexuality are different phenomena, and our data show that only a portion of the transvestites have homosexual histories (p. 679).

There is some question whether the scant record of female homosexuality among pre-literate groups adequately reflects the fact. It may merely reflect the taboos of the European or American anthropologists who accumulated the data, and the fact that they have been notably reticent in inquiring about sexual practices which are not considered "normal" by Judeo-Christian standards. Moreover, the informants in the anthropologic studies have usually been males, and they would be less likely to know the extent of female homosexual activities in their cultures. It is, nonetheless, quite possible that such activities are actually limited among the females of these pre-literate groups, possibly because of the wide acceptance of pre-marital heterosexual relationships, and probably because of the social importance of marriage in most primitive groups.[9]

---

7   Ford and Beach 1951:130 note that 64 per cent of a sample of 76 societies consider homosexuality acceptable for certain persons.

8   The sexual life of the Mohave was intensively studied by Devereux 1936, 1937.

9   Ford and Beach 1951:133, 143, also note that female homosexuality seems less frequent than male homosexuality among pre-literates.

RELATION TO AGE AND MARITAL STATUS

As in any other type of sexual situation, there are: (1) individuals who have been erotically aroused by other individuals of the same sex, whether or no they had physical contact with them; (2) individuals who have had physical contacts of a sexual sort with other individuals of the same sex, whether or no they were erotically aroused in those contacts; and (3) individuals who have been aroused to the point of orgasm by their physical contacts with individuals of the same sex. These three types of situations are carefully distinguished in the statistics given here.

ACCUMULATIVE INCIDENCE IN TOTAL SAMPLE

Some of the females in the sample had been conscious of specifically erotic responses to other females when they were as young as three and four (Table 13). The percentages of those who had been erotically aroused had then steadily risen, without any abrupt development, to about thirty years of age. By that time, a quarter (25 per cent) of all the females had recognized erotic responses to other females. The accumulative incidence figures had risen only gradually after age thirty. They had finally reached a level at about28 per cent (Table 29.6, Figure 29.1).[10]

The number of females in the sample who had made specifically sexual contacts with other females also rose gradually, again without any abrupt development, from the age of ten to about thirty. By then some 17 per cent of the females had had such experience (Tables 126, 131, Figure 29.1). By age forty, 19 per cent of the females in the total sample had had some physical contact with other females which was deliberately and consciously, at least on the part of one of the partners, intended to be sexual.[11]

Homosexual activity among the females in the sample had been largely confined to the single females and, to a lesser extent, to previously married females who had been widowed, separated, or divorced, Both the incidences and frequencies were distinctly low among the married females (Table 29.1, Figure 29.2). Thus, while the accumulative incidences of homosexual contacts had reached 19 per cent in the total sample by age forty, they were 24 per cent for the females who had never been married by that age, 3 per cent for the married females, and 9 per cent for the previously married females. The age at which the females had married seemed to have had no effect on

---

10   Our accumulative incidence figures for homosexual responses among females are close to those in two other studies: Davis 1929:247 (26 per cent at age 36). Gilbert Youth Research 1951 (13 per cent, college students).

11   Our accumulative incidence figures for overt homosexual contacts among females are of the same general order as those from other studies: Davis 1929:247 (20 per cent, unmarried college and graduate females, average age 36). Bromley and Britten 1938:117 (4 per cent, college females). Landis et al. 1940:262, 286 (4 per cent, single females), England acc. Rosenthal 1951:58 (20 per cent, British females). Gilbert Youth Research 1951 (6 per cent, college females).

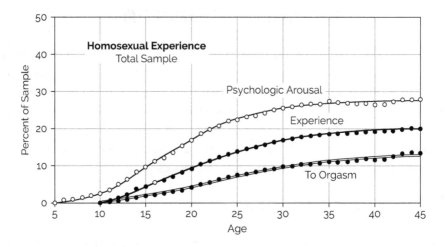

FIGURE 29.1   Accumulative incidence: homoscxual experience, arousal, and orgasm

Data from Table 29.6.

the pre-marital incidences of homosexual activity, even though we found that the pre-marital heterosexual activities (petting and pre-marital coitus) had been stepped up in anticipation of an approaching marriage. The chief effect of marriage had been to stop the homosexual activities, thereby lowering the active incidences and frequencies in the sample of married females.

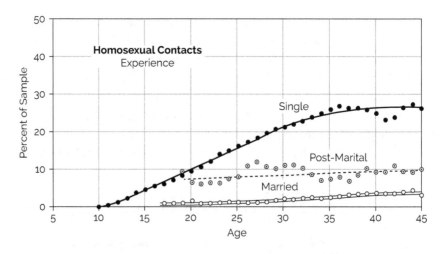

FIGURE 29.2   Accumulative incidence: homoscxual experience, by marital status

Data from Table 29.1.

A half to two-thirds of the females who had had sexual contacts with other females had reached orgasm in at least some of those contacts. By twenty years of age there were only 4 per cent of the total sample who had experienced orgasm in homosexual relations, and by age thirty-five there were still only 11 per cent with such experience (Table 29.6, Figure 29.1). The accumulative incidences finally reached 13 per cent in the middle forties. Since there were differences in the incidences among females of the various educational levels (Table 29.6, Figure 29.4), and since our sample includes a disproportionate number of the females of the college and graduate groups where the incidences seem to be higher than in the grade school and high school groups, the figures for this sample are probably higher than those which might be expected in the U. S. population as a whole.

ACTIVE INCIDENCE TO ORGASM

Since there is every gradation between the casual, non-erotic physical contacts which females regularly make and the contacts which bring some erotic response, it has not been possible to secure active incidence or frequency data on homosexual contacts among the females in the sample except where they led to orgasm. However, comparisons of the accumulative incidence data for experience and for orgasm (Table 29.6, Figure 29.1) suggest that the active incidences of the homosexual contacts may, at least in the younger groups, have been nearly twice as high as the active incidences of the contacts which led to orgasm.

In the total sample, not more than 2 to 3 per cent had reached orgasm in their homosexual relations during adolescence and their teens (Table 29.3), although five times that many may have been conscious of homosexual arousal and three times that many may have had physical contacts with other girls which were specifically sexual. After age twenty, the active incidences of the contacts which led to orgasm had gradually increased among the females who were still unmarried, reaching their peak, which was 10 per cent, at age forty. Then they began to drop. Between the ages of forty-six and fifty, about 4 per cent of the still unmarried females were actively involved in homosexual relations that led to orgasm. We do not have complete histories of single females who were reaching orgasm in homosexual relations after fifty years of age, but we do have incomplete information on still older women who were making such contacts with responses to orgasm while they were in their fifties, sixties, and even seventies.

Among the married females, slightly more than 1 per cent had been actively involved in homosexual activities which reached orgasm in each and every age group between sixteen and forty-five (Table 29.3).

On the other hand, among the females who had been previously married and who were then separated, widowed, or divorced, something around 6 per cent were having homosexual contacts which led to orgasm in each of the groups from ages sixteen to thirty-five (Table 29.3). After that some 3 to 4 per cent were involved, but by the middle fifties, only 1 per cent of the previously married females were having contacts which were complete enough to effect orgasm.

FREQUENCY TO ORGASM

Among the unmarried females in the sample who had ever experienced orgasm from contacts with other females, the average (active median) frequencies of orgasm among the younger adolescent girls who were having contacts had averaged nearly once in five weeks (about 0.2 per week), and they had increased in frequency among the older females who were not yet married (Table 29.3), In the late twenties they had averaged once in two and a half weeks (0.4 per week), and had stayed on about that level for the next ten years. This means that the active median frequencies of orgasm derived from the homosexual contacts had been higher than the active median frequencies of orgasm derived from nocturnal dreams and from heterosexual petting, and about the same as the active median frequencies of orgasm attained in masturbation.[12]

The active mean frequencies were three to six times higher than the active median frequencies, because of the fact that there were some females in each age group whose frequencies were notably higher than those of the median females (Table 29.3). The individual variation had depended in part upon the fact that the frequencies of contact had varied, and in part upon the fact that some of these females had regularly experienced multiple orgasms in their homosexual contacts.

In most age groups, three-quarters or more of the single females who were having homosexual experience to the point of orgasm were having it with average frequencies of once or less per week (Figure 29.3). There were individuals, however, in every age group from adolescence to forty-five, who were having homosexual contacts which had led to orgasm on an average of seven or more per week. From ages twenty-one to forty there were a few individuals who had averaged ten or more and in one instance as many as twenty-nine orgasms per week from homosexual sources. In contrast to the record for most other types of sexual activities, the most extreme variation in the homosexual relationships had not occurred in the youngest groups, but in the groups aged thirty-one to forty.

As in most other types of sexual activity among females (except coitus in marriage), the homosexual contacts had often occurred sporadically. Several contacts might be made within a matter of a few days, and then there might be no such contacts for a matter of weeks or months. In not a few instances the record was one of intense and frequently repeated contacts over a short period of days or weeks, with a lapse of several years before there were any more. On the other hand, there were a fair number of histories in which the homosexual partners had

---

12 The limited frequency data previously published were not calculated on any basis comparable to our 5-year calculations.

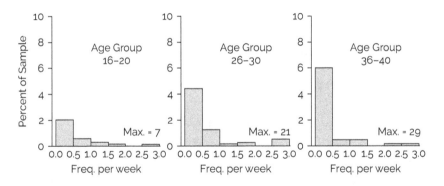

FIGURE 29.3   Individual variation: frequency of homosexual contacts to orgasm

For three age groups of single females. Each class interval includes the upper but not the lower frequency. For incidences of females not having homosexual experience or reaching orgasm in such contacts, see Table 29.3.

lived together and maintained regular sexual relationships for many years, and in some instances for as long as ten or fifteen years or even longer, and had had sexual contacts with considerable regularity throughout those years. Such long-time homosexual associations are rare among males. A steady association between two females is much more acceptable to our culture and it is, in consequence, a simpler matter for females to continue relationships for some period of years. The extended female associations are, however, also a product of differences in the basic psychology of females and males (Chapter 16).

Among the married females in the sample, there were a few in each age group—usually not more than one in a hundred or so—who were having homosexual contacts to the point of orgasm (Table 29.3). Even in those small active samples, however, the range of individual variation was considerable. Most of the married females had never had more than a few such contacts, but in nearly every age group there were married females who were having contacts with regular frequencies of once or twice or more per week. There were a few histories of married females who were completely homo-sexual and who were not having coitus with their husbands, although they continued to live with them as a matter of social convenience. In some of these cases there were good social adjustments between the spouses even though the sexual lives of each lay outside of the marriage.

Among the females in the sample who had been previously married and who were then widowed, separated, or divorced, the frequencies of homosexual experience were distinctly higher than among the married females (Table 29.3). In some cases these females, after the dissolution of their marriages, had established homes with other women with whom they had then had their first homosexual contacts and with whom they subsequently maintained regular homosexual relationships. Some of the women had been divorced because of their homosexual interests, although homosexuality in the female is only rarely a factor in divorce. It should be emphasized, however, that a high proportion of the unmarried females who live together never have contacts which are in any sense sexual.

PERCENTAGE OF TOTAL OUTLET

Homosexual contacts are highly effective in bringing the female to orgasm (p. 467), In spite of their relatively low incidence, they had accounted for an appreciable proportion of the total number of orgasms of the entire sample of unmarried females. Before fifteen years of age, the homosexual contacts had been surpassed only by masturbation and heterosexual coitus as sources of outlet, and they were again in that position among the still single females after age thirty (Table 171, Figure 110). Among these single females, orgasms obtained from homosexual contacts had accounted for some 4 per cent of the total outlet of the younger adolescent females, some 7 per cent of the outlet of the unmarried females in their early twenties, and some 19 per cent of the total outlet of the females who were still unmarried in their late thirties (Table 29.3).

Among the married females in the sample, homosexual contacts had usually accounted for less than one-half of one per cent of all their orgasms (Table 29.3).

However, among the females who had been previously married, homosexual contacts had become somewhat more important again as a source of outlet. They had accounted for something around 2 per cent of the total outlet of the younger females in the group, and for nearly 10 per cent of the outlet of the females who were in their early thirties (Table 29.3).

NUMBER OF YEARS INVOLVED

For most of the females in the sample, the homosexual activity had been limited to a relatively short period of time (Table 29.4). For nearly a third (32 per cent) of those who had had any experience, the experience had not occurred more than ten times, and for many it had occurred only once or twice. For nearly a half (47 per cent, including part of the above 32 per cent), the experience had been confined to a single year or to a part of a single year. For another quarter (25 per cent), the activity had been spread through two or three years, These totals, interesting to note, had not materially differed between females who were in the younger, and females who were in the older age groups at the time they contributed their histories. This means that for most of them, most of the homosexual activity had occurred in the younger years. There were a quarter (28 per cent) whose homosexual experience had extended for more than three years. There were histories of a few females whose activities had extended for as many as thirty or forty years, and more extended samples of older females would undoubtedly show cases which had continued for still longer periods of time.

NUMBER OF PARTNERS

In the sample of single females, a high proportion (51 per cent) of those who had had any homosexual experience had had it with only a single partner, up to the time at which they had contributed their histories to the record. Another 20 per cent had had it with two different partners. Only 29 per cent had had three or more partners in their homosexual relations, and only 4 per cent had had more than ten partners (Table 29.5).[13]

In this respect, the female homosexual record contrasts sharply with that for the male. Of the males in the sample who had had homosexual experience, a high proportion had had it with several different persons, and 22 per cent had had it with more than ten partners (p. 683). Some of them had had experience with scores and in many instances with hundreds of different partners. Apparently, basic psychologic factors account for these differences in the extent of the promiscuity of the female and the male (Chapter 16).

RELATION TO EDUCATIONAL LEVEL

The incidences of homosexual activity among the females in the sample had been definitely correlated with their educational backgrounds. This was more true than with any of their other sexual activities.

ACCUMULATIVE INCIDENCE

Homosexual responses had occurred among a smaller number of the females of the grade school and high school sample, a distinctly larger number of the college sample, and still more of the females who had gone on into graduate work (Table 29.6). At thirty years of age, for instance, there were 10 per cent of the grade school sample, 18 per cent of the high school sample, 25 per cent of the college sample, and 33 per cent of the graduate group who had recognized that they had been erotically aroused by other females.[14]

Overt contacts had similarly occurred in a smaller number of the females of the lower educational levels and a larger number of those of the upper educational

13 Davis 1929:251 gives closely parallel data (63 per cent with one partner, 18 per cent with two partners, 19 per cent with three or more partners). Statistically unsupported impressions of a high degree of promiscuity in female homosexuality may be found in: Bloch 1908:530 (female homosexuals change partners more frequently than male homosexuals). Alibert 1926:22. Kisch 1926:192. Chideckel 1935:122. But the greater durability of relationships among female homosexuals is also noted in: Smitt 1951:102.

14 Davis 1929:308 also finds a higher incidence of adult homosexual responses among better educated females (38 per cent of college group, 15 per cent of non-college group).

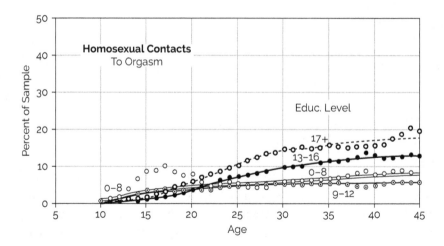

FIGURE 29.4   Accumulative incidence: homosexual contacts to orgasm, by educational level

Based on total sample, including single, married, and previously married females. Data from Table 29.6.

levels. At thirty years of age, the accumulative incidence figures had reached 9 per cent, 10 per cent, 17 per cent, and 24 per cent in the grade school, high school, college, and graduate groups, respectively.

At thirty years of age, homosexual experience to the point of orgasm had occurred in 6 per cent of the grade school sample, 5 per cent of the high school sample, 10 per cent of the college sample, and 14 per cent of the graduate sample (Table 29.6, Figure 29.4).

We have only hypotheses to account for the extension of this type f sexual activity in the better educated groups. We are inclined to believe that moral restraint on pre-marital heterosexual activity is the most important single factor contributing to the development of a homosexual history, and such restraint is probably most marked among the younger and teen-age girls of those social levels that send their daughters to college. In college, these girls are further restricted by administrators who are very conscious of parental concern over the heterosexual morality of their offspring. The prolongation of the years of schooling, and the consequent delay in marriage (Figure 46), interfere with any early heterosexual development of these girls. This is particularly true if they go on into graduate work. All of these factors contribute to the development of homosexual histories. There may also be a franker acceptance and a somewhat lesser social concern over homosexuality in the upper educational levels.

ACTIVE INCIDENCE TO ORGASM

Between adolescence and fifteen years of age, homosexual contacts to orgasm were more common in the sample of high school females and in the limited sample of grade

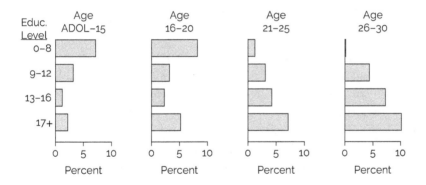

FIGURE 29.5 Active incidence: homosexual contacts to orgasm, by educational level

Data based on single females; see Table 29.2.

school females (Table 29.2, Figure 29.5). However, between the ages of twenty-one and thirty-five, while the active incidences stood at something between 3 and 6 per cent among the high school females, they had risen to something between 7 and 11 per cent in the college and graduate school groups.

FREQUENCY TO ORGASM

Between adolescence and fifteen years of age, the active median frequencies of homosexual contacts to orgasm among the females in the sample were higher in the grade school and high school groups, and lower among the sexually more restrained young females of the upper educational levels (Table 29.2). Subsequently these discrepancies had more or less disappeared, and after age twenty the frequencies had averaged once in two or three weeks for the median females of all the educational levels represented in the sample.

PERCENTAGE OF TOTAL OUTLET

Among the younger teen-age girls, 14 per cent of the orgasms of the grade school group had come from homosexual contacts, while only 1 or 2 per cent of the orgasms of the college and graduate groups had come from such sources (Table 29.2). Subsequently, these differences were reversed, and between thirty and forty years of age the still unmarried females of the graduate group were deriving 18 to 21 per cent of their total outlet from homosexual sources. If one-fifth of the outlet of this group came from homosexual sources, and only a little more than one-tenth (11 per cent) of the females in the group were having such activity, it is evident that the females who were having homosexual experience were reaching orgasm more frequently than those who were depending on other types of sexual activity for their outlet.

RELATION TO PARENTAL OCCUPATIONAL CLASS

In the available sample there seems to be little or nothing in the accumulative or active incidences, or the frequencies of the homosexual contacts, which suggests that there is any correlation with the occupational classes of the homes in which the females were raised (Tables 132, 133). There is only minor evidence that the accumulative incidences of contacts to the point of orgasm may have involved a slightly higher percentage of the females who came from upper white collar homes, and a smaller percentage of those who came from the homes of laboring groups—at age forty, a matter of 14 per cent in the first instance, and under 10 per cent in the second instance (Table 29.7).

The active incidences in the younger age groups were higher among the females who had come from the homes of laborers; but after the age of twenty the differences had largely disappeared, and after the age of twenty-five the females who had come from upper white collar homes were the ones most often involved (Table 29.8).

RELATION TO DECADE OF BIRTH

In the available sample, the accumulative incidences of homosexual contacts to the point of orgasm had been very much the same for the females who were born in the four decades on which we have data. There is no evidence that there are any more females involved in homosexual contacts today than there were in the generation born before 1900 or in any of the intermediate decades (Table 29.9, Figure 29.6).[15] Similarly, the number of females having homosexual contacts in particular five-year periods of their lives (the active incidences), the frequencies of such contacts, and the percentages of the total outlet which had been derived from homosexual contacts, do not seem to have varied in any consistent fashion during the four decades covered by the sample (Table 29.10).

It is not immediately obvious why this, among all other types of sexual activity, should have been unaffected by the social forces which led to the marked increase in the incidences of masturbation, heterosexual petting, pre-marital coitus, and even nocturnal dreams among American females immediately after the first World War, and which have kept these other activities on the new levels or have continued to keep them rising since then.

---

15 Statistically unsubstantiated statements that female homosexuality is on the increase may be found, for instance, in: Parke 1900:319. Havelock Ellis 1915 (2):261–262. Potter 1933:6–9, 150. McPartland 1947:143, 150. Norton 1949: 61.

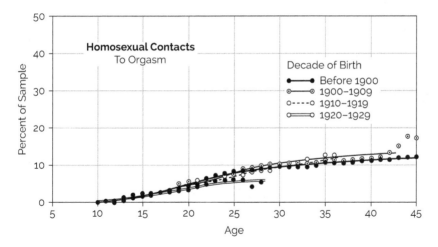

FIGURE 29.6   Accumulative incidence: homosexual contacts to orgasm, by decade of birth

Based on total sample, including single, married, and previously married females. Data from Table 29.9.

RELATION TO AGE AT ONSET OF ADOLESCENCE

There do not seem to be any consistent correlations between either the accumulative incidences, the active incidences, or the frequencies of homosexual contacts, and the ages at which the females in the sample had turned adolescent (Tables 136, 137). Among males we found (1948:320) that those who turned adolescent at earlier ages were more often involved in homosexual contacts as well as in masturbation and pre-marital heterosexual contacts. The absence of such a correlation among females may be significant (see Chapter 18).

RELATION TO RURAL-URBAN BACKGROUND

The accumulative incidences of homosexual contacts to the point of orgasm were a bit higher among the city-bred females in the sample (Table 29.13, Figure 29.7). The active incidences appear to have been a bit higher among the rural females in their teens, but they were higher among urban females after the age of twenty (Table 29.14). The data, however, are insufficient to warrant final conclusions.

RELATION TO RELIGIOUS BACKGROUND

The educational levels and religious backgrounds of the females in the sample were the social factors which were most markedly correlated with the incidences of their homosexual activity.

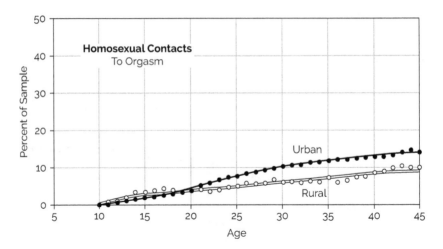

FIGURE 29.7 Accumulative incidence: homosexual contacts to orgasm, by rural-urban background

Based on total sample, including single, married, and previously married females. Data from Table 29.13.

ACCUMULATIVE INCIDENCE

In the Protestant, Catholic, and Jewish groups on which we have samples, fewer of the devout females were involved in homosexual contacts to the point of orgasm, and distinctly more of the females who were least devout religiously (Table 29.15, Figures 29.8–10). For instance, by thirty-five years of age among the Protestant females some 7 per cent of the religiously devout had had homosexual relations to orgasm, but 17 per cent of those who were least actively identified with the church had had such relations. The differences were even more marked in the Catholic groups: by thirty-five years of age, only 5 per cent of the devoutly Catholic females had had homosexual relations to the point of orgasm, but some 25 per cent of those who were only nominally connected with the church. The differences between the Jewish groups lay in the same direction.

There is little doubt that moral restraints, particularly among those who were most actively connected with the church, had kept many of the females in the sample from beginning homosexual contacts, just as some were kept from beginning heterosexual activities. On the other hand, as we have already noted, some of the females had become involved in homosexual activities because they were restrained by the religious codes from making pre-marital heterosexual contacts, and such devout individuals had sometimes become so disturbed in their attempt to reconcile their behavior and their moral codes that they had left the church, thereby increasing the incidences of homosexual activity among the religiously inactive groups.

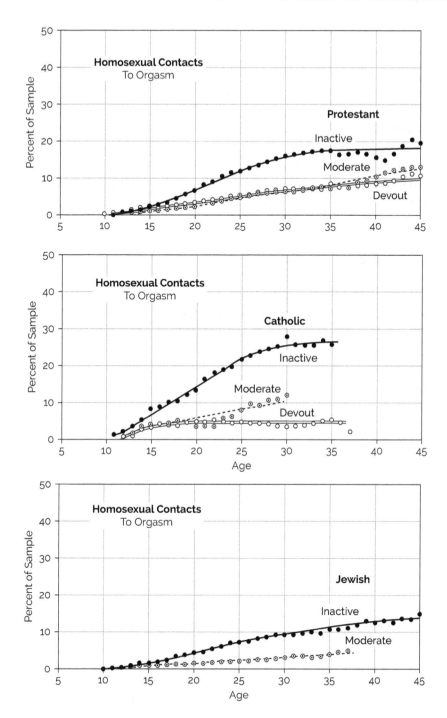

FIGURE 29.8-10   Accumulative incidence: homosexual contacts to orgasm, by religious background

Based on total sample, including single, married, and previously married females. Data from Table 29.15.

ACTIVE INCIDENCE.

In eleven out of the twelve groups on which we have data available for comparisons, the active incidences of homosexual contacts to the point of orgasm were lower among the more devout females and higher among those who were religiously least devout (Table 29.16, Figure 29.11). For instance, among the younger adolescent groups, there were 3 per cent of the devoutly Catholic females who were having homosexual relations to the point of orgasm, but 8 per cent of the inactive Catholics. Similarly, at ages twenty-six to thirty, among the still unmarried Protestant groups, 5 per cent of the more devout females were involved, but 13 per cent of the least devout females (Table 29.16).

ACTIVE MEDIAN FREQUENCY TO ORGASM

In the sample, there does not seem to have been any consistent correlation between the active median frequencies of homosexual activities and the religious backgrounds of the females in the various groups (Table 29.16).

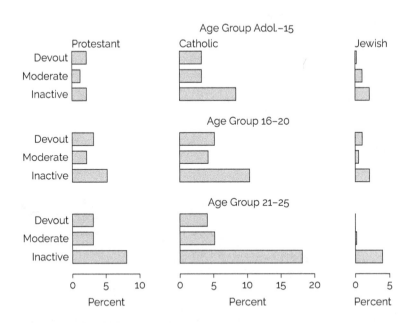

FIGURE 29.11   Active incidence: homosexual contacts to orgasm, by religious background

Data based on single females; see Table 29.16.

PERCENTAGE OF TOTAL OUTLET.

The percentage of the total outlet which had been derived by the various groups of females from their homosexual relations was, in most instances, correlated with the number of females (the active incidences) who were involved in such activity (Table 29.16); but among the religiously more devout females, and especially in the older age groups, the percentage of the total outlet derived from homosexual sources was in excess and often in considerable excess of what the incidences might have led one to expect. This had depended in part upon the fact that an unusually large number of the religiously devout were not reaching orgasm in any sort of sexual activity (Table 165), and for those who had accepted homosexual relations and reached orgasm in them, those relations had become a chief source of all the orgasms experienced by the group. It is also possible that a selective factor was involved, and that the sexually more responsive females were the ones who had most often accepted homosexual relations.

TECHNIQUES IN HOMOSEXUAL CONTACTS

The techniques utilized in the homosexual relations among the females in the sample were the techniques that are ordinarily utilized in heterosexual petting which precedes coitus, or which may serve as an end in itself. The homosexual techniques had differed primarily in the fact that they had not included vaginal penetrations with a true phallus.

The physical contacts between the females in the homosexual relations had often depended on little more than simple lip kissing and generalized body contacts (Table 29.5). In some cases the contacts, even among the females who had long and exclusively homosexual histories, had not gone beyond this. In many instances the homosexual partners had not extended their techniques to breast and genital stimulation for some time and in some cases for some period of years after the relationships had begun. Ultimately, however, among the females in the sample who had had more extensive homosexual experience, simple kissing and manual manipulation of the breast and genitalia had become nearly universal (in 95 to 98 per cent); and deep kissing (in 77 per cent), more specific oral stimulation of the female breast (in 85 per cent), and oral stimulation of the genitalia (in 78 per cent) had become common techniques. In something more than half of the histories (56 per cent), there had been genital appositions which were designed to provide specific and mutual stimulation (Table ISO). But vaginal penetrations with objects which had served as substitutes for the male penis had been quite rare in the histories.[16]

---

16   Further data on the nature of female homosexual techniques may be found in: Forberg 1884(2):113–115, 135, 141, 143. Parke 1906:322. Rohleder 1907(2): 466, 484. 494. Bloch 1908:529. Talmey 1910:154–155. Havelock Ellis 1915(2) i257–258. Krafft-Ebing 1922:400. Kronfeld 1923:58. Kisch 1926: 195–190. Eberhard 1927:354, 360. Kelly 1930:137. Deutsch 1933:40; 1944: 348. Sadler 1944:96. Hirschfeld

It is not generally understood, either by males or by females who have not had homosexual experience, that the techniques of sexual relations between two females may be as effective as or even more effective than the petting or coital techniques ordinarily utilized in heterosexual contacts. But if it is recalled that the clitoris of the female, the inner surfaces of the labia minora, and the entrance to the vagina are the areas which are chiefly stimulated by the male penetrations in coitus (pp. 574 ff.), it may be understood that similar tactile or oral stimulation of those structures may be sufficient to bring orgasm. However, for females who find satisfaction in having the deeper portions of the vagina penetrated during coitus (pp. 579–584), the lack of this sort of physical stimulation may make the physical satisfactions of homosexual relationships inferior to those which are available in coitus.

Nevertheless, comparisons of the percentages of contacts which had brought orgasm in marital coitus among the females who had been married for five years, and in the homosexual relations of females who had had about the same number of years of homosexual experience, show the following:

The higher frequency of orgasm in the homosexual contacts may have depended in part upon the considerable psychologic stimulation provided by such relationships,

% of Contacts Leading to Orgasm	In Fifth Year of Marital Coitus	In More Extensive Homosexual Experience
	Percent of Females	
0	17	7
1–29	13	7
30–59	15	8
60–89	15	10
90–100	40	68
Number of cases	1448	133

but there is reason for believing that it may also have depended on the fact that two individuals of the same sex are likely to understand the anatomy and the physiologic responses and psychology of their own sex better than they understand that of the opposite sex. Most males are likely to approach females as they, the males, would like to be approached by a sexual partner. They are likely to begin by providing immediate genital stimulation. They are inclined to utilize a variety of psychologic stimuli which may mean little to most females (Chapter 16). Females in their heterosexual relationships are actually more likely to prefer techniques which are closer to those which are commonly utilized in homosexual relationships. They would prefer a considerable

1944:232–233. Bergler 1948:200. See also the classical references in footnote 22.

amount of generalized emotional stimulation before there is any specific sexual contact. They usually want physical stimulation of the whole body before there is any specifically genital contact. They may especially want stimulation of the clitoris and the labia minora, and stimulation which, after it has once begun, is followed through to orgasm without the interruptions which males, depending to a greater degree than most females do upon psychologic stimuli, often introduce into their heterosexual relationships (p. 668).

It is, of course, quite possible for males to learn enough about female sexual responses to make their heterosexual contacts as effective as females make most homosexual contacts. With the additional possibilities which a union of male and female genitalia may offer in a heterosexual contact, and with public opinion and the mores encouraging heterosexual contacts and disapproving of homosexual contacts, relationships between females and males will seem, to most persons, to be more satisfactory than homosexual relationships can ever be. Heterosexual relationships could, however, become more satisfactory if they more often utilized the sort of knowledge which most homosexual females have of female sexual anatomy and female psychology.

THE HETEROSEXUAL-HOMOSEXUAL BALANCE

There are some persons whose sexual reactions and socio-sexual activities are directed only toward individuals of their own sex. There are others whose psychosexual reactions and socio-sexual activities are directed, throughout their lives, only toward individuals of the opposite sex. These are the extreme patterns which are labeled homosexuality and heterosexuality. There remain, however, among both females and males, a considerable number of persons who include both homosexual and heterosexual responses and/or activities in their histories. Sometimes their homosexual and heterosexual responses and contacts occur at different periods in their lives; sometimes they occur coincidentally. This group of persons is identified in the literature as bisexual.

That there are individuals who react psychologically to both females and males, and who have overt sexual relations with both females and males in the course of their lives, or in any single period of their lives, is a fact of which many persons are unaware; and many of those who are academically aware of it still fail to comprehend the realities of the situation. It is a characteristic of the human mind that it tries to dichotomize in its classification of phenomena. Things either are so, or they are not so. Sexual behavior is either normal or abnormal, socially acceptable or unacceptable, heterosexual or homosexual; and many persons do not want to believe that there are gradations in these matters from one to the other extreme.[17]

---

17   Attempts to categorize female homosexuality as congenital, Teal, genuine, acquired, situational, temporary, latent, partial, complete, total, absolute, regressive, progressive, pseudo-homosexuality, psychosexual hermaphroditism, bisexuality, inversion, perversity, etc., may be found, for instance, in: Féré 1904: 188. Parke 1906:320. Bloch 1908:489. Carpenter 1908:55. Freud 1910:2. Talmey 1910:143,

In regard to sexual behavior it has been possible to maintain this dichotomy only by placing all persons who are exclusively heterosexual in a heterosexual category, and all persons who have any amount of experience with their own sex, even including those with the slightest experience, in a homosexual category. The group that is identified in the public mind as heterosexual is the group which, as far as public knowledge goes, has never had any homosexual experience. But the group that is commonly identified as homosexual includes not only those who are known or believed to be exclusively homosexual, but also those who are known to have had any homosexual experience at all. Legal penalties, public disapproval, and ostracism are likely to be leveled against a person who has had limited homosexual experience as quickly as they are leveled against those who have had exclusive experience. It would be as reasonable to rate all individuals heterosexual if they have any heterosexual experience, and irrespective of the amount of homosexual experience which they may be having. The attempt to maintain a simple dichotomy on these matters exposes the traditional biases which are likely to enter whenever the heterosexual or homosexual classification of an individual is involved.

HETEROSEXUAL-HOMOSEXUAL RATING

Only a small proportion of the females in the available sample had had exclusively homosexual histories. An adequate understanding of the data must, therefore, depend upon some balancing of the heterosexual and homosexual elements in each history. This we have attempted to do by rating each individual on a heterosexual-homosexual scale which shows what proportion of her psychologic reactions and/or overt behavior was heterosexual, and what proportion of her psychologic reactions and/or overt behavior was homosexual (Figure 29.12). We have done this for each year for which there is any record. This heterosexual-homosexual rating scale was explained in our volume on the male (1948:636–659), but before applying it to the data on the female it seems desirable to summarize again the principles involved in the construction and use of the scale.

¶ The ratings represent a balance between the homosexual and heterosexual aspects of an individual's history, rather than the intensity of his or her psychosexual reactions or the absolute amount of his or her overt experience.

¶ Individuals who fall into any particular classification may have had various and diverse amounts of overt experience. An individual who has had little or no experience may receive the same classification as one who has had an abundance of

152. Moll 1912:125–130. Krafft-Ebing 1922:285–289, 336. Kelly 1930:136, 220. Robinson 1931:230–231. Marañón 1932:199. Potter 1933:151. Henry 1941(2):1023–1026. Hirschfeld 1944:281–282. Negri 1949: 163, 187. The concept of a continuum from exclusive heterosexuality to exclusive homosexuality is less often encountered, but is suggested, for instance, in: Freud 1924(2):207–208. Marañón 1929:170. Blanchard and Manasses 1930:109.

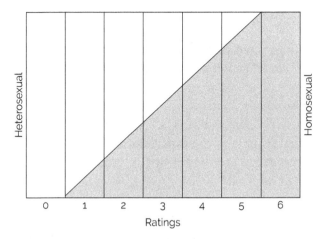

FIGURE 29.12   Heterosexual-homosexual rating scale

Definitions of the ratings are as follows: 0 = entirely heterosexual. 1 = largely heterosexual, but with incidental homosexual history. 2 = largely heterosexual, but with a distinct homosexual history. 3 = equally heterosexual and homosexual. 4 = largely homosexual, but with distinct heterosexual history. 5 = largely homosexual, but with incidental heterosexual history. 6 = entirely homosexual.

experience, provided that the heterosexual and homosexual elements in each history bear the same relation to each other.

¶ The ratings depend on the psychologic reactions of the individual and on the amount of his or her overt experience. An individual may receive a rating on the scale even if he or she has had no overt heterosexual or homosexual experience.

¶ Since the psychologic and overt aspects of any history often parallel each other, they may be given equal weight in many cases in determining a rating. But in some cases one aspect may seem more significant than the other, and then some evaluation of the relative importance of the two must be made. We find, however, that most persons agree in their ratings of most histories after they have had some experience in the use of the scale. In our own research, where each year of each individual history has been rated independently by two of us, we find that our independent ratings differ in less than one per cent of the year-by-year classifications.

¶ An individual may receive a rating for any particular period of his or her life, whether it be the whole life span or some smaller portion of it. In the present study it has proved important to give ratings to each individual year, for some individuals may materially change their psychosexual orientation in successive years.

¶ While the scale provides seven categories, it should be recognized that the reality includes individuals of every intermediate type, lying in a continuum between the two extremes and between each and every category on the scale.

The categories on the heterosexual-homosexual scale (Figure 29.12) may be defined as follows:

> 0. Individuals are rated as 0's if all of their psychologic responses and all of their overt sexual activities are directed toward persons of the opposite sex. Such individuals do not recognize any homosexual responses and do not engage in specifically homosexual activities. While more extensive analyses might show that all persons may on occasion respond to homosexual stimuli, or are capable of such responses, the individuals who are rated 0 are those who are ordinarily considered to be completely heterosexual.

> 1. Individuals are rated as 1's if their psychosexual responses and/or overt experience are directed almost entirely toward individuals of the opposite sex, although they incidentally make psychosexual responses to their own sex, and/or have incidental sexual contacts with individuals of their own sex. The homosexual reactions and/or experiences are usually infrequent, or may mean little psychologically, or may be initiated quite accidentally. Such persons make few if any deliberate attempts to renew their homosexual contacts. Consequently the homosexual reactions and experience are far surpassed by the heterosexual reactions and/or experience in the history.

> 2. Individuals are rated as 2's if the preponderance of their psychosexual responses and/or overt experiences are heterosexual, although they respond rather definitely, to homosexual stimuli and/or have more than incidental homosexual experience. Some of these individuals may have had only a small amount of homosexual experience, or they may have had a considerable amount of it, but the heterosexual element always predominates. Some of them may turn all of their overt experience in one direction while their psychosexual responses turn largely in the opposite direction; but they are always erotically aroused by anticipating homosexual experience and/or in their physical contacts with individuals of their own sex.

> 3. Individuals are rated as 3's if they stand midway on the heterosexual-homosexual scale. They are about equally heterosexual and homosexual in their psychologic responses and/or in their overt experience. They accept or equally enjoy both types of contact and have no strong preferences for the one or the other.

> 4. Individuals axe rated as 4's if their psychologic responses are more often directed toward other individuals of their own sex and/or if their

sexual contacts are more often had with their own sex. While they prefer contacts with their own sex, they, nevertheless, definitely respond toward and/or maintain a fair amount of overt contact with individuals of the opposite sex.

5. Individuals are rated as 5's if they are almost entirely homosexual in their psychologic responses and/or their overt activities. They respond only incidentally to individuals of the opposite sex, and/or have only incidental overt experience with the opposite sex.

6. Individuals are rated as 6's if they are exclusively homosexual in their psychologic responses, and in any overt experience in which they give any evidence of responding. Some individuals may be rated as 6's because of their psychologic responses, even though they may never have overt homosexual contacts. None of these individuals, however, ever respond psychologically toward, or have overt sexual contacts in which they respond to individuals of the opposite sex.

X. Finally, individuals are rated as X's if they do not respond erotically to either heterosexual or homosexual stimuli, and do not have overt physical contacts with individuals of either sex in which there is evidence of any response. After early adolescence there are very few males in this classification (see our 1948:658), but a goodly number of females belong in this category in every age group (Table 29.17, Figure 29.14). It is not impossible that further analyses of these individuals might show that they do sometimes respond to socio-sexual stimuli, but they are unresponsive and inexperienced as far as it is possible to determine by any ordinary means.

PERCENTAGE WITH EACH RACING

It should again be pointed out, as we did in our volume on the male (1948:650), that it is impossible to determine the number of persons who are "homosexual" or "heterosexual." It is only possible to determine bow many persons belong, at any particular time, to each of the classifications on a heterosexual-homosexual scale. The distribution of the available female sample on the heterosexual-homosexual scale is shown in Table 29.17 and Figure29.13. These incidence figures differ from the incidence figures presented in the earlier part of this chapter, because the heterosexual-homosexual ratings are based on psychologic responses and overt experience, while the accumulative and active incidences previously shown are (with the exception of Table 29.6 and Figure 29.1) based solely on overt contacts.

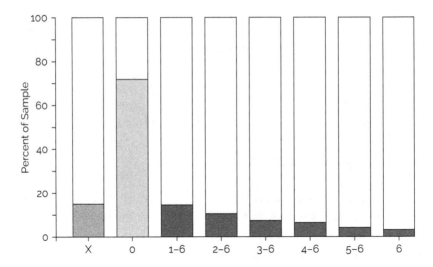

FIGURE 29.13 Active incidence: heterosexual-homosexual ratings, single females, age twenty-five

For definitions of the ratings, see p. 471. Data from Table 29.17.

The following generalizations may be made concerning the experience of the females in the sample, up to the time at which they contributed their histories to the present study.

Something between 11 and 20 per cent of the unmarried females and 8 to 10 per cent of the married females in the sample were making at least incidental homosexual responses, or making incidental or more specific homosexual contacts—*i.e.,* rated 1 to 6—in each of the years between twenty and thirty-five years of age. Among the previously married females, 14 to 17 per cent were in that category (Table 29.17).

Something between 6 and 14 per cent of the unmarried females, and 2 to 3 per cent of the married females, were making more than incidental responses, and/or making more than incidental homosexual contacts—*i.e.,* rated 2 to 6—in each of the years between twenty and thirty-five years of age. Among the previously married females, 8 to 10 per cent were in that category (Table 29.17).

Between 4 and 11 per cent of the unmanned females in the sample, and 1 to 2 per cent of the married females, had made homosexual responses, and/or had homosexual experience, at least as frequently as they had made heterosexual responses and/or had heterosexual experience—*i.e.,* rated 3 to 6—in each of the years between twenty and thirty-five years of age. Among the previously married females, 5 to 7 per cent were in that category (Table 29.17).

Between 3 and 8 per cent of the unmarried females in the sample, and something under 1 per cent of the married females, had made homosexual responses and/or had homosexual experience more often than they had responded heterosexually and/or had heterosexual experience—*i.e.,* rated 4 to 6—in each of the years between

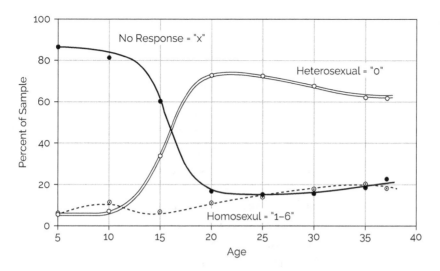

FIGURE 29.14 Active incidence: heterosexual-homosexual ratings, single females

For definitions of the ratings, X, o, and 1–6, see p. 471. Data from Table 29.17.

twenty and thirty-five years of age. Among the previously married females, 4 to 7 per cent were in that category (Table 29.17).

Between 2 and 6 per cent of the unmarried females in the sample, but less than 1 per cent of the married females, had been more or less exclusively homosexual in their responses and/or overt experience—*i.e.,* rated 5 or 6—in each of the years between twenty and thirty-five years of age. Among the previously married females, 1 to 6 per cent were in that category (Table 29.17).[18]

Between 1 and 3 per cent of the unmarried females in the sample, but less than three in a thousand of the married females, had been exclusively homosexual in their psychologic responses and/or overt experience—*i.e.,* rated 6—in each of the years between twenty and thirty-five years of age. Among the previously married females, 1 to 3 per cent were in that category (Table 29.17).

Between 14 and 19 per cent of the unmarried females in the sample, and 1 to 3 per cent of the married females, had not made any socio-sexual responses (either heterosexual or homosexual)—*i.e.,* rated X—in each of the years between twenty and thirty-five years of age. Among the previously married females, 5 to 8 per cent were in that category (Table 29.17).

---

18 That fewer females than males are exclusively homosexual is also noted in: Havelock Ellis 1915(2):195. Potter 1933:151. Hesnard 1933:189. Cory 1951:88.

EXTENT OF FEMALE VS. MALE HOMOSEXUALITY.

The incidences and frequencies of homosexual responses and contacts, and consequently the incidences of the homosexual ratings, were much lower among the females in our sample than they were among the males on whom we have previously reported (see our 1948:650–651). Among the females, the accumulative incidences of homosexual responses had ultimately reached 28 per cent; they had reached 50 per cent in the males. The accumulative incidences of overt contacts to the point of orgasm among the females had reached 13 per cent (Table 29.6, Figure 29.1); among the males they had reached 37 per cent This means that homosexual responses had occurred in about half as many females as males, and contacts which had proceeded to orgasm had occurred in about a third as many females as males. Moreover, compared with the males, there were only about a half to a third as many of the females who were, in any age period, primarily or exclusively homosexual.

A much smaller proportion of the females had continued their homosexual activities for as many years as most of the males in the sample.

A much larger proportion (71 per cent) of the females who had had any homosexual contact had restricted their homosexual activities to a single partner or two; only 51 per cent of the males who had had homosexual experience had so restricted their contacts. Many of the males had been highly promiscuous, sometimes finding scores or hundreds of sexual partners.

There is a widespread opinion, which is held both by clinicians and the public at large, that homosexual responses and completed contacts occur among more females than males.[19] This opinion is not borne out by our data, and it is not supported by previous studies which have been based on specific data.[20] This opinion may have originated in the fact that females are more openly affectionate than males in our culture. Women may hold hands in public, put arms about each other, publicly fondle and kiss each other, and openly express their admiration and affection for other females without being accused of homosexual interests, as men would be if they made such an open display of their interests in other men. Males, interpreting what they observe in terms of male psychology, are inclined to believe that the female behavior reflects emotional interests that must develop sooner or later into overt sexual relationships. Nevertheless, our data indicate that a high proportion of

---

19 For instance, Clark 1937:70, and Bergler 1951 ;317, feel that the incidences of homosexuality among females exceed those among males. Others differentiate various types of homosexuality, and feel that incidental or temporary homosexuality is commoner in the female, as in; Bloch 1908:525, and Hirschfeld 1944:281. Others who estimate that homosexuality is equally common in 1924(2) ;202. Kelly 1930:143. Sadler 1944:92.

20 All specific studies have arrived at incidence figures for the male which exceed those for the female: Hamilton 1929: 492—493 (57 per cent male, 37 per cent female). Bromley and Britten 1938:117, 210 (13 per cent male, 4 per cent female). Gilbert Youth Research 1951 (12 per cent male, 6 per cent female).

this show of affection on the part of the female does not reflect any psychosexual interest, and rarely leads to overt homosexual activity.

Not a few heterosexual males are erotically aroused in contemplating the possibilities of two females in a homosexual relation; and the opinion that females are involved in such relationships more frequently than males may represent wishful thinking on the part of such heterosexual males. Psychoanalysts may also see in it an attempt among males to justify or deny their own homosexual interests.

The considerable amount of discussion and bantering which goes on among males in regard to their own sexual activities, the interest which many males show in their own genitalia and in the genitalia of other males, the amount of exhibitionistic display which so many males put on in locker rooms, in showier rooms, at swimming pools, and at informal swimming holes, the male's interest in photographs and drawings of genitalia and sexual action, in erotic fiction which describes male as well as female sexual prowess, and in toilet wall inscriptions portraying male genitalia and male genital functions, may reflect homosexual interests which are only infrequently found in female histories. The institutions which have developed around male homosexual interests include cafes, taverns, night clubs, public baths, gymnasia, swimming pools, physical culture and more specifically homosexual magazines, and organized homosexual discussion groups; they rarely have any counterpart among females. Many of these male institutions, such as the homosexually oriented baths and gymnasia, are of ancient historic origin, but there do not seem to have been such institutions for females at any time in history. The street and institutionalized homosexual prostitution which is everywhere available for males, in all parts of the world, is rarely available for females, anywhere in the world.[21] All of these differences between female and male homosexuality depend on basic psychosexual differences between the two sexes.

SOCIAL SIGNIFICANCE OF HOMOSEXUALITY

Society may properly be concerned with the behavior of its individual members when that behavior affects the persons or property of other members of the social oganization, or the security of the whole group. For these reasons, practically all societies everywhere in the world attempt to control sexual relations which are secured through the use of force or undue intimidation, sexual relations which lead to unwanted pregnancies, and sexual activities which may disrupt or prevent marriages or otherwise threaten the existence of the social organization itself. In various societies, however, and particularly in our own Judeo-Christian culture, still other types of sexual activity are condemned by religious codes, public opinion, and the law

---

21 In addition to our own data, female homosexual clubs and bars are recorded in: Bloch 1908:530. Caofeynon 1934:22. Hirschfeld 1944:285. McPartland 1947:149–150. Cory 1951:122 (more rare than male homosexual clubs and bars). Female homosexual prostitution is also noted, for example, in: Martineau 1886:31. Parke 1906:313. Rohleder 1907(2):493; 1925:338–339. Bloch 1908:530. Hirschfeld 1944:282.

because they are contrary to the custom of the particular culture or because they are considered intrinsically sinful or wrong, and not because they do damage to other persons, their property, or the security of the total group.

The social condemnation and legal penalties for any departure from the custom are often more severe than the penalties for material damage done to persons or to the social organization. In our American culture there are no types of sexual activity which are as frequently condemned because they depart from the mores and the publicly pretended custom, as mouth-genital contacts and homosexual activities. There are practically no European groups, unless it be in England, and few if any other cultures elsewhere in the world which have become as disturbed over male homosexuality as we have here in the United States. Interestingly enough, there is much less public concern over homosexual activities among females, and this is true in the United States and in Europe and in still other parts of the world.[22]

In an attempt to secure a specific measure of attitudes toward homosexual activity, all persons contributing histories to the present study were asked whether they would accept such contacts for themselves, and whether they approved or disapproved of other females or males engaging in such activity. As might have been expected, the replies to these questions were affected by the individual's own background of experience or lack of experience in homosexual activity, and the following analyses are broken down on that basis.

ACCEPTANCE FOR ONESELF.

Of the 142 females in the sample who had had the most extensive homosexual experience, some regretted their experience and some had few or no regrets. The record is as follows:

Regret	Percent
None	71
Slight	6
More or less	3
Yes	20
Number of cases	142

---

22   For ancient Greece, Rome, and India, female homosexuality is recorded in: Ovid [1st cent, B.C., Roman]: Heroides, XV, 15–20, 201 (1921:183, 195) (Sappho recounts her past loves). Plutarch [1st cent, a.d., Greek]: Lycuxgus, 18.4 (1914:(1)265). Martial [1st cent a.d., Roman]: I,90(1919(1):85–87; 1921:33); VII, 67 (1919(1):469–471; 1921:193–194); VII, 70 (1919(1) :471: 1921:194). Juvenal [1st-2nd cent, A.D., Roman3: Satires, VI, 308–325 (1789:272–275; 1817:239–240). Lucian [2nd cent. A.D.. Greek]: Amores (1895:190); Dialogues of Courtesans, V (1895:100–105). Kama Sutra of Vatsyayana [1st-6th cent, A.D., Sanskrit] 1883–1925:62, 124. For additional accounts of Sappho of Lesbos, see; Wharton 1885, 1895. Miller and Robinson 1925, Weigall 1932.

Among the females who had never had homosexual experience, there were only 1 per cent who indicated that they intended to have it, and 4 per cent more who indicated that they might accept it if the opportunity were offered (Table 29.19).

But among the females who had already had some homosexual experience, 18 per cent indicated that they expected to have more. Another 20 per cent were uncertain what they would do, and some 62 per cent asserted that they did not intend to continue their activity. Some of the 18 per cent who indicated that they would continue were making a conscious and deliberate choice based upon their experience and their decision that the homosexual activity was more satisfactory than any other type of sexual contact which was available to them. Some of the others were simply following the path of least resistance, or accepting a pattern which was more or less forced upon them.

The group which had had homosexual experience and who expected to continue with it represented every social and economic level, from the best placed to the lowest in the social organization. The list included store clerks, factory workers, nurses, secretaries, social workers, and prostitutes. Among the older women, it included many assured individuals who were happy and successful in their homosexual adjustments, economically and socially well established in their communities and, in many instances, persons of considerable significance in the social organization. Not a few of them were professionally trained women who had been preoccupied with their education or other matters in the day when social relations with males and marriage might have been available, and who in subsequent years had found homosexual contacts more readily available than heterosexual contacts. The group included women who were in business, sometimes in high positions as business executives, in teaching' positions in schools and colleges, in scientific research for large and important corporations, women physicians, psychiatrists, psychologists, women in the auxiliary branches of the Armed Forces, writers, artists, actresses, musicians, and women in every other sort of important and less important position in the social organization.[23] For many of these women, heterosexual relations or marriage would have been difficult while they maintained their professional careers. For many of the older women no sort of socio-sexual contacts would have been available if they had not worked out sexual adjustments with the companions with whom they had lived, in some instances for many years. Considerable affection or strong emotional attachments were involved in many of these relationships.

On the other hand, some of the females in the sample who had had homosexual experience had become much disturbed over that experience. Often there was a feeling of guilt in having engaged in an activity which is socially, legally, and religiously disapproved, and such individuals were usually sincere in their intention

---

23 As examples of the statistically unsupported opinion that homosexuality is more common among females in aesthetic professions, see: Eberhard 1924:548. Rohleder 1925:381–382. Moreck 1929:312. Hesnard 1933:189, Chesser 1947;257. Martinez 1947:103. McPartland 1947:154. Beauvoir 1952:411.

not to continue their activities. Some of them, however, were dissatisfied with their homosexual relations merely because they had had conflicts with some particular sexual partner, or because they had gotten into social difficulties as a result of their homosexual activities.

Some 27 per cent of those who had had more extensive homosexual experience had gotten into difficulty because of it (Table 29.20). Some of these females were disturbed because they had found it physically or socially impossible to continue relationships with the partner in whom they were most interested, and refused to contemplate the possibility of establishing new relationships with another partner. In a full half of these cases, the difficulties had originated in the refusal of parents or other members of their families to accept them after they had learned of their homosexual histories.

On the other hand, among those who had had homosexual experience, as well as among those who had not had experience, there were some who denied that they intended to have or to continue such activity, because it seemed to be the socially expected thing to disavow any such intention. Some of these females would actually accept such contacts if the opportunity came and circumstances were propitious. It is very difficult to know what an individual will do when confronted with an opportunity for sexual contact.

APPROVAL FOR OTHERS

As a further measure of female reactions to homosexual activity, each subject was asked whether she approved or disapproved or was neutral in regard to other persons, of her own or of the opposite sex, having homosexual activity. Each of the female subjects was also asked to indicate whether she would keep friends, female or male, after she had discovered that they had had homosexual experience. Since the question applied to persons whom they had previously accepted as friends, it provided a significant test of current attitudes toward homosexual behavior. From these data the following generalizations may be drawn:

1. The approval of homosexual activity for other females was much higher among the females in the sample who had had homosexual experience of their own. Some 23 per cent of those females recorded definite approval, and only 15 per cent definitely disapproved of other females having homosexual activity (Table 29.19, Figure 29.15).
2. Females who had had experience of their own approved of homosexual activity for males less often than they approved of it for females. Only 18 per cent completely approved of the male activity, and 22 per cent definitely disapproved (Table 29.19, Figure29.15).
3. The females who had never had homosexual experience were less often inclined to approve of it for other persons. Some 4 per cent expressed approval of homosexual activity for males, but approximately 42 per cent definitely

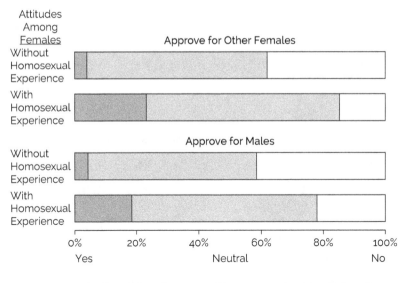

FIGURE 29.15 Attitudes of females toward homosexual contacts for others

Data from Table 29.19.

disapproved (Table 29.19). Some 4 per cent approved of activities for females, and 39 per cent disapproved.

4. Among the females who had had homosexual experience, some 88 per cent indicated that they would keep female friends after they had discovered their homosexual histories; 4 per cent said they would not (Table 29.19, Figure 29.16). Some of these latter responses reflected the subject's dissatisfaction with her own homosexual experience, but some represented the subject's determination to avoid persons who might tempt her into renewing her own activities.

5. Among the females who had had homosexual experience, 74 per cent indicated that they would continue to keep male friends after they had discovered that they had homosexual histories, and 10 per cent said they would not (Table 29.19, Figure 29.16). The disapproval of males with homosexual histories often depends upon the opinion that such males have undesirable characteristics, but this objection could not have been a factor in the present statistics because the question had concerned males whom the subject had previously accepted as friends.

6. Females who had never had homosexual experience were less often willing to accept homosexual female friends. Only 55 per cent said they would keep such friends, and 22 per cent were certain that they would not keep them (Table 29.19, Figure 29.16). This is a measure of the intolerance with which our Judeo-Christian culture views any type of sexual activity which departs from the custom.

7. Some 51 per cent of the females who had never had homosexual experience said that they would keep homosexual males as friends, 26 per cent said they

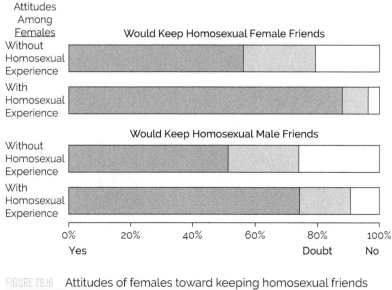

FIGURE 29.16   Attitudes of females toward keeping homosexual friends

Data from Table 29.19.

would not, and 23 per cent were doubtful (Table 29.19, Figure 29.16). As we have noted before (1948:663–664), this sort of ostracism by females often becomes a factor of considerable moment in forcing the male who has had some homosexual experience into exclusively homosexual patterns of behavior.

MORAL INTERPRETATIONS

The general condemnation of homosexuality in our particular culture apparently traces to a series of historical circumstances which had little to do with the protection of the individual or the preservation of the social organization of the day. In Hittite, Chaldean, and early Jewish codes there were no over-all condemnations of such activity, although there were penalties for homosexual activities between persons of particular social status or blood relationships, or homosexual relationships under other particular circumstances, especially when force was involved.[24]

---

24   For the rather broad acceptance of homosexuality in many parts of the ancient Near East, see: Pritchard 1950:73–74, 98–99, for the Giigamesh Epic (2nd millennium B.C. or earlier) which contains passages suggesting homosexual relations between the heroes Giigamesh and Enkidu. Homosexuality is not mentioned in the codes of Lipit-Ishtar or Hammurabi, and the injunction in the Hittite code (Pritchard 1950:196) is aimed only at men who have contact with their sons. The Middle Assyrian laws (12th century B.C. or earlier) likewise mention male homosexuality which Was punishable by castration (see: Barton 1925:Chapter 15, item 19), but a more modem translation suggests that this punishment was preceded by homosexual contact between the convicted man and his punishers (Pritchard 1950:181). Epstein 1948:135–136 assumes a general taboo on male homosexuality among the ancient Hebrews, but admits that this taboo is not to be found in the Covenant Code or in

The more general condemnation of all homosexual relationships originated in Jewish history in about the seventh century B.C., upon the return from the Babylonian exile. Both mouth-genital contacts and homosexual activities had previously been associated with the Jewish religious service, as they had been with the religious services of most of the other peoples of that part of Asia, and just as they have been in many other cultures elsewhere in the world.[25] In the wave of nationalism which was then developing among the Jewish people, there was an attempt to dis-identify themselves with their neighbors by breaking with many of the customs which they had previously shared with them. Many of the Talmudic condemnations were based on the fact that such activities represented the way of the Canaanite, the way of the Chaldean, the way of the pagan, and they were originally condemned as a form of idolatry rather than a sexual crime. Throughout the middle ages homosexuality was associated with heresy.[26] The reform in the custom (the mores) soon, however, became a matter of morals, and finally a question for action under criminal law.

Jewish sex codes were brought over into Christian codes by the early adherents of the Church, including St. Paul, who had been raised in the Jewish tradition on matters of sex.[27] The Catholic sex code is an almost precise continuation of the more ancient Jewish code.[28] For centuries in Medieval Europe, the ecclesiastic law dominated on all questions of morals and subsequently became the basis for the English common law, the statute laws of England, and the laws of the various states of the United States. This accounts for the considerable conformity between the Talmudic and Catholic codes and the present-day statute law on sex, including the laws on homosexual activity.[29]

Condemnations of homosexual as well as some other types of sexual activity are based on the argument that they do not serve the prime function of sex, which is interpreted to be procreation, and in that sense represent a perversion of what is taken to be "normal" sexual behavior. It is contended that the general spread of homosexuality

---

Deuteronomy, but only in the somewhat later Leviticus 18:22 and 20:13. See also Genesis 10:1–25, and Judges 19:17–25, for the protection of a male guest from forced homosexual relations. Deuteronomy 23:17–18 simply prohibits men of the Israelites from becoming temple prostitutes, but goes no further.

25   Male homosexual temple prostitutes, "kadesh," were at one time a part of Jewish religion, as may be gathered from II Kings 23:7, and from the warning in Deuteronomy 23:17—18, This is discussed by Westermarck 1917(2):488, and by Epstein 1948:135–136. The subsequent condemnation of homosexuality occurs repeatedly, as in: I Kings 14:24; 15:12; 22:46. Leviticus 18:22; 20:13. See also the Talmud, Sanhedrin 54a, 78a, 82a, Yebamoth 25a, 54b, Sotah 26b, etc.

26   The condemnation of homosexuality as idolatry is noted by Westermarck 1917(2):487–488, and by Epstein 1948:136.

27   For St. Paul's condemnation of homosexuality, see Romans I:26–27. I Corinthians 6:9. I Timothy 1:10.

28   The Catholic codes explicitly condemn male and female homosexuality. See such accepted Catholic sources as: Arregui 1927:153, Davis 1946(2):246.

29   For the relationship between Jewish and Catholic codes, and the statute law, see also: Westermarck 1917 (2): 480—489. May 1931: ch. 2, 3,

would threaten the existence of the human species, and that the integrity of the home and of the social organization could not be maintained if homosexual activity were not condemned by moral codes and public opinion and made punishable under the statute law. The argument ignores the fact that the existent mammalian species have managed to survive in spite of their widespread homosexual activity, and that sexual relations between males seem to be widespread in certain cultures (for instance, Moslem and Buddhist cultures) which are more seriously concerned with problems of overpopulation than they are with any threat of underpopulation. Interestingly enough of these are also cultures in which the institution of the family is very strong.

LEGAL ATTITUDES

While it is, of course, impossible for laws to prohibit homosexual interests or reactions, they penalize, in every state of the Union, some or all of the types of contact which are ordinarily employed in homosexual relations. The laws are variously identified as statutes against sodomy, buggery, perverse or unnatural acts, crimes against nature, public and in some instances private indecencies, grossly indecent behavior, and unnatural or lewd and lascivious behavior. The penalties in most of the states are severe, and in many states as severe as the penalties against the most serious crimes of violence,[30] The penalties are particularly severe when the homosexual relationships involve an adult with a young minor.[31] There is only one state, New York, which, by an indirection in the wording of its statute, appears to attach no penalty to homosexual relations which are carried on between adults in private and with the consent of both of the participating parties; and this sort of exemption also appears in Scandinavia and in many other European countries. There appears to be no other major culture in the world in which public opinion and the statute law so severely penalize homosexual relationships as they do in the United States today.

It might be expected that the moral and legal condemnations of homosexual activity would apply with equal force to both females and males. The ancient Hittite code, however, condemned only male homosexual activity and then only when it occurred under certain circumstances, and made no mention of homosexual activity among females. Similarly the references to homosexual activity in the Bible and in the Talmud apply primarily to the male. The condemnations were severe and usually called for the death of the transgressing male, but they rarely mentioned female activity, and when they did, no severe penalties were proposed.[32] In medieval European

---

30 For a convenient and almost complete summary of the statutes concerning homosexuality in the forty-eight states, see: Cory 1951 appendix B.

31 For the problem involved in the relationships of adults and minors, see; Guttmacher and Weihofen 1952:156.

32 The stringent penalty for homosexuality given in Leviticus 18:22 and 20:13 applies only to the male. Reference to female homosexuality does not appear until much later: Romans 1:26, where it is considered a "vile affection." The Talmud is relatively lenient regarding females, stating that female

history there are abundant records of death imposed upon males for sexual activities with other males, but very few recorded cases of similar action against females.[33] In modern English and other European law, the statutes continue to apply only to males[34]; but in American law, the phrasing of the statutes would usually make them applicable to both female and male homosexual contacts.[35] The penalties are usually invoked against "all persons," "any person," "whoever," 'one who," or "any human being" without distinction of sex. Actually there are only five states [36] in the United States where the statutes do not cover female homosexual relationships, and it is probable that the courts would interpret the statutes in nearly all of the other states to apply to females as well as to males.

These American statutes appear, however, to have gone beyond public opinion in their condemnation of homosexual relations between females, for practically no females seem to have been prosecuted or convicted anywhere in the United States under these laws. In our total sample of several hundred females who had had homosexual experience, only three had had minor difficulties and only one had had more serious difficulty with the police (Table 29.20), and none of the cases had been brought to court. We have cases of females who were disciplined or more severely penalized for their homosexual activities in penal or other institutions, or while they were members of the Armed Forces of the United States, and we have cases in which social reactions constituted a severe penalty, but no cases of action in the courts.

Our search through the several hundred sodomy opinions which have been reported in this country between 1696 and 1952 has failed to reveal a single case sustaining the conviction of a female for homosexual activity. Our examination of the records of all the females admitted to the Indiana Women's Prison between 1874 and 1944 indicates that only one was sentenced for homosexual activity, and that was for activity which had taken place within the walls of another institution. Even in such a large city as New York, the records covering the years 1930 to 1939 show only one case of a woman convicted of homosexual sodomy, while there were over 700 convictions

---

homosexual activity is a "mere obscenity" disqualifying a woman from marrying a priest. See Yebamoth 76a. Maimonides, according to Epstein 1948:188, felt that a female guilty of homosexuality should be flogged and excluded from the company of decent women, which is a penalty far less severe than the death penalty required for the male.

33 Such medieval penalties for homosexuality are mentioned, for instance, in: Havelock Ellis 1915(2):346–347. Westermarck 1917(2):481–482. For a case of capital punishment levied on a female, see: Wharton 1932(1): 1036–1037, footnote 18.

34 There are specific statutes against female homosexuality only in Austria, Greece, Finland, and Switzerland.

35 The applicability of the laws to both females and males are also noted in: Sherwin 1951:13. Ploscowe 1951:204. Pilpel and Zavin 1952:220.

36 The states in which the statutes apparently do not apply to female homosexuality are; Conn., Ga., Ky., S. C., and Wis. Heterosexual cunnilingus has been held not "the crime against nature" in Illinois, Mississippi, and Ohio, and the decisions would supposedly apply to homosexual cunnilingus. In Arkansas, Colorado, Iowa, and Nebraska there is also some doubt as to the status of female homosexuality.

of males on homosexual charges, and several thousand cases of males prosecuted for public indecency, or for solicitation, or for other activity which was homosexual.[37] In our own more recent study of the enforcement of sex law in New York City we find three arrests of females on homosexual charges in the last ten years, but all of those cases were dismissed, although there were some tens of thousands of arrests and convictions of males charged with homosexual activity in that same period of time.

It is not altogether clear why there are such differences in the social and legal attitudes toward sexual activities between females and sexual activities between males, They may depend upon some of the following, and probably upon still other factors:

1. In Hittite, Jewish and other ancient cultures, women were socially less important than males, and their private activities were more or less ignored.
2. Both the incidences and frequencies of homosexual activity among females are in actuality much lower than among males. Nevertheless, the number of male cases which are brought to court are, even proportionately, tremendously higher than the number of female cases that reach court.
3. Male homosexual activity more often comes to public attention in street solicitation, public prostitution, and still other ways.
4. Male homosexual activity is condemned not only because it is homosexual, but because it may involve mouth-genital or anal contacts. It is not so widely understood that female homosexual techniques may also involve mouth-genital contacts.
5. Homosexual activities more often interfere with the male's, less often interfere with the female's marrying or maintaining a marriage.
6. The Catholic Code emphasizes the sin involved in the wastage of semen in all male activities that are non-coital; it admits that female non-coital activities do not involve the same species of sin.
7. There is public objection to the effeminacy and some of the other personality traits of certain males who have homosexual histories; there is less often objection to the personalities of females who have homosexual histories.[38]
8. The public at large has some sympathy for females, especially older females, who are not married and who would have difficulty in finding sexual contacts if they did not engage in homosexual relations.

---

37 New York City data are to be found in the report of the Mayor's Committee on Sex Offenses 1944:75.

38 The statistically unsupported opinion that females with homosexual histories frequently or usually exhibit masculine physical characters, behavior, or tastes appears, however, in such authors as the following: Féré 1904:189. Parke 1909:266, 300–501, 321. Bloch 1908:526. Carpenter 1908:30–31. Talmey 1910:158–161. Freud 1910:11. Havelock Ellis 1915(2) :251–254. Krafft-Ebing 1922:336, 398–399. Kisch 1926:192. Kelly 1930:138. Moll 1931:226 ff. Potter 1933:158. Hesnard 1933:180. Caufeynon 1934:132. S. Kahn 1937:69, 134. Hutton 1937:126, 129. Henry 1941(2):1062, 1075, 1081. Deutsch 1944:325. Negri 1949:187. Keiser and Schaffer 1949:287, 289. Bergler 1951:318. Higher masculinity" ratings on masculinity-femininity tests are reported by: Terman and Miles 1936:577–578. Henry 1941(2):1033–1034.

9. Many heterosexual males are erotically aroused when they consider the possibilities of two females in sexual activities. In not a few instances they may even encourage sexual contacts between females. There are fewer cases in our records of females being aroused by the contemplation of activities between males.

10. There are probably more males and fewer females who fear their own capacities to respond homosexually. For this reason, many males condemn homosexual activities in their own sex more severely than they condemn them among females.

11. Our social organization is presently much concerned over sexual relationships between adults and young children. This is the basis for a considerable portion of the action which is taken against male homosexual contacts; but relationships between older women and very young girls do not so often occur.

BASIC SOCIAL INTERESTS

When a females homosexual experience interferes with her becoming married or maintaining a marriage into which she has entered, social interests may be involved. On the other hand, our social organization has never indicated that it is ready to penalize, by law, all persons who fail to become married.

When sexual relationships between adult females do not involve force or undue coercion, and do not interfere with marital adjustments that might have been made, many persons, both in Europe and in our American culture, appear to be fairly tolerant of female homosexual activities. At any rate, many of those who feel that a question of morality may be involved, fail to believe that the basic social interests are sufficient to warrant any rigorous legal action against females who find a physiologic outlet and satisfy their emotional needs in sexual contacts with other females.

Summary and Comparisons of Female and Male

Homosexual Responses and Contacts

	In Females	In Males
Physiologic and Psychologic Bases		
Inherent capacity to respond to any sufficient stimulus	Yes	Yes
Preference developed by psychologic conditioning	Yes	Yes
Among mammals homosexual behavior widespread	Yes	Yes
Anthropologic Background		
Data on homosexual behavior	Very few	Some
Heterosexual more acceptable in most cultures	Yes	Yes
Homosexual behavior sometimes permitted	Yes	Yes
Social concern over homosexual behavior	Less	More
Relation to Age and Marital Status		
Accumulative incidence		
Homosexual response, by age 45	28%	±50%
Homosexual experience, by age 45	20%	
Single	26%	±50%
Married	3%	±10%
Previously married	10%	
Homo, exper. to orgasm, by age 45	13%	±37%
Active incidence, to orgasm		
Single		
Age 16–20	3%	22%
Age 36–40	10%	40%
Age 46–50	4%	36%
Married	1–2%	2–8%
Previously married, age 16–50	3–7%	5–28%
Frequency to orgasm, per week		
Single		
Age Adol.–15	0.2	0.1
Age 21–30	0.3–04	0.4–0.7
Age 31–40	0.3–0.4	0.7–1.0
Married freq. lower than in single	Somewhat	Markedly

Summary and Comparisons (*Continued*)

	In Females	In Males
Percent of total outlet, before age 40		
Single, gradual increase	4–19%	5–22%
Married	Under 1%	Under 1%
Previously married, gradual increase	2–10%	9–26%
Number of years involved		
1 year or less	47%	
2 to 3 years	25%	
Number of partners		
1–2	71%	51%
Over 10	4%	22%
Relation to Educational Level*		
Accumul. incid- to orgasm, by age 30		
Grade school	6%	27%
High school	5%	39%
College	10% }	
Graduate	14% }	34%
Act. incid. and % of outlet, higher		
Before age 20	In less educ.	In less educ.
After age 20	In better educ.	In less educ.
Frequency to orgasm higher	In less educ.	In less educ.
Relation to Parental Occupational Class	Little	Little or none
Relation to Decade of Birth	None	Little or none
Relation to Age at Onset of Adolescence	None	Higher incid. and freq. in early-adol.
Relation to Rural-Urban Background	Little	Incid. and freq. higher in urban
Relation to Religious Background		
Accum. and act. incid. higher among less dev.	Yes	Yes
Frequency to orgasm (active median)	No relation	Little relation
Percentage of total outlet	Higher among devout	No relation

Summary and Comparisons (*Continued*)

	In Females	In Males
Techniques in Homosexual Contacts	Yes	Yes
Essentially same as in hetero. petting		
Kissing and general body contacts	Extensive	
Genital techniques utilized	Later or never	Early and ± always
More effective than marital coitus	Yes	No
Hetero.-Homo. Ratings, *e.g.*, ages 20–35		
X: no socio-sexual response		
Single	14–19%	3—4%
Married	1–3%	0%
Previously married	5–8%	1–2%
0: entirely heterosexual experience		
Single	61–72%	53–78%
Married	89–90%	90–92%
Previously married	75–80%	
1–6: at least some homosexual	11–20%	18–42%
2–6: more than incidental homosexual	6–14%	13–38%
3–6: homo. as much or more than hetero.	4–11%	9–32%
4–6: mostly homosexual	3–8%	7–26%
5–6: ± exclusively homosexual	2–6%	5–22%
6: exclusively homosexual	1–3%	3–16%
Social Significance of Homosexuality		
Social concern in Anglo-Amer. culture	Little	Great
Most exper. indiv. regret least	Yes	Yes
Intent to have, highest among those with exper.	Yes	
Approval for others, most often :		
By those with experience	Yes	Yes
For own sex	Yes	No
Moral and Legal Aspects of Homosexuality		
Injunction against, in:		
Ancient Near Eastern codes	No	Sometimes
Old Testament	No	Yes
Talmud	Yes	Yes
St. Paul and Christian codes	Yes	Yes
Formerly considered heresy	Yes	Yes

Summary and Comparisons (*Continued*)

	In Females	In Males
Death in ancient and medieval liist.	Rarely	Yes
Legally punishable in	43 states	48 states
Laws enforced	Almost never	Frequently

*Beginning at this point, the data apply to single females and males only, unless otherwise indicated

TABLE 29.1 **Accumulative Incidence: Homosexual Contacts By Marital Status**

Age	Total Sample	While Single	While Married	Post-Marital	Total Sample	While Single	While Married	Post-Marital
	%		*Percent*				*Cases*	
12	I	I			5733	5732		
15	5	5			5685	5681		
20	9	9	I	7	4318	3941	556	77
25	14	16	I	8	2779	1464	1338	174
30	17	21	2	11	2045	670	1216	221
35	19	26	2	7	1470	381	912	205
40	19	24	3	9	951	207	571	179
45	20	26	3	10	572	128	312	130

Table based on total sample, including single, married, and previously married females.

TABLE 29-2. **Active Incidence, Frequency, and Precentage of Outlet Homosexual Contacts to Orgasm**

Single Females, by Educational Level

Age During Activity	Educ. Level	Active Incid.%	Active Median Freq. Per Wk.	% of Total Outlet	Cases in Total Sample
Adol.-15	0–8	7	0.7	14	162
	9–12	3	0.3	6	983
	13–16	2	0.1	1	3271
	17+	1	0.2	2	1128
16–20	0–8	8	0.7	9	143
	9–12	3	0.3	4	976
	13–16	2	0.1	3	3299
	17+	5	0.3	6	1149
21–25	9–12	3	0.5	7	537
	13–16	4	0.4	8	1204
	17+	7	0.3	7	1002
26–30	9–12	4		12	181
	13–16	7	0.5	10	313
	17+	10	0.3	13	531
31–35	9–12	6		6	65
	13–16	7		11	139
	17+	11	0.3	18	309
36–40	13–16	12		17	68
	17+	11	0.3	21	205
41–45	17+	7		7	122
46–50	17+	5		5	80

Italic figures throughout the series of tables indicate that the calculations are based on less than 50 cases. No calculations are based on less than 11 cases. The dash (–) indicates a percentage or frequency smaller than any quantity which would be shown by a figure in the given number of decimal places.

TABLE 29.3 Active Incidence, Frequency, and Percentage of Outlet Homosexual Contacts to Orgasm by Age and Marital Status

Age During Activity	Active Sample			Total Sample		Cases in Total Sample
	Active Incid. %	Median Freq. Per Wk.	Mean Frequency Per Wk.	Mean Freq. Per Wk.	% of Total Outlet	
SINGLE FEMALES						
Adol.–15	2	0.2	0.6 ± 0.09	—	4	5677
16–20	3	0.2	0.6 ± 0.08	—	4	5613
21–25	5	0.3	1.0 ± 0.16	—	7	2810
26–30	8	0.4	1.3 ± 0.30	0.1 ± 0.03	11	1064
31–35	9	0.3	1.6 ± 0.63	0.1 ± 0.06	14	539
36–40	10	0.4	2.5 ± 0.96	0.3 ± 0.10	19	315
41–45	6			0.1 ± 0.04	6	179
46–50	4			—	4	109
51–55	0			0.0	0	58
56–60	0			0.0	0	27
MARRIED FEMALES						
16–20	1			—	—	578
21–25	1	0.3	0.9 ± 0.29	—	—	1654
26–30	1	0.2	1.2 ± 0.64	—	1	1662
31–35	1	0.3	1.0 ± 0.51	—	—	1246
36–40	2	0.1	0.4 ± 0.19	—	—	851
41–45	1			—	—	497
46–50	—			—	—	260
51–55	1			—	1	118
56–60	2			—	3	49
PREVIOUSLY MARRIED FEMALES						
16–20	6			—	2	72
21–25	6	0.7	1.1 ± 0.38	0.1 ± 0.03	4	239
26–30	6	2.0	2.3 ± 0.59	0.1 ± 0.05	9	328
31–35	7	1.1	2.4 ± 0.80	0.2 ± 0.06	10	304
36–40	3			—	2	245
41–45	4			0.1 ± 0.05	6	195
46–50	4			—	3	126
51–55	1			—	—	82
56–60	0			0.0	0	53

TABLE 29.4 **Number of Years Involved in Homosexual Contacts**
Including activity with and without orgasm

Number of Times or Year	Total Sample	Age at Reporting			
		Adol.–20	21–30	31–40	41–50
		Percent			
1–10 times	32	26	35	32	33
1 year or less	47	48	51	44	44
2–3 years	25	26	27	21	25
4–5 years	10	15	7	9	9
6–10 years	9	11	11	8	7
11–20 years	7		4	14	8
21+ years	2			4	7
Number of cases	709	137	202	202	122

TABLE 29.5 **Partners and Techniques in Homosexual Contacts**

PARTNERS		TECHNIQUES		
Number	%	Technique Utilized	By Females with Limited Exper.	By Females with Extensive Exper.
			%	%
1 only	51	Kissing: simple		95
2	20	Kissing; deep		77
3	9	Breast: manual stimul.	27	97
4	5	Breast: oral stimul.	7	85
5	4	Genital: manual stimul.	67	98
6–10	7	Genital: oral stimul.	16	78
11–20	3	Genital apposition	24	56
21+	1			
Cases with exper.	591		499	145

Data on kissing unavailable on females with limited experience.

TABLE 29.6. **Accumulative Incidence: Homosexual Arousal, Experience, and Orgasm**

By Educational Level

Age	Total Sample %	Educational Level Percent				Total Sample Cases	Educational Level Cases			
		0–8	9–12	13–16	17+		0–8	9–12	13–16	17+
					Homosexual Arousal					
8	2	1	1	1	2	5720	179	999	3226	1124
10	3	2	3	2	4	5699	179	999	3226	1124 ·
12	5	3	6	4	6	5674	179	999	3226	1124
15	10	11	10	9	11	5614	173	998	3226	1124
20	17	13	14	17	21	4267	127	849	2168	1123
25	23	9	16	24	28	2743	117	678	1020	928
30	25	10	18	25	33	2017	109	494	697	717
35	27	10	21	28	33	1447	91	317	487	552
40	27	10	18	28	32	937	67	189	301	380
45	28		17	28	36	565		124	165	231
					Homosexual Contacts: Experience					
12	1	2	1	1	1	5733	179	1007	3267	1142
15	5	9	5	4	4	5685	175	1006	3267	1142
20	9	11	7	9	12	4318	129	854	2194	1141
25	14	8	8	14	19	2779	119	683	1035	942
30	17	9	10	17	24	2045	111	500	707	727
35	19	9	12	17	25	1470	93	322	493	562
40	19	10	10	19	24	951	68	193	304	386
45	20		8	20	27	572		127	166	234
					Homosexual Contacts to Orgasm					
12	1	2	1	—	—	5779	178	1012	3301	1152
15	2	9	3	1	2	5733	174	1011	3301	1152
20	4	8	4	3	6	4359	128	860	2220	1151
25	7	5	5	7	10	2803	118	687	1046	952
30	10	6	5	10	14	2058	110	502	713	733
35	11	7	5	11	15	1480	92	323	498	567
40	12	7	5	13	15	956	68	194	305	389
45	13		6	13	19	574		127	166	236

Table based on total sample, including single, married, and previously married females.

TABLE 29.7   Accumulative Incidence, Homosexual Contacts to Orgasm

By Parental Occupational Class

Age	PARENTAL CLASS				PARENTAL CLASS			
	2 + 3	4	5	6 + 7	2 + 3	4	5	6 + 7
	Percent				Cases			
12	1	—	—	1	973	812	1526	2684
15	5	2	1	2	943	810	1523	2671
20	5	3	4	4	711	631	1139	2018
25	6	6	7	9	511	421	722	1225
30	9	6	9	12	379	313	506	907
35	10	6	9	13	268	197	345	692
40	9	4	10	14	174	119	206	470
45	7	4	15	17	108	71	117	282

Table based on total sample, including single, married, and previously married females.
The occupational classes are as follows: 2 + 3 = unskilled and semi-skilled labor. 4 = skilled labor. 5 = lower white collar class. 6+7 = upper white collar and professional classes.

TABLE 29.8   Active Incidence and Percentage of Outlet Homosexual Contacts to Orgasm

Single Females, by Parental Occupational Class

Age	Parental Class	Active Incid. %	% of Total Outlet	Cases in Total Sample	Age	Parental Class	Active Incid. %	% of Total Outlet	Cases in Total Sample
Adol.									
−15	2 + 3	5	8	947	26–30	2 + 3	5	11	195
	4	2	3	796		4	6	8	181
	5	2	2	1506		5	7	6	275
	6 + 7	1	2	2654		6 + 7	10	14	447
16–20	2 + 3	5	5	881	31–35	2 + 3	4	14	96
	4	3	4	796		4	3	1	91
	5	2	3	1512		5	9	11	148
	6 + 7	3	4	2649		6 + 7	13	17	224
21–25	2 + 3	4	3	461	36–40	2 + 3	5	25	62
	4	4	6	422		5	9	6	85
	5	4	4	735		6 + 7	12	23	141
	6 + 7	5	9	1283					

TABLE 29.9 **Accumulative Incidence; Homosexual Contacts to Orgasm By Decade of Birth**

Age	DECADE OF BIRTH				DECADE OF BIRTH			
	Bf. 1900	1900–1909	1910–1919	1920–1929	Bf. 1900	1900–1909	1910–1919	1920–1929
	Percent				*Cases*			
12	—	—	—	1	456	783	1341	3072
15	2	2	2	3	456	783	1341	3058
20	5	6	4	3	456	783	1340	1780
25	8	9	7	6	456	783	1191	373
30	9	10	10		456	783	819	
35	11	11	13		456	754	270	
40	11	12			456	499		
45	12	17			435	139		

Table based on total sample, including single, married, and previously married females.

TABLE 29.10 Active Incidence and Percentage of Outlet Homosexual Contacts to Orgasm

Single Females, by Decade of Birth

Age	Decade of Birth	Active Incid. %	% of Total Outlet	Cases in Total Sample
Adol.–15	Bf.1900	2	1	436
	1900–1909	1	3	760
	1910–1919	2	3	1319
	1920–1929	2	6	3049
16–20	Bf. 1900	4	3	451
	1900–1909	5	6	772
	1910–1919	3	5	1328
	1920–1929	2	4	2999
21–25	Bf. 1900	5	6	366
	1900–1909	6	7	617
	1910–1919	6	7	987
	1920–1929	3	7	843
26–30	Bf. 1900	6	18	218
	1900–1909	8	10	344
	1910–1919	9	10	448
	1920–1929	7	9	54
31–35	Bf. 1900	8	19	151
	1900–1909	8	14	228
	1910–1919	11	8	160
36–40	Bf. 1900	8	19	123
	1900–1909	9	17	165
41–45	Bf. 1900	4	6	116
	1900–1909	8	3	63

TABLE 29.11 Accumulative Incidence: Homosexual Contacts to Orgasm By Age at Onset of Adolescence

Age	ADOLESCENT					ADOLESCENT				
	By 11	At 12	At 13	At 14	At 15+	By 11	At 12	At 13	At 14	At 15+
	Percent					Cases				
12	2	1				1203	1681			
15	3	2	2	2	2	1185	1666	1738	792	348
20	5	3	5	5	4	876	1227	1321	649	283
25	8	6	8	8	8	511	741	848	465	235
30	11	9	9	11	10	355	488	650	368	196
35	12	11	11	11	11	250	322	470	281	156
40	14	11	12	12	10	151	199	297	191	117
45	13	14	14	13	11	93	111	174	119	76

Table based on total sample, including single, married, and previously married females.

TABLE 29.12   Active Incidence and Percentage of Outlet Homosexual Contact to Orgasm

Single Females, by Age at Onset of Adolescence

Age During Activity	Age at Adol.	Active Incid. %	% of Total Outlet	Cases in Total Sample
Adol.–15	8–11	3	6	1203
	12	2	3	1684
	13	2	2	1747
	14	2	6	796
	15+	2	3	262
16–20	8–11	3	4	1166
	12	2	4	1638
	13	3	4	1700
	14	5	6	777
	15+	3	4	345
21–25	8–11	5	11	526
	12	3	5	770
	13	5	6	851
	14	7	7	460
	15+	6	5	203
26–30	8–11	10	12	196
	12	9	24	266
	13	5	5	323
	14	10	11	192
	15+	7	6	87
31–35	8–11	10	11	99
	12	7	28	122
	13	8	2	162
	14	13	16	109
36–40	8–11	11	9	65
	12	14	45	66
	13	6	2	96
	14	13	25	62

TABLE 29.13 Accumulative Incidence: Homosexual Contacts to Orgasm

By Rural-Urban Background

Age	Rural	Urban	Rural	Urban	Age	Rural	Urban	Rural	Urban
	Percent		*Cases*			*Percent*		*Cases*	
12	1	1	399	5200	30	6	10	168	1796
15	3	2	397	5161	35	7	12	124	1285
20	4	4	335	3873	40	8	13	84	825
25	5	8	223	2465	45	10	14	60	488

Table based on total sample, including single, married, and previously married females.

TABLE 29.14 Active Incidence and Percentage of Outlet Homosexual Contacts to Orgasm

Single Females by Rural-Urban Background

Age During Activity	Backgrnd.	Active Incid. %	% of Total Outlet	Cases in Total Sample
Adol.–15	Rural	3	7	388
	Urban	2	4	5132
16–20	Rural	4	5	386
	Urban	3	4	5080
21–25	Rural	3	3	229
	Urban	5	7	2484
26–30	Rural	2	2	104
	Urban	9	12	915
31–35	Rural	2	—	64
	Urban	10	15	453

TABLE 29.15 Accumulative Incidence: Homosexual Contacts to Orgasm By Religious Background

	PROTESTANT			CATHOLIC			JEWISH	
AGE	Dev.	Moder.	Inact.	Dev.	Moder.	Inact.	Moder.	Inact.
	Percent							
12	1	1	1	1	1	2	—	—
15	2	1	2	3	4	8	1	2
20	3	2	7	5	4	13	2	5
25	5	5	12	5	8	22	2	7
30	7	6	16	3	12	28	3	9
35	7	9	17	5		25	4	11
40	8	10	16					13
45	11	13	20					15
	Cases							
12	1234	1166	1090	390	153	171	575	985
15	1217	1156	1083	385	151	171	574	981
20	922	923	976	284	114	146	334	692
25	566	587	739	177	76	107	187	413
30	424	435	552	124	51	79	136	294
35	337	315	419	78		52	77	205
40	237	212	274					127
45	150	132	153					74

Table based on total sample, including single, married, and previously married females.

TABLE 29.16   Active Incidence, Frequency, and Percentage of Outlet
Homosexual Contacts to Orgasm
Single Females, by Religious Background

Age During Activity	Religious Group	Active Incid. %	Active Median Freq. per WK.	% of Total Outlet	Cases in Total Sample
Adol.–15	Protestant				
	Devout	2	0.3	6	1218
	Moderate	3	0.4	4	1147
	Inactive	2	0.2	2	1063
	Catholic				
	Devout	3	0.3	13	382
	Moderate	3		6	150
	Inactive	8	0.4	6	169
	Jewish				
	Devout	0		0	107
	Moderate	1		—	571
	Inactive	2	0.1	2	978
16–20	Protestant				
	Devout	3	0.2	6	1197
	Moderate	2	0.2	2	1133
	Inactive	5	0.2	5	1065
	Catholic				
	Devout	5	0.6	15	372
	Moderate	4		6	139
	Inactive	10	0.7	8	160
	Jewish				
	Devout	1		—	107
	Moderate	—		—	571
	Inactive	2	0.2	2	972
21–25	Protestant				
	Devout	3	0.3	10	604
	Moderate	3	0.4	4	615
	Inactive	8	0.4	8	676
	Catholic				
	Devout	4		15	196
	Moderate	5		12	57
	Inactive	18	0.5	13	91

TABLE 29.16 Active Incidence, Frequency, and Percentage of Outlet *(continued)*

Age During Activity	Religious Group	Active Incid. %	Active Median Freq. per Wk.	% of Total Outlet	Cases in Total Sample
	Jewish				
	Moderate	0		0	192
	Inactive	4	0.3	6	396
26–30	Protestant				
	Devout	5	0.4	17	221
	Moderate	4	0.4	4	249
	Inactive	13	0.5	13	309
	Catholic				
	Devout	5		29	79
31–35	Protestant				
	Devout	7		34	121
	Moderate	6		2	127
	Inactive	15	0.4	11	159
36–40	Protestant				
	Devout	7		37	76
	Moderate	6		2	77
	Inactive	16	0.5	18	102

TABLE 29.17   Active Incidence: Heterosexual-Homosexual Ratings By Marital Status

Age	0	1-6	RATING 1	2	3	4	5	6	X (%)	Cases
	Percent				*Percent*				*%*	*Cases*
SINGLE FEMALES										
5	7	6	—	—	2	—	—	3	87	5914
10	7	11	—	1	2	—	—	8	82	5820
15	34	6	2	1	1	—	—	2	60	5714
20	72	11	5	2	1	1	1	1	17	3746
25	72	14	4	3	1	3	1	2	14	1315
30	67	18	5	4	2	3	2	2	15	622
35	61	20	6	3	3	2	3	3	19	370
37	61	17	5	3	2	2	2	3	22	290
MARRIED FEMALES										
	Percent				*Percent*				*%*	*Cases*
17	80	11	9	1	0	0	0	1	9	89
20	89	8	5	1	1	—	—	—	3	545
25	90	8	6	1	—	—	—	—	2	1331
30	90	9	6	2	—	—	—	—	1	1215
35	89	10	7	2	—	—	—	—	1	908
40	89	9	6	2	—	0	—	—	2	569
45	89	9	6	2	—	0	—	1	2	311
50	88	8	4	3	0	0	1	0	4	154
PREVIOUSLY MARRIED FEMALES										
	Percent				*Percent*				*%*	*Cases*
20	80	14	6	1	3	3	0	1	6	81
25	75	17	7	3	0	1	3	3	8	178
30	78	14	6	2	1	2	1	2	8	224
35	78	17	9	3	0	1	2	2	5	204
40	76	14	8	2	2	0	1	1	10	177

Definitions of the ratings are as follows: 0 = entirely heterosexual. 1-6 = with homosexual history, of any sort. 1 = largely heterosexual, but with incidental homosexual history. 2 = largely heterosexual, but with a distinct homosexual history. 3 = equally heterosexual and homosexual. 4 = largely homosexual, but with distinct heterosexual history. 5 = largely homosexual, but with incidental heterosexual history. 6 = entirely homosexual. X = without either. See p. 471.

TABLE 29.18 Active Incidence: Females with Some Homosexual Rating By Educational Level and Marital Status

Age	Total Sample	Educational Level			Total Sample	Educational Level		
		9–12	13–16	17+		9–12	13–16	17+
				SINGLE FEMALES				
	%	Percent			Cases	Cases		
5	6	5	6	8	5914	1014	3302	1152
10	11	12	11	12	5820	1014	3301	1151
15	6	6	5	8	5714	1005	3299	1150
20	11	7	10	13	3746	641	1943	1079
25	14	8	14	17	1315	229	423	621
30	18	8	17	21	622	85	167	343
35	20		28	20	370		82	237
				MARRIED FEMALES				
	%	Percent			Cases	Cases		
20	8	7	9	11	545	194	253	63
25	8	5	10	11	1331	408	563	296
30	9	6	10	11	1215	342	475	331
35	10	6	11	13	908	235	346	271
40	9	4	12	10	569	139	204	188
45	9	4	10	13	311	83	111	93
				PREVIOUSLY MARRIED FEMALES				
	%	Percent			Cases	Cases		
25	17	11	18		178	64	65	
30	14	14	12	16	224	76	73	61
35	17	16	20	17	204	55	72	60
40	14		13	18	177		61	62

The table includes all females with heterosexual-homosexual ratings of 1 to 6. These females had had some homosexual history, either psychologic or overt, in the particular year shown. Those with a rating of 1 had minimum homosexual histories; those with a rating of 6 had the maximum and therefore exclusive homosexual histories. See Table 29.17.

TABLE 29.19 Attitudes of Females Toward Homosexual Activity
Correlation of Attitudes with Subject's Own Homosexual
Experience

ATTITUDES	ACCEPT FOR SELF		APPROVE HOMOSEXUAL ACTIVITY				WOULD KEEP FRIENDS WHO HAD HOMOSEXUAL EXPERIENCE			
			For Other Females		For Males		Female Friends		Male Friends	
	Subject		Subject		Subject		Subject		Subject	
	With exp.	No exp.	With exp.	No exp.	With exp.	No exp.	With exp.	No exp.	With exp.	No exp.
	%	%	%	%	%	%	%	%	%	%
Yes	18	1	23	4	18	4	88	55	74	51
Uncertain	20	4	62	57	60	54	8	23	16	23
No	62	95	15	39	22	42	4	22	10	26
Number of cases	683	4500	653	4758	616	4718	251	941	122	935

TABLE 29.20 Social Difficulties Resulting from Homosexual Experience

Source of Difficulty	Total Cases	Cases of Major Difficulty	Cases of Minor Difficulty
Home	21	13	8
School	8	4	4
Business	6	2	4
Police	4	1	3
Institutional	3	1	2
No. of cases of difficulties	42	21	21
No. of females with diffic.	38		
No. of females without diffic.	104		
% of females with diffic.	27		

There were 710 females in the sample with homosexual experience, but only the 142 with the most extensive experience are included in these calculations. None of those with more minor experience had run into such social difficulties.

READING 30

Vernon Rosario, "Rise and Fall of the Medical Model," *The Gay & Lesbian Review Worldwide*, (Nov./Dec. 2012): 39–41.

Reprinted in its entirety, this essay by historian Vernon Rosario describes the history of medical models of homosexuality in the twentieth century.

Rise and Fall of the Medical Model

Vernon Rosario

One of the most dramatic revolutions in lesbian and gay history, and perhaps the greatest victory of the gay rights movement, is the transformation in psychiatric approaches to homosexuality. Indeed, many current historians argue that late-19th-century doctors constructed modern homosexual identity. "Sodomites" and "pederasts" had long been studied by legal, religious, and medicoforensic experts as criminal or immoral because of their "perverse" acts. However, it was only in the 19th century that the "sexual invert" or "homosexual" emerged in the medical literature as a distinct category of human being. According to historian Michel Foucault, "the homosexual of the 19th century became a personage: a past, a case history and a childhood, a character, a form of life; also a morphology, with an indiscrete anatomy and perhaps a mysterious physiology."

The accuracy and generalizability of this claim has been much debated as historians have examined new documents suggesting that individuals well before the 19th century or beyond the influence of European medicine had already developed identities as same-sex-loving people (whatever they or we might like to call that identity).

It is, however, clear that Victorian doctors themselves believed that they had discovered a new phenomenon. Their writings also make it clear that they were baffled, disgusted, and terrified by it. Nevertheless, the emerging leaders in psychiatry and sexology believed that "contrary sexual sensation" had to be a profound mental aberration and had to have some biological explanation. Take, for example, one of the first discussions of "contrary sexual sensation" in the American medical press, an exchange of letters published in *The Medical Record* of New York in 1881 . A physician (clearly embarrassed by the subject matter) wrote under the pseudonym Dr. H to describe "a curious case of prolonged masturbation" currently under his care. The patient was "a highly cultivated gentlemen of high moral character, the father of three or four healthy children, the result of an unusually happy marriage." However, the patient had a lifelong fondness for "indoor games, female pursuits, and even attire," especially corsets and tight ladies' boots with French heels. He had largely managed to abstain from masturbating with these articles until he married and fathered two children. Then he abandoned himself to cross-dressing in painfully tight female clothing and even attended church in a black silk dress. He carried several pictures of himself as a ballet girl, as Queen Elizabeth, as the Goddess of Liberty, etc. The dismayed and perplexed Dr. H turned to the conventional remedies of the day: bromides and dietary manipulations (still known to us through Drs. Kellogg and Graham), but to no avail. He concluded his cry for professional assistance: "Have any of your readers had a similar case within their experience? I proposed the name of Gynomania for it."

Dr. H never got to coin a new disease. Instead, a subsequent issue of the journal carried a reply from the president of the New York Neurological Society, Dr. Edward C. Spitzka, who was clearly better read in the latest medical literature. He was quick to pronounce a diagnosis of "contrary sexual sensation" and noted that twenty such cases had been described by German and French "alienists." He lamented that there were undoubtedly more, but they went undetected and were not committed to asylums. They were a result of a "degenerative psychosis" (a hereditary neuropsychiatric disease) and were incurable.

One curious and telling aspect of the case is that Dr. H never described any same-sex affections in his patient. However, as the terms "contrary sexual sensation" or "sexual inversion" suggest, any kind of cross-gendered behavior, tastes, or erotic attraction invoked the suspicion of homosexuality. Relying on recent discoveries that all embryos are "bi-sexual" (i.e., possess both male and female primordial genital tissue), doctors viewed inverts as "psychosexual hermaphrodites." Using this model, physicians desperately searched for hints of cross-sexed anatomical, neurological, or endocrinological traits that might "objectively" betray a person's homosexuality (especially if accused of sodomy). More importantly, such crossed-sexed biology might suggest therapies for restoring "normal" masculinity or femininity. These included castration and ovariotomies, implants of "normal" testicles, and hormone therapy. Even into the 20th century, homosexuality remained an obsession of psychiatry: the latest techniques of biological and analytic psychiatry were deployed to explain and treat it, and it became a key pathology for explaining myriad other mental illnesses.

A biological explanation of homosexuality, however, did not necessarily imply its pathologization. From the mid-19th century until today, homosexual researchers and heterosexual scientists sympathetic to the social plight of gays, hoping to promote wider acceptance, have tried to prove the "natural," biological, and unalterable quality of homosexuality. They have generally insisted that homosexuality is not a pathology but a natural biological variant.

Particularly before World War II, there were a number of positive depictions of homosexuality in the medical literature. William J. Robinson, chief of the Department of Genito-Urinary Diseases and Dermatology of the Bronx Hospital, was a friend of Magnus Hirschfeld, a prominent German homosexual sexologist. As editor of the *American Journal of Urology and Sexology*, Robinson frequently published items on homosexuality, including a poignant letter in 1919 from an anonymous invert, who wrote: "[It] is my belief that two men who love each other have as much right to live together as a man and a woman have. Also that it is as beautiful when looked at in the right light and far more equal! ... May I not have as high an ideal in my love towards men, as a man towards a woman? Higher no doubt, than most men have toward women!"

Dr. Florence Beery, who also supported the biological model of congenital bisexuality, was even more enthusiastic in defending homosexuals. Writing in the *Medico-Legal Journal* of 1924, she enthused: "Homo-sexuals are keen, quick, intuitive, sensitive, exceptionally tactful and have a great deal of understanding. ... Contrary to the general impression, homosexuals are not necessarily morbid; they are generally fine, healthy specimens, well developed bodily, intellectual, and generally with a very high standard of conduct." She dismissed the search for cross-sexed anatomical traits and insisted that generally the "homo-genic woman" had a thoroughly feminine body. It was her temperament that was "active, brave, originative, decisive," Beery declared. "Such a woman is fitted for remarkable work in professional life or as a manageress of institutions, even as a ruler of a country." Beery, like many other advocates of biological explanations of homosexuality, was vehemently opposed to the new psychoanalytic views of homosexuality.

In 1905, Freud published his groundbreaking *Three Essays on the Theory of Sexuality*, which introduced the notions of infantile sexuality, the oral, anal, and phallic stages of development, the castration complex, and penis envy. Although Freud had not treated any inverts before this time, inversion was the subject of the critical first essay as well as the final section of the third essay, on the "Prevention of Inversion." Freud argued that the "sexual aberrations" were not discrete degenerative pathologies but represented fixations on universal, primitive, infantile stages of erotism. The newborn had the capacity to find any part of the body erotogenic and, furthermore, all children went through a phase of "latent homosexuality" until "normal" heterosexual object choice developed at puberty. While Freud was quite radical in suggesting the universality of homosexuality, he was still a man of his time, for he believed that only heterosexual, reproductive sexuality was normal and healthy. Homosexuality represented a form of arrested sexual development resulting from traumatic parent-child dynamics. Nevertheless, Freud did not believe that homosexuals were necessarily unhappy and dysfunctional people; nor did they need to be "cured."

Dr. Abraham Brill, one of Freud's early American promoters and translators, was even more adamant in his assessment. Writing in the *Journal of Nervous and Mental Disease* (1919), he reaffirmed that, "everyone is more or less homosexual, which enabled them to live in friendly relations with their fellow beings of the same sex." Most homosexuals, he claimed, did not want to be cured; nor could they be. The only homosexuals who did seek therapy were of the "compulsive neurotic type." Psycho-analyzing homosexuals who were forced into therapy and who did not want to be cured was "simply a waste of time and money." Brill argued that it was more useful to encourage the family to be broad-minded. Writing at the end of the Roaring Twenties, Dr. Clarence P. Oberndorf noted in the *Urologie and Cutaneous Review* (1929) that, at least in educated circles, American attitudes towards sex were far less Victorian. He even criticized as outdated Radclyffe Hall's portrayal of the "distressed and fatalistic wail" of the lesbian heroine in *The Well of Loneliness* (1928).

Upon Freud's death in 1939, and with the U.S. entry into World War II, psychoanalytic views of homosexuality took a distinct turn for the worse. Psychoanalyst Sandor Rado in 1940 challenged Freudian orthodoxy by denying the universality of infantile bisexuality and by insisting that homosexuality was distinctly pathological and potentially curable. Typically, analysts blamed homosexuality on a close-binding, overprotective mother and a detached, hostile father. Some psychoanalysts even advocated the additional use of hormone and shock therapies for recalcitrant patients who "posed too much resistance to treatment."

Psychoanalysis also gained enormous professional clout thanks to its involvement in the war effort. The Selective Service wanted to screen out inductees who might buckle under pressure and undermine company morale. "Homosexual proclivities" were among the mental handicaps to be referred for more expert scrutiny and exclusion. Dr. Manfred Guttmacher complained in *Neuropsychiatry in World War II* (1966, edited by Robert S. Anderson) that "there was that pathetic group of homosexuals who had denied their abnormality to induction examiners and who had blindly hoped to adjust by living a robust life among thousands of normal military men. ... Others with strong latent tendencies developed psychosomatic disorders and acute anxiety states." Psychiatrists also assessed for "reclaimability" the thousands of armed forces members diagnosed with "pathological sexuality" (mostly homosexuality).

The stresses of war and crowded all-male living conditions seem to have prompted numerous cases of "acute anxiety states" with "homosexual panic." The term first appeared in Dr. Edward Kempf's textbook *Psychopathology* (1920), which described typical cases in which a young man became convinced that friends or comrades believed he was homosexual, stared at him oddly, whispered insults like "cock sucker," "woman," or "fairy," and tried to engage him in fellatio or sodomy. Kempf explained that it resulted from "the pressure of uncontrollable perverse sexual cravings." In the most severe cases, it became chronic and was indistinguishable from dementia precox or schizophrenia. Ten years earlier, Freud had proposed that paranoia was frequently the result of repressed homosexuality being transformed through the defense mechanisms of reaction formation ("I hate him") and projection ("he hates me"). Analysts increasingly believed that schizophrenia in general was caused by homosexuality. One analyst even called schizophrenia the "twin brother" of homosexuality.

Homosexuality soon became the culprit for just about every other psychopathology. In addition to psychotic disorders, it was connected to all neurotic disorders, alcoholism, even promiscuous heterosexuality (or Casanova syndrome). Thus Dr. Benjamin Karpman was exaggerating only slightly when he declared in 1937: "The problems of psychiatry will not be solved until we solve the problem of homosexuality."

The problem of homosexuality only grew after the war, particularly following the publication of *Sexual Behavior in the Human Male* (1948), by Alfred Kinsey, Wardell Pomeroy, and Clyde Martin. The "Kinsey Report" reported astoundingly high rates of homosexual behavior (as well as masturbation and other perversities). It quickly became a global bestseller and inspired the formation of "homophile" groups such as the Mattachine Society. Many psychiatrists and sexologists objected to its findings and were offended by Kinsey 's sharp critiques of both hormonal and psychoanalytic explanations of homosexuality. Most notably, Kinsey argued that sexual orientation was not binary (either hetero- or homosexual) or fixed over one's lifespan. The thought that homosexuals were numerous and not all flamingly evident no doubt fueled the gay purges that began in 1950. Like "Reds," "sex perverts" might be corrosive yet invisible.

Further challenges to the pathological view of homosexuality came from psychologist Evelyn Hooker at UCLA. Through one of her students, she was introduced to the gay community of Los Angeles, and began conducting psychological testing of these non-clinical subjects in the 1940's. Previous research had been based on prison cases or homosexuals seeking psychiatric treatment. Hooker's gay subjects, however, were not significantly different in their psychological adjustment from her heterosexual controls. Hooker began to publish her findings in the late 1950's and was a welcome speaker at homophile group meetings. She chaired a National Institutes of Mental Health research panel on homosexuality, whose initially suppressed report in 1969 decried the widespread mistreatment of homosexuals and called for decriminalization and greater social acceptance as the way to improve their mental health.

At the time, a variety of behaviorist conversion therapies were being actively promoted. Electric shock aversion therapy (first used to treat alcoholism in the 1920's), chemical aversion therapy with emetics (developed in the 50's), covert sensitization, and other conditioning therapies all tried to re-orient erotic attraction by associating homoerotic images with discomfort. They generally failed in the long run and provoked the most visceral opposition by gay rights activists. At the 1970 American Psychiatric Association (APA) annual meeting, Dr. Nathaniel McConaghy's presentation on aversive conditioning exploded in gay pandemonium as activists accused him of being a vicious torturer.

The work of Kinsey, Hooker, and others all emboldened a new breed of post-Stonewall gay activists ready to engage in dramatic and confrontational tactics, including disrupting APA meetings and demanding equal time to refute the theories of homosexual pathology. With the assistance of key supporters within the APA, a panel of "non-patient" gays spoke at the 1971 APA meeting. At the 1972 meeting, a similar panel included a gay psychiatrist who wore a mask to preserve his anonymity. That year the APA's Nomenclature Committee began considering the pathological status of homosexuality as presented in the *Diagnostic and Statistical Manual of Psychiatric Disorders*, 2nd edition (DSM II). With growing support for reform among psychiatrists, after extensive debate at the 1973 meeting, and with much behind-the-scenes lobbying both for and against de-pathologization, the APA Board of Trustees voted on December 15, 1973, to delete homosexuality from the DSM. Sensitive to many psychiatrists' profound theoretical and emotional commitment to the pathological nature of homosexuality, the Board added the classification of "sexual orientation disturbance" (later labeled "ego-dystonic homosexuality") for individuals who are disturbed by their same-sex orientation. Newspapers around the world reported the decision, with one writer wryly noting it was the single greatest cure in the history of psychiatry.

Many prominent psychoanalysts, such as Charles Socarides and Irving Bieber, were not pleased with this outcome and mounted a vocal battle against the change, ultimately forcing it to a vote by the APA membership. In 1974, a majority of APA members ratified the declassification of homosexuality. The American Psychological Association followed suit in 1975, and the social workers' association did so in 1977. Gay and lesbian caucuses have sprung up within all these organizations and have been formally recognized. Out gay and lesbian researchers have explored the mental health challenges and successes of gay people within a homophobic culture. The American Psychoanalytic Association proved most resistant: only in 1992 did it officially reverse its long-standing, unspoken policy of excluding homosexuals from advancement in psychoanalytic institutes. The most recent edition of the DSM (1994) eliminated any diagnosis of homosexuality, and the APA has officially criticized gay "conversion therapy" as useless and harmful.

In the span of a century, the diagnosis of homosexuality had come full circle, from being "discovered" as a profound psychiatric illness to being declared nothing of the sort. This history serves as a powerful example of the social and political malleability of supposedly objective scientific knowledge. It is wise to keep this in mind as we witness a revival, at the end of the century, in research on the biology of homosexuality. Although now conducted by openly gay scientists, such as Richard Pillard, Simon LeVay, and Dean Hamer, its methods, subject selection, and models of homosexuality are all subject to cultural, sociological, and historical biases. While biomedical research on homosexuality may, like the work of Hirschfeld or Freud a century ago, be genuinely proffered as a humane and scientific corrective to cultural prejudice, there is no telling how it will be used in the century ahead.

SIDEBAR

In the span of a century, the diagnosis of homosexuality came full circle, from being "discovered" as a profound psychiatric illness to being declared nothing of the sort.

REFERENCES

Bayer, Ronald. *Homosexuality and American Psychiatry: The Politics of Diagnosis*. Princeton University Press, 1987.

Bérubé, Allan. *Coming Out under Fire: The History of Gay Men and Women in World War II*. Free Press, 1990.

D'Emilio, John. "The Homosexual Menace: The Politics of Sexuality in Cold War America," in *Passion and Power: Sexuality in History*, Kathy Peiss. et al, eds. Temple University Press, 1989.

Foucault, Michel. *Histoire de la sexualité: La volonté de savoir*. Gallimard, 1976 (translated as *A History of Sexuality*, Vol. 1: *An Introduction*).

PART VIII

SEXUAL REVOLUTIONS

The end of the twentieth century witnessed new concerns with population growth, as exemplified in Paul Ehrlich's book *The Population Bomb*. At the same time, the sexual revolution of the 1970s brought more openness about sexual expression, birth control, and sexuality. Tensions between tradition and sexual openness remained, however, and are evident in debates over sex education and gender nonconformity.

READING 31

Paul Ehrlich, *The Population Bomb* (1968), Excerpts.

Paul Ehrlich (1932–) is an American biologist best known for his work on population growth. In his book *The Population Bomb*, he argued for the negative consequences of unchecked population growth.

The Population Bomb

Paul Ehrlich

I have understood the population explosion intellectually for a long time. I came to understand it emotionally one stinking hot night in Delhi a few years ago. My wife and daughter and I were returning to our hotel in an ancient taxi. The seats were hopping with fleas. The only functional gear was third. As we crawled through the city, we entered a crowded slum area. The temperature was well over 100, and the air was a haze of dust and smoke. The streets seemed alive with people. People eating, people washing, people sleeping. People visiting, arguing, and screaming. People thrusting their hands through the taxi window, begging. People defecating and urinating. People clinging to buses. People herding animals. People, people, people, people. As we moved slowly through the mob, hand horn squawking, the dust, noise, heat, and cooking fires gave the scene a hellish aspect. Would we ever get to our hotel? All three of us were, frankly, frightened. It seemed that anything could happen—but, of course, nothing did. Old India hands will laugh at our reaction. We were just some overprivileged tourists, unaccustomed to the sights and sounds of India. Perhaps, but the problems of Delhi and Calcutta are our problems too. Americans have helped to create them; we help to prevent their solution. We must all learn to identify with the plight of our less fortunate fellows on Spaceship Earth if we are to help both them and ourselves to survive.

TOO MANY PEOPLE

Americans are beginning to realize that the underdeveloped countries of the world face an inevitable population-food crisis. Each year food production in these countries falls a bit further behind burgeoning population growth, and people go to bed a little bit hungrier. While there are temporary or local reversals of this trend, it now seems inevitable that it will continue to its logical conclusion: mass starvation. The rich may continue to get richer, but the more numerous poor are going to get poorer. Of these poor, a *minimum* of ten million people, most of them children, will starve to death during each year of the 1970s. But this is a mere handful compared to the numbers that will be starving before the end of the century. And it is now too late to take action to save many of those people.

However, most Americans are not aware that the U.S. and other developed countries also have a problem with overpopulation. Rather than suffering from food shortages, these countries show symptoms in the form of environmental deterioration and increased difficulty in obtaining resources to support their affluence.

In a book about population there is a temptation to stun the reader with an avalanche of statistics. I'll spare you most, but not all, of that. After all, no matter how you slice it, population is a numbers game. Perhaps the best way to impress you with numbers is to tell you about the "doubling time"—the time necessary for the population to double in size.

It has been estimated that the human population of 8000 B.C. was about five million people, taking perhaps one million years to get there from two and a half million. The population did not reach 500 million until almost 10,000 years later—about 1650 A.D. This means it doubled roughly once every thousand years or so. It reached a billion people around 1850, doubling in some 200 years. It took only 80 years or so for the next doubling, as the population reached two billion around 1930. We have not completed the next doubling to four billion yet, but we now have well over three and a half billion people. The doubling time at present seems, to be about 35 years.[1] Quite a reduction in doubling times: 1,000,000 years, 1,000 years, 200 years, 80 years, 35 years. Perhaps the meaning of a doubling time of around 35 years is best brought home by a theoretical exercise. Let's examine what might happen on the absurd assumption that the population continued to double every 35 years into the indefinite future.

If growth continued at that rate for about 900 years, there would be some 60,000,000,000,000,000 people on the face of the earth. Sixty million billion people. This is about 100 persons for each square yard of the Earth's surface, land and sea. A British physicist, J. H. Fremlin,[2] guessed that such a multitude might be housed in a continuous 2,000-story building covering our entire planet. The upper 1,000 stories would contain only the apparatus for running this gigantic warren. Ducts, pipes, wires, elevator shafts, etc., would occupy about half of the space in the bottom 1,000 stories. This would leave three or four yards of floor space for each person. I will leave to your imagination the physical details of existence in this ant heap, except to point out that all would not be black. Probably each person would be limited in his travel. Perhaps he could take elevators through all 1,000 residential stories but could travel only within a circle of a few hundred yards' radius on any floor. This would permit, however, each person to choose his friends from among some ten million people!

And, as Fremlin points out, entertainment on the worldwide TV should be excellent, for at any time "one could expect some ten million Shakespeares and rather more Beatles to be alive."

Could growth of the human population of the Earth continue beyond that point? Not according to Fremlin. We would have reached a "heat limit." People themselves, as well as their activities, convert other forms of energy into heat which must be dissipated. In order to permit this excess heat to radiate directly from the top of the "world building" directly into space, the atmosphere would have been pumped into flasks under the sea well before the limiting population size was reached. The precise limit would depend on the technology of the day. At a population size of one billion billion people, the temperature of the "world roof" would be kept around the melting point of iron to radiate away the human heat generated.

But, you say, surely Science (with a capital "S") will find a way for us to occupy the other planets of our solar system and eventually of other stars before we get all that crowded. Skip for a moment the virtual certainty that those planets are uninhabitable. Forget also the insurmountable logistic problems of moving billions of people off the Earth. Fremlin has made some interesting calculations on how much time we could buy by occupying the planets of the solar system. For instance, at any given time it would take only about 50 years to populate Venus, Mercury, Mars, the moon, and the moons of Jupiter and Saturn to the same population density as Earth.[3]

What if the fantastic problems of reaching and colonizing the other planets of the solar system, such as Jupiter and Uranus, can be solved? It would take only about 200 years to fill them "Earth-full." So we could perhaps gain 250 years of time for population growth in the solar system after we had reached an absolute limit on Earth. What then? We can't ship our surplus to the stars. Professor Garrett Hardin[4] of the University of California at Santa Barbara has dealt effectively with this fantasy. Using extremely optimistic assumptions, he has calculated that Americans, by cutting their standard of living down to 18% of its present level, could in *one year* set aside enough capital to finance the exportation to the stars of *one day's* increase in the population of the world.

Interstellar transport for surplus people presents an amusing prospect. Since the ships would take generations to reach most stars, the only people who could be transported would be those willing to exercise strict birth control. Population explosions on space ships would be disastrous. Thus we would have to export our responsible people, leaving the irresponsible at home on Earth to breed.

Enough of fantasy. Hopefully, you are convinced that the population will have to stop growing sooner or later and that the extremely remote possibility of expanding into outer space offers no escape from the laws of population growth. If you still want to hope for the stars, just remember that, at the current growth rate, in a few thousand years everything in the visible universe would be converted into people, and the ball of people would be expanding with the speed of light! Unfortunately, even 900 years is much too far in the future for those of us concerned with the population explosion. As you will see, the next *nine* years will probably tell the story.

Of course, population growth is not occurring uniformly over the face of the Earth. Indeed, countries are divided rather neatly into two groups: those with rapid growth rates, and those with relatively slow growth rates. The first group, making up about two-thirds of the world population, coincides closely with what are known as the "underdeveloped countries" (UDCs). The UDCs are not industrialized, tend to have inefficient agriculture, very small gross national products, high illiteracy rates and related problems. That's what UDCs are technically, but a short definition of underdeveloped is "hungry." Most Latin American, African, and Asian countries fall into this category. The second group consists of the "overdeveloped countries" (ODCs). ODCs are modem industrial nations, such as the United States, Canada, most European countries, Israel, the USSR, Japan, and Australia. They consume a disproportionate amount of the world's resources and are the major polluters. Most, but by no means all,[4] people in these countries are adequately nourished.

Doubling times in the UDCs range around 20 to 35 years. Examples of these times (from the 1970 figures released by the Population Reference Bureau) are: Kenya, 23 years; Nigeria, 27; Turkey, 26; Indonesia, 24; Philippines, 21; Brazil, 25; Costa Rica, 19; and El Salvador, 21. Think of what it means for the population of a country to double in 25 years. In order just to keep living standards at the present inadequate level, the food available for the people must be doubled. Every structure and road must be duplicated. The amount of power must be doubled. The capacity of the transport system must be doubled. The number of trained doctors, nurses, teachers, and administrators must be doubled. This would be a fantastically difficult job in the United States—a rich country with a fine agricultural system, immense industries, and access to abundant resources. Think of what it means to a country with none of these.

READING 32

Radicalesbians, "The Woman-Identified Woman" (1970).

The Radicalesbians was an American group of lesbian feminists who challenged all feminists to engage with sexuality and lesbianism as political issues in their 1970 manifesto, "The Woman-Identified Woman."

The Woman Identified Woman

Radicalesbians

What is a lesbian? A lesbian is the rage of all women condensed to the point of explosion. She is the woman who, often beginning at an extremely early age, acts in accordance with her inner compulsion to be a more complete and freer human being than her society—perhaps then, but certainly later—cares to allow her. These needs and actions, over a period of years, bring her into painful conflict with people, situations, the accepted ways of thinking, feeling and behaving, until she is in a state of continual war with everything around her, and usually with her self. She may not be fully conscious of the political implications of what for her began as personal necessity, but on some level she has not been able to accept the limitations and oppression laid on her by the most basic role of her society—the female role. The turmoil she experiences tends to induce guilt proportional to the degree to which she feels she is not meeting social expectations, and/or eventually drives her to question and analyze what the rest of her society more or less accepts. She is forced to evolve her own life pattern, often living much of her life alone, learning usually much earlier than her "straight" (heterosexual) sisters about the essential aloneness of life (which the myth of marriage obscures) and about the reality of illusions. To the extent that she cannot expel the heavy socialization that goes with being female, she can never truly find peace with herself. For she is caught somewhere between accepting society's view of her—in which case she cannot accept herself—and coming to understand what this sexist society has done to her and why it is functional and necessary for it to do so. Those of us who work that through find ourselves on the other side of a tortuous journey through a night that may have been decades long. The perspective gained from that journey, the liberation of self, the inner peace, the real love of self and of all women, is something to be shared with all women—because we are all women.

It should first be understood that lesbianism, like male homosexuality, is a category of behavior possible only in a sexist society characterized by rigid sex roles and dominated by male supremacy. Those sex roles dehumanize women by defining us as a supportive/serving caste in relation to the master caste of men, and emotionally cripple men by demanding that they be alienated from their own bodies and emotions in order to perform their economic/political/military functions effectively. Homosexuality is a by-product of a particular way of setting up roles (or approved patterns of behavior) on the basis of sex; as such it is an inauthentic (not consonant with "reality") category. In a society in which men do not oppress women, and sexual expression is allowed to follow feelings, the categories of homosexuality and heterosexuality would disappear.

But lesbianism is also different from male homosexuality, and serves a different function in the society. "Dyke" is a different kind of put-down from "faggot", although both imply you are not playing your socially assigned sex role... are not therefore a "real woman" or a "real man." The grudging admiration felt for the tomboy, and the queasiness felt around a sissy boy point to the same thing: the contempt in which women—or those who play a female role—are held. And the investment in keeping women in that contemptuous role is very great. Lesbian is a word, the label, the condition that holds women in line. When a woman hears this word tossed her way, she knows she is stepping out of line. She knows that she has crossed the terrible boundary of her sex role. She recoils, she protests, she reshapes her actions to gain approval. Lesbian is a label invented by the Man to throw at any woman who dares to be his equal, who dares to challenge his prerogatives (including that of all women as part of the exchange medium among men), who dares to assert the primacy of her own needs. To have the label applied to people active in women's liberation is just the most recent instance of a long history; older women will recall that not so long ago, any woman who was successful, independent, not orienting her whole life about a man, would hear this word. For in this sexist society, for a woman to be independent means she can't be a woman—she must be a dyke. That in itself should tell us where women are at. It says as clearly as can be said: women and person are contradictory terms. For a lesbian is not considered a "real woman." And yet, in popular thinking, there is really only one essential difference between a lesbian and other women: that of sexual orientation—which is to say, when you strip off all the packaging, you must finally realize that the essence of being a "woman" is to get fucked by men.

"Lesbian" is one of the sexual categories by which men have divided up humanity. While all women are dehumanized as sex objects, as the objects of men they are given certain compensations: identification with his power, his ego, his status, his protection (from other males), feeling like a "real woman," finding social acceptance by adhering to her role, etc. Should a woman confront herself by confronting another woman, there are fewer rationalizations, fewer buffers by which to avoid the stark horror of her dehumanized condition. Herein we find the overriding fear of many women toward being used as a sexual object by a woman, which not only will bring her no male-connected compensations, but also will reveal the void which is woman's real situation. This dehumanization is expressed when a straight woman learns that a sister is a lesbian; she begins to relate to her lesbian sister as her potential sex object, laying a surrogate male role on the lesbian. This reveals her heterosexual conditioning to make herself into an object when sex is potentially involved in a relationship, and it denies the lesbian her full humanity. For women, especially those in the movement, to perceive their lesbian sisters through this male grid of role definitions is to accept this male cultural conditioning and to oppress their sisters much as they themselves have been oppressed by men. Are we going to continue the male classification system of defining all females in sexual relation to some other category of people? Affixing the label lesbian not only to a woman who aspires to be a person, but also to any situation of real love, real solidarity, real primacy among women, is a primary form of divisiveness among women: it is the condition which keeps women within the confines of the feminine role, and it is the debunking/scare term that keeps women from forming any primary attachments, groups, or associations among ourselves.

Women in the movement have in most cases gone to great lengths to avoid discussion and confrontation with the issue of lesbianism. It puts people up-tight. They are hostile, evasive, or try to incorporate it into some 'broader issue." "They would rather not talk about it. "If they have to, they try to "dismiss it as a 'lavender herring,'" But it is no side issue. It is absolutely essential to the success and fulfillment of the women's liberation movement that this issue be dealt with. As long as the label "dyke" can be used to frighten women into a less militant stand, keep her separate from her sisters, keep her from giving primacy to anything other than men and family—then to that extent she is controlled by the male culture. Until women see in each other the possibility of a primal commitment which includes sexual love, they will be denying themselves the love and value they readily accord to men, thus affirming their second-class status. As long as male acceptability is primary—both to individual women and to the movement as a whole—the term lesbian will be used effectively against women. Insofar as women want only more privileges within the system, they do not want to antagonize male power. They instead seek acceptability for women's liberation, and the most crucial aspect of the acceptability is to deny lesbianism—i. e., to deny any fundamental challenge to the basis of the female. It should also be said that some younger, more radical women have honestly begun to discuss lesbianism, but so far it has been primarily as a sexual "alternative" to men. This, however, is still giving primacy to men, both because the idea of relating more completely to women occurs as a negative reaction to men, and because the lesbian relationship is being characterized simply by sex, which is divisive and sexist. On one level, which is both personal and political, women may withdraw emotional and sexual energies from men, and work out various alternatives for those energies in their own lives. On a different political/psychological level, it must be understood that what is crucial is that women begin disengaging from male—defined response patterns. In the privacy of our own psyches, we must cut those cords to the core. For irrespective of where our love and sexual energies flow, if we are male-identified in our heads, we cannot realize our autonomy as human beings.

But why is it that women have related to and through men? By virtue of having been brought up in a male society, we have internalized the male culture's definition of ourselves. That definition consigns us to sexual and family functions, and excludes us from defining and shaping the terms of our lives. In exchange for our psychic servicing and for performing society's non-profit-making functions, the man confers on us just one thing: the slave status which makes us legitimate in the eyes of the society in which we live. This is called "femininity" or "being a real woman" in our cultural lingo. We are authentic, legitimate, real to the extent that we are the property of some man whose name we bear. To be a woman who belongs to no man is to be invisible, pathetic, inauthentic, unreal. He confirms his image of us—of what we have to be in order to be acceptable by him—but not our real selves; he confirms our womanhood—as he defines it, in relation to him—but cannot confirm our personhood, our own selves as absolutes. As long as we are dependent on the male culture for this definition, for this approval, we cannot be free.

The consequence of internalizing this role is an enormous reservoir of self-hate. This is not to say the self-hate is recognized or accepted as such; indeed most women would deny it. It may be experienced as discomfort with her role, as feeling empty, as numbness, as restlessness, as a paralyzing anxiety at the center. Alternatively, it may be expressed in shrill defensiveness of the glory and destiny of her role. But it does exist, often beneath the edge of her consciousness, poisoning her existence, keeping her alienated from herself, her own needs, and rendering her a stranger to other women. They try to escape by identifying with the oppressor, living through him, gaining status and identity from his ego, his power, his accomplishments. And by not identifying with other "empty vessels" like themselves. Women resist relating on all levels to other women who will reflect their own oppression, their own secondary status, their own self-hate. For to confront another woman is finally to confront one's self—the self we have gone to such lengths to avoid. And in that mirror we know we cannot really respect and love that which we have been made to be.

As the source of self-hate and the lack of real self are rooted in our male-given identity, we must create a new sense of self. As long as we cling to the idea of "being a woman," we will sense some conflict with that incipient self, that sense of I, that sense of a whole person. It is very difficult to realize and accept that being "feminine" and being a whole person are irreconcilable. Only women can give to each other a new sense of self. That identity we have to develop with reference to ourselves, and not in relation to men. This consciousness is the revolutionary force from which all else will follow, for ours is an organic revolution. For this we must be available and supportive to one another, give our commitment and our love, give the emotional support necessary to sustain this movement. Our energies must flow toward our sisters, not backward toward our oppressors. As long as woman's liberation tries to free women without facing the basic heterosexual structure that binds us in one-to-one relationship with our oppressors, tremendous energies will continue to flow into trying to straighten up each particular relationship with a man, into finding how to get better sex, how to turn his head around—into trying to make the "new man" out of him, in the delusion that this will allow us to be the "new woman." This obviously splits our energies and commitments, leaving us unable to be committed to the construction of the new patterns which will liberate us.

It is the primacy of women relating to women, of women creating a new consciousness of and with each other, which is at the heart of women's liberation, and the basis for the cultural revolution. Together we must find, reinforce, and validate our authentic selves. As we do this, we confirm in each other that struggling, incipient sense of pride and strength, the divisive barriers begin to melt, we feel this growing solidarity with our sisters. We see ourselves as prime, find our centers inside of ourselves. We find receding the sense of alienation, of being cut off, of being behind a locked window, of being unable to get out what we know is inside. We feel a realness, feel at last we are coinciding with ourselves. With that real self, with that consciousness, we begin a revolution to end the imposition of all coercive identifications, and to achieve maximum autonomy in human expression.

READING 33

Jonathan Zimmerman, "A Right to Knowledge: Culture, Diversity, and Education in the Age of AIDS, 1984–2010," in *Too Hot to Handle: A Global History of Sex Education* (Princeton University Press, 2016), 115–129.

This excerpt from historian Jonathan Zimmerman describes different responses from sex educators to the AIDS crisis that began in the 1980s.

A Right to Knowledge? Culture, Diversity, and Sex Education in the Age of AIDS, 1984–2010

Jonathan Zimmerman

In September 1994, twenty thousand delegates gathered in Cairo, Egypt, for the International Conference on Population and Development (ICPD). Discarding the family-planning model that had marked most such meetings since the 1960s, the conference adopted a new emphasis on "reproductive rights." All human beings should be able to choose when and how they reproduced, the convention resolved; to make informed choices, they also needed access to sex education from the beginning of their reproductive years. "Information and services should be made available to adolescents to help them understand their sexuality," the ICPD declared. "This should be combined with the education of young men to respect women's self-determination and to share responsibility with women in matters of sexuality and reproduction." Scandinavians took the lead in promoting this rights-based approach at the meeting, which heard opening-day speeches from the Norwegian prime minister and from Denmark's minister for overseas development. The resolutions also represented a triumph for American officials at the Ford Foundation, who laid the groundwork for the ICPD by funding local Egyptian groups to "raise awareness" of sex education and especially AIDS. Sex education was "the only available protection" against AIDS, one Egyptian grant recipient noted. It would also help combat "sex perversion," he added, particularly homosexuality.[1]

Yet the final comment also underscored the limits of consensus at the ICPD. Egypt would eventually join with four other majority-Muslim countries in denouncing the idea of "individual" rights to sexual knowledge and self-determination; such a claim "could be interpreted as applying to sexual relations outside the framework of marriage," an Iranian delegate explained, "and this is totally unacceptable." Two mostly Catholic countries (El Salvador and Guatemala) also issued dissents from the resolutions, as did the delegation from the Vatican;

Jonathan Zimmerman, *from Too Hot to Handle: A Global History of Sex Education,*

pp. 115-129, 183-187. Copyright © 2015 by Princeton University Press. Reprinted

with permission.

earlier in the year, Philippines cardinal Jaime Sin called on Catholics to reject the ICPD along with "the shackles of this new global citizenship." The conference also heard a stinging rebuke from Pakistani premier Benazir Bhutto, who reiterated her support for population control even as she condemned Western leaders for pushing their own libertinism on the conservative East. "This conference must not be viewed by the teeming masses of the world as a universal social charter seeking to impose adultery, abortion, sex education and other such matters on individuals, societies, and religions which have their own social ethos," Bhutto warned. "The world needs consensus. It does not need a clash of cultures."[2]

It got one, anyway, although not the kind that Bhutto imagined. Two years after he declared a "cultural war" in the United States at the Republican National Convention, right-wing columnist Pat Buchanan proclaimed that the ICPD had united conservatives across borders—indeed, across cultures. "While this may be a bold agenda at Washington dinner parties, to traditional societies in Latin America, Africa and the Islamic world, it is the essence of decadent, godless Western materialism," Buchanan wrote, condemning the Cairo resolutions. Prior to the ICPD, Vatican officials met with representatives of the World Muslim League and other Islamic groups; in a joint statement, they condemned the "extreme individualism" and "moral decadence" of the conference. The papal envoy in Teheran also met with Iranian officials, who declared their "full endorsement" for the Vatican in its battle against the ICPD. As an Islamic leader in the United Kingdom wrote three years later, the Cairo controversy generated a "common platform" with "like-minded non-Muslim faith groups." It also emboldened them to challenge school officials, who had stepped up sex education in the face of the AIDS crisis. "Both sides—the authorities as well as the community—speak of promoting 'the moral,'" the Muslim leader wrote. "Whose morals is the child going to subscribe to?"[3]

The same question had surrounded sex education since its inception, of course. But it assumed a new meaning and urgency in the age of AIDS, which made most governments adopt some kind of school-based sex instruction. Suddenly, the question was no longer whether schools would teach about sex; it was what they would teach, and how, and to what end. Abandoning their long-standing opposition to the subject, conservative Christian activists in the West backed new forms of "abstinence-only" sex education. They also made common cause with different faith groups, at home and overseas, belying the popular notion of a "clash of cultures" between them. The real conflict pitted liberal and secular voices against the Global Right, which rallied religious conservatives behind older notions of sexual continence and obedience. For their own part, liberals struggled to respect ethnic and religious "diversity" even as they proclaimed a universal right to sexual choice and information. "How can a sexuality, reproduction and health perspective based on individual rights become a global norm?" a Swedish educator wondered in 2004, on the ten-year anniversary of the Cairo conference. Sadly, the Swede admitted, large parts of the globe still resisted that viewpoint. In an age of diversity, a single shared standard of sex education—or, even a personal "right" to the same—remained a chimera.[4]

THE AIDS CRISIS AND SEX EDUCATION, I: EUROPE AND THE USA

In 1987, US Surgeon General C. Everett Koop traveled to Japan to address a conference on HIV/AIDS. A leader in the effort to combat the disease back home, Koop was shocked when the Japanese Minister of Health raised a glass of sake in honor of his American guest and said, "AIDS, no problem in Japan." Koop bluntly replied that AIDS *was* a problem there, noting that businessmen consorted with prostitutes in Hawaii and then returned to Japan to infect their wives with HIV. And just as in America, he added, the only way to fight AIDS was via education. To be sure, Koop added, "lack of understanding and official denial" hampered AIDS prevention everywhere; in the United States, for example, his 1986 report on AIDS—calling on schools to start teaching about it in the third grade—had triggered outrage among his fellow conservatives, and even a few death threats against Koop himself. But that was all the more reason to press forward, he argued, citing the Hippocratic oath that was administered to physicians around the world. "We will not abandon the sick or disabled, whoever they are," Koop declared, "or however they got their problem." He added a jab at "homophobia" in Japan, although—as he later admitted—he also feared that his words "were falling on deaf ears."[5]

Koop might have been right. Nearly two decades later, Japanese textbooks took pains to debunk "myths" about AIDS—it wasn't spread by mosquito bites or by shaking hands, for example—but remained silent about how it *was* transmitted, and about who was suffering from it. But even these elliptical remarks represented a much more explicit discussion than what had been taught under Japanese "Purity Education," which had since assumed a more common name: sex education. Elsewhere, the subject continued to appear under older euphemisms—especially family life education and population education—and added a few new ones, including "adolescent reproductive health" and "life skills." As before, many of these names were designed to mask, downplay, or avoid sex-related content. But in the age of HIV/AIDS, such content increased—both in detail and in volume—in almost every corner of the globe. Not surprisingly, much of this instruction simply warned young people against having sex. On the one hand, an American educator wrote in 1996, the spread of HIV/AIDS helped erode "the taboo surrounding sexuality" in schools; on the other, it also reinforced traditional notions about it. Most sex education still focused on "the biology of sexuality" and on "controlling sexual activity through fear," the American educator wrote, reviewing several new initiatives overseas.[6]

The same was true in the United States, where a burst of new sex education laws and policies bore a distinctly conservative flavor. In 1986, when Koop released his AIDS report, just three states and the District of Columbia mandated sex education; by 1992, all but four states required or recommended it. These years also witnessed the rise of so-called abstinence-only sex education, fueled by federal measures that provided funds for the same. By 1999 one in three American school districts was using an abstinence-only curriculum like *Sex Respect,* which touted the idea of "secondary virginity": even if you had already had sex, you could reclaim virgin status by abstaining until marriage. It also issued controversial—and mostly flawed—data about condom failure, insisting that "safe sex" was a contradiction in terms. "There's another good reason not to have sex," the curriculum's creator told an interviewer in a news report she sent to C. Everett Koop. "You can die." Koop himself recommended abstinence outside of marriage but also argued for teaching students about condoms and even anal sex, so they knew how to protect themselves; as he told a reporter, "you can't talk about the dangers of snake poisoning and not mention snakes." His position drove a wedge into the Republican Party and created political headaches for President Ronald Reagan, who blithely announced that he had neither read Koop's HIV/AIDS report nor spoken to him about it. But it also underscored the limits of sex education in the era of AIDS; even in a plea for abstinence, there was only so much sexual information that Americans would allow their children to receive.[7]

In the United Kingdom, likewise, HIV/AIDS sparked a spike in both sex education and the squabbles surrounding it. In 1986, under pressure from Conservatives in Parliament, the government made local education authorities responsible for sex education and also declared that parents could exempt their children from it. When the Education Department issued a pamphlet the following year to guide instruction about AIDS, it emphasized that such instruction remained optional for schools and families alike; in the classroom, meanwhile, many teachers continued to avoid sex education for fear of offending local officials and parents. But it clearly received more attention than ever before; as in the United States, one British educator observed, the question became "how sex education is carried out and not whether it is carried out." A 1996 measure required sex education for all high school students—subject to parental right of withdrawal—but added that it should be taught "in such a manner as to encourage those pupils to have due regard to moral considerations and the value of family life." In 2000, yet another law declared that students should also be "protected from teaching materials which are inappropriate to [their] religious and cultural background." As another educator noted, these mandates made schools "walk a fine line"; stressing the value of family and morality, they also had to respect the varied moralities of different families.[8]

In the more liberal societies of northern Europe, meanwhile, HIV/AIDS brought renewed and often highly explicit attention to safe-sex practices. In the Netherlands, a popular television news program for children staged a condom demonstration on a model of an erect penis; a Danish cartoon book showed "Oda and Ole" making love, using a condom; Finnish authorities sent a sex education leaflet and a condom to all adolescents on their sixteenth birthdays; and in Sweden, teachers passed around condoms in class and urged students to experiment with them. "Take these home and masturbate with them on, so you can see which kinds feel good and what kind you like," one teacher told the boys in her charge. "And girls, you too take some home and open them up and handle them and make sure that you feel comfortable with them, so you won't feel shy when the time comes to put them on your boyfriends." Elsewhere in Europe, finally, countries that had formerly resisted or sharply restricted sex education found that they could no longer do so. Ireland issued its first sex education guidelines in 1987, cautioning that "such education should not be secular and would require religious input"; Poland developed a sex education syllabus to delay sexual debut and promote marital fidelity, which would both allegedly help control AIDS; and in France, minister for education and future presidential candidate Ségolène Royal launched a campaign to distribute a "pocket guide to contraception" in the schools. Across Europe and around the globe, a 1997 United Nations study observed, the spread of HIV/AIDS had "convinced otherwise reluctant governments" to institute—or to expand—sex education.[9]

THE AIDS CRISIS AND SEX EDUCATION, II: THE DEVELOPING WORLD

The starkest change occurred in the so-called developing world, especially in the epicenter of the AIDS epidemic: Africa. By 2004, 80 percent of people living with AIDS were between fifteen and twenty-four years of age; three-quarters of them lived in Africa, where 70 percent of children entered primary school and two-thirds of those children reached the fifth grade. So schools represented "the single location where the largest proportion of young people can be reached," as two African health specialists wrote. Countries that had formerly taught "population education"—with only a smattering of sex-related information—began to teach much more explicitly about the subject, often supplanting families and other traditional modes of socialization. "In a changing modern world, parents need help with this formidable task," noted one observer in Botswana, where AIDS and divorce had spawned a dramatic increase in single-parent households. "The stable, predictable world is gone." Botswanan schools integrated material about sex and HIV/AIDS into science, home economics, and religious education; so did Kenya, which also taught the subject via geography, history, civics, Swahili, and math. "A hospital had 35 inpatients tested for HIV," one math teacher told his class, in a typical word problem. "Ten percent of these were HIV-negative. How many were HIV positive?" Whatever their subject, almost all such lessons ended with the same advice: abstinence, except in marriage. "If children are 'taught' that it is OK for them to change partners and fall into bed when the emotions move them (provided they use a condom!), what hope is there for that young person ... ever to form a firm lasting relationship based on mutual trust?" asked the minister of health in Zimbabwe, which barred "safe-sex" lessons from schools. "We have to promote *lasting, permanent marriage* since this is the only sound basis for the family, which in turn is the building block upon which the whole structure of the nation is based."[10]

Echoing American abstinence-only organizations, other African countries warned about infertility—a hugely stigmatizing condition in many parts of the continent—and other potentially harmful consequences of sexual activity, particularly illegal abortions and HIV. More often, though, African schools condemned out-of-wedlock sex in moral and religious terms. "The biological aim is to present sex within a creative framework and to vindicate the existence of the Omnipotent and Omnipresent," declared a school textbook in Ghana, where sex education was taught via social studies. "The religious restrictions are strict but they protect the person from a lot of problems." The textbook went on to cite biblical passages indicting fornication, masturbation, and "homosexuality and lesbianism." To be sure, sexual relations represented a constant temptation for young people; quoting a popular Ghanaian proverb, the textbook acknowledged that "there is nothing on this earth which is as sweet as sex." But that was precisely why schools needed to steel adolescents against it. Sexually active teens "become disrespectful, indulge in drug abuse, gambling, stealing, truancy, homosexualism, prostitution or promiscuity leading to contraction of HIV/AIDS, abortion, and death," another textbook warned. A third text admonished students to resist Internet pornography, urging them to "turn to God in prayer" if they faltered; yet another book condemned parents who provided condoms to their children as protection against HIV/AIDS. "Our children are practicing fornication and we are conniving at this by giving them every encouragement," the book blared.[11]

Elsewhere in the developing world, sex education was less overtly moralistic. But nobody could miss its overall moral: no sex out of marriage. Some of the most sexually explicit instruction occurred in Iran, where curricula emphasized "the consent and readiness of the woman" and "the enjoyment of each partner." But Iranians also stressed that such activity must be restricted to marital unions, echoing educators around the Third World. "By the rules of traditional religion, law and culture, a girl and boy must be a virgin," a 1994 population education curriculum in the Philippines declared. "There must be no sex aside from your husband and wife." Schools in India replaced population education with "Adolescent Education," which provided more information about sex and especially HIV. But it also warned against "sexual indiscipline," which educators blamed for "family and social disorganization, crimes, physical and mental diseases and widespread discontent, cruelties, miseries, and unhappiness." In China, where educators had long ignored or resisted sex, a 1988 national directive on "Adolescence Education" instructed all schools to address it. Part of the impetus came from China's one-child policy and its related effort to delay the age of marriage, which increased the likelihood of sex *before* marriage. The sex education initiative also aimed to counter "negative Western sexual culture"—especially film and video—that flooded China in the 1980s and 1990s, as one educator wrote. Reinscribing abstinence and continence, sex education would provide a timely antidote to "the 'sexual freedom' of capitalism," the educator added.[12]

Around the globe, non-Westerners promoted "corrective sex education"—as one Kenyan called it—as a check on the incursions of Western popular culture. The argument echoed early twentieth-century colonial officials, who promoted school-based sex instruction to challenge the sexual suggestiveness of imported books, magazines, and movies. Now the same cudgel was taken up by postcolonial educators, who feared that the "cultural invasion" of the West had "wreaked havoc on impressionable young minds," as one Indian observer wrote; sex education would "clear misconceptions," he added, and revive the "moral fibre of the child." The danger increased with growing access to satellite television and especially the Internet, which made pornography easily available to millions of young people—even in highly mon-itored societies like China. "The 'Great Firewall' of internet supervision is failing to serve its primary stated purpose," a Chinese journalist wrote, noting the growing pop-ularity of digital pornography among the young. But the same report underscored the slow development of sex education in Chinese schools, which continued to evade the subject well after they were directed to provide it. Although its advocates promoted sex education as a "fire extinguisher" against the blazes of "sexual liberation"—as another wry Chinese observer noted—many educators and parents rejected it as a symptom of that same libertine disease. Sex education is "a surrender to the dominance of the corrupt, 'promiscuous West,'" a Lebanese critic wrote, noting that· consultants from the United Nations had helped devise curricula for the subject.[13]

A GLOBAL "RIGHT" TO SEX EDUCATION?

Western and international experts often played key roles in the creation of new sex education programs in the developing world. Nongovernmental organizations (NGOs) from the West had worked closely with local allies since the 1940s to seed "grassroots" sex education groups, even as they tried to disguise the Western role in cultivating them. In the era of AIDS, however, foreign NGOs increasingly offered direct aid and advice to state agencies and officials. With a grant from the Carnegie Corporation, for example, the Washington, DC-based Pan American Health Organi-zation began a project in 1985 to develop curricula and train teachers for family life education in four Caribbean countries. Most of all, the project sought "to help chil-dren and young people to develop healthy attitudes and values about their sexuality," as a curriculum guide stated. Prefiguring the 1994 Cairo conference, a 1986 teacher workshop highlighted the shared principle that undergirded this goal: sex as a basic right of every person, to determine and develop as he or she wished. "The individual should be able to see clearly what he wants to do and why and what he wants to avoid and why," the Caribbean workshop declared. "Every human being is a unique individ-ual with rights to freedom privacy, personal fulfillment, and the right to be treated as our equal."[14]

This perspective was especially prominent in projects sponsored by Sweden, which became a global emblem of rights-centered sex education during these years. As in the 1960s and 1970s, the Swedish Association for Sexuality Education (RFSU) hosted trainings and study tours that stressed the right of each individual to a "healthy sexual life," as an appreciative Israeli visitor wrote in 1986. But the RFSU also accelerated its overseas activity, spurred by the murder of the Swedish prime minister, Olaf Palme—a longtime advocate for sex education around the world—as well as the centennial of the birth of RFSU founder Elise Ottesen-Jensen. Borrowing Ottesen-Jensen's nickname, the RFSU launched an "Ottar Fund" to promote sex education in Kenya; over the next several years, the group would also start projects in Tanzania, Zambia, and Lithuania. Here it joined hands with the Swedish International Development Cooperation Agency (SIDA), the government's foreign-aid arm, which matched the private funds raised for Kenya and also sponsored sex education projects in Vietnam and Malawi. In the face of AIDS, Swedish educators stressed, it was not enough to change sexual behavior; the key was to alter sexual *attitudes*. "Whole nations have to be reoriented and retrained," a 2004 SIDA publication declared. "Sex is Good—Sex is Joy—Sex is Fun—Sex is Love—Sex is Power—Protected Sex is Life!"[15]

Other European countries promoted similar projects via their own NGOs and foreign-aid organizations, emphasizing sexual rights for all. Funded mainly by the German Technical Cooperation Agency, a 1996 "African Youth Conference on Sexual Health" in Ghana called for "comprehensive sexuality education at all levels." Again, the focus was on changing values, beliefs, and attitudes—particularly about gender— so that individuals could determine their own sexual destinies. "On our continent and elsewhere, males are taught to be dominant, controlling, and unemotional, while females are encouraged to be subservient, dependent, and emotional," a participant at the conference observed. "Young people have to change their attitudes and perceptions of each other as males and females." By the mid-1990s, "positive, healthy sexuality for all people"—as a Ford Foundation document called it—had become the standard goal for international sex educators around the world. But in the United States, especially, educators who promoted that ideal overseas were forced to acknowledge that their own country fell far short of it; with the rise of abstinence-only education, America had arguably moved in the opposite direction. So Americans often cited a different country—Sweden—as the prime example of proper sex education, which the United States and the rest of humanity would be wise to follow. "Imagine a world," an American sex educator wrote in 1990,

> where: School sexuality education is compulsory. Contraceptives are readily available. Abortion is free until the 18th week of pregnancy. There is a law that states, "Cohabitation between people of the same sex is entirely acceptable from society's point of view." Teenage births and sexually transmitted diseases among teens are rare. Sound too good to be true? That world exists today in Sweden.[16]

The goal of sex education as a human right reached an apotheosis of sorts in 2008, when the International Planned Parenthood Federation issued its "Declaration on Sexual Rights." Developed with funds from the Ford Foundation, the statement said that sexuality was an "integral part of personhood," and that "the pleasure deriving from it is a central aspect of being human." As one observer noted, the idea of negative rights—that is, freedom from discrimination, violence, and coercion—was easily accepted by the IPPF membership. But positive rights—especially "self-expression and the pursuit of pleasure"—were "more contentious," she added. The controversy would spill across front pages of the world the following year, when UNESCO released a draft report of its "International Guidelines on Sexuality Education." Issued first in Sweden in June 2009, the guidelines echoed the now-standard assumptions that "sexuality extends from birth to death"—and that human beings at every age needed proper information to develop and determine it. Included were brief discussions of masturbation, abortion, and contraception, which drew the ire of conservative foes around the world. "This is like telling our kids not to smoke and yet providing them with cigarette filters," a Singaporean critic complained. He went on to blast the "U.S.-centrism" of the UNESCO guidelines, which were authored by two American educators. In the United States, finally, conservatives blasted the guidelines as "culturally insensitive" toward minorities. "We think it's a kind of one-size-fits-all approach that's damaging to cultures, religions and to children," one critic declared. In this new struggle, conservatives would sound the tocsin of multiculturalism and diversity. They would also join hands across cultural differences, creating a powerful new global force against sex education.[17]

DIVERSITY AND THE GLOBAL RIGHT, I: INTERNAL FERMENT

Since the 1960s, conservatives like Mary Whitehouse had forged alliances with like-minded critics of sex education across the West. But the new right-wing alliance linked activists around the globe, spurred by unpredicted—and unprecedented—population flows between the developing and developed worlds. Until the 1980s, as envious American educators frequently noted, most countries in Europe remained fairly homogenous. So they had the "luxury" of teaching sex education without inciting major parental or political objections, as one reporter wrote in 1987. The comment understated the degree of dissent within purportedly "united" societies such as Denmark, where parental objections to school-based sex instruction had spawned the landmark *Kjeldsen* case in the 1970s. But it also ignored the fact that European societies were becoming immigrant hubs, rendering sex education far more controversial than it had ever been. This trend was also frequently overlooked by American sex educators, who were eager to contrast the heated controversies of US sex education with the supposed consensus that reigned in less diverse—and more "rational"—European countries. Following a 1998 study tour in the Netherlands, France, and Germany, for example, two Americans jealously reported that "religion and politics have little influence on policies related to adolescent sexuality"; indeed, all three countries regarded sex education as a "health issue," not as a political one. The "overwhelming majority of the people" supported comprehensive sexuality education, including frank discussions of sexual practices and the ways to perform them safely. [18]

The report neglected the long history of parental resistance to sex education in

France, especially, where a 2002 survey found that students received a grand total of two hours of instruction in the subject per year. Most of all, though, the Americans failed to notice the astounding growth of ethnic, religious, and cultural diversity in the supposedly "monocultural" societies of western Europe. Resistance to sex education was especially sharp inside Great Britain's burgeoning Muslim community, which skyrocketed from half a million in 1981 to nearly three million in 2011. In 1994, the editor of Britain's *Muslim Education Quarterly* blamed sex education on "the decadence of European civilization"; that same year, the Muslim Parliament of Great Britain resolved that Muslim children would be "better off without the sex education presently offered in state schools." Echoing Islamic critics of the 1994 ICPD resolutions in Cairo, British Muslims complained that sex education violated a core principle of their faith: abstinence outside of marriage. "In Islam extra-marital sex is considered to be a dreadful sin," *MEQ* editorialized in 1996. "Adultery is condemned by stoning to death ... and fornication among unmarried people is penalized. by whipping." Most of all, though, Muslims objected to the allegedly "value-free" philosophy of modem sex education; by privileging "individual choice" about sex, schools insulted religious communities that did not leave such choices to the individual. Here Islamic critics echoed mainstream sex education opponents like Conservative leader Michael Howard, who noted the "natural ties of friendship, common outlook, and values" between Muslim and Christian conservatives.[19]

Elsewhere in the West, too, growing Muslim communities joined hands with white right-wingers to condemn sex education. In Canada, Somalian refugees argued that sex instruction—like school dances and parties—promoted "promiscuity and corruption"; even as she tried to shield her teenaged children from sex, an Iranian immigrant added, their teachers were explaining it in excessive detail. Australian Muslims were outraged to find schools addressing masturbation and oral sex as well as "the etiquette of dating," which violated the Islamic prohibition on unchaperoned male-female contact; Muslims also blasted schools' emphasis on "personal autonomy," which seemed to privilege students' own desires over communal authority. But the sharpest controversies occurred in Continental Europe, where the Muslim population increase was also the fastest. In Sweden, home to a half million Muslims by 2001, critics said that schools were pushing "free sex"; in Norway, where the Islamic population in the capital city of Oslo rose 34 percent in just two years, Muslims blasted sex educators for providing contraceptives as well as lessons on their use; and in Holland, which had reached a rough modus vivendi on sex education in the 1980s, Muslims mounted energetic new challenges to it. "It is ironic that public sex education became acceptable in the Netherlands at the same time as large groups of Muslim immigrants, with ideals of modesty and obligatory innocence, became resident in the country," one observer wrote. They were now making common cause with Pentecostals in Holland's so-called Bible Belt, home to the last native-born holdouts against sex education.[20]

Eastern Europe also witnessed a spike in religious controversy over the subject, finally, spurred less by immigration than by revolution; with the fall of repressive Communist governments, churches were freed to attack school-based sex instruction. To Catholic leaders in Poland, even the bland, conservative sex curriculum instituted under Communism reflected the "moral decay" of "atheist rule." Quoting numerous Vatican attacks on the subject, Catholics succeeded in revoking Poland's compulsory sex education law in 1993; when the subject was reinstituted a few months later, as part of a strict new antiabortion measure, most schools enlisted priests to teach the "Catholic view" of sex. In Russia, meanwhile, leaders in the Orthodox Church stoked nationalist flames against the alleged "western ideological subversion" of sex educa-tion. "Children! The enemies of God, enemies of Russia for hundreds of years have tried to conquer our native land with the help of fire and the sword," the Moscow patriarch declared in a 2000 attack on sex education. "Now they want to annihilate our people with the help of depravity." Most critics trained their fire at a pilot project sponsored by UNESCO to assist sex education in a handful of schools; others hinted at darker forces, accusing "Western secret services" of clandestine efforts to impose it. Yet as several Orthodox priests observed in 1996, even Western nations that had long taught sex education were now facing citizen attacks upon it. So while Russians struggled to rebut this foreign menace, they needed to work with foreigners who were menaced by it as well.[21]

NOTES

1   Report of the International Conference on Population and Development. Cairo, 5-13 September 1994 (New York: United Nations, 1995), 49; Stanley Johnson, *The Politics of Population: The International Conference on Population and Development* (London: Earthscan, 1995), 153-54; Jocelyn DeJong memorandum, March 23, 1994, reel 7009; Aziz Ahmed Khattab, "Sex Education in Egypt. [Thirty Years' Personal Experience]" (MS, n.d. [1995]), reel 6855, both in grant 09451109, Ford Foundation Archives, New York.

2   Swedish Association for Sexuality Education, *Breaking Through: A Guide to Sexual and Reproductive Health and Rights* (Stockholm: RFSU, 2004), 15-17; Report of the International Conference on Population and Development, 146; "The Poor Lose Out in Battle between Church and State," *Guardian*, October 31, 1994, p. 9; Michelle Goldberg, *The Means of Reproduction: Sex, Power, and the Future of the World* (New York: Penguin, 2009), 104; "Pakistani Leader Attends Conference Despite Isla-mists," *Christian Science Monitor*, September 6, 1994, p. 7.

3   Johnson, *The Politics of Population*, 157; Goldberg, *Means of Reproduction*, 112; Fatima Amer, "The Problems of Sex Education within the Context of Islamic Teachings— Towards a Clearer Vision of the British Case," *Muslim Education Quarterly* 14, no. 2 (1997): 16, 24, 26.

4   Swedish Association for Sexuality Education, *Passion for Rights: Ten Years of Fighting for Sexual and Reproductive Health* (Stockholm: RFSU, 2004), 69.

5   "AIDS lecture October 6, 1987" (MS, 1989), pp. 1–2, folder 3, box 148, C. Everett Koop Papers, National Library of Medicine, Bethesda, Maryland.

6   Yoshiro Hatano and Tsuguo Shimazaki, "Japan," in *The Continuum Complete International Encyclopedia of Sexuality*, ed. Robert T. Francoeur and Raymond J. Noonan (Bloomington, IN: Kinsey Institute, 2004), online edition; James L. Shortridge, "Siecus Is Pioneering a Worldwide Sexuality Education Effort," SIECUS Report 24, no. 3 (1996): 2.

7   "Family Feuds," *New York Times*, August 5, 1990, p. EDUC26; Debra W. Haffner, "1992 Report Card on the States: Sexual Rights in America," SIECUS Report 20, no. 3 (1992); "Abstinence Is Focus of U.S. Sex Education," *New York Times*, December 15, 1999, p. A18; "U.S. Shows Respect," Daily Journal (Kankakee, IL), February 10, 1987, enclosed with Coleen Kelly Mast to C. Everett Koop, February 19, 1987, folder 7, box 84, Koop Papers; "Sex and Schools," *Time*, November 24, 1986, "AIDS. Education—Newspaper Clippings" folder, box 101, *AIDS History Project Collection, One: National Gay and Lesbian Archives, Los Angeles*; "Dr. Koop Defends His Crusade on AIDS," *New York Times*, April 6, 1987, p. B8.

8   "Sex Lesson Rules Mean Pupils May Miss Aids Advice," *Guardian*, March 7, 1987, p. 2; "Condoms Pose Sex Lesson Problem in Catholic Schools," Guardian, April 16, 1987, p. 4; "Children 'Need Lessons on Aids,'" *Guardian*, July 15, 1987, p. 4; Paul Meredith, "Children's Rights and Education," in *Legal Concepts of Childhood*, ed. Julia Fonda (Portland, OR: Hart Publishing, 2001), 211–12.

9   Hugo Roling, "The Problem of Sex Education in the Netherlands in the 20th Century," in *Cultures of Child Health in Britain and the Netherlands in the 20th Century*, ed. Marijke Gijswijt-Hofstra and Hilary Marland (Amsterdam: Rodopi, 2003), 255; Jay Friedman, "Cross-Cultural Perspectives on Sexuality Education," *SIECUS Report 20*, no. 6 (1992): 9; Osmo Kontula, *Reproductive Health Behaviour of Young Europeans*, vol. 2 (Strasbourg: Council of Europe, 2004), 48; Kristin Luker, *When Sex Goes to School* (New York: Norton, 2006), 209; Thomas Phelim Kelly, "Ireland," in Francoeur and Noonan, *Continuum Complete International Encyclopedia of Sexuality*; Anna Titkow, "Poland," in *From Abortion to Contraception: A Resource to Public Policies and Reproductive Behavior in Central and Eastern Europe from 1917 to the Present*, ed. Henry David (Westport, CT: Greenwood, 1999), 187; Corinne Nativel, "Teen Pregnancy and Reproductive Policies in France," in *When Children Become Parents: Welfare State Responses to Teenage Pregnancy*, ed. Anne Dagueree and Corinne Nativel (Bristol, UK: Policy Press, 2006), 127; United Nations Family Planning Association, *Thematic Evaluation of Adolescent Reproductive Health Programmes* (New York: UNFPA, 1997), 24.

10 Melanie Gallant and Eleanor Maticka-Tyndale, "School-Based HIV Prevention Programmes for African Youth," *Social Science and Medicine* 58 (April 2004): 1337–38; Monica Dynowski Smith, *Profile of Youth in Botswana* (Gabarone: Intersectoral

Committee on Family Life Education, 1989), 5; *Final Report of the UNESCO Regional Seminar on HIV/AIDS and Education within the School System for English-Speaking Countries in Eastern and Southern Africa* (Paris: UNESCO, 1995), 12-13, 72; Colleen McLaughlin et al., *Old Enough to Know: Consulting Children about Sex and AIDS Education in Africa* (Cape Town: HSRC Press, 2012), 41.

11 Christopher Mensah Chrismek, *Sex Education and Social Harmony*, vol. 1 (Accra, Ghana: Chrismek Rights' Foundation, 2004), 15, 27-28, 36-39; Michael Aketewah, *Current Social Studies for West African Senior Schools* (Kumasi, Ghana: 4th Born Printing Press, 2007 [2004]), 114; Gifty Gyamera, Religious and Moral Education for Senior Secondary Schools (Accra, Ghana: Gogan Publishing, 2007), 94; Luke Gyesi-Appiah, *HIV/AIDS—Condom or Abstinence* (Cape Coast, Ghana: L. Nyakod Printing Works, 2007), 12.

12 Margaret E. Greene et al., *In This Generation: Sexual and Reproductive Health Policies for a Youthful World* (Washington, DC: Population Action International, 2002), 28-29; James T. Sears, "In(ter)ventions of Male Sexualities and HIV Education: Case Studies in the Philippines," in *A Dangerous Knowing: Sexuality, Pedagogy, and Popular Culture*, ed. Debbie Epstein and James T. Sears (London and New York: Cassell, 1999), 106; S. P. Ruhela and Ahrar Husain, *Sex Education in India in the 21st Century* (Delhi: Indian Publishers Distributors, 2002), ix; Nancy E. Riley and Edith Bowles, "Premarital Sexual Behavior in the People's Republic of China: A Review of Critical Problems and Issues," p. 13, in "Conference on Adolescent Sexuality in Asia" (MS, September 24-28, 1990), Research Information Services, East-West Center, Honolulu, Hawai'i; Joanna McMillan, *Sex, Science, and Morality in China* (London: Routledge, 2006), 57.

13 Margaret Gecaga, "Sex Education in the Context of Changing Family Roles," in *Responsible Leadership in Marriage and Family*, ed. Mary N. Getui (2005; Nairobi, Kenya: Acton Publishers, 2008), 55; Shishir Bhate, "Should a Child Be Told about 'The Birds and the Bees?'" in Ruhela and Husain, Sex Education in India in the 21st Century, 4-5; "Progress or Pornography?" *News China*, December 1, 2011, p. 18; Alessandra Aresu, "Sex Education in Modern and Contemporary China: Interrupted Debates across the Last Century," *International Journal of Educational Development* 29, no. 5 (2009): 539; Azzah Shararah Baydoun, "Sex Education in Lebanon: Between Secular and Religious Discourses," in *Deconstructing Sexuality in the Middle East*, ed. Pinar Ilkkaracan (Hampshire, UK: Ashgate, 2008), 91.

14 *Office of the Secretary MEMORANDUM*, October 18, 1985, folder 4, box 1323; Inter-Agency Working Group, "Core Curriculum Guide for Strengthening Health and Family Life Education in Teacher Training Colleges in the Eastern Caribbean" (MS, 1993), p. 73, folder 5, box 1321; "Workshop for Primary School Teachers in Health and Family Life Education, 12-14 November 1986" (MS, 1986), pp. 2-3, folder 8, box 1322, all in *Carnegie Corporation of New York Papers*, Rare Books and Manuscripts Library, Columbia University.

15 Ruth Landau, "Trip Report" (n.d., 1987), enclosed with Landau to Kerstin Strid, January 27, 1987, volume 22, IPPF Correspondence; "Ottar Fund," People 13, no. 2 (1986), enclosed with Maj Fant and Kerstin Strid to "World List of Family Planning Addresses," June 6, 1986, volume 18, Foreign Correspondence, both in Papers of Riksförbundet för Sexuell Upplysning [RFSU], Labour Movement Archives and Library, Stockholm, Sweden; Le Thi Nham Tuyet and Vuong Xuan Tinh, eds., *Reproductive Culture in Vietnam* (Hanoi: Gioi Publishers, 1999), foreword [n.p.]; Anna Runeborg, *Sexuality—A Super Force: Young People, Sexuality, and Rights in the Era of HIV/AIDS* (Stockholm: Swedish International Development Cooperation Agency, 2002), 27, 34–35.

16 Summary of Proceedings of the First African Youth Conference on Sexual Health (Accra, Ghana: GUNSA National Secretariat, 1996), 28; Ford Foundation, *Sexuality and Social Change: Making the Connection; Strategies for Action and Investment* (New York: Ford Foundation, 1995), 32–33; Debra Haffner, "Should We Do It the Swedish Way?" *SIECUS Report* 18, no. 5 (1990): 10.

17 Carmen Barroso, "From Reproductive to Sexual Rights," in *Routledge Handbook of Sexuality, Health and Rights*, ed. Peter Aggleton and Richard Parker (London: Routledge, 2010), 386; "International Guidelines on Sex Education Reignite Debate," Singapore News, September 4, 2009; "Unesco Assailed over Sex Education Guidelines," *International Herald Tribune*, September 3, 2009, p. 8.

18 "Swedes Instill a Sense of Responsibility," New York Times, November 8, 1987, p. EDUC19; Maureen A. Kelly and Michael McGee, "Report from a Study Tour: Teen Sexuality Education in Netherlands, France, and Germany," SIECUS Report 27, no. 2 (December 1998/January 1999): 11–12.

19 Nativel, "Teen Pregnancy and Reproductive Policies in France," 125; Syed Ali Ashraf, "Sex Education and the Decadence of European Civilization," *Muslim Education Quarterly* 11, no. 4 (1994): 1; J. Mark Halstead, "Values and Sex Education in a Multicultural Society," in *Sex Education and Religion*, ed. Michael J. Reiss and Shaikh Abdul Mabud (Cambridge: Islamic Academy, 1998), 238; Syed Ali Ashraf, "The Islamic Concept of Sex as the Basis of Sex Education," *Muslim Education Quarterly* 13, no. 2 (1996): 2; Shaikh Abdul Mabud, "An Islamic View of Sex Education," in *Sex Education and Religion*, 114; "'Cameron Did Not Want a Yes Man': Sayeeda Warsi, David Cameron's New Shadow Minister for Community Cohesion, Is the First Muslim to Sit in Either a Cabinet or Shadow Cabinet," *Guardian*, July 11, 2007, p. 10.

20 Isabel Kaprielian-Churchill, "Refugees in Education in Canadian Schools," *International Review of Education* 42, no. 4 (1996): 361; Shahnaz Khan, "Muslim Women: Negotiations in the Third Space," *Signs* 23, no. 2 (1998): 480; Fida Sanjakdar, "'Teacher Talk': The Problems, Perspectives, and Possibilities for Developing a Comprehensive Sexual Health Education Curriculum for Australian Muslim Students," *Sex Education* 9, no. 3 (2009): 265–66; "Liberal Sexual Mores Present a 'Threat' to Swedish Muslims," *Jakarta Post*, June 24, 2001, p. 1; Tiffany Bartz, "Sex Education in

Multicultural Norway," *Sex Education* 7, no. 1 (2007): 18–20, 24; Roling, "The Problem of Sex Education in the Netherlands," 255; Jan Steutel and Ben Spiecker, "Sex Education, State Policy, and the Principle of Mutual Consent," *Sex Education* 4, no. 1 (2004): 52; Rachel Parker et al., "Sexuality Education in Europe: An Overview of Current Policies," *Sex Education* 9, no. 3 (2008): 237.

21 "Church Turns the Clock Back on Poland's Sexual Taboos," *Observer* (UK), May 2, 1993, p. 18; "Behind the Priests' Back," *Guardian*, October 3, 1995, p. B5; Kontula, *Reproductive Health Behaviour of Young Europeans*, 56; Igor S. Kon, "Russia," in Francoeur and Noonan, *Continuum Complete International Encyclopedia of Sexuality*; Igor S. Kon, "Sexual Culture and Politics in Contemporary Russia," in *Sexuality and Gender in Postcommunist Eastern Europe and Russia*, ed. Aleksandar Stulhofer and Theo Sandfort (New York: Haworth Press, 2005), 119.

READING 34

Genny Beemyn, "Transgender History in the United States," in *Trans Bodies, Trans Selves* (Oxford University Press, 2014).

This essay from historian Genny Beemyn offers a history of transgender and gender nonconforming people in the United States.

Transgender History in the United States

Genny Beemyn

INTRODUCTION

Can there be said to be a "transgender history," when "transgender" is a contemporary term and when individuals in past centuries who would perhaps appear to be transgender from our vantage point might not have conceptualized their lives in such a way? And what about individuals today who have the ability to describe themselves as transgender, but choose not to for a variety of reasons, including the perception that it is a White, middle-class Western term and the belief that it implies transitioning from one gender to another? Should they be left out of "transgender history" because they do not specifically identify as transgender?

These questions complicate any attempt to write a history of individuals who would have been perceived as gender nonconforming in their eras and cultures. While it would be inappropriate to limit this chapter to people who lived at a time and place when the concept of "transgender" was available and used by them, it would also be inappropriate to assume that people who are "transgender," as we currently understand the term, existed throughout history. For this reason, we cannot claim that gender nonconforming individuals were "transgender" or "transsexual" if these categories were not yet named or yet to be embraced. However, where possible, we can seek to distinguish between individuals whose actions would seem to indicate that they would be what we would call "transgender," "transsexual," or a "crossdresser" today and those who might have presented as a gender different from the one assigned to them at birth for reasons other than a sense of gender difference (such as to escape narrow gender roles or pursue same-sex sexual relationships). While all these can admittedly be fine lines, the distinctions are worth trying to make clear when presenting any specific "transgender history."

Genny Beemyn, from *Transgender History in the United States: A Special Unabridged Version of a Book Chapter from Trans Bodies, Trans Selves*, ed. Laura Erickson-Schroth, pp. 1-36, 532-536. Copyright © 2014 by Oxford University Press. Reprinted with permission.

FRAMING GENDER NONCONFORMITY IN THE PAST: TWO STORIES

From the earliest days of the American colonies, violations of established gender systems and attempts to prevent and contain such transgressions have been a part of life in what would become the United States. One of the first recorded examples involved a servant in the Virginia colony in the 1620s who claimed to be both a man and a woman and, at different times, adopted the traditional roles and clothing of men and women and variously went by the names of Thomas and Thomasine Hall. Unable to establish Hall's "true" gender, despite repeated physical examinations, and unsure of whether to punish him/her for wearing men's or women's apparel, local citizens asked the court at Jamestown to resolve the issue. Perhaps because it too was unable to make a conclusive determination, or perhaps because it took Hall at his/her word that Hall was bi-gendered or what would be known today as intersexed, the court ordered Hall in 1629 to wear both a man's breeches and a woman's apron and cap. This unique ruling affirmed Hall's dual nature and subverted traditional gender categories, but by fixing Hall's gender and denying him/her the freedom to switch between male and female identities, the decision simultaneously punished Hall and reinforced gender boundaries. It also forever marked Hall publicly as an oddity in the Virginia settlement, and likely made him/her the subject of ridicule and pity (Brown, 1995; Reis, 2007; Rupp, 1999).

Reflecting how dominant gender expectations had changed little in the intervening three hundred years, another individual named Hall would confound authorities at the turn of the twentieth century. Murray Hall lived as a man for thirty years, becoming a prominent New York City politician, operating a commercial "intelligence office," and marrying twice. Hall was not discovered to have been assigned female at birth until his death in 1901 from breast cancer, for which he had avoided medical treatment for several years, seemingly out of a fear that the gender assigned to him at birth would become public. His wives apparently were aware of Hall's secret and respected how he expressed his gender. No one else knew, including the daughter he raised, and his friends and colleagues were shocked at the revelation. While some officials and a coroner's jury subsequently chose to see Hall as female, his daughter, friends, and political colleagues continued to recognize him as a man. Said an aide to a New York State Senator, "If he was a woman he ought to have been born a man, for he lived and looked like one" (Cromwell, 1999; Katz, 1976: 234).

READING GENDER NONCONFORMITY

The experiences of Thomas/Thomasine Hall and Murray Hall demonstrate the diversity of gender expression and identity over time, the multiple ways that these societies have read gender, and the efforts of the judicial system to regulate and simplify it in response. But it is not just legal authorities that have had trouble understanding and addressing the complexities of gendered lives. Historians have often ignored or dismissed instances of non-normative gender expression, especially among individuals assigned female at birth, who they regarded as simply seeking male privilege if they lived as men. It was not until lesbian and gay historians in the 1970s and 1980s sought to identify and celebrate individuals from the past who had had same-sex relationships that their gender nonconformity began to receive more than cursory attention.

In seeking to normalize same-sex sexuality by showing that people attracted to others of the same sex existed across time and cultures, lesbian and gay historians, especially those who wrote before transgender people began calling attention to their own histories, have frequently considered all individuals who crossdressed or who lived as a gender different from the one assigned to them at birth to have done so in order to pursue same-sex relationships, even when evidence suggests that their actions were not principally motivated by same-sex attraction (Califia, 1997). Thus, ironically, some lesbian and gay historians have engaged in a process of erasure that is little different from the silencing practiced by the heterosexist historians whose work they were challenging and revising. For example, Jonathan Ned Katz (1976) includes Murray Hall in his documentary history, *Gay American History: Lesbians and Gay Men in the USA*, as part of a section on "Passing Women," and referring to him by female pronouns, states that "reports of Hall's two 'marriages' and her being 'sweet on women' suggest Lesbianism" (232). Other historians, including Jeffrey Escoffier (2004), John D'Emilio and Estelle Freedman (1988), and Elizabeth Lapovsky Kennedy (1998), have likewise considered Hall to have been a passing woman and a lesbian.

But such authors ignore significant contradictions. If Hall was simply passing, then why did he present so completely as a male that even his adopted daughter did not know? Why did the individuals who were closest to him continue to insist that he was a man after his death? And if being with a woman was his only motivation, then why did he avoid medical treatment that would have likely saved his life in order to prevent anyone from finding out that he had been assigned female at birth? These questions complicate a simplistic explanation of Hall as a lesbian who sought to avoid social condemnation by presenting as a man.

READING CONTEMPORARY GENDER NONCONFORMITY: THE EXAMPLE OF BILLY TIPTON

The experiences of Billy Tipton, a jazz musician who lived as a man for more than fifty years and who was not discovered to have been assigned female until his death in 1989, are reminiscent of those of Murray Hall. Similarly, Tipton avoided doctors and died from a treatable medical condition, rather than risk disclosure. He also apparently had to turn away from what could have been his big break in the music industry, for fear that the exposure would "out" him. In later years, he chose to live in poverty, rather than claim Social Security benefits, seemingly for the same reason (Middlebrook, 1998).

Tipton, like Hall, kept knowledge of his anatomy from even his family members. He was apparently able to prevent several women with whom he had long-term relationships and his three adopted sons from discovering that he had been assigned female at birth by dressing and bathing behind a locked door and by using a prosthetic device that enabled him to simulate having a penis during sexual activities. In addition, Tipton kept his chest bound with a bandage, stating that he had suffered permanent injuries in a car accident. With his last partner, he also used this story to explain why he could not have sex.

Also similar to Hall, Tipton, who did not leave behind any documentation of how he identified or explain his choices to anyone, has been the subject of competing gender narratives. Literary critic Marjorie Garber (1992), for example, treats Tipton as a "transvestite" and lesbian historian Lillian Faderman (1991) considers him to have been a woman who felt compelled to pass as a man in order to succeed as a musician in the 1930s. A biography of Tipton by Diane Wood Middlebrook (1998) creates an even more muddled portrait. Arbitrarily employing both male and female pronouns, Middlebrook admits that Tipton may have seen himself as a man or may have been a transgender person, even stating that at least two of his partners, his sons, and some of his former band members continue to think of him as a man, but she never seriously explores these possibilities. Instead, Middlebrook conjectures that Tipton was engaging in a performance, "playing the role of Billy," and once in that role, could not escape it (217).

But other authors respect Tipton's apparent identity. Anthropologist Jason Cromwell (1999), an FTM (female-to-male) person himself, criticizes Middlebrook and other writers who consider Tipton to be either a closeted lesbian or a prime example of the extent to which women have gone to make a living in a male bastion like the music industry. He states:

> Billy Tipton's life speaks for itself. The male privileges that accrue from living as a man do not justify spending fifty years living in fear, hiding from loved ones, taking extreme measures to make sure that no one knows what their body is or looks like, and then dying from a treatable medical condition (a bleeding ulcer). When someone like Tipton dies or is discovered, they are discounted as having been "not real men" or "unreal men." Despite having lived for years as men, the motivations of these individuals are read as being wrought of socioeconomic necessity or the individuals are considered to be lesbians. Does this mean that "anatomy is not destiny" while one is alive but "anatomy is destiny" after death? (89–90).

According to all the information we have available, Tipton sought to live his life as a man and to die as one. To characterize him otherwise implies that this history does not matter or, worse, that it is a lie. Not only does this view deny Tipton's agency, but it also negates the experiences of all transgender people, for it means that regardless of how someone might express or identify their gender, only the gender assigned to that individual at birth matters. Ironically, many of the lesbian individuals and communities that have claimed Tipton, Murray Hall, and other female-assigned men as one of their own after their deaths may have rejected and sought to exclude Tipton and Hall from "women's space" while they were alive (Cromwell, 1998).

A FRAMEWORK FOR IDENTIFYING A TRANSGENDER HISTORY

While evidence strongly suggests that Tipton and Hall saw themselves as men, it can sometimes be difficult to determine how someone may have identified, especially given the absence of autobiographical accounts. In contemplating whether female-assigned individuals from the past who presented as male might have been what we would call transsexual today, Cromwell (1999) offers three questions to consider: if the individuals indicated that they were men, if they attempted to modify their bodies to look more traditionally male, and if they tried to live their lives as men, keeping the knowledge of their female bodies a secret, even if it meant dying rather than seeking necessary medical care (81). Using this framework, Tipton and Hall would be best categorized from a contemporary perspective as transgender men.

Cromwell's questions can apply equally as well to individuals assigned male at birth who presented as female. Such instances are significantly less documented in Western cultures, perhaps because of the difficulty of being read as female before the advent of hormones and hair-removal techniques. One well-known example is Jenny Savalette de Lange, a member of Parisian high society who lived as a woman for at least fifty years and who was not discovered to have been assigned male at birth until her death in 1858. She had obtained a new birth certificate that designated her as female and had been engaged to men six times, but never married, seemingly to avoid her birth gender from being discovered (Bullough, 1975).

Cromwell helps us distinguish individuals like Tipton, Hall, and de Lange, who we would now presumably call transsexual because they saw their identities as a gender other than that assigned at birth, from cisgender people who presented as a gender other than that assigned at birth for economic, social, or sexual reasons, but who did not identify as that other gender or seek to permanently alter their gender. But his questions do not speak to the differences between transsexual people and individuals we now refer to as cross-dressers. To make this distinction in regards to historical figures, two other questions can be added: if the individuals continued to crossdress when it was publicly known that they crossdressed or if they crossdressed consistently but only in private, so that no one else knew, except perhaps their families. In either case, the important demarcation is that the people who crossdressed did not receive any privilege or benefit from doing so, other than their own comfort and satisfaction.

One individual who seems to fit the label of crossdresser is Hannah Snell/James Gray. Snell, a resident of Worcester, England, began dressing as a man in 1745 to search for her husband, a Dutch sailor who had deserted her while she was pregnant (Anonymous, 1989 [1750]). For the next five years, Snell served under the name of James Gray in both the British navy and army, working variously as a servant, watchman, and deckhand, and was wounded in battle in India. After learning from another sailor that her husband had been executed for murder, Snell/Gray returned to England, at which point she disclosed her assigned gender to her shocked but ultimately supportive shipmates. The "female soldier" became a sensation after her story was published, and Snell/Gray took advantage of her fame to earn an income by appearing on the stage in her military uniform. Upon retiring, Snell/Gray continued to wear traditionally male apparel and purchased a "public house . . . for which [she] had a signboard painted with a British tar on one side and a brave marine on the other, while beneath was inscribed: The Widow in Masquerade or the Female Warrior" (Thompson, 1974: 105). Though Snell/ Gray initially presented as male for personal gain (to be able to look for her husband), she seems to best be referred to as a crossdresser because Snell/ Gray did not identify as a man, but continued to cross-dress even after her birth gender was known.

An example of a female-presenting crossdresser is a thirty-three-year-old US journalist who was a patient of German physician Magnus Hirschfeld, the leading authority on crossdressers in the late nineteenth and early twentieth centuries. Included as "Case 14" in Hirschfeld's 1910 *The Transvestites*, the journalist stated: "From my earliest youth I had the urge to step forth in women's clothing, and whenever the opportunity presented itself, I procured for myself elegant underclothing, silk petticoats, and whatever was in fashion." He experienced "a certain discomfort" in "men's clothing," but felt "a feeling of peace" when he could dress as female. His wife knew about his crossdressing and decided to remain with him (94).

NON-BINARY GENDERS IN NATIVE AMERICAN CULTURES

These examples of individuals who might be considered a part of transgender history all come from European and European-American cultures that rejected and often punished gender nonconformity. Some non-Western societies, though, welcomed and had recognized roles for individuals who assumed behaviors and identities different from those of the gender assigned to them at birth. Many Native American cultures at the time of European conquest enabled male-assigned individuals and, to a lesser extent, female-assigned individuals to dress, work, and live, either partially or completely, as a different gender.

One of the earliest known descriptions of non-binary genders in a Native American society was recorded by Spanish conquistador Cabeza de Vaca, who wrote about seeing "effeminate, impotent men" who are married to other men and "go about covered-up like women and they do the work of women, and they draw the bow and they carry very heavy load" among a group of Coahuiltecan Indians in what is today Southern Texas in the 1530s (Lang, 1998: 67). As with de Vaca's account, most of the subsequent reports of gender diversity in Native American cultures were by Europeans—whether conquistadors, explorers, missionaries, or traders—whose worldviews were shaped by Christian doctrines that espoused adherence to strict gender roles and condemned any expressions of sexuality outside of married male-female relationships. Consequently, they reacted to instances of non-binary genders, in the words of gay scholar Will Roscoe (1998), "with amazement, dismay, disgust, and occasionally, when they weren't dependent on the natives' goodwill, with violence" (4).

Among the extreme reactions was that of Spanish conquistador Vasco Núñez de Balboa. In his trek across the Isthmus of Panama in 1513, de Balboa set his troop's dogs on forty male-assigned Cueva Indians for being "sodomites," as they had assumed the roles of women. The murders were subsequently depicted in an engraving by Theodore de Bry. Another Spanish conquistador, Nuño de Guzmán, burned alive a male-assigned individual who presented as female—considering the person to be a male prostitute—while traveling through Mexico in the 1530s (Saslow, 1999).

In one of the less judgmental accounts, Edwin T. Denig, a fur trader in present day Montana in the mid-nineteenth century, expressed astonishment at the Crow Indians' acceptance of a "neuter" gender. "Strange country this," he stated, "where males assume the dress and perform the duties of females, while women turn men and mate with their own sex!" (Roscoe, 1998: 3). Another matter-of-fact narrative was provided by Jacques Le Moyne de Morgues, an artist who accompanied a French expedition to Florida in 1564, who noted that what he referred to as "hermaphrodites" were "quite common" among the Timucua Indians (Katz, 1976: 287).

As these different accounts indicate, Europeans did not agree on what to make of cultures that recognized non-binary genders. Lacking comparable institutional roles in their own societies, they labeled the aspects that seemed familiar to them: male-assigned individuals engaged in same-sex sexual behavior ("sodomites") or individuals that combined male and female elements ("hermaphrodites"). Anthropologists and historians in the twentieth century would repeat the same mistake, interpreting these individuals as "homosexuals" or "transvestites," or as "berdaches," a French adaptation of the Arabic word for a male prostitute or a young male slave used for sexual purposes (Roscoe, 1987).

By failing to see beyond their own Eurocentric biases and prejudices, these observers take the recognition of gender diversity by many Native American societies out of their specific cultural contexts. While male-assigned individuals who assumed female roles often married other male-assigned individuals, these other men presented as masculine and the relationships were generally not viewed in Native American cultures as involving two people of the same gender. The same was true of female-assigned individuals who assumed male roles and married other female-assigned individuals. Because many Native American groups recognized genders beyond male and female, these relationships would best be categorized as what anthropologist Sabine Lang (1999: 98) calls "hetero-gender" relationships, and not as "same-sex" relationships, as they were often described by European and Euro-American writers from the seventeenth through the late twentieth century.

The ways that the Native American societies that accepted gender diversity characterized non-binary genders varied by culture and by time. Within most of these cultures, male- and female-assigned individuals who assumed different genders were not considered to be women or men; rather, they constituted separate genders that combined female and male elements. This fact is reflected in the words that Native American groups developed to describe multiple genders. For example, the terms for male-assigned individuals who took on female roles used by the Cheyenne (*heemaneh*), the Ojibwa (*agokwa*), and the Yuki (*i-wa-musp*) translate as "half men, half women" or "men-women." Other Native American groups referred to male-assigned individuals who "dress as a woman," "act like a woman," "imitate a woman," or were a "would-be woman" (Lang, 1998). Similarly, the Zuni called a female-assigned individual who took on male roles a *katsotse*, or "boy-girl" (Lang, 1999).

The exact number of Native American cultures that recognized non-binary genders is a subject of debate among contemporary historians and anthropologists, as data remains limited, especially regarding female-assigned individuals who presented as male, and scholars differ on what should count as gender diversity. Figures range from 113 Native American groups in North America that had female roles for male-assigned individuals and thirty that had male roles for female-assigned individuals to 131 and 63, respectively. Lang identifies sixty Native American cultures in North America that had additional genders for female-assigned individuals, including eleven that had recognized roles for female-assigned but not male-assigned individuals.

Writers also disagree on how these individuals lived their lives and the statuses that they held. Among gay male scholars, there has been a tendency to invoke a timeless and universally revered position for male-assigned individuals who assumed female roles, envisioning them as "gay" predecessors from a past when people who pursued same-sex relationships were accepted and a valued part of their societies. For example, Roscoe (1988) calls the Zuni "berdache" a "traditional gay role" (57), and anthropologist Walter Williams (1986) states that a view of the "berdache" as a "sacred people" was "widespread among the aboriginal peoples of the New World" (31). Williams also creates a mythology around female-assigned individuals who assumed male roles. He refers to them as "amazons," which denies the status they held in many Native American cultures as belonging to genders other than female.

Some transgender authors, even such pioneering writers as Kate Bornstein and Leslie Feinberg, similarly romanticize Native American societies that recognized non-binary genders and look to the individuals who assumed different genders as "transgender" precursors (Towle & Morgan, 2006). In a sense, like Williams and Roscoe, they see what they want to see. In her autobiographical work *Gender Outlaw*, Bornstein (1994), a writer and performance artist, places herself within an eternal, unchanging transgender history. "My ancestors were performers," she states, for "[t]he earliest shamanic rituals involved women and men exchanging genders. Old, old rituals. . . . We're talking cross-cultural here" (143). While Feinberg (1996), a leading activist and writer, notes the dangers of such cultural appropriation, she nevertheless creates a reductionist narrative in her book *Transgender Warriors*, which, as the title indicates, focuses on "courageous trans warriors of every sex and gender – those who led battles and rebellions throughout history" (xi).

Contrary to the depiction of individuals who assumed different genders as holding a highly esteemed, sacred position across culture and history, available evidence suggests that while they were apparently accepted in most Native American societies in which they have been known to exist, their statuses and roles differed from group to group and over time. Some Native American cultures considered them to possess supernatural powers and afforded them special ceremonial roles; in other cultures, they were less revered and viewed more secularly (Lang 1998). In these societies, the status of individuals who assumed different genders seems to have reflected their gender role, rather than a special gender status. If women predominated in particular occupations, such as being healers, shamans, and handcrafters, then male-assigned individuals who took on female roles engaged in the same professions. In a similar way, the female-assigned individuals who took on male roles became hunters and warriors (Lang, 1999).

In at least a few Native American cultures, individuals who assumed different genders appear to have been denigrated or even despised. According to historian Richard Trexler (1995), male-assigned individuals who presented as female in parts of the Inca Empire and among the Aztecs and Pueblos were forced to be the sexual subordinates of local lords or were relegated to the most subservient duties. While data is limited, it seems to have been a common practice for Native American societies to give young people a choice about assuming a different gender role. But in some areas, families that had many sons but no daughters might have required a male child to take on a female role, which could have been a lifelong change.

Just as the cultural status of individuals who assumed different genders seems to have varied greatly, so too did the extent to which they took on these roles. Some adopted their roles completely, others only partly or part of the time. In some cases, dressing as a different gender was central to assuming the gender role; in others it was not. Marrying or having relationships with other male-assigned or other female-assigned individuals was likewise common in some cultures, but less so in others. "Gender variance is as diverse as Native American cultures themselves," states Sabine Lang (1999). "About the only common denominator is that in many Native American tribal cultures systems of multiple genders existed" (95–96).

THE DEVELOPMENT OF DRAG COMMUNITIES IN THE US

The cultural inclusion of individuals who assumed different genders in some Native American societies stands in contrast to the general lack of recognition within the White-dominated American colonies in the seventeenth and eighteenth centuries. To the extent to which such individuals were acknowledged in the colonies, it was largely to condemn their behavior as unnatural and sinful. For example, the charges filed in Middlesex County, Massachusetts in 1692 against a female-assigned individual named Mary Henly for wearing "men's clothing" stated that such behavior was "seeming to confound the course of nature" (Reis, 2007: 152).

Relatively few instances of gender nonconformity are documented in the colonial and post-colonial periods. A number of the cases that became known involved female-assigned individuals who were discovered to be living as a different gender only when their bodies were examined following an injury or death, like Murray Hall and Billy Tipton of later times. Many male-assigned individuals seemingly had less ability to present effectively in public as female because of their facial hair and physiques, so likely presented as female mostly in private.

The lack of a public presence for individuals who assumed different genders began to change in the mid nineteenth century as a growing number of single people left their communities of origin to earn a living, gain greater freedom, or simply see the world. Able to take advantage of the anonymity afforded by new surroundings, these migrants had greater opportunities to fashion their own lives, which included engaging in same-sex relationships and presenting as a gender different from the one assigned to them at birth.

Some headed out West, where, according to historian Peter Boag (2012), "cross-dressers were not simply ubiquitous, but were very much a part of daily life on the frontier" (1–2). Others moved from rural to urban areas, primarily to pursue wage labor. In a groundbreaking 1983 article, gay historian John D'Emilio argues that the industrialization of US cities in the nineteenth century made it possible for the emergence of same-sex sexual communities; transgender historian Susan Stryker (2008) suggests that similar circumstances likely benefited individuals who lived different gendered lives, enabling them to meet and socialize with others like themselves.

The two groups were often not separate or distinguished from each other, and they created and frequented some of the same social spaces. The most popular of these gathering places were masquerade balls, or "drags" as they were commonly known. Adapting the tradition of costume balls from the larger society, individuals who would be referred to today as gay men, transsexual women, and female-presenting crossdressers all began to organize drags in large cities in the late nineteenth century (Chauncey, 1994). One of the earliest known drags took place in Washington, D.C. on New Year's Eve in 1885. The event was documented by the Washington *Evening Star* because a participant, "Miss Maud," was arrested while returning home the following morning. Dressed in "a pink dress trimmed with white lace, with stockings and undergarments to match," the male-assigned, thirty-year-old Black defendant was charged with vagrancy and sentenced to three months in jail, even though the judge, the newspaper reported, "admired his stylish appearance" (Roscoe, 1991: 240).

The growing visibility of male-assigned individuals who presented as female at drags in the late nineteenth century was not limited to Washington. By the 1890s, they and non-crossdressing men who were attracted to other men had also begun organizing their own drag events in New York City. According to historian George Chauncey (1994), these drags drew enormous numbers of Black and White participants and spectators, especially during the late 1920s and early 1930s, when at least a half dozen events were staged each year in some of the city's largest and most respectable halls including Madison Square Garden and Harlem's Savoy Ballroom. By 1930, public drag balls were also being held in Chicago, New Orleans, Baltimore, Philadelphia, and other US cities, bringing together hundreds of crossdressing individuals and their escorts, and often an equal or greater number of curious onlookers (Anonymous, 1933; Drexel, 1997; Matthews, 1927). Organizers would typically obtain a license from the police to prevent participants from being arrested for violating ordinances against crossdressing, and uniformed officers would even provide crowd control outside the halls and help ensure order inside.

While female-assigned individuals who presented as male did not hold drag balls in the late nineteenth and early twentieth centuries, they were by no means invisible in society. Some performed as male impersonators, while others crossdressed both on and off stage but did not seek to be read as men. One of the most notable in the latter group was Gladys Bentley, a Black blues singer and pianist who became well-known during the Harlem Renaissance of the 1920s. Bentley, an open lesbian, performed in a white tuxedo and top hat in some of Harlem's most popular bars and regularly wore "men's" clothing out in public with her female partner (Garber, 1988).

The enactment of laws in many US cities beginning in the 1850s that made it a crime for a person to appear in public "in a dress not belonging to his or her sex" reflected the increasing visibility of crossdressers and the resulting efforts to contain them (Stryker, 2008: 32). Another indication of the growing presence in the late nineteenth century of individuals who assumed gender behaviors and identities different from the gender assigned to them at birth was the interest that US and European physicians began to show in their experiences. Like the drag balls themselves, the research conducted by these doctors did not make clear distinctions between gender nonconformity and same-sex sexuality.

SEXOLOGY CONSIDERS GENDER NONCONFORMITY

The sexologists, as they came to be known, characterized attraction to others of the same sex as merely a sign of "gender inversion"—that is, having a gender inverted or opposite of the gender assigned at birth. A separate category did not initially exist for gender-normative women and men who pursued same-sex relationships; only gender nonconforming individuals were recognized as possessing what was considered to be a deviant sexuality (Rupp, 1999; Rupp, 2009). One of the leading advocates of this theory was Karl Heinrich Ulrichs, a German lawyer who explained his own interest in other men as stemming from having "a female soul enclosed within a male body." Anticipating descriptions of transsexuality a century later, Ulrichs argued in the 1860s that men who desired other men, whom he called "urnings," might be male by birth, but identified as female to varying degrees (Meyerowitz, 2002; Stryker, 2008: 37).

Other nineteenth-century writers followed Ulrichs's lead in separating physical from mental sex. The sexologist who had the greatest influence on the Western medical profession's views toward sexual and gender difference in the late nineteenth century was Austro-German psychiatrist Richard von Krafft-Ebing. In his widely-cited study, *Psychopathia Sexualis*, which was first published in 1886, Krafft-Ebing defined and sought to distinguish between what he saw as types of psychosexual disorders, including a number of categories that incorporate aspects of what we would now refer to as cross-dressing and transsexuality. Like Ulrichs, Krafft-Ebing considered same-sex attraction to be a manifestation of an inner sense of gender difference, and he created a framework of increasing severity of cross-gender identification (and, in his view, increasing pathology), from individuals who had a strong preference for clothing of the "other sex," to individuals whose feelings and inclinations became those of the "other sex," to individuals who believed themselves to be the "other sex" and who claimed that the sex assigned to them at birth was wrong. Krafft-Ebing characterized this last group as especially disturbed and saw their "delusion of transformation of sex" as a form of psychosis (Heidenreich, 1997: 270; Stryker, 2008; von Krafft-Ebing, 2006).

Not until the pioneering work of German physician and sexologist Magnus Hirschfeld in the early twentieth century did gender difference start to be less pathologized by the medical profession and considered a separate phenomenon from same-sex sexuality. In his epic 1910 work *Transvestites*, Hirschfeld coined the word "transvestite"—from the Latin "trans" or "across" and "vestis" or "clothing"— to refer to individuals who are overcome with a "feeling of peace, security and exaltation, happiness and well-being . . . when in the clothing of the other sex" (125). A hundred years later, this description remains one of the most insightful explanations of what we now call crossdressing. Although Hirschfeld "readily admit[ted] that this name ["transvestite"] indicate[d] only the most obvious aspect," he recognized that how they expressed their sense of gender was what set them apart from other "sexual intermediaries," including individuals with same-sex desires (Cromwell, 1999: 21).

Hirschfeld (1991 [1910]) saw transvestism as completely distinct from "homosexuality," a term that began to be commonly used in the medical literature in the early twentieth century to categorize individuals who were attracted to others of the same sex but who were still thought to be gender inverted in different ways. Through his research, Hirschfeld, who was homosexual himself, not only found that transvestites could be of any sexual orientation (including asexual), but also that most were heterosexual from the standpoint of their gender assigned at birth. In his study of seventeen individuals who crossdressed, he considered none to be homosexual from the standpoint of their assigned gender and "at the most" one—the lone female-assigned person in his sample—to be bisexual. Some of his male-assigned research subjects had experimented with relationships with men; however, they realized over time that their desire to present as feminine women did not include partnering with men. Ten of the participants were married, and Hirschfeld had met six of the wives, who had "adapt[ed] to their special kind of husbands, in spite of their initial opposition, finally even meeting them half-way" (130).

It is significant that Hirschfeld included a female-assigned person in his study, as most subsequent researchers would consider crossdressing to be an exclusively male phenomenon. Also contrary to ensuing studies, especially those by psychoanalysts, Hirschfeld recognized that transvestites were not suffering from a form of psychopathology, nor were they masochists or fetishists. While some of them derived erotic pleasure from cross-dressing, not all did, and Hirschfeld was not convinced that it was a necessary part of transvestism.

Despite being ahead of his time in many ways, Hirschfeld did not distinguish between individuals who crossdressed but who identified as their birth gender (people who would be referred to today as crossdressers) and individuals who identified as a gender different from the one assigned to them at birth and who lived cross-gendered lives, which included crossdressing (today's transsexual individuals). Among the seventeen people in his study, four had lived part of their lives as a different gender, including the female-assigned participant, and would now likely be thought of as transsexual. Hirschfeld did coin the term *seelischen Transsexualismus* or "spiritual transsexualism" in the 1920s, but he used it to refer to an aspect of "inversion," rather than considering it a specific gender identity (Meyerowitz, 2002: 19).

THE DEVELOPMENT OF GENDER-AFFIRMING SURGERIES AND HORMONE THERAPY

Hirschfeld's Institute for Sexual Science, the world's first institute devoted to sexology, also performed the earliest recorded genital transformation surgeries. The first documented case was that of Dorchen Richter, a male-assigned individual from a poor German family who had desired to be female since early childhood, lived as a woman when she could, and hated her male anatomy. She underwent castration in 1922 and had her penis removed and a vagina constructed in 1931. Following her first surgery, Richter was given a job at the institute as a domestic worker and served as an example for other patients (Meyerowitz, 2002: 19).

The institute's most well-known patient was Einar Wegener, a Dutch painter who began to present and identify as Lili Elbe in the 1920s, and after being evaluated by Hirschfeld, underwent a series of male-to-female surgeries. In addition to castration and the construction of a vagina, she had ovaries inserted into her abdomen, which at a time before the synthesis of hormones, was the only way that doctors knew to try to change estrogen levels. It is extremely doubtful that the operation had any real effect, but Elbe felt that it made her both a woman and young again and proceeded with a final operation to create a uterus in an attempt to be a mother and no different from other women (Hoyer, 1953; Kennedy, 2007). She died from heart failure in 1931 in the aftermath of the surgery. Before her death, though, Elbe requested that her friend Ernst Ludwig Hathorn Jacobson develop a book based on her diary entries, letters, and dictated material. Jacobson published the resulting work, *A Man Changes His Sex*, in Dutch and German in 1932 under the pseudonym Niels Hoyer. It was translated into English a year later as *Man into Woman: An Authentic Record of a Change of Sex* and is the first known book-length account of a gender transition (Meyerowitz, 2002).

Elbe was one of Hirschfeld's last patients. With the rise of Nazism, Hirschfeld's ability to do his work became increasingly difficult and then impossible after Adolph Hitler personally called Hirschfeld "the most dangerous Jew in Germany" (Stryker 2008, 40). Fearing for his life, Hirschfeld left the country. In his absence, the Nazis destroyed the Institute in 1933, holding a public bonfire of its contents. Hirschfeld died in exile in France two years later.

Although opportunities for surgical transition diminished with the destruction of Hirschfeld's Institute, two breakthroughs in hormonal research in the 1930s gave new hope to gender-nonconforming individuals. First, the discovery by endocrinologists that "male" hormones occurred naturally in women and that "female" hormones occurred naturally in men challenged the dominant scientific thinking that there were two separate and mutually exclusive biological sexes. The findings refuted the medical profession's assumption that only men could be given "male" hormones and women given "female" hormones, making cross-gender medical treatments possible (Rubin, 2006). At the same time, the development of synthetic testosterone and estrogen enabled hormone therapy to become more affordable and, over time, more widely available. In the 1930s and 1940s, few European and US physicians were willing to provide hormones to patients seeking to physically transition, but a small number of gender nonconforming individuals found ways to obtain them (Kennedy, 2007).

The first female-assigned individual known to have taken testosterone for the purpose of transforming his body was Michael Dillon, a doctor from an aristocratic British family, who had entered medicine in order to better understand his own masculine identity and how he could change his body to be like other men. In 1939, he began taking hormones that he received from a physician, and within a few months was readily seen as a man by strangers. For Dillon, though, it was just the beginning of his efforts to masculinize his appearance. He had a double mastectomy in 1942 and underwent more than a dozen operations to construct a penis beginning in 1946. His were the first recorded female-to-male genital surgeries performed on a non-intersex person (Kennedy, 2007; Shapiro, 2010).

The same year that Dillon began his phalloplasty, he also published a book on the treatment of gender nonconforming individuals, *Self: A Study in Ethics and Endocrinology*. Despite its title, *Self* did not include a discussion of Dillon's own experiences. Instead, his focus was on the need for society to understand people who, like himself, felt that they were a gender different from that assigned to them at birth. Dillon argued that such individuals were not mentally unbalanced, but "would develop naturally enough if only [they] belonged to the other sex." He was especially critical of the psychologists who believed that they could change the sense of self of gender nonconforming individuals through therapy, when what their clients really needed was access to hormones and genital surgeries. Making an argument that would become commonplace in the years that followed, Dillon reasoned that "where the mind cannot be made to fit the body, the body should be made to fit, approximately, at any rate to the mind, despite the prejudices of those who have not suffered these things" (53). *Self*, though, was not widely circulated, and Dillon himself sought to avoid public attention, even taking the extraordinary step of going into exile in India in 1958, when the media discovered his secret and ran stories about a transsexual being the heir to a British title.

THE RISE OF THE CONCEPT OF TRANSSEXUALITY

Instead of Dillon, the leading advocate in the 1950s and 1960s for "adjust[ing] the body to the mind" of gender nonconforming people through hormones and surgeries became Harry Benjamin, a German-born, US endocrinologist. Benjamin (1966), like Dillon, saw attempts to "cure" such individuals by psychotherapy as "a useless undertaking" (91), and began prescribing hormones to them and suggesting surgeons abroad, as no physician in the United States at that time would openly perform gender transition operations. Along with US physician David O. Cauldwell, Benjamin referred to those who desired to change their sex as "transsexuals" in order to distinguish them from "transvestites." The difference between the groups, according to Benjamin, was that "true transsexuals feel that they *belong* to the other sex, they want to *be* and *function* as members of the opposite sex, not only to appear as such. For them, their sex organs . . . are disgusting deformities that must be changed by the surgeon's knife" (13–14).

Cauldwell was apparently the first medical professional to use the word "transsexual" (which he initially spelled "transexual") in its contemporary sense. In a 1949 article in *Sexology* magazine entitled "Psychopathia Transexualis" (playing off of Krafft-Ebing's *Psychopathia Sexualis*), Cauldwell (2006) presented the case history of "Earl," a "psychopathic transexual" who "grew up thinking of herself [sic] as a boy" and "was desperate to become a male" (41–42). Earl had approached Cauldwell, who was known for writing approvingly about operations on intersex individuals, to seek his help in finding a surgeon who would remove Earl's breasts and ovaries and create a penis in place of his vagina. But as Cauldwell related in the article, he refused to assist Earl. In sharp contrast to Benjamin, Cauldwell believed that transsexuals were mentally ill and considered surgery for individuals like Earl to be mutilation and a criminal action.

The opposing attitudes on gender-affirming surgeries between Benjamin and Cauldwell reflected fundamental differences in how sex and gender were viewed by the medical profession in the mid twentieth century. Most physicians supported Cauldwell's position that biological sex was the defining aspect of someone's gender and was immutable, outside of cases of intersex individuals, where the "true" sex of the person may not be immediately known. Increasingly, though, this belief was challenged by doctors and researchers like Benjamin who distinguished between biological sex and "psychological sex," or as it came to be known, "gender identity." As more and more transsexual individuals were acknowledged and studied, these physicians and scientists developed the evidence to begin to gradually shift the dominant medical view to the contrary argument: that gender identity and not biological sex was the critical element of someone's gender and was immutable. Transsexual individuals thus needed to be able to change the sex of their bodies to match their sense of self (Meyerowitz, 2002).

THE STORIES WE TELL: HISTORICAL DIALOGUES ABOUT TRANSGENDER IDENTITY

Trans people spend a lot of time helping others to understand what it's like to be trans. In my research, I've found there are three primary narratives trans people have turned to in order to share their stories. Not every trans person relies exclusively on these ways of explaining themselves, nor do they necessarily follow only one plot—but these narratives show us how our history has influenced the ways we talk about sex and gender.

The "hermaphroditic narrative" emerged in Germany with the story of Lili Elbe, one of the first transgender people to record her story. In 1922, Elbe was castrated, and in 1931 she had her penis removed and a vagina constructed. Elbe's autobiography was translated into English in 1933, and her story spread in the United States. Elbe said she was a female "personality" born into a hermaphroditic (or what today would be called intersex) body, a body with both male and female reproductive organs. The hermaphroditic narrative—having a hermaphroditic body and a desire for men -- allowed Elbe to receive a vagina reconstruction operation in the West.

The hermaphroditic narrative began to wane in the years following World War II, and the "sex-gender misalignment" narrative took hold. In 1949, psychiatrist David Cauldwell defined "trans-sexual" people as those who are physically of one sex and psychologically of the opposite sex. Harry Benjamin, an endocrinologist, helped spread this "born in the wrong body" narrative. In the early 1950s he diagnosed as transsexual only those who explained themselves using a narrative along the lines of: "I am a woman born into the wrong (male) body; this causes me extreme psychological duress. After you help me acquire a female body, I will be returned to my true self and live as a happy and productive, heterosexual citizen." (Not much mention was made of female-to-male trans people, yet.) In order to be diagnosed as transsexual by doctors like Benjamin, one had to use this narrative; and because only those with the diagnosis could access sex reassignment surgery, trans people felt pressure to use it. This narrative perpetuated a limited understanding of what it meant to be transsexual that persists today.

The "queer narrative" began in the 1960s, when the assumed norms of binary gender and heterosexuality came under scrutiny. People started telling stories of who they were that did not align with the hetero-norm. LGB psychiatrists worked to remove "homosexual" from *The Diagnostic and Statistical Manual of Mental Disorders III* (DSM-III), and transgender activists began working to remove "transsexual" from the *DSM-IV*. The "queer narrative" hit academia when writer Sandy Stone called for posttranssexuality, or the acceptance of a wider range of expressions of sex and gender. After Stone's article, the lines between academia and social activism began to blur, and many people started working in both arenas: Kate Bornstein called for gender play, Judith Halberstam suggested we all live the fiction of gender, and Riki Wilchins advocated for the right to choose gender and body meaning.

Over time, the ways in which we talk about transsexual identity and experience have changed. Each narrative has had personal and political significance, offering possibilities and limitations; for instance, the "sex-gender misalignment" narrative aided in gaining medical assistance for transitioning but also reinforced heteronormative ways of thinking about sex and gender. There is no single narrative that fits every trans body and no narrative that remains free from political and personal limitations. It is critical to be aware of how we share and listen to experiences of sex and gender, because the narratives we use can have powerful consequences.

Jodi Kaufmann is an Associate Professor at Georgia State University.

CHRISTINE JORGENSEN: THE TRANSSEXUAL PHENOMENON

Although Harry Benjamin was referring to the issue of transsexuality in general and not to Christine Jorgensen in particular with the title of his pioneering 1966 work *The Transsexual Phenomenon*, it would not be an exaggeration to characterize her as such. Through the publicity given to her transition, she brought the concept of "sex change" into everyday conversations in the United States, served as a role model for many other transsexual individuals to understand themselves and pursue medical treatment, and transformed the debate about the efficacy of providing hormones and gender-affirming surgeries to individuals who identified as a gender different from the one assigned to them at birth. Following the media frenzy over Jorgensen, much of the US public began to recognize that "sex change" was indeed possible.

Jorgensen herself had spent many years questioning her sense of gender difference before realizing that an answer could be found through science and medicine. Born in 1926 to Danish-American parents in New York City, Jorgensen struggled with an intense feeling that she should have been born female. Among the childhood experiences that she recounts in her 1967 autobiography were preferring to play with girls, wishing that she had been sent to a girls' camp rather than one for boys, and having "a small piece of needlepoint" that she cherished taken away by an unsympathetic elementary school teacher. The teacher called in Jorgensen's mother and asked her confrontationally, "do you think that this is anything for a red-blooded boy to have in his desk as a keepsake?" (18).

Although not mentioned in her autobiography, Jorgensen also apparently began wearing her sister's clothing in secret when she was young and, by her teens, had acquired her own small wardrobe of "women's" clothing. Many transsexual individuals dress as the gender with which they identify from a young age, but Jorgensen may have been concerned that readers would confuse her for a "transvestite" or an effeminate "homosexual." She did indicate being attracted to men in her autobiography, and acknowledged years later having had "a couple" of same-sex sexual encounters in her youth (Meyerowitz, 2002: 57). However, by her early 20s, Jorgensen gradually became aware that she was a heterosexual woman, rather than a crossdresser or gay man, and began to look for all she could find about "sex changes."

Jorgensen read about the first studies to examine the effects of hormone treatments and about "various conversion experiments in Sweden," which led her to obtain commercially synthesized female hormones and to travel "first to Denmark, where [she] had relatives, and then to Stockholm, where [she] hoped [she] would find doctors who would be willing to handle [her] case" (81, 94). While in Denmark, though, Jorgensen learned that doctors in that country could help her, and came under the care of leading endocrinologist Christian Hamburger, who treated her with increasingly higher doses of female hormones for two years, beginning in 1950. Hamburger also arranged for her to have operations to remove her testicles and penis and to reshape her scrotum into labia.

While recovering in December 1952, Jorgensen went from being an unknown American abroad to "the most talked-about girl in the world." A trade magazine for the publishing industry announced in 1954 that Jorgensen's story over the previous year "had received the largest worldwide coverage in the history of newspaper publishing." Looking back years later on the media's obsession, Jorgensen (1967) remained incredulous: "A tragic war was still raging in Korea, George VI died and Britain had a new queen, sophisticated guided missiles were going off in New Mexico, Jonas Salk was working on a vaccine for infantile paralysis. . . . [yet] Christine Jorgensen was on page one" (249, 144).

Given that Jorgensen was by no means the first person to undergo a gender transition and that some cases had been widely covered in the media, it would seem surprising that she would be the subject of so much attention. Part of the reason Jorgensen became such a sensation was that she had been a US serviceman, the epitome of masculinity in post–World War II America (though Jorgensen served in the US and never saw combat), and had been reborn into a "blonde bombshell," the symbol of 1950s White feminine sexiness (Meyerowitz, 2002: 62). The initial newspaper story, published in The *New York Daily News* on December 1, 1952, highlighted this dramatic transformation, with its headline, "Ex-GI Becomes Blonde Beauty," and its accompanying "before" and "after" photographs. A grainy Army picture of a nerdish-looking, male-bodied Jorgensen in uniform is contrasted with a professionally taken profile picture of a feminine Jorgensen looking like Grace Kelly.

Subsequent news stories also fixated on Jorgensen's appearance, as journalists sought to judge the extent to which she had truly "become female." In most of the initial accounts, she was not only described as looking like a woman, but as an extremely attractive one. The press marveled at her movie-star qualities, including a male reporter who indicated in a story published a year after the news of her transition broke that he "Could Have Gone for the He-She Girl." Readers were likewise captivated; the more the media reported, the more people wanted to know about her and "how she managed to become such a beautiful woman" (Docter, 2008: 115; Meyerowitz, 2002: 63).

The tremendous attention that Jorgensen's transition received also reflected the public's newfound fascination with the power of science. A tidal wave of remarkable inventions—from television and the transistor radio to the atomic bomb—had made scientists in the 1950s seem capable of anything, so why not the ability to turn a man into a woman? However, in the aftermath of the first use of nuclear weapons, Jorgensen's "sex change" was also pointed to as evidence that science had gone too far in its efforts to alter the natural environment. Jorgensen thus served as a symbol for both scientific progress and a fear that science was attempting to play God. By being at the center of postwar debates over technological advancement, she remained in the spotlight well after the initial reports of her transition and was able to have a successful stage career based on her celebrity status (Meyerowitz, 2002).

Anxieties over changing gender roles were another factor that contributed to Jorgensen's celebrity. At a time when millions of US women who had been recruited to work in factories during the war were being pushed back into the home in order to make way for returning servicemen, gender expectations for both women and men were in a state of flux. Suddenly, the assumed naturalness of what it meant to be male and female was being called into question. Not only could women do "men's" work, but men could become women. As historian Susan Stryker argues, "Jorgensen's notoriety in the 1950s was undoubtedly fueled by the pervasive unease felt in some quarters that American manhood, already under siege, could quite literally be undone and refashioned into its seeming opposite through the power of modern science" (Stryker, 2000: viii).

TRANSSEXUALITY IN 1950S TAIWAN

The first case of transsexuality in Chinese-speaking communities was reported in post–World War II Taiwan. In 1953, four years after Mao Zedong's political regime took over mainland China and the Nationalist government under Chiang Kai-shek was forced to relocate its base, news of the success of native doctors in converting a man into a woman made headlines in Taiwan. On August 14 that year, the *United Daily News* (*Lianhebao*) surprised the public by announcing the discovery of an intersex soldier, Xie Jianshun, in Tainan, Taiwan. Within a week, the paper adopted a radically different rhetoric, now with a headline claiming that "Christine Will Not Be America's Exclusive: Soldier Destined to Become a Lady." Considered by many to be the "first" Chinese transsexual, Xie was frequently dubbed the "Chinese Christine." This allusion to the contemporaneous American ex-G.I. celebrity Christine Jorgensen, who had traveled to Denmark for her sex reassignment surgery and became a worldwide household name immediately after due to her personality and glamorous looks, reflected the growing influence of American culture on the Republic of China at the peak of the Cold War.

Within days, the characterization of Xie in the Taiwanese press changed from an average citizen whose ambiguous sex provoked uncertainty and anxiety throughout the nation, to a transsexual cultural icon whose fate would indisputably contribute to the global staging of Taiwan on par with the United States. The publicity surrounding Xie's transition worked as a pivotal fulcrum in shifting common understandings of transsexuality (including its gradual separation from intersexuality), the role of medical science, and their evolving relation to the popular press in mid-twentieth century Chinese-speaking culture.

Dripping with national and trans-Pacific significance, Xie's experience made *bianxingren* (transsexual) a household term in the 1950s. She served as a focal point for numerous new stories that broached the topics of changing sex and human intersexuality. People who wrote about her debated whether she qualified as a woman, whether medical technology could transform sex, and whether the "two Christines" were more similar or different. These questions led to persistent comparisons of Taiwan with the United States, but Xie never presented herself as a duplicate of Jorgensen. As Xie knew, her story highlighted issues that pervaded postwar Taiwanese society: the censorship of public culture by the state, the unique social status of men serving in the armed forces, the limit of individualism, the promise and pitfalls of science, the normative behaviors of men and women, and the boundaries of acceptable sexual expression. Her story attracted the press, but the public's avid interest in sex and its plasticity prompted reporters to dig deeply. As the press coverage escalated, new names and previously unheard of medical conditions grabbed the attention of journalists and their readers.

The wide-ranging debates on sex transformation that preoccupied Republican-era (1912–49) sexologists and popular writers in mainland China were transferred to the island of Taiwan along with the Nationalist government's migration. The saga of Xie Jianshun and other "sex change" reports that sprung up in the Taiwanese press exemplify the emergence of transsexuality as a form of modern sexual embodiment in Chinese society. Xie's story, in particular, became a lightning rod for many post-WWII anxieties about gender and sexuality, and called dramatic attention to issues that would later drive the feminist and gay and lesbian movements in the decades ahead.

Howard Chiang is Assistant Professor of History at the University of Warwick and editor of Transgender China *(2012).*

THE POST-CHRISTINE ERA

While many in 1950s America were deeply troubled by what Jorgensen's transition meant for traditional gender roles, many transsexual individuals, particularly transsexual women, experienced a tremendous sense of relief. They finally had a name for the sense of gender difference that most had felt from early childhood and recognized that their feelings were shared by others.

> *"[Coverage surrounding Jorgensen's return to the US was] a true lifesaving event. . . [t] he only thing that kept me from suicide at 12 was the publicity of Christine Jorgensen. It was the first time I found out that there were others like me—I was no longer alone,"* (Trans Bodies, Trans Selves online survey, 2013).

> *"[I remember feeling] 'giddy'. . . because for the first time ever I realized it was possible,"* (Trans Bodies, Trans Selves online survey, 2013).

Many other transsexual individuals also saw themselves in Jorgensen and hoped to gain access to hormones and surgical procedures. In the months following her return to the United States, Jorgensen received "hundreds of tragic letters . . . from men and women who also had experienced the deep frustrations of lives lived in sexual twilight." Doctor Hamburger was likewise inundated with requests from individuals seeking to transition; in the ten and a half months following his treatment of Jorgensen, he received more than 1,100 letters from transsexual people, many of whom sought to be his patients (Jorgensen, 1967: 149–50).

While hearing about Jorgensen helped many transsexual individuals understand themselves and offered a sense of hope that they too could change their sex, few were able to obtain immediate relief. Deluged with a flood of requests from people throughout the world, the Danish government banned such procedures for non-citizens. In the United States, many physicians simply dismissed the rapidly growing number of individuals seeking gender-affirming surgeries as being mentally ill. Other, more sympathetic doctors were reluctant to operate because of a fear that they would be criminally prosecuted for destroying healthy tissue under state "mayhem" statutes or sued by patients unsatisfied with the surgical outcomes. Thus, despite the tremendous demand, only a few dozen, mostly secretive "sex changes" were performed in the US in the years after Jorgensen first made headlines (Stryker, 2008).

Not until the mid 1960s, when the dominant US medical paradigm related to trans-sexuality began to shift, did gender-affirming surgery become more available. The constant mainstream media coverage in the decade following the disclosure of Jorgensen's transition made it increasingly difficult for the medical establishment to characterize transsexual people as a few psychologically disordered individuals. That mental health professionals could not point to even one transsexual person who had been "cured" of a desire to change sex further discredited a psychological disorder explanation. At the same time, the first published studies of the effects of gender-affirming surgery demonstrated the benefits of medical intervention. Harry Benjamin, who worked with more transsexual individuals than any other physician in the United States, found that among fifty-one of his MTF (male-to-female) patients who underwent surgery, 86 percent had "good" or "satisfactory" lives afterward. He concluded: "I have become convinced from what I have seen that a miserable, unhappy male [assigned at birth] transsexual can, with the help of surgery and endocrinology, attain a happier future as a woman," (Benjamin, 1966: 135; Meyerowitz, 2002). The smaller number of FTM (female-to-male) patients he saw likewise felt better about themselves and were more psychologically well-adjusted following surgery.

Despite Benjamin's efforts to find surgeons in the United States for his MTF patients, most were forced to travel to other countries for gender-affirming surgery through the mid 1960s. However, within months of the publication of Benjamin's *The Transsexual Phenomenon* in 1966, the Johns Hopkins University opened the first gender identity clinic in the US to diagnose and treat transsexual individuals and to conduct research related to transsexuality. Similar programs were soon established at the University of Minnesota, Stanford University, the University of Oregon, and Case Western University, and within ten years, more than forty university-affiliated gender clinics existed throughout the United States (Bullough & Bullough, 1998; Denny, 2006; Stryker, 2008).

The sudden proliferation of health care services for transsexual individuals reflected not only the effect of Benjamin's work and the influence of a prestigious university like Hopkins on other institutions, but also the behind-the-scenes involvement of millionaire philanthropist Reed Erickson. A transsexual man and a patient of Benjamin, Erickson created a foundation that paid for Benjamin's research and helped fund the Hopkins program and other gender identity clinics. The agency also disseminated information related to transsexuality and served as an indispensable resource for individuals who were coming out as transsexual (Stryker, 2008).

The establishment of gender identity clinics at leading universities called attention to the health care needs of transsexual people and helped to legitimize gender-affirming surgery. At the same time, though, the clinics also institutionalized a model of transsexuality that excluded many from the definition of "transsexual" and denied them access to hormones and surgery. This model had its roots in Benjamin's (1966) concept of a "true transsexual"—someone who has felt themselves to be in the "wrong" body from their earliest memories and who is attracted to individuals of the same birth sex but as a member of the "other" sex (i.e., someone who is heterosexual after transition). As detailed by writer Dallas Denny (2006), the gender identity clinics adopted this presumption of heterosexuality and a binary understanding of gender that expected transsexual people to conform to stereotypical gender norms. Denny states:

> To qualify for treatment, it was important that applicants report that their gender dysphorias manifested at an early age; that they have a history of playing with dolls as a child, if born male, or trucks and guns, if born female; that their sexual attractions were exclusively to the same biological sex; that they have a history of failure at endeavors undertaken while in the original gender role; and that they pass or had potential to pass successfully as a member of the desired sex (177).

Unable to meet these narrow and biased criteria, the vast majority of transsexual people were turned away from the gender identity clinics. In its first two and half years, Johns Hopkins received almost 2,000 requests for gender-affirming surgery, but performed operations on only 24 individuals (Meyerowitz, 2002).

Transsexual men especially encountered difficulties. In the aftermath of the extraordinary publicity given to Jorgensen and the transsexual women who followed her in the spotlight in the 1950s and 1960s, transsexuality became seen as a primarily male-to-female phenomenon. The medical establishment gave little consideration to transsexual men, and in the late 1960s, physicians at one of the country's leading programs, UCLA's Gender Identity Research Clinic, debated whether trans men should even be considered transsexuals (Meyerowitz, 2002).

Admittedly, many trans men did not recognize themselves as transsexual either. While they may have known about Jorgensen and other transsexual women, they did not know anyone who had transitioned from female-to-male or that such a transition was even possible. This sense of being "the only one" was especially common among the transsexual men who grew up in the 1950s and 1960s (Beemyn & Rankin, 2011).

The transsexual men who did transition often did not pursue surgery to construct a penis because the process was expensive, involved multiple surgeries, and produced imperfect results. Moreover, few doctors were skilled in performing phalloplasties. In the United States, the first "bottom surgeries" for trans men were apparently not undertaken until the early 1960s, and even when the gender identity clinics opened, the programs did only a handful of such operations (Meyerowitz, 2002). The vast majority of transsexual men had to be satisfied with hormone therapy and the removal of their breasts and internal reproductive organs, which surgeons already commonly performed on women. However, since the effects of hormones (especially increased facial hair and lower voices) and "top surgery" enabled trans men to be seen more readily by others as men, these steps were considered more critical by most transsexual men.

The likelihood of passing as one's desired sex was a main criterion in gaining access to gender-affirming surgery. Physicians also counseled or sometimes required their patients to avoid socializing with other transsexual individuals and expected that they would consider themselves "normal" women and men and blend into society following surgery (Denny, 2006). In order to fit in, they were encouraged to hide and lie about their transsexual pasts. They were told to invent a boyhood or girlhood for themselves matching their post-transition gender, to sever ties whenever possible with old acquaintances and develop new friendships with individuals who were unaware of their personal histories, and even to change jobs and move to another city to avoid the possibility of being outed. Given the extreme social stigma against transsexual people, many did not need much encouragement to "disappear" if they could.

Some transsexual individuals did organize in the late 1960s to assist others in finding support and gaining access to services, but most of these efforts were small and short-lived. In 1967, transgender people in San Francisco formed Conversion Our Goal, or COG, the first known transsexual support group in the United States. However, within a year, the organization had disintegrated into two competing groups, neither of which existed for very long. More successful was the National Transsexual Counseling Unit, a San Francisco-based social service agency established in 1968 with funding from Reed Erickson. That same year in New York City, Mario Martino, a female-to-male transsexual and registered nurse, and his wife founded Labyrinth, a counseling service for trans men. It was the first known organization in the United States to focus on the needs of transsexual men and worked with upwards of one hundred transitioning individuals (Martino, 1977; Stryker, 2008).

ORGANIZING AMONG CROSSDRESSING INDIVIDUALS

The first enduring transgender organization in the United States was started by female-presenting crossdressers or "transvestites," as they were then known. In 1952, the year that Jorgensen became an international media phenomenon, a group of crossdressers in the Los Angeles area led by Virginia Prince quietly created a mimeographed newsletter, *Transvestia: The Journal of the American Society for Equity in Dress*. Although its distribution was limited to a small number of crossdressers on the group's mailing list and it lasted just two issues, *Transvestia* was apparently the first specifically transgender publication in the United States and served as a trial run for wider organizing among crossdressers.

In 1960, Prince relaunched *Transvestia* as a bi-monthly magazine with twenty-five subscribers, who contributed four dollars each to provide start-up capital. Sold through adult bookstores and by word of mouth, *Transvestia* grew to several hundred subscribers within two years and to more than one thousand from across the country by the mid 1960s (Ekins & King, 2005; Prince, 1962; Prince & Bentler, 1972). Prince wrote regular columns for the magazine but relied on readers for much of the content, which included life stories, fiction, letters to the editor, personal photographs, and advice on crossdressing. The involvement of its subscribers, many of whom came out publicly for the first time on the magazine's pages, had the effect of creating a loyal fan base and contributed to its longevity. Prince's commitment also sustained *Transvestia*; she served as its editor and publisher for twenty years, retiring after its one hundredth issue in 1979 (Hill, 2007).

Through *Transvestia*, Prince was able to form a transgender organization that continues more than fifty years later. A year after starting the magazine, she invited several Los Angeles subscribers to a clandestine meeting in a local hotel room. The female-presenting crossdressers were requested to bring stockings and high heels, but were not told that the others would be there. When the meeting began, Prince had them don the female apparel, thus outing themselves to each other and forcing them to maintain their shared secret. Initially known as the Hose and Heels Club, the group was renamed the Foundation for Personality Expression (FPE or Phi Pi Epsilon) the following year by Prince, who envisioned it as the Alpha Chapter of a sorority-like organization that would have chapters throughout the country. By the mid 1960s, several other chapters had been chartered by Prince, who set strict membership requirements. Only individuals who had subscribed to and read at least five issues of *Transvestia* could join, and then they had to have their application personally approved by Prince and be interviewed by her or an area representative. Prince kept control over the membership through the mid 1970s, when FPE merged with a Southern California crossdressing group, Mamselle, to become the Society for the Second Self or Tri-Ess, the name by which it is known today (Ekins & King, 2005; Stryker, 2008). Continuing the practice of FPE, Tri-Ess is modeled on the sorority system and currently has more than twenty-five chapters throughout the country.

CROSSDRESSING FOR SUCCESS

At about the age of 5, I began to recognize myself as being different some-how from boys. As a child growing up in the 1950s I had no clue as to what was going on inside. I began to do research secretly in the mid 1960s, when I was in my early teens, to try to figure out what was going on, but what I found only said that my condition was an illness and curable. I finally dis-covered Masters and Johnson's research, which spoke of "transvestism" in a more humane and positive light. The term still felt clinical, but I saw myself reflected enough in the description to think "maybe that's what I am." I no longer felt fearful, and a sense of freedom to explore this inexplicable "gift" took over. No sense of guilt or remorse remained.

While attending UC Berkeley, I would secretly dress as female and go out. Via literature and sordid sex-shop glossy magazines, I found out that there were indeed others, past and present, who had dealt or were dealing with their own gender identities. The first person I met whom I felt some af-finity or commonality with was a drag queen in San Francisco. She clocked me right off and took me aside. She was kind, and the education awarded by her kindness was that we are all the same deep down. I carry and try to share that message to this day.

My now ex-partner was my support system for many years, and she learned about Tri-Ess on the Internet. There was a chapter, Sigma Rho Delta (SRD), near me in Raleigh, North Carolina. I wasn't looking for support or un-derstanding, just simple camaraderie, and SRD provided that for me. It was fun.

The group began with a handful of members, but soon grew exponen-tially as word got out via the street and the Internet. We went from three to forty members. I served as vice president of membership and later as president.

Tri-Ess was founded as an organization for heterosexual male crossdress-ers and their significant others. But the group's guidelines did not prevent us from being more inclusive, and our chapter decided to welcome people of all gender presentations and sexual proclivities into our young organization.

All persuasions and ages passed through our door. Twenty-somethings to people over 70 years young. Timid, garden-variety crossdressers in hid-ing from years of accumulated fear. Bold and boisterous politicos. Fetish practitioners. The white glove and party manner set. Those in transition or considering it. Musical and artistic types. Truck drivers and doctors. Com-puter geeks and business owners. Individuals with disabilities or who were physically ailing. They and more came and went. It was a revolving door, which we kept open for over ten years.

We landed in restaurants, clubs, and at theatres. We played music to-gether and laughed a lot at ourselves. We had picnics. Members who were so inclined bravely attended events of a political nature, such as lobby days at the state legislature, where we asked our elected officials their positions on the pending ENDA (Employment Non-Discrimination Act) and LGBT-inclusive hate crimes bill. We even crashed a high-dollar-per-plate Human Rights Campaign fundraiser that featured Representative Barney Frank and confronted him about his stance on transgender inclusion in the aforemen-tioned legislation. We had a sense of strength within our own diversity. We had some kind of insight that told us this time would not come again, that it was time to act. We were kicked out of some meeting places because of prejudice, but we never succumbed to failure. Like a cat, we always landed on our feet.

Although membership declined and the group eventually disbanded, our lasting impressions and friendships have carried on past the decade of Sig-ma Rho Delta's existence. We still stay in touch and visit one another. We are proud of our unique heritage and the challenges that we met together and as individuals. We found pride in ourselves.

Angelika Van Ashley

Transvestia and FPE/Tri-Ess reflected Prince's narrow beliefs about crossdressing. In her view, the "true transvestite" is "exclusively heterosexual," "frequently . . . mar-ried and often fathers," and "values his male organs, enjoys using them and does not desire them removed," (Ekins & King, 2005: 9). She not only excluded admittedly gay and bisexual male crossdressers and transsexual women, but also was scornful of them; she openly expressed anti-gay sentiment and was a leading opponent of gen-der-affirming surgery. By making sharp distinctions between "real transvestites" and other groups, Prince addressed the two main fears of the wives and female partners of heterosexual male crossdressers: that their husbands and boyfriends will leave them for men or that their partners would become women. In addition, she sought to downplay the erotic and sexual aspects of crossdressing for some people in order to lessen the stigma commonly associated with transvestism and to normalize the one way in which White, middle-class heterosexual male crossdressers like herself were not privileged in society. In the mid 1960s, *Transvestia* was promoted as being "dedi-cated to the needs of the sexually (that's heterosexual) normal individual," (Ekins & King, 2005: 7; Stryker, 2008).

Prince further attempted to dissociate transvestism from sexual activity through the creation of the term "femmiphile"—literally "lover of the feminine." "Femmi-phile" did not catch on, but the word "crossdresser" slowly replaced "transvestite" as the preferred term among most transgender people and supporters. As gay and bisexual men who presented as female increasingly referred to themselves as drag queens, "crossdresser" began to be applied only to heterosexual men—achieving the separation that Prince desired.

Prince deserves a tremendous amount of credit for bringing formerly isolated cross-dressers together, helping this segment of the community recognize that they are not pathological or immoral, creating a national organization that has provided support to tens of thousands of members and their partners, and increasing the visibility of heterosexual male crossdressers. At the same time, by preventing gay and bisexual crossdressers from joining her organizations, she helped ensure that they would identify more with the gay community than with the crossdressing community and form their own groups; thus Prince's prejudice and divisiveness foreclosed the possible development of a broad transgender or lesbian, gay, bisexual, and transgender (LGBT) political coalition in the 1960s.

The largest and oldest continuing organization consisting primarily of gay male crossdressers or drag queens, the Imperial Court System, was founded by José Sarria in San Francisco in 1965. Beginning with other chapters (known as "realms") in Portland, Oregon, and Los Angeles, the court system has grown today to more than 65 local groups in the United States, Canada, and Mexico; reflecting this expansion, its name is now the International Court System (2010). The primary mission of each chapter is to raise money for LGBT, HIV/AIDS, and other charities through annual costume balls and other fundraising events. Involvement often pays personal dividends as well. According to Steven Schacht (2002), a sociologist who has participated in the group, "courts also serve as an important conduit for gay and lesbian individuals to do drag and as a venue for formal affiliation and personal esteem (largely in the form of various drag titles; i.e. Empress, Emperor, Princess, and Prince) often unavailable to such individuals in the dominant culture," (164).

In the 1950s and 1960s, lesbian, gay, and bisexual crossdressers also found a home in bars, restaurants, and other venues that catered to (or at least tolerated) such a clientele. Sarria, for example, performed in drag at San Francisco's Black Cat Bar in the 1950s and early 1960s and helped turn it into a social and cultural center for the city's gay community until harassment from law enforcement and local authorities forced the bar to close (Boyd, 2003). Lesbian, gay, and bisexual individuals—both those who did drag and those who did not—similarly carved out spaces in other US cities, despite regular police crackdowns against them.

By the late 1960s, Black drag queens were also organizing their own events. Growing out of the drag balls held in New York City earlier in the century, these gatherings began in Harlem and initially focused on extravagant feminine drag performances. As word spread about the balls, they attracted larger and larger audiences and the competitions became fiercer and more varied. The drag performers "walked" (competed) for trophies and prizes in a growing number of categories beyond most feminine (known as "femme realness") or most glamorous, including categories for "butch queens"—gay and sometimes trans men who look "real" as different class-based male archetypes, such as "business executive," "school boy," and "thug."

The many individuals seeking to participate in ball culture led to the establishment of "houses," groups of Black and Latino "children" who gathered around a "house mother" or less often a "house father," in the mid 1970s. These houses were often named after their leaders, such as Crystal LaBeija's House of LaBeija, Avis Pendavis's House of Pendavis, and Dorian Corey's House of Corey, or took their names from leading fashion designers like the House of Chanel or the House of St. Laurent. The children, consisting of less experienced drag performers, walked in the balls under their house name, seeking to win trophies for the glory of the house and to achieve "legendary" status for themselves. Given that many of the competitors were poor youth who came from broken homes or who had been thrown out of their homes for being gay or transgender, the houses provided a surrogate family and a space where they could be accepted and have a sense of belonging (Cunningham, 1995; Trebay, 2000).

The ball culture spread to other cities in the 1980s and 1990s and achieved mainstream visibility in 1990 through Jennie Livingston's documentary *Paris Is Burning* and Madonna's mega-hit song and video "Vogue." In recent years, many of the New York balls have moved out of Harlem, but continue to include dozens of local houses and groups from other cities competing in a wide array of categories. Reflecting changes in the wider Black and Latino cultures, hip hop and R & B have become more prominent in the ball scene, and a growing number of performers are butch queens who imitate rap musicians (Cunningham, 1995; Trebay, 2000).

TRANSGENDER POWER!

The 1969 Stonewall Riots in New York City were not a unique event but the culmination of more than a decade of militant opposition by poor and working-class LGBT people in response to discriminatory treatment and police brutality. Much of this resistance took the form of spontaneous, everyday acts of defiance that received little attention at the time, even in LGBT communities. Susan Stryker, for example, recounts two confrontations with the police that, until recently, were largely unknown. One night in May of 1959, two Los Angeles police officers went into Cooper's Donuts—an all-night coffeehouse popular with drag queens and gay male hustlers, many of whom were Latino/a or African American—and began harassing and arresting the patrons in drag. The customers responded by fighting back, first by throwing doughnuts and ultimately by engaging in skirmishes with the officers that led the police to retreat and to call in backup. In the melee, the drag queens who had been arrested were able to escape (Faderman & Timmons, 2006; Stryker, 2008).

A similar incident occurred in San Francisco in 1966 at the Tenderloin location of Gene Compton's Cafeteria—a twenty-four-hour restaurant that, like Cooper's, was frequented by drag queens and male hustlers, as well as the people looking to pick them up. According to Stryker, the management called the police one August night, as it had done in the past, to get rid of a group of young drag queens who were seen as loitering. When a police officer tried to remove one of the queens forcibly, she threw a cup of coffee in his face and a riot ensued. Patrons pelted the officers with everything at their disposal, including chairs, sugar shakers, plates, and cups, and wrecked the cafeteria and its plate-glass windows. Vastly outnumbered, the police ran outside to call for reinforcements, only to have the drag queens chase after them, beating the officers with their purses and kicking them with their high heels. The incident served to empower the city's drag community and motivated many to begin to organize for their rights.

Three years later, the riots at the Stonewall Inn in the Greenwich Village neighborhood of New York City inspired gender nonconforming people across the country to activism on an even greater scale. As with the earlier confrontations in Los Angeles and San Francisco, the immediate impetus for the Stonewall uprising was oppression by the local police. But the events that began in the early morning hours of June 28, 1969 and continued on and off for six days also reflected long-simmering anger. "Back then we were beat up by the police, by everybody.... You get tired of being just pushed around," recalls Sylvia Rivera, a Puerto Rican transgender woman who was a leader in the riots and the LGBT organizing that occurred afterward. "We were not taking any more of this shit" (Carter, 2004; Feinberg, 1998: 107; Stryker, 2006).

Rivera and many of the other Stonewall participants were active in the women's movement, the civil rights movement, and the anti–Vietnam War movement, and recognized that they would have to demand their rights as LGBT people too. Rivera states: "We had done so much for other movements. It was time.... I always believed that we would have [to] fight back. I just knew that we would fight back. I just didn't know it would be that night" (Feinberg, 1998: 107, 109).

The police raided the Stonewall Inn and as usual began arresting the bar's workers, customers who did not have identification, and those who were crossdressed. Unlike in the past, the other patrons did not scatter, but instead congregated outside and, with other LGBT people from the neighborhood, taunted the police as they tried to place the arrestees into a patrol wagon.

Accounts differ as to what incited the onlookers to violence; it is likely that events happened so fast that there was not one single precipitating incident. As the crowd grew, so did their anger toward the police for their rough treatment of the drag queens and at least one butch lesbian whom they had arrested. People began to throw coins at the officers, and when this failed to halt the brutality, they hurled whatever they could find—cans, bottles, cobblestones, and bricks from a construction site on the next block. Unaccustomed to LGBT people resisting police brutality and fearful for their safety, the eight police officers retreated and barricaded themselves into the bar. In a reversal of roles, the LGBT crowd then tried to break in after them, while at least one person attempted to set the bar on fire. The arrival of police reinforcements likely kept those inside the bar from firing on the protesters. However, even the additional officers, who were members of an elite riot-control unit, could not immediately quell the uprising. The police would scatter people by wading into the crowd swinging their billy clubs, but rather than flee the area, the demonstrators simply ran around the block and, regrouping behind the riot squad, continued to jeer and throw objects. At one point, the police turned around to a situation for which their training undoubtedly did not prepare them: a chorus line of drag queens, calling themselves the "Stonewall girls," kicked up their heels—a la the Rockettes—and sang mockingly at the officers. Eventually, the police succeeded in dispersing the crowd, but only for the night. The rioting was similarly violent the following evening—some witnesses say more so—and sporadic and less combative demonstrations continued for the next several days (Duberman, 1993).

The effects of the Stonewall Riots were both immediate and far-reaching. Among the first to notice a change in the LGBT community was Deputy Inspector Seymour Pine, the police officer who led the raid on the bar that night. "For those of us in public morals, things were completely changed," Pine stated after the rebellion. "Suddenly [LGBT people] were not submissive anymore," (Duberman, 1993: 203).

LGBT youth, in particular, felt a sense of empowerment and were unwilling to remain in the closet. At the time of the Stonewall Riots, gay rights groups—often chapters of the Student Homophile League—existed at just six colleges in the United States, almost all of which were large universities in the Northeast. By 1971, groups had been formed at hundreds of colleges and universities throughout the country (Beemyn, 2003). Reflecting the sense of militancy that had fueled the uprising, many of the new groups named themselves after the Gay Liberation Front (GLF) that was formed in New York City a month after the riots, and typically had a more radical political agenda than the earlier student organizations. Many of these groups were also initially more welcoming to crossdressers, drag queens, and transsexuals than the pre-Stonewall groups, and a number of transgender people helped form Gay Liberation Fronts.

Transgender people also established their own organizations in the immediate aftermath of the Stonewall Riots. Sylvia Rivera and Marsha P. Johnson, an African American transgender woman who had likewise been involved in the riots, founded Street Transvestite Action Revolutionaries (STAR) in New York City in 1970 to support and to fight for the rights of the many young transgender people who were living on the city's streets. Rivera and Johnson hustled to open STAR House, a place where the youth could receive shelter, clothing, and food without needing to hustle themselves. The house remained open for two or three years and inspired similar efforts in Chicago, California, and England. Also in New York City in 1970, Lee Brewster and Bunny Eisenhower founded the Queens Liberation Front and led a campaign that decriminalized crossdressing in New York. Brewster also began *Drag*, one of the first politically oriented trans publications, in 1970 (Feinberg, 1998; Zagria, 2009). During this same time, trans man Jude Patton, along with Sister Mary Elizabeth Clark (formerly known as Joanna Clark), used funding from Erickson to start disseminating information to trans people (Moonhawk River Stone, personal communication, May 12, 2013; Jamison Green, personal communication, June 6, 2013).

FROM A PHENOMENON TO AN EMPIRE: THE ANTI-TRANSGENDER BACKLASH

Despite the central role of gender nonconforming people in the Stonewall Riots and their involvement in the initial political organizing that followed, much of the broader movement soon abandoned them in an attempt to appear more acceptable to mainstream society. Six months after the riots, a group comprised mostly of White middle-class gay men formed the Gay Activists Alliance (GAA) in New York City to work "completely and solely" for their own equal rights (Duberman, 1993: 232). The group did not consider transgender people to be relevant to its mission; GAA would not even provide a loan to pay the rent to keep STAR House open or support a dance to raise the funds. Transgender people also did not feel welcomed in the group. Marsha P. Johnson remembered that she and Rivera were stared at when they attended GAA meetings, being the only people in drag and sometimes the only people of color there (Jay & Young, 1972). Similar gay groups that excluded transgender people subsequently formed in other cities.

Transgender women often faced rejection in the 1970s from members of lesbian organizations as well, many of whom viewed them not as "real women" but as "male infiltrators." One of the most well-known victims of such prejudice was Beth Elliott, an openly transsexual lesbian activist and singer who joined the San Francisco chapter of the groundbreaking lesbian group the Daughters of Bilitis in 1971 and became its vice president and the editor of its newsletter. Although Elliott had been accepted for membership, she was forced out the following year as part of a campaign in opposition to her involvement in the 1973 West Coast Lesbian Feminist Conference. Elliott was on the conference's planning committee and a scheduled performer, but when she took the stage, some audience members attempted to shout her down, saying that she was a man. Others defended her. Elliott managed to get through her performance, but the controversy continued. In the keynote speech, feminist Robin Morgan viciously attacked Elliott, referring to her as a "male transvestite" who was "leeching off women who have spent entire lives *as women* in women's bodies." Morgan concluded her diatribe by declaring: "I charge him as an opportunist, an infiltrator, and a destroyer—with the mentality of a rapist," (Gallo, 2006; Stryker, 2008: 104–05). Morgan called on the conference attendees to vote to eject Elliott. Although more than two-thirds reportedly chose to allow her to remain, Elliot was emotionally traumatized by the experience and decided to leave anyway.

The campaign against Elliott marked the start of the exclusionist policing of "women's spaces" by some lesbian separatists. Another target was Sandy Stone, a sound engineer who, as part of the all-women Olivia Records, helped create the genre of women's music in the mid 1970s. Stone had disclosed her transsexuality to the record collective and had its support, but when her gender history became widely known, Olivia was deluged with hate mail from lesbians—some threatening violence, others threatening a boycott, if Stone was not fired. The collective initially defended her, but fearing that they would be put out of business, they reluctantly asked Stone to resign, which she did in 1979 (Califia, 1997; Devor & Matte, 2006).

Many lesbians had left activist organizations like GLF and GAA in the early and mid 1970s because of the sexism of gay men, but one area of agreement between the two groups was their rejection of transgender people. In 1973, lesbian separatists and more conservative gay men in San Francisco organized an alternative Pride parade that banned transgender people and individuals in drag; in subsequent years, this event became the city's main Pride celebration. At the New York City Pride rally in 1973, Jean O'Leary of Lesbian Feminist Liberation read a statement that denounced drag queens as an insult to women, which nearly provoked a riot and further marked the exclusion of transgender people from the "lesbian and gay" rights movement (Clendinen & Nagourney, 1999; Stryker, 2008).

Arguably the most vitriolic and influential attack on transgender people was Janice Raymond's *The Transsexual Empire: The Making of the She-Male*, published in 1979 and reissued in 1994. Raymond, a leading scholar in women's studies, fomented the witch hunt against Sandy Stone and effectively made transsexual women pariahs in many lesbian feminist communities. Whereas Robin Morgan argued that transsexual women who entered "women's spaces" had "the mentality of a rapist," Raymond went further, stating that they *are* rapists. In one of the most infamous passages, she claims: "All [female] transsexuals rape women's bodies by reducing the real female form to an artifact, appropriating this body for themselves." She also contends that their supposedly secretive presence in lesbian feminist spaces constitutes an act of forced penetration that "violates women's sexuality and spirit" (104).

For Raymond, transsexual women are not women but "castrated" and "deviant" men who were a creation of the medical and psychological specialties that arose in support of gender-affirming surgeries—"the transsexual empire" to which her title refers. Ignoring centuries of gender nonconformity in cultures around the world, she erroneously considers transsexuality to be a recent phenomenon stemming from the development of genital surgeries.

In an attempt to discredit transsexuality, Raymond repeatedly seeks to link it with Nazism. Based on dubious evidence, she initially insists that "at least one transsexual operation was done in the camps," but seemingly anticipating being challenged on the accuracy of this statement, she then becomes less definitive, claiming that "some transsexual research and technology may well have been initiated and developed in the camps," (152). Still, a lack of proof does not deter her from comparing the gender identity clinics to the Nazi eugenics movement and the extermination of millions of people in the Holocaust: "What we are witnessing in the transsexual context is a science at the service of a patriarchal ideology of sex-role conformity in the same way that breeding for blond hair and blue eyes became a so-called science at the service of Nordic racial conformity," (149).

This association fits in with Raymond's paranoid conspiracy theory that male medical doctors were using transsexual women to create docile, male-identified "artificial" women—a la *The Stepford Wives*—in order to infiltrate lesbian communities and undermine feminism. She even seriously suggests that feminists who speak out against trans-sexuality might one day be sent for brainwashing: "It is not inconceivable that gender identity clinics, again in the name of therapy, could become centers of sex-role control for nontranssexuals," (Califia, 1997: 97; Raymond, 2006). To resist being taken over by the evil "transsexual empire," Raymond advocates for a drastic reduction in the availability of gender-affirming surgery and recommends that transsexual individuals instead undergo "gender reorientation" (Stryker, 2008: 110).

Raymond's inflammatory rhetoric and false allegations had a significant effect, not just within lesbian communities, but also within the medical profession. Despite being portrayed as part of the "transsexual empire," the medical establishment largely opposed the gender identity clinics because of the same anti-transgender prejudice. Moreover, as stated above, the clinics performed only a small number of surgeries, turning away thousands of applicants. Influenced in part by Raymond's anti-transsexual attacks, the clinics performed even fewer surgeries and began to shut down altogether, starting with the Johns Hopkins program in 1979—the same year that *The Transsexual Empire* was published.

Another factor in the closing of the Hopkins program and other gender identity clinics was the publication of a study in 1979 by its director, Jon Meyer, and his secretary, Donna Reter, that purportedly showed "no objective improvement" among individuals who had undergone gender-affirming surgery at Hopkins as compared to a group of transsexuals who had been turned down for surgery or had changed their mind (Denny, 2006: 176). Meyer and Reter's study has been widely criticized for the arbitrary nature of its rating scale, as well as for its value judgments: individuals who did not improve their socio-economic standing, who continued to see a therapist, or who were unmarried or with a same-sex partner were deemed to be less well-adjusted. In addition, noticeably absent was any measure of the participants' satisfaction or happiness, despite Meyer and Reter admitting that only one of the individuals who underwent gender-affirming surgery expressed any regrets at having done so (and in this person's case, because the surgery had been performed poorly). Other studies from the period found much more positive outcomes from surgery (Bullough & Bullough, 1998; Rudacille, 2005).

The bias of Meyer and Reter's study was confirmed by a subsequent investigative report, which concluded that "the ending of surgery at the GIC [gender identity clinic] now appears to have been orchestrated by certain figures at Hopkins who, for personal rather than scientific reasons, staunchly opposed any form of sex reassignment," (Denny, 2006: 176). One of these figures was Paul McHugh, the chair of the Psychiatry Department at Hopkins and the doctor who oversaw the clinic. After ending the program, McHugh admitted that this had been his intention since being hired in 1975. In a subsequent interview, he stated, "my personal feeling is that surgery is not a proper treatment for a psychiatric disorder, and it's clear to me that these patients have severe psychological problems that don't go away following surgery," (Zagria, 2010).

McHugh's position that transsexual people were mentally disordered was a widespread belief among psychiatrists in the 1970s, despite the decades-long history of physicians successfully treating transsexuality as a physical concern. In 1980, this illness model was codified into the third edition of the American Psychiatric Association's *Diagnostic and Statistical Manual of Mental Disorders* (*DSM*), which defined "transsexualism" as a "disorder" characterized by "a persistent sense of discomfort and inappropriateness about one's anatomic sex and a persistent wish to be rid of one's genitals and to live as a member of the other sex," (261–62). Despite the efforts of some transgender activists and allies to remove the diagnosis (just as "homosexuality" had been removed before the third edition), transsexuality continued to be listed as a psychological disorder in subsequent editions. The 1994 version of the *DSM* replaced the category "transsexualism" with "gender identity disorder," but the diagnostic criteria remained largely unchanged. "A strong and persistent cross-gender identification" was evidence of a psychopathology (532). The 2013 edition of the *DSM* makes significant progress in destigmatizing transsexuality by replacing "gender identity disorder" with "gender dysphoria," which is described as emotional distress resulting from "a marked incongruence between one's experienced/expressed gender and assigned gender." However, the latest version still largely pathologizes gender nonconformity among children and includes a category of "Transvestic Disorder," which, according to trans activist Kelley Winters (2010, 2012), "labels gender expression not stereotypically associated with assigned birth sex as inherently pathological and sexually deviant."

FEMINISM AND TRANS IDENTITY OVER TIME

It may seem obvious that feminist and trans politics go together like peanut butter and jelly. In both feminist and trans politics, there is a concern with gender oppression, so there appears to be a common cause. Trans women not only experience transphobia but also sexism; many trans *men* have had first-hand experience with sexism prior to transition (and even after transition if they are transphobically viewed as "really women"). So it might be surprising to learn that some (non-trans) feminists have viewed trans people in hostile, transphobic ways.

Continued

In the 1970s and 1980s, influential "second wave" (non-trans) feminists such as Robin Morgan, Mary Daly, and Janice Raymond represented trans women as rapists and boundary-violators trying to invade women's space. Trans men were disregarded as mere tokens used to hide the patriarchal nature of the phenomenon of transsexuality. Raymond's *The Transsexual Empire: The Making of the She-Male* systemizes these hostile views and in trans circles it is widely regarded as a "classic" of transphobic literature. Raymond's overall claim is that transsexuality ought to be "morally mandated" out of existence. In her view, transsexuality arises as a consequence of unhappiness with existing "sex-roles." So to her, the problem is not medical in nature – it is social. And the social problem is *sexism*. By treating transsexuality as a medical problem, the sex-role system is maintained rather than destroyed, and what needs to be done, instead, according to Raymond, is to eradicate the sex-role system and this can be done only through education. For Raymond the goal is to completely get away from sex-roles. And because of this, she thinks that trans people who undergo medical transformation violate their own bodily integrity.

Things have changed quite a bit since then. While there are still non-trans feminists with these types of views, they are now in the minority. Much of this has to do with the emergence of so-called "third wave feminism." Queer theory, which developed in the nineties, played an important role in the development of trans theory and transgender politics (also during the nineties). Indeed, it has become a central tenet that transgender people are those who challenge the existing categories of "woman" and "man" – that is, those who are "beyond the binary." One of the most important consequences of this development is that it became possible to view trans people as oppressed in a way that was not reduced to sexism. *Other* forms of gender oppression besides sexism were recognized.

Perhaps the most important strand of "third wave feminism" is the view that one cannot focus on only one kind of oppression (sexism) to the exclusion of others (racism). Women of color critiqued the early ("second wave") feminism as racially biased. The core idea is that kinds of oppression (e.g. sexism) cannot be understood and opposed without focusing on *other* kinds of oppression (such as racism) (The Combahee River Collective is one group that wrote about this). A woman of color not only has to confront sexism, she has to confront racism. And sometimes racism and sexism can be experienced as inseparable. This means that the attempt to focus only on sexism is something that would only ever make sense to somebody who never had to deal with racism in the first place. It would only make sense to someone who had White privilege.

This leads to the rejection of the view that there is a common universal experience of womanhood. Women of color who experience racism and sexism bound up together have different experiences of womanhood than do White women who experience White privilege and sexism bound up together. And this provides an important framework for "trans/feminism" which focuses on the *intersections* of trans and sexist oppression. One important lesson of Emi Koyama's work is that any form of trans/feminism which marginalizes other forms of oppression, such as racism, does so at its own peril.

Despite these positive developments, there remains an important challenge for "trans/feminism." Many trans people simply don't identity as "beyond the binary" at all—they identify as plain men and women. Obviously the "beyond the binary" idea doesn't provide much help to those trans people who, in this view, are regarded as "gender conservative." If trans oppression and resistance are not framed in terms of the dreaded binary, then how should they be understood? How do we understand trans oppression/resistance if *both* "beyond the binary" and "trapped in the wrong body" are found to be inadequate?

We might need a completely new theory.

Talia Bettcher is a Philosophy Professor at Cal State Los Angeles.

TRANSGENDER ACTIVISM IN THE LATE TWENTIETH CENTURY

The 1970s to the early 1980s can be considered the contemporary nadir for transgender people. However, the period did have a few bright spots. Except for Jorgensen's autobiography, the stories of transsexual women that were published in the 1960s and early 1970s were lurid exposés of female impersonators, strippers, and prostitutes with tabloid titles like *"I Changed My Sex!"* and *"I Want to Be a Woman!"* (Sherman, 1964; Star, 1963). But the 1970s marked the beginning of a steady stream of non-sensational transsexual books, mostly by individuals who had been successful in society as men before transitioning to female. More transgender people also began to turn to activism at this time to counter the stigma and hostility they experienced.

This new wave of transsexual autobiographies began with the 1974 publications of Jan Morris's *Conundrum* and Canary Conn's *Canary*. Morris, a renowned British author and travel writer who had accompanied the first known expedition to reach the summit of Mount Everest in 1953, describes how she sublimated her sense of herself as female through constant travel before undergoing gender-affirming surgery in 1972. Conn, a rising teenage rock star, transitioned in her early 20s, which seems to have led to the end of her singing career, whereas Morris continued to be a successful writer. Another autobiography, *Mirror Image*, written in 1978 by award-winning

Chicago Tribune newspaper reporter Nancy Hunt, did not receive as much publicity, but more than other writers, Hunt discusses how transitioning affected her romantic relationships.

The most well-known autobiography of the era was Renée Richards' *Second Serve*, published in 1983. Richards achieved international notoriety for successfully suing the Women's Tennis Association when it barred her from competing in the 1976 US Women's Open under a newly introduced "women-born women" policy. The court decision was groundbreaking and opened the door for other transsexual athletes. Surprisingly, Richards devotes relatively few pages to the case or her tennis career. Instead, she dedicates the majority of her memoir to describing her struggle to accept herself as female, which came only after three failed attempts to go back to living as a man.

While the best-selling autobiographies by Jorgensen, Morris, and Richards, and to a lesser extent the memoirs by Conn and Hunt, drew significant attention to the lives of transsexual women, the lack of autobiographies by transsexual men contributed to their invisibility. The only full-length narrative by a trans man published in the United States prior to the 1990s was Mario Martino's 1977 book *Emergence: A Transsexual Autobiography* (Stryker, 2008). Just as Morris, Hunt, and Richards pursued traditionally male careers in order to conform to societal gender expectations and to try to convince themselves and others of their masculinity, Martino entered a convent school, hoping to suppress his feelings and be more feminine. Not surprisingly, he was unsuccessful, and after transitioning, began to provide support to other transsexual men.

Shortly before Martino's book was published, Steve Dain became the first public trans man. Dain was a high school girls' physical education teacher who fought to retain his job after transitioning in 1976, appearing on talk shows across the country. Although he ultimately won the right to teach again, he could not find a school that would hire him, so became a chiropractor with his own business. He died in 2007 of metastatic breast cancer at age 68 (Jamison Green, personal communication, June 6, 2013).

As discussed above, another high point for transgender people in the 1970s and early 1980s was the expansion of organizing efforts by heterosexual, as well as bisexual and gay male crossdressers, which transformed local groups into national organizations. Crossdressers also started Fantasia Fair (2011), a weeklong series of social, entertainment, and education events in Provincetown, Massachusetts. First held in 1975, "The Fair" has become the oldest continuing transgender event in the United States. Transsexual women likewise established many more support groups—sometimes inclusive of heterosexual male crossdressers who chose not to affiliate with Tri-Ess, and other times inclusive of transsexual men. But few trans men joined these groups, as they were dominated by transsexual women and, with meetings focused on topics such as female make-up and clothing tips, failed to address the needs of transsexual men.

A few trans male support groups were started in the 1970s and early 1980s, including groups in Los Angeles, New York City, and Toronto (Green, 2004). The first trans male educational and support organization in the United States, which was called simply "FTM," was begun in San Francisco in 1986 by Lou Sullivan, a gay transsexual man. The group published the quarterly *FTM Newsletter*, which became the leading source of information related to trans men and had hundreds of subscribers from around the world. In 1990, Sullivan also compiled the first guide for trans men, *Information for the Female-to-Male Crossdresser and Transsexual*, and wrote the first book explicitly about a trans male individual—a biography of Jack Bee Garland, a female-assigned journalist and social worker who lived as a man for 40 years in San Francisco in the late nineteenth and early twentieth centuries (Stryker, 2008). Sullivan died from complications from AIDS at the age of 39 in 1991.

Under the subsequent leadership of Jamison Green (2004), FTM, which changed its name to FTM International in 1994, became the largest trans male organization in the world. Green went on to become a more public figure than Sullivan had been, convening the first trans male conference in 1995 (thanks to a grant from Dallas Denny), educating police officers and lawmakers, and working to reform the World Professional Association for Transgender Health (WPATH) Standards of Care. Following in the footsteps of Stephen Whittle, Green was elected as the second trans President of WPATH.

A larger rights movement also grew significantly in the 1990s, facilitated by the increasing use of the term "transgender" to encompass all individuals whose gender identity or expression differs from the social norms of the gender assigned to them at birth. This wider application of "transgender" developed among writers and activists beginning in the mid 1980s and started to catch on more widely in the early 1990s. In her groundbreaking article "The Transgender Alternative," published in the trans community journals *Chrysalis Quarterly* and *Tapestry* in 1991, Holly Boswell suggested that "transgender" is a term that "encompasses the whole spectrum" of gender diversity and brings together all gender nonconforming people (Stryker, 2008: 123). This understanding became most strongly associated with socialist writer and activist Leslie Feinberg, who called on all people who face discrimination for not conforming to gender norms to organize around their shared oppression in hir 1992 pamphlet *Transgender Liberation: A Movement Whose Time Has Come* and in hir subsequent books, *Transgender Warriors* and *Trans Liberation*. The expansive meaning of the term was further popularized by writers such as Kate Bornstein and Martine Rothblatt, and this usage became commonplace by the late 1990s (Bornstein, 1994; Feinberg, 1992, 1996, 1998; Rothblatt, 1994).

The broad-based political movement that Feinberg envisioned came to fruition in response to continued acts of discrimination and violence against transgender people. Reflecting the persistence of anti-transgender bias among some lesbian feminists, transsexual women were banned from the National Lesbian Conference in 1991 and a postoperative transsexual woman, Nancy Jean Burkholder, was expelled that same year from the Michigan Womyn's Music Festival. The festival, an annual weeklong women's outdoor music and cultural event, has been a pilgrimage for thousands of lesbians since it began in 1976. While the event had always been for "womyn only," Burkholder's removal was the first known exclusion of a transsexual woman; afterward, festival organizers articulated a policy limiting attendance to "womyn-born womyn" (Rubin, 2006).

The growth of an out transgender community over the course of little more than a decade is demonstrated by the different responses to the expulsions of Stone and Burkholder from lesbian-feminist cultural institutions. While few spoke publicly in Stone's defense in 1979, the ouster of Burkholder in 1991 was widely denounced and led to protests at "Michigan" itself. Transgender activists passed out thousands of "I might be transsexual" buttons to festival goers the next year, and following the removal of four more transsexual women in 1993, they created what became known as "Camp Trans" across from the entrance to the festival.

The initial Camp Trans consisted of several dozen transsexual women and supporters who leafleted Michigan attendees and held workshops and readings that attracted hundreds of women from the other side of the road. The significance of this protest was noted by Riki Wilchins, one of the main organizers: "Camp Trans was the first time transpeople ever coordinated and pulled off a national event. Not only that, it was the first time that significant numbers of the hard-core lesbian-feminist community backed us," (Boyd, 2006; Califia, 1997: 227; Denny, 2006). The organizers of the Michigan Womyn's Music Festival, though, refused to change their policy, leading transgender activists to re-establish Camp Trans in 1999. The festival leadership finally gave in to the pressure in the mid 2000s and now no longer actively enforces their policy, while continuing to insist that only womyn-born womyn should attend. The situation today is "Don't Ask, Don't Tell": the festival organizers do not press the issue, and a number of transsexual women have attended the festival without calling significant attention to themselves. Camp Trans (2011) continues to be held to advocate, as their slogan states, for "room for all kinds of womyn."

It was not only lesbian feminists who discriminated against transgender people in the early 1990s. When lesbian and gay leaders were planning to hold a March on Washington in 1993, transgender activists, with the support of bisexual allies, sought to have the word "transgender" added to the name of the event. Although some local organizing committees supported transgender inclusion, the march's national steering committee voted by a significant margin to have the name be the "March on Washington for Lesbian, Gay, and Bi Equal Rights and Liberation." Like their banishment from the Michigan Womyn's Music Festival, their exclusion from the title of the march prompted many transgender people to become more politically active and for the transgender community to become more organized.

Another major incident that mobilized a large number of transgender people was the murder of twenty-one-year-old Brandon Teena near Falls City, Nebraska in the early hours of New Year's Day in 1994. Teena lived as a man, but was outed as being assigned female at birth when the county sheriff's office reported his arrest on a misdemeanor to the local newspaper. Following the disclosure, two men whom Teena thought to be friends, John Lotter and Tom Nissen, beat and raped him, and a week after he reported the sexual assault to the sheriff, the two killed Teena and two others. Transgender people and allies were incensed not only by the horrific murders and the bias of the police for failing to arrest Lotter and Nissen after the rape, but also by the initial media coverage, in which Teena was often portrayed as a butch lesbian and referred to as "her" (Califia, 1997).

Teena's murder touched off a series of important protests. In response to the particularly transgender-insensitive reporting of the *Village Voice*, members of Transexual Menace, a direct action group that Riki Wilchins and Denise Norris had just started in New York City, picketed outside of the newspaper's offices. The group and other transgender activists also held a vigil outside of the Nebraska courthouse where Lotter was standing trial in 1995. Wilchins called the event "a turning point for trans activism," because it was the first highly visible national demonstration organized by trans-gender people and helped draw unprecedented media attention to an anti-transgender hate crime (Califia, 1997: 232). Teena's life and death became the subject of news stories, books, and movies, including Kimberly Peirce's 1999 film *Boys Don't Cry*, in which Hilary Swank played Teena and won an Academy Award for Best Actress. What also made this case different was that Teena's killers received significant sentences—Nissen was given life imprisonment without the possibility of parole and Lotter the death penalty.

In addition to Camp Trans and Transexual Menace, a number of other transgender institutions and groups were established in the early and mid 1990s. Dallas Denny created the American Educational Gender Information Service (AEGIS) in Decatur, Georgia in 1990 to disseminate information about transgender people, which included publishing *Chrysalis Quarterly* and *The Transgender Treatment Bulletin* (AEGIS, 1999). One of the largest annual transgender events, the Southern Comfort conference, began in Atlanta in 1991, and the International Conference on Transgender Law and Employment Policy, a yearly meeting to discuss strategies for creating transgender-supportive laws, was convened by attorney Phyllis Frye in Houston from 1992–1997 (Frye, 2001; Stryker, 2008). Also in 1992, Bet Power founded the East Coast FTM Group, the first FTM-only support group in the Eastern United States, in Northampton, Massachusetts. Today, it is the second oldest continuing transmasculine organization in the world (B. Power, personal communication, June 15, 2011). In 1995, Riki Wilchins began the Gender Public Advocacy Coalition (GenderPAC), a national organization whose accomplishments included producing some of the first reports on hate crimes against gender nonconforming people and holding an annual National Gender Lobby Day to urge members of Congress to address gender-based violence and discrimination.

The 1990s also saw the highly visible, direct-action tactics pioneered by radical groups like ACT-UP (AIDS Coalition to Unleash Power) and Queer Nation begin to infuse the transgender movement. The first transgender organization to reflect this new queer activism was Transgender Nation, a subgroup of San Francisco's Queer Nation chapter, which was formed in 1992 by Anne Ogborn to fight anti-trans prejudice within the chapter and within society (Stryker, 2008). Soon, Transgender Nation chapters were established in several other cities, most notably in Washington, D.C., where the group helped lead the response to the death of Tyra Hunter, a transsexual woman who died in 1995 after D.C. paramedics denied her medical treatment following the discovery that she was transgender. Although Transgender Nation was short-lived, it inspired the creation of two other chapter-based transgender activist groups, Transexual Menace and It's Time America!, and led the transgender movement to become more visible and confrontational.

But the most significant factor in the development of a national transgender movement may have been the rise of the Internet in the mid 1990s. As sociologist Eve Shapiro (2010) states, the Internet revolutionized the movement by "allow[ing] transgender people to connect with one another more easily, especially those who live in geographically isolated places," and by "giv[ing] individuals ways to experiment with defining their gender," (132). Shapiro shows how online activism mobilized large numbers of people and generated substantial media attention in the debate over the American Psychiatric Association's pathologizing of transgender people in the *DSM*.

A 2006 national transgender study by Genny Beemyn and Sue Rankin also documented the importance of the Internet, especially for the participants under fifty years old, for whom the Web was their primary method of meeting others like themselves and accessing resources. The older participants less commonly socialized virtually, but many first recognized themselves as transgender and realized that they were not alone through exploring the Web. The study respondents in their forties or older often described feeling isolated or being in denial about their identities for decades—until they discovered online resources. Tina, an interviewee who had cross-dressed for forty years, captured the sentiments of many participants: "I learned from reading, but I was *liberated* by the Internet!" (Beemyn & Rankin, 2011: 57–58).

The Internet also helped to give voice to trans people of color. Monica Roberts, a Black trans woman from Houston who transitioned in 1994, started the award-winning blog TransGriot, which has become one of the most well-known hubs for news and information about trans people of color (Roberts, n.d.).

Like the growth of the Internet, the development of queer studies in the early 1990s helped create a space for transgender people. Texts by queer theorists, such as Gloria Anzaldúa (1987), Diana Fuss (1989), Judith Butler (1990), Eve Kosofsky Sedgwick (1990), and Teresa de Lauretis (1991), laid the groundwork for transgender scholarship and greatly influenced how gender and sexuality were considered in academia. Transgender studies emerged as its own discipline in the late 1990s and early 2000s through conferences, academic listservs, special journal issues, and articles and books by the first generation of scholars whose primary area of research was transgender people. These scholars included Susan Stryker (1994), C. Jacob Hale (1996), Aaron Devor

(1997), Judith Halberstam (1998), Jay Prosser (1998), Jason Cromwell (1999), Viviane Namaste (2000), and Stephen Whittle (2002).

THE START OF TRANS-ACTIVISM, 1994–1995

It started, as serious things often do, with a murder and a fight. The fight was the simple part. An attendee at the Michigan Womyn's Music Festival was stopped by two women from Security and asked if she was really a man. She refused to affirm or deny. So, asserting that they thought she was a man, Nancy Jean Burkholder was forcibly evicted from the event. Afterward, the Festival quietly and retroactively announced a new policy it called "womyn-born-womyn"—a weird, supposedly feminist-y sounding neologism which everyone concerned understood to mean "no trannies allowed." Janis Walworth, a friend who had accompanied Nancy, reached out to several activists about coming to the next year's Festival to raise awareness—few people even knew what had happened or were aware of the policy.

Four of us showed up that year. We camped out across the road from the main gate in the National Forest. Not to miss a beat, Festival Security was soon talking with Park Rangers and asking them to throw us out, but fortunately there were no grounds for doing so. We planned several workshops, distributed a few fliers to surprised attendees driving and walking by, and sat back to see what would happen next. What happened was that hundreds of women walked miles out of the Festival to attend our workshops, hang out, and offer support. A few even came to stay. Our little campground became crowded every evening. It became obvious that this was something that could scale, and we began laying plans for a bigger, better presence the next year. Transgender people were pushing back.

In fact, the idea of transgender protest had been circulating in the community. Transgender Nation, modeled on (and some said a reaction to transphobia in) Queer Nation, had been launched by Anne Ogborn in San Francisco. It had some early successes, but hadn't really caught on. This was still at a time when many if not most of us still hoped to "pass." There were relatively few public transgender activists. Susan Stryker had written a manifesto just a few years earlier in which she pointed to trans-visibility as a critical factor in launching transgender advocacy. But transgender people organizing politically and in public to confront cisgender bigotry (as opposed to coming together socially inside hotel conferences) was rare.

Some of us decided to print up a batch of "Transexual Menace" T-shirts, modeled on a combination of the Lavender Menace (who confronted NOW

Continued

over its exclusion of lesbians) and the genderfuck of Rocky Horror Picture Show. We began handing them out any time we came together politically for events. They were visible, cheeky, and determinedly tongue-in-cheek, both outing ourselves but also mocking straights for their fear and loathing of transsexuals... and an instant hit. Being "out, loud, and proud" was new for transpeople used to being very closeted.

I announced I was going to take a carload of T-shirts to the Southern Comfort conference in Atlanta with some of the NY Menace to see how they would play on a larger stage. This immediately launched widespread rumors that the Menace was coming to "disrupt" the conference and ruin the event. That was okay – the more hysteria the better. We could mock trans-paranoia as well as cis paranoia. When I arrived every one of the dozens of T-shirts was gone within 24 hours. Not just transsexuals, but academics, and even straight male crossdressers (and their wives!) who had been closeted all their lives wore the black, blood-dripping red T-shirts... *over their dresses*... out of the hotel, all over Atlanta.

This was entirely new. Clearly, something was shifting in trans political consciousness. Pride was challenging, if not entirely replacing, passing. Within two years activists had started Menace chapters in 39 cities. Shifting, indeed.

Around this time, the Village Voice published a piece about the 1994 murder of FTM Brandon Teena, rubbing salt in the wound by positioning Brandon as a "hot butch," a lesbian dreamboat, and referring to him as "Tee-na" and "she" and "her" throughout. The Menace promptly picketed both the Voice and the piece's author. Many other gay and lesbian media outlets ignored the murder entirely because he wasn't (wait for it...) gay or lesbian.

The murder trial of Brandon's assailants, John Lotter and Tom Nissen, was set to start in Falls City, NE. We decided there needed to be a visible, public response from the community. With Boston's Nancy Nangeroni and Tony Baretto-Neto, a transgender deputy sheriff from Florida (who provided security), we announced a Memorial Vigil outside the courthouse on the first day of the trial. We didn't know what would happen or if anyone would show. Forty-two people showed up, including Leslie Feinberg (author of Stone Butch Blues) and a quiet unknown filmmaker named Kimberly Pierce working on a script tentatively titled Boys Don't Cry.

Apparently, transsexuals in black Menace T-shirts was not a common sight in Falls City, Nebraska. By noon, the local neo-Nazis showed up, spitting at us out of the windows of their trucks and trying to run us off the sidewalks. Tony had liaised with the Sheriff's office beforehand and when a group of the skinheads advanced toward us on foot, a line of Deputy Sheriffs was all that stood between us and serious violence. It was chilling, knowing we were depending on the same Sheriff's office that had outed Brandon and led to his death, perhaps even some of the same officers. Afterward, Tony founded Transgender Officers Protect & Serve (TOPS).

Back in Michigan, plans were forming for what was inevitably becoming known as "Camp Trans." That year, 30 of us showed up, again camping out across from the main gate. This time, instead of a few workshops, we had scheduled three solid days of workshops, musical events, and teach-ins, with a special speak-out by Leslie Feinberg. We drew almost a thousand attendees over three days, many of whom went back in wearing Menace T-shirts; even supportive members of Security wore them openly. Then, on the last day, a group of leather-clad Lesbian Avengers asked why we didn't just come inside. Kidding, I asked them why they didn't just send an escort. To my shock, they agreed instantly. That evening, four dozen of them showed up and escorted Leslie Feinberg, myself, and 10 other members of Camp Trans into the Festival and to a presentation attended by hundreds of waiting fans and supporters. The trans-discrimination policy, while still official policy, was for all intents broken.

Alas, the train of trans murders was not. Brandon's death was a wake-up call. Once we started paying attention to and tracking transgender murders, it was shocking how many there were. Deborah Forte, Channelle Pickett, Christian Paige, James Percy Rivers, Tarayon Corbitt, Quincy Taylor, Tyra Hunter—and that was just 1995.

This was not as immediately obvious as it seems. The Internet was new, there was no Google (that was three years in the future), and many people still didn't have or use email. Finding out about new victims meant calling activists in different cities or looking for local news that began with the vague and stigmatizing words: "The body of man wearing women's clothing. . ."

Nancy, Tony, and I decided whenever a transgender person was murdered, we would fly in to coordinate another memorial vigil. Transgender people from the local community always came out to support the events, and it created fresh media coverage and attention that had been absent.

Yet it quickly became apparent that we couldn't expect to wage a struggle against violence and discrimination from a psychiatric category. We could portray ourselves in media as patients suffering from a medical disorder, or as an oppressed minority demanding their political and civil rights, but it was very difficult to do both simultaneously. The American Psychiatric Association was conveniently holding their annual conference in New York that year. With signboards declaring "Keep Your Diagnoses OFF our Bodies!" and accusing them of "GenderPathoPhilia" (defined "as an unnatural need or desire to

Continued

pathologize any kind of gender that makes you feel uncomfortable"), the NYC Menace picketed the APA. Our list of demands was brief: depathologize transsexuality, just as long ago they had depathologized homosexuality.

It soon became apparent that you couldn't stop the war from a M*A*S*H tent. Transpeople kept dying with regularity – one every few months. We needed to be on the front lines, or at least put transgender issues onto the national agenda. All our actions had been local—one event, one city. I asked New York's Lynn Walker how we could start a more national movement and she answered (quite brilliantly, in retrospect), "start doing things at the national level." Out of that comment came two developments. First was GenderPAC, the first national organization devoted to political advocacy for the right to *gender identity and expression*. It was formalized at a meeting of the community held outside Philadelphia in 1995. The second was National Gender Lobby Day, with activist Jane Fee and Phyllis Frye (now Texas' first transgender judge).

One hundred and four transgender activists and their partners showed up. The *New York Times* led their national news with us. Strangely titled "Shunning *He* and *She* They Fight for Respect," it was accompanied by the picture of a bearded Jamison Green sitting quietly in a suit on the D.C. METRO (which no doubt confused many readers). It was our first real print coverage of transgender political activism. Today you can't pick up the *Times, Washington Post, TIME, Slate* or any other major outlet without reading trans news. But that was the first big piece.

Street activism was all about being insubordinate and loud; it was serious theater, to compel media attention. Capitol Hill was a different game. This was being *professionally trans*, sitting in a business suit in Congressional offices and patiently explaining our community's needs. It was new and intimidating, but also tremendously validating and exhilarating. We were no longer Kate Bornstein's *gender outlaws;* we were citizens, voters, taxpayers. We were legitimate. In spite of that, I frankly expected us all to get arrested on Capitol Hill when we inevitably had to use the women's rooms, especially the many male cross-dressers who had (bravely) shown up. But that didn't happen. And that morning, as the sun rose over the Capitol dome, all of us stood together nervously before a bank of microphones and media cameras, taking turns answering questions before marching off to our first Congressional appointments. It was a sight: 100 transgender people walking off together to meet their elected representatives. A doorway had opened. A community was on the move. Something new had begun.

Riki Wilchins, MA, has written three books on gender theory, founded GenderPAC and The Transexual Menace, and was selected by TIME *as one of "100 Civic Innovators for the 21st Century."*

LGB AND T

The work of transgender activists, writers, and scholars led a growing number of lesbian and gay individuals and groups to become supportive of the rights of transgender people and to consider them a part of what became known as the LGBT community. While many lesbian feminists in the 1970s and 1980s were influenced by *The Transsexual Empire*, many young lesbians in the mid and late 1990s—some of whom had yet to be born when Raymond's book was published—had their attitude toward transgender people shaped by Leslie Feinberg's *Stone Butch Blues* and Kate Bornstein's *Gender Outlaw*. Feinberg's semi-autobiographical 1993 novel tells the moving story of Jess Goldberg, an individual who journeys from being a butch lesbian in the years before the Stonewall Riots, to passing as a man in order to survive the economic recession of the 1970s, to living outside of a gender binary in the 1980s. Bornstein's 1994 work combines memoir, performance, and commentary to offer insights into how society constructs gender. Many young queer women activists, as well as transgender individuals, considered these books necessary reading, and many instructors in LGBT and sexuality studies assigned them in courses in the 1990s.

Another point of connection between trans men and young queer women that resulted in the latter becoming more supportive of transgender people was involvement in drag king culture. Individuals assigned female at birth have long experimented with gender and sought to blur gender lines by performing in "men's" clothing. The contemporary phenomenon of drag king performances emerged in the mid 1980s in London and San Francisco, and within a decade, drag king shows and competitions involving both transgender men and cisgender lesbians were regularly held in major cities in the United States, Canada, Europe, and Australia (Ashburn 2010). "In the last fifteen years, drag king culture has created a rope bridge of intellectual dialogue between the lesbian and transgender communities," states Sile Singleton, an African American transgender person who organizes and performs as Luster/Lustivious de la Virgion in drag king shows. "Because drag kinging by its very nature invites self-exploration into gender, it has nurtured a noticeably less negative backlash toward transgendered bodies" (S. Singelton, personal communication, July 18, 2011). The first international event, the International Drag King Extravaganza, took place in Columbus, Ohio in 1999. It brought together many drag king performers and troupes, as well as individuals who studied, filmed, and photographed drag kings, for the first time (Troka, 2003).

The efforts of transgender activists and allies resulted in many national, state, and local organizations in the United States that had focused primarily on the rights of lesbians, bisexuals, and gay men to begin to address gender identity issues. The National Gay and Lesbian Task Force added transgender people to its mission statement in 1997, and PFLAG (Parents, Families, and Friends of Lesbians and Gays) did so the following year. Other national organizations were initially more hesitant to include transgender people in their work. The largest lesbian and gay rights group,

MALE, FEMALE, OR OTHERWISE

I was born in 1961, and grew up during the cresting height of the civil rights movement, the women's liberation movement, the Black Panthers, the hippie movement, and anti–Vietnam war protests. Sitting at the dinner table, my formative years were filled with the background noise of Walter Cronkite's reports on social unrest and the demands for equality sweeping, not just the good old US of A, but the world. In every newspaper, there were headlines about people demanding to be seen and treated fairly.

However, the reality of my situation was not about personal freedom. My staunchly democratic and liberal mother was terrified by my "mannishness." Her usual re-programming tactics included several verbal assaults referencing my walk and stance (like a peacock), my sweating and smell (like a football player), and my voice and laughter (like Barry White). While I will admit that her unabashed disappointment in the way her "first born turned out" did smart a bit—well a lot—that's another tale. I actually only pretended to be bothered by her attempts to "save me." Secretly, I was relieved that I was recognizable as male, because somewhere I have always known, regardless of an anatomically correct appendage (or, in my case, lack thereof) on the heavenly chart, I am male. Now I won't say it is as simple as that, because for all the soul brother energy I ooze, I am most comfortable when packing in hot pants and 10-inch-high, matching lime pleather go-go boots. I couldn't feel more he than when the bangs of my circa 1971 magenta "Geraldine Jones"-styled wig begin to fall into my 3-inch-long "Patti Labelle"-styled eyelashes, with my chest bound tight into a 36-inch wall of pectoral bulk. Even if I opted for a sensible pair of Cinderella slippers and something unassuming from Casual Corner, there is no wholeness without Mr. Softie. What is most amazing about all of this is that I had little conscious knowledge of these facts, prior to my 1992 involvement with a little historical Midwestern phenom that became known as the H.I.S. Kings Show.

H.I.S. Kings, a female-to-male, crossdressing, gender-bending, lip-synching, and entertainment troupe, was one of the country's first drag king ensembles when it formed in Columbus, Ohio in 1992. The troupe was the accidental brainchild of a couple of bored women's studies graduate students and three in-your-face rad-ass lesbians named Helen, Ivett, and Sue (hence, "H.I.S."). We had no idea that the wardrobe we decided to explore would be so critical to whom we see ourselves as now in terms of sex, sexuality, and gender identity. Personally, I was just trying to shake an overall image, of my "gay and second-wave feminist" self in a lavender batik moo moo playing co-opted ceremonial drums and pushing tofu at placenta parties. This is not to say that we brain-children did not appreciate that ultra-Gaia space. But it was the 1990s. We just wanted to capture some of the fun, high energy, and sexy explorations of the gay-boy-club settings. We wanted to dance dripping hot, sexual, and wild. We were purposefully invested in creating acts that not only pushed beyond conventional notions of masculinity and femininity, but that also disrupted expected depictions of lesbian and gay behavior. On a basic level, we didn't see why gay men "owned" pop culture and gay entertainment. The cathartic nature of the spaces the H.I.S. Kings Show fostered opened up a plane where performers, crew, staff, Kings Courts, and our audiences could be whatever they needed and wanted to be with far less questioning as to whether it was "appropriate behavior" for a girl or a lesbian. After all, in the previous decade, the proponents of third-wave feminism had blazed a path that embraced contradiction and conflict as they worked to include multiculturalism and change.

What I wanted was to be a "queen." Not the Cleopatra-type, per se—although I must admit that the idea of four sets of bulky muscles careening me around to my appointments on an overstuffed, chenille-covered chaise lounge did have a certain appeal. I was more inspired to attain the beauty, grace, ultra-femininity, and pure chutzpah of Flip Wilson's Geraldine, disco-soul entertainer extraordinaire Sylvester, and Columbus, Ohio's favorite circa '80s and '90s female impersonator, the fabulous Miss Georgia Jackson. At the time, it never occurred to me that they were all, at the very least, born males who enjoyed the art of passable crossdressing. I never thought about that. What I tuned into was their energy and womanish-ways or, more accurately, their approach to softening squared bones and hip-wide stances. I would practice to emulate perfectly their movements—the slow swivel of their chin-to-shoulder demur look, their toe-to-heel tip-tap walk, and the rush of air that entwined with their speech, lifting it away from any telltale baritone in their voices.

The first show opened at a dyke bar named Summit Station in Columbus on September 13, 1992. That night five scared "kids," including a birthday girl, a brand new DJ, and three budding drag kings, took the stage with no real idea of what they were doing. However, when the light bulb lit and the opportunity arrived to share all of me as the show's premiere "Hostess with the Mostest," Lustivious Dela Virgion, with the audiences of what, by the second show, would be christened The H.I.S. King Show, I did not hesitate. All I knew was that for 7–20 hours a week, I was surrounded by people who were similar in their chemistry to me. When would I ever again be able to hang out with folks who were open to and accepting "beings" who exhibited multiple genders? There was no turning back. At its height, the experience was exhilarating. At its close, exasperating. All in all, it was a fantastic "coming of gender" trip. And now nearly 20 years later, I know I experienced freedom, as we dared to celebrate masculinity: male, female, and otherwise.

Sile Singleton

the Human Rights Campaign (HRC), amended its mission statement in 2001 and GLAAD (formerly the Gay and Lesbian Alliance Against Defamation) only did so in 2013. On the state and local level, most of the organizations established since the mid 1990s have included transgender people in their names and missions. Cases in point are the professionally staffed offices and centers that have been founded at US and Canadian colleges and universities to further sexual and gender diversity. Among the 26 offices and centers created before 1995, all but three had names indicating that their constituencies were "gay and lesbian" or "gay, lesbian, and bisexual" individuals. Today there are more than 150 such centers and offices, and all are transgender inclusive in both their names and mission statements (Beemyn, 2002; Consortium of Higher Education LGBT Resource Professionals, 2011).

However, the proliferation of LGBT organizations has not always resulted in greater attention to the needs of transgender people; in some cases, the "T" seems to stand for "token," rather than "transgender." The most infamous example of transgender inclusion being little more than rhetoric involved the Human Rights Campaign. In 1994, the organization drafted and had allies in Congress introduce the Employment Non-Discrimination Act (ENDA), a bill to protect workers based on their sexual orientation. Transgender leaders were incensed by the exclusion of "gender identity" and lobbied Congress and the public for it to be added—only to have HRC work to thwart their efforts. Following the failure of the bill by one vote in the Senate, HRC continued to insist on shutting out transgender people when the legislation was reintroduced the next year, fearing that a more inclusive bill would lose votes. In response, transgender activists and allies picketed fourteen of the organization's fundraising events, until HRC agreed to support an amendment to add "gender identity" as a protected class (Califia, 1997). Neither the amendment nor the original bill was approved by Congress, and the legislation was stalled for the next decade.

In 2006, ENDA was revived by openly gay Representative Barney Frank, who, after deciding that the transgender-inclusive version would not readily pass, put forward a measure without transgender protection. Despite the Human Rights Campaign's promise that it would support only transgender-inclusive legislation, the organization endorsed Frank's bill. HRC's about-face showed that some within the mostly older, more conservative lesbian and gay establishment continued to see transgender people as dispensable. However, nearly 400 LGBT groups—virtually every major LGBT organization other than HRC—formed a coalition called United ENDA (2010) to advocate for the restoration of gender identity protection. Although the effort failed to change the bill (which passed the House of Representatives in 2007 but died in the Senate), it represented an unprecedented level of support for transgender rights, and the coalition succeeded in having gender identity language included in ENDA thereafter, demonstrating that much had changed since the movement first abandoned transgender people in the 1970s.

BIBLIOGRAPHY

American Educational Gender Information Service. (1999). What is AEGIS? Retrieved June 21, 2011, from http://www.gender.org/aegis

American Psychiatric Association (1980). *Diagnostic and statistical manual of mental disorders*, Third Edition. Washington, DC: Author.

American Psychiatric Association (1994). *Diagnostic and statistical manual of mental disorders*, Fourth Edition. Washington, DC: Author.

American Psychiatric Association (2010). DSM-5 development. Retrieved June 10, 2011, from http://www.dsm5.org/ProposedRevisions/Pages/proposedrevision.aspx?rid=482

Anonymous. (1989 [1750]). *The female soldier; or, the surprising life and adventures of Hannah Snell*. Los Angeles: William Andrews Clark Memorial Library.

Anonymous. (1933, April 8). Police keep crowd of 200 from third sex. *The Afro-American*, p. 9.

Anzaldúa, G. (1987). *Borderlands/la frontera: The new mestiza*. San Francisco: Spinsters/Aunt Lute.

Ashburn, E. (2010). Drag shows: Drag kings and male impersonators. In C. J. Summers (Ed.), *glbtq: An encyclopedia of gay, lesbian, bisexual, transgender, and queer culture*. Retrieved July 9, 2011, from http://www.glbtq.com/arts/drag_kings.html.

Beemyn, B. (2002). The development and administration of campus LGBT centers and offices. In R. Sanlo, S. Rankin, & R. Schoenberg (Eds.), *Our place on campus: Lesbian, gay, bisexual, transgender services and programs in higher education* (pp. 25–32). Westport, CT: Greenwood Press.

Beemyn, B. (2003). The silence is broken: A history of the first lesbian, gay, and bisexual college student groups. *Journal of the History of Sexuality*, 12, 205–223.

Beemyn, B. G. (2008). Genderqueer. In J. O'Brien (Ed.), *Encyclopedia of gender and society*, Vol. 2 (pp. 370–71). Thousand Oaks, CA: Sage Publications.

Beemyn, G. (2013). Campus Pride Trans Policy Clearinghouse. Retrieved November 18, 2013, from http://www.campuspride.org/tpc

Beemyn, G., & Rankin, S. (2011). *The lives of transgender people*. New York: Columbia University Press.

Benjamin, H. (1966). *The transsexual phenomenon*. New York: Julian Press.

Besnier, N. (1994). Polynesian gender liminality through time and space. In G. Herdt (Ed.), *Third sex, third gender: Beyond sexual dimorphism in culture and history* (pp. 285–328). New York: Zone Books.

Bleys, R. C. (1995). *The geography of perversion: Make-to-male sexual behavior outside the West and the ethnographic imagination, 1750–1918*. New York: New York University Press.

Boag, P. (2011). *Re-dressing America's Frontier Past*. Berkeley: University of California Press.

Bolin, A. (1988). *In search of Eve: Transsexual rites of passage*. New York: Bergin & Garvey.

Bolin, A. (1994). Transcending and transgendering: Male-to-female transsexuals, dichotomy and diversity. In G. Herdt (Ed.), *Third sex, third gender: Beyond sexual dimorphism in culture and history* (pp. 447–85). New York: Zone Books.

Bolin, A. (1997). Transforming transvestism and transsexualism: Polarity, politics, and gender. In B. Bullough, V. L. Bullough, & J. Elias (Eds.), *Gender blending* (pp. 25–32). Amherst, NY: Prometheus Books.

Bornstein, K. (1994). *Gender outlaw: On men, women and the rest of us*. New York: Routledge.

Boswell, H. (1998). The transgender paradigm shift toward free expression. In D. Denny (Ed.), *Current concepts in transgender identity* (pp. 55–61). New York: Garland Publishing.

Boyd, N. A. (2003). *Wide open town: A history of queer San Francisco to 1965*. Berkeley: University of California Press.

Boyd, N. A. (2006). Bodies in motion: Lesbian and transsexual histories. In S. Stryker and S. Whittle (Eds.), *The transgender studies reader* (pp. 420–33). New York: Routledge.

Boylan, J. F. (2003). *She's not there: A life in two genders*. New York: Broadway Books.

Boylan, J. F. (2013). *Stuck in the Middle with You: A Memoir of Parenting in Three Genders*. New York: Crown.

Brown, K. (1995). "Changed . . . into the fashion of man": The politics of sexual difference in a seventeenth-century Anglo-American settlement. *Journal of the History of Sexuality*, 6 (21), 171–93.

Bullough, B., & Bullough, V. L. (1998). Transsexualism: Historical perspectives, 1952 to present. In D. Denny (Ed.), *Current concepts in transgender identity* (pp. 15–34). New York: Garland Publishing.

Bullough, V. L. (1975). Transsexualism in history. *Archives of Sexual Behavior*, 4 (5), 561–71.

Bullough, V. L., & Bullough, B. (1993). *Cross dressing, sex, and gender*. Philadelphia: University of Pennsylvania Press.

Butler, J. (1990). *Gender trouble: Feminism and the subversion of identity*. New York: Routledge.

Califia, P. (1997). *Sex changes: The politics of transgenderism*. San Francisco: Cleis Press.

Callender, C., & Kochems, L. M. (1983). The North American berdache. *Current Anthropology*, 24, 443–56.

Camp Trans. (2011). Camp Trans history: Trans inclusion in womyn's music and MMWF. Retrieved June 19, 2011, from http://www.camp-trans.org/pages/ct-history.html

Carter, D. (2004). *Stonewall: The riots that sparked the gay revolution*. New York: St. Martin's Press.

Cauldwell, D.O. (2006). Psychopathia transsexualis. In S. Stryker and S. Whittle (Eds.), *The transgender studies reader* (pp. 40–44). New York: Routledge.

Chauncey, G. (1994). *Gay New York: Gender, urban culture, and the making of the gay male world, 1890–1940*. New York: HarperCollins.

Chiñas, B. N. (1995). Isthmus Zapotec attitudes toward sex and gender anomalies. In S. O. Murray (Ed.), *Latin American male homosexualities* (pp. 293–302). Albuquerque: University of New Mexico Press.

Clendinen, D., & Nagourney, A. (1999). *Out for good: The struggle to build a gay rights movement in America*. New York: Simon and Schuster.

Conn, C. (1974). *Canary: The story of a transsexual*. Los Angeles: Nash Publishing.

Consortium of Higher Education LGBT Resource Professionals. (2011). Directory. Retrieved July 10, 2011, from http://www.lgbtcampus.org/directory

Cromwell, J. (1998). Fearful others: Medico-psychological constructions of female-to-male transgenderism. In D. Denny (Ed.), *Current concepts in transgender identity* (pp. 117–44). New York: Garland Publishing.

Cromwell, J. (1999). *Transmen and FTMs: Identities, bodies, genders, and sexualities*. Urbana: University of Illinois Press.

Cunningham, M. (1995). The slap of love. Open City. Retrieved March 18, 2012, from http://opencity.org/archive/issue-6/the-slap-of-love

D'Emilio, J. (1983). Capitalism and gay identity. In A. Snitow, C. Stansell, and S. Thompson (Eds.), *Powers of desire: The politics of sexuality* (pp. 100–13). New York: Monthly Review Press.

D'Emilio, J., & Freedman, E. B. (1988). *Intimate matters: A history of sexuality in America*. New York: Harper and Row.

de Lauretis, T. (Ed.). (1991). Queer theory: Lesbian and gay sexualities. *differences: A Journal of Feminist Cultural Studies*. 3 (2),

Denny, D. (1997). Transgender: Some historical, cross-cultural, and contemporary models and methods of coping and treatment. In B. Bullough, V. L. Bullough, & J. Elias (Eds.), *Gender blending* (pp. 33–47). Amherst, NY: Prometheus Books.

Denny, D. (2006). Transgender communities of the United States in the late twentieth century. In P. Currah, R. M. Juang, & S. P. Minter (Eds.), *Transgender rights* (pp. 171–91). Minneapolis: University of Minnesota Press.

Devor, A. H., & Matte, N. (2006). ONE Inc. and Reed Erickson: The uneasy collaboration of gay and trans activism, 1964–2003. In S. Stryker and S. Whittle (Eds.), *The transgender studies reader* (pp. 387–406). New York: Routledge.

Devor, H. (1997). *FTM: Female-to-male transsexuals in society.* Bloomington: Indiana University Press.

Dillon, M. (1946). *Self: A study in ethics and endocrinology.* London: William Heinemann Medical Books.

Docter, R. F. (2008). *Becoming a woman: A biography of Christine Jorgensen.* New York: Haworth.

Drexel, A. (1997). Before Paris burned: Race, class, and male homosexuality on the Chicago South Side, 1935–1960. In B. Beemyn (Ed.), *Creating a place for ourselves: Lesbian, gay, and bisexual community histories* (pp. 119–44). New York: Routledge.

Duberman, M. (1993). *Stonewall.* New York: Dutton.

Ekins, R., & King, D. (2005). Virginia Prince: Transgender pioneer. In R. Ekins & D. King (Eds.), *Virginia Prince: Pioneer of transgendering* (pp. 5–15). Binghamton, NY: Haworth Medical Press.

Escoffier, J. (2004). New York City. In C. J. Summers (Ed.), *glbtq: An encyclopedia of gay, lesbian, bisexual, transgender, and queer culture.* Retrieved December 16, 2010, from www.glbtq.com/social-sciences/new_york_city.html.

Faderman, L. (1991). *Odd girls and twilight lovers: A history of lesbian life in twentieth-century America.* New York: Columbia University Press.

Faderman, L., & Timmons, S. (2006). *Gay L.A.: A history of sexual outlaws, power politics, and lipstick lesbians.* New York: Basic Books.

Fantasia Fair. (2011). History of Fantasia Fair. Retrieved June 21, 2011, from http://fantasiafair.org/History_of_Fantasia_Fair.aspx

Feinberg, L. (1992). *Transgender liberation: A movement whose time has come.* New York: World View Forum.

Feinberg, L. (1993). *Stone butch blues.* Ithaca, NY: Firebrand.

Feinberg, L. (1996). *Transgender warriors: Making history from Joan of Arc to RuPaul.* Boston: Beacon Press.

Feinberg, L. (1998). *Trans liberation: Beyond pink or blue.* Boston: Beacon Press.

Frye, P. (2001). History of the International Conference on Transgender Law and Employment Policy, Inc. Retrieved June 21, 2011, from http://www.transgenderlegal.com/ictlephis1.htm

Fuss, D. (1989). *Essentially speaking: Feminism, nature and difference.* New York: Routledge.

Gallo, M. M. (2006). Different daughters: A history of the Daughters of Bilitis and the rise of the lesbian rights movement. New York: Carroll and Graf.

Garber, E. (1988). Gladys Bentley: The bulldagger who sang the blues. *OUT/LOOK,* 1, 52–61.

Garber, M. (1992). *Vested interests: Cross-dressing and cultural anxiety.* New York: Routledge.

Gender Public Advocacy Coalition. (2006). *50 under 30: Masculinity and the war on America's youth.* Washington, DC: Gender Public Advocacy Coalition.

Gómez Regalado, A. (n.d.). Transcending. Retrieved December 16, 2010, from http://www.2spirits.com/TrascendiendoEnglishversion.pdf

Grant, J. M., Mottet, L. A., & Tanis, J. (2010). Injustice at every turn: A report of the national transgender discrimination survey—executive summary. Retrieved July 16, 2011, from http://transequality.org/PDFs/Executive_Summary.pdf

Green, J. (2004). *Becoming a visible man.* Nashville, TN: Vanderbilt University Press.

Grémaux, R. (1994). Woman becomes man in the Balkans. In G. Herdt (Ed.), *Third sex, third gender: Beyond sexual dimorphism in culture and history* (pp. 241–81). New York: Zone Books.

Halberstam, J. (1998). *Female masculinity.* Durham, NC: Duke University Press.

Hale, C. J. (1996). Are Lesbians Women? *Hypatia.* 11 (2), 94–121.

Heidenreich, L. (1997). A historical perspective on Christine Jorgensen and the development of an identity. In B. Bullough, V. L. Bullough, & J. Elias (Eds.), *Gender blending* (pp. 267–76). Amherst: Prometheus Books.

Hill, R. S. (2007). As a man I exist; as a woman I live: Heterosexual transvestism and the contours of gender and sexuality in postwar America. Diss. University of Michigan.

Hirschfeld, M. (1991 [1910]). *Transvestites: The erotic drive to cross dress* (M. A. Lombardi-Nash, Trans.). Buffalo, NY: Prometheus Books.

Hoyer, N. (Ed.). (1953). *Man into woman: An authentic record of a change of sex*. New York: Popular Library.

Hunt, N. (1978). *Mirror image*. New York: Holt, Rinehart and Winston.

International Court System (2010). 45 years of noble deeds. Retrieved May 21, 2011, from http://www.impcourt.org/icis/about/index.html

Jay, K., & Young, A. (1972). Rapping with a street transvestite revolutionary: An interview with Marcia Johnson. In K. Jay & A. Young (Eds.), *Out of the closets: Voices of gay liberation* (pp. 112–20). New York: Douglas/Links.

Jorgensen, C. (1967). *Christine Jorgensen: A personal autobiography*. New York: Paul S. Eriksson.

Kailey, M. (2005). *Just add hormones: An insider's guide to the transsexual experience*. Boston: Beacon Press.

Katz, J. N. (1976). *Gay American history: Lesbians and gay men in the U.S.A.* New York: T.Y. Crowell.

Kennedy, E. L. (1998). Lesbianism. In G. Mink, M. Navarro, W. Mankiller, B. Smith, & G. Steinem (Eds.), *The reader's companion to U.S. women's history* (pp. 327–30). New York: Houghton Mifflin.

Kennedy, P. (2007). *The first man-made man: The story of two sex changes, one love affair, and a twentieth-century medical revolution*. New York: Bloomsbury.

Krieger, N. (2011). *Nina here nor there: My journey beyond gender*. Boston: Beacon Press.

Ladin, J. (2012). *Through the door of life: A Jewish journey between genders*. Madison: University of Wisconsin Press.

Lang, S. (1998). *Men as women, women as men: Changing gender in Native American cultures*. Austin: University of Texas Press.

Lang, S. (1999). Lesbians, men-women and two-spirits: Homosexuality and gender in Native American cultures. In E. Blackwood and S. E. Wieringa (Eds.), *Female desires: Same-sex relations and transgender practices across cultures* (pp. 91–116). New York: Columbia.

Martino, M., with Harriett. (1977). *Emergence: A transsexual autobiography*. New York: Crown Publishers.

Matthews, R. (1927, March 19). Men dance with male "flappers" at artists' ball. *The Baltimore Afro-American*, p. 20.

Matzner, A. (2001). *'O au no keia: Voices from Hawai'i's mahu and transgender communities*. Bloomington, IN: Xlibris Corporation.

Meyerowitz, J. (2002). *How sex changed: A history of transsexuality in the United States*. Cambridge, MA: Harvard University Press.

Middlebrook, D. W. (1998). *Suits me: The double life of Billy Tipton*. New York: Houghton Mifflin.

Minter, S. P. (2006). Do transsexuals dream of gay rights? Getting real about transgender inclusion. In P. Currah, R. M. Juang, & S. P. Minter (Eds.), *Transgender rights* (pp. 141–70). Minneapolis: University of Minnesota Press.

Morris, J. (1974). *Conundrum: From James to Jan—an extraordinary personal narrative of transsexualism*. New York: Harcourt Brace Jovanovich.

Namaste, V. K. (2000). *Invisible lives: The erasure of transsexual and transgendered people*. Chicago: University of Chicago Press.

Nanda, S. (1994). Hijras: An alternative sex and gender role in India. In G. Herdt (Ed.), *Third sex, third gender: Beyond sexual dimorphism in culture and history* (pp. 373–417). New York: Zone Books.

Nanda, S. (1999). *Neither man nor woman: The Hijras of India*. Stamford, CT: Wadsworth Publishing.

National Gay and Lesbian Task Force (2012). Jurisdictions with explicitly transgender-inclusive nondiscrimination laws. Retrieved November 18, 2013, from http://thetaskforce.org/downloads/reports/fact_sheets/all_jurisdictions_w_pop_6_12.pdf

National Gay and Lesbian Task Force (2013). State nondiscrimination laws in the U.S. Retrieved November 18, 2013, from http://thetaskforce.org/downloads/reports/issue_maps/non_discrimination_6_13.pdf

Pecheur, J. (2004). The third gender. Retrieved December 16, 2010, from http://www.myhusband-betty.com/2004/05/28/third-gender-muxe-in-mexico

Prince, C. V. (1962). 166 men in dresses. *Sexology*, 3, 520–25.

Prince, V., & Bentler, P. M. (1972). Survey of 504 cases of transvestism. *Psychological Reports*. 31 (3), 903–17.

Prosser, J. (1998). *Second skins: The body narratives of transsexuality*. New York: Columbia University Press.

Raymond, J. G. (1994). The *transsexual empire: The making of the she-male*. New York: Teachers College Press.

Raymond, J. G. (2006). Sappho by surgery: The transsexually constructed lesbian-feminist. In S. Stryker and S. Whittle (Eds.), *The transgender studies reader* (pp. 131–43). New York: Routledge.

Reddy, G. (2005). *With respect to sex: Negotiating Hijra identity in South India*. Chicago: University of Chicago Press.

Reis, E. (2007). Hermaphrodites and "same-sex" sex in early America. In T. A. Foster (Ed.), *Long before Stonewall: Histories of same-sex sexuality in early America* (pp. 144–63). New York: New York University Press.

Richards, R., with Ames, J. (1983). *Second serve: The Renée Richards story*. New York: Stein and Day.

Roscoe, W. (1988). The Zuni man-woman. *OUT/LOOK*, 1, 56–67.

Roscoe, W. (1991). *The Zuni man-woman*. Albuquerque: University of New Mexico Press.

Roscoe, W. (1997). Bibliography of berdache and alternative gender roles among North American Indians. *Journal of Homosexuality*, 14 (3/4), 81–171.

Roscoe, W. (1998). *Changing ones: Third and fourth genders in Native North America*. New York: St. Martin's Press.

Rothblatt, M. (1994). *The apartheid of sex: A manifesto on the freedom of gender*. New York: Crown.

Rubin, G. (2006). Of catamites and kings: Reflections on butch, gender, and boundaries. In S. Stryker and S. Whittle (Eds.), *The transgender studies reader* (pp. 471–81). New York: Routledge.

Rubin, H. (2006). The logic of treatment. In S. Stryker and S. Whittle (Eds.), *The transgender studies reader* (pp. 482–98). New York: Routledge.

Rudacille, D. (2005). *The riddle of gender: Science, activism, and transgender rights*. New York: Pantheon Books.

Rupp, L. J. (1999). *A desired past: A short history of same-sex love in America*. Chicago: University of Chicago Press.

Rupp, L. J. (2009). *Sapphistries: A global history of love between women*. Vancouver: University of British Columbia Press.

Saslow, J. M. (1999). *Pictures and passions: A history of homosexuality in the visual arts*. New York: Viking Press.

Schacht, S. P. (2002). Four renditions of doing female drag: Feminine appearing conceptual variations of a masculine theme. In P. Gagné & R. Tewksbury (Eds.), *Gendered sexualities* (pp. 157– 80). Amsterdam: JAI Press.

Sedgwick, E. K. (1990). *Epistemology of the closet*. Berkeley: University of California Press.

Serlin, D. H. (1995). Christine Jorgensen and the Cold War closet. *Radical History Review*, 62, 136–65.

Shapiro, E. (2010). *Gender circuits: Bodies and identities in a technological age*. New York: Routledge.

Sherman, G. (1964). *"I want to be a woman!" The autobiography of female impersonator Gayle Sherman*. Chicago: Novel Books.

Silverman, V., & Stryker, S. (Directors). (2005). *Screaming queens: The riots at Compton's Cafeteria* [Motion picture]. United States: Frameline.

Sinnott, M. J. (2004). *Toms and dees: Transgender identity and female same-sex relationships in Thailand*. Honolulu: University of Hawaii Press.

Star, H. J. (1963). *"I changed my sex!" The autobiography of stripper Hedy Jo Star, formerly Carl Hammonds*. Chicago: Novel Books.

Stephen, L. (2002). Sexualities and genders in Zapotec Oaxaca. *Latin American Perspectives*, 29 (2), 41–59.

Stryker, S. (1994). My words to Victor Frankenstein above the village of Chamounix: Performing transgender rage. *GLQ: A Journal of Lesbian and Gay Studies*. 1 (3), 237–54.

Stryker, S. (2000). Introduction. In *Christine Jorgensen, Christine Jorgensen: A personal autobiography* (pp. v-xiii). San Francisco: Cleis Press.

Stryker, S. (2008). *Transgender history*. Berkeley, CA: Seal Press.

Sullivan, L. (1990). *From female to male: The life of Jack Bee Garland*. Boston: Alyson Publications.

Thompson, C. J. S. (1974). *The mysteries of sex: Women who posed as men and man who impersonated women*. New York: Causeway Books.

Totman, R. (2003). *The third sex: Kathoey: Thailand's ladyboys*. London: Souvenir Press.

Towle, E. B., & Morgan, L. M. (2006). Romancing the transgender native: Rethinking the use of the "third gender" concept. In S. Stryker and S. Whittle (Eds.), *The transgender studies reader* (pp. 666–84). New York: Routledge.

Trans Bodies, Trans Selves Online Survey (2013). http://transbodies.com/surveys/.

Trans Respect versus Transphobia Worldwide. (2013). Transgender Europe's Trans Murder Monitoring Project reveals 238 killings of trans people in the last 12 months. Retrieved November 18, 2013, from http://www.transrespect-transphobia.org/uploads/downloads/2013/TDOR2013english/TvT-TDOR2013PR-en.pdf

Trebay, G. (2000). Legends of the ball: Paris is still burning. *Village Voice*. Retrieved March 18, 2012, from http://www.villagevoice.com/2000-01-11/news/legends-of-the-ball/

Trexler, R. C. (1995). *Sex and conquest: Gendered violence, political order, and the European conquest of the Americas*. Ithaca, NY: Cornell University Press.

Troka, D. J. (2003). The history of the first International Drag King Extravaganza. Retrieved July 10, 2011, from http://www.idke.info/about_us.html#history

United ENDA (2010). United ENDA. Retrieved July 16, 2011, from http://unitedenda.org

von Krafft-Ebing, R. (2006). Selections from Psychopathia Sexualis with Special Reference to Contrary Sexual Instinct: A Medico-Legal Study. In S. Stryker and S. Whittle (Eds.), *The transgender studies reader* (pp. 21–27). New York: Routledge.

Whittle, S. (2002). *Respect and equality: Transsexual and transgender rights*. London, UK: Cavendish Publishing.

Williams, W. L. (1986). *The spirit and the flesh: Sexual diversity in American Indian culture*. Boston: Beacon Press.

Winters, K. (2010). Ten reasons why the Transvestic Disorder diagnosis in the DSM-5 has got to go. Retrieved March 5, 2013, from http://gidreform.wordpress.com/2010/10

Winters, K. (2012). An update on gender diagnoses, as the DSM-5 goes to press. Retrieved March 5, 2013, from http://gidreform.wordpress.com/2012/12/05/an-update-on-gender-diagnoses-asthe-dsm-5-goes-to-press

Zagria. (2009). Lee Brewster. A gender variance who's who. Retrieved March 5, 2013, from http://zagria.blogspot.com/2009/10/lee-brewster-1943-2000-retailer.html

Zagria. (2010). Johns Hopkins – part 2: 1966–1979. A gender variance who's who. Retrieved June 9, 2011, from http://zagria.blogspot.com/2010/07/johns-hopkins-part-2-1966-1979.html

CPSIA information can be obtained
at www.ICGtesting.com
Printed in the USA
LVHW011955130819
627515LV00007B/29/P